JAMES E. POTTER

Standing Firmly
by the Flag

Nebraska Territory
and the Civil War,
1861–1867

University of Nebraska Press | Lincoln & London

Publication of this volume was assisted by the
Virginia Faulkner Fund, established in memory of Virginia Faulkner,
editor in chief of the University of Nebraska Press.

Library of Congress Cataloging-in-Publication Data
Potter, James E. (James Edward), 1945–
Standing firmly by the flag: Nebraska Territory and the Civil War, 1861–1867 / James E.
Potter.
p. cm.
Includes bibliographical references and index.
ISBN 978-0-8032-4090-2 (pbk.: alk. paper) 1. Nebraska—History—Civil War, 1861–1865.
2. Nebraska—History—19th century. I. Title.
E518.P67 2012
978.2′02—dc23   2012021979

Set in Swift.

To my colleagues at the Nebraska State Historical Society

The patriotism of those who assist our country now, when she is defending the Constitution and the Union against traitors and rebels, and who stand firmly by that flag and those institutions which have descended to us from the hands of *Washington*, will be held in grateful remembrance by the great and good everywhere.

—Nebraska governor Alvin Saunders, Message to
the Territorial Legislature, December 2, 1861

CONTENTS

⌒

List of Illustrations | ix

Preface | xi

Acknowledgments | xix

Introduction: Nebraska Territory on the Eve of War | 1

1. 1861: "Civil War Is upon Us" | 15

2. 1862: "Nobly Did the First Nebraska Sustain
Its Reputation" | 45

3. 1863: "Let Us Battle . . . for 'The Constitution As It Is,
and The Union As It Was'" | 77

4. 1864: "You May Expect a General Indian Outbreak in
All This Western Country" | 117

5. 1865: "Peace Will Soon Again Bless the Land" | 167

6. 1866: "A Change of Government . . . Is Being
Freely Discussed" | 225

7. 1867: "Nebraska Has a Singularly Bright and
Prosperous Future" | 265

Epilogue: The New State and the Old Soldiers | 283

Notes | 293

Bibliography | 335

Index | 347

ILLUSTRATIONS

〰

Maps

1. The First Nebraska Regiment's theater of operations, 1861–64 | 29

2. Post of Plum Creek, ca. 1865 | 151

3. The central and northern Plains, 1865 | 169

Figures

1. "Volunteer!" *Nebraska Advertiser* (Brownville) | 22

2. Pvt. John Hutton, First Nebraska Volunteer Infantry | 38

3. Pvt. James Hutton, First Nebraska Volunteer Infantry | 39

4. Alvin Saunders | 43

5. Gen. John M. Thayer | 52

6. Counterattack of Wallace's division at Fort Donelson | 55

7. Pvt. Jacob Coffman, Second Nebraska Volunteer Cavalry | 70

8. Augustus Harvey | 87

9. J. Sterling Morton | 90

10. Officers of the Second Nebraska Volunteer Cavalry | 94

11. Headquarters, Second Nebraska Volunteer Cavalry | 98

12. The Battle of White Stone Hill | 100

13. Nancy Jane Fletcher Morton | 144

14. Fort Mitchell | 148

15. George L. Miller | 160

16. Clement L. Vallandigham | 164

17. Downtown Omaha | 184

18. Freight wagons at Nebraska City | 189

19. Flag of the First Nebraska Veteran Volunteer Cavalry | 199

20. William H. H. Waters | 211

21. *Omaha Daily Herald* building | 216

22. Thomas W. Tipton | 249

23. Algernon S. Paddock | 257

24. Union Pacific excursion to the 100th meridian | 263

25. African Americans in Brownville | 278

26. Great Seal of the state of Nebraska | 280

PREFACE

I had originally intended this book to focus on the First Nebraska Regiment of volunteers, Nebraska's primary military
contribution to Civil War history. Beginning in the 1960s with
the advent of the Civil War centennial, and periodically since
then, part of the regiment's story has been told via *Nebraska
History* articles and in *Marching with the First Nebraska: A Civil
War Diary* (University of Oklahoma Press, 2007), a book I coed-
ited with Edith Robbins. The latter presents the diary and letters of Pvt. August Scherneckau, a German immigrant who
served in the First Nebraska from 1862 to 1865. Despite these
efforts, I thought there was still a place for a comprehensive
history of the regiment from its acceptance into the Union
army in the summer of 1861 until its soldiers were finally discharged from federal service in July 1866.

As I mined newspapers and other documents for informa-
tion and insights about the First Nebraska, it became clear that
the regiment's contribution was only part of a more complex
and interesting story. Aside from their military aspects, the
Civil War years had a significant effect on Nebraska's political,

social, and economic development and its transition from territory to state, the first to be admitted after the war was over. Yet what happened in Nebraska between March 4, 1861, when President Abraham Lincoln was inaugurated, and March 1, 1867, when President Andrew Johnson issued the statehood proclamation, has not received much attention. Hence I decided to forego the detailed history of the First Nebraska Regiment in favor of a broader look at Civil War Nebraska, a project I hope will appeal to a wider audience.

Those with a good grasp of American history will recognize the May 30, 1854, act of Congress creating the territories of Nebraska and Kansas as a signal event in the intensifying sectional crisis that led to civil war some seven years later. By repealing the Missouri Compromise of 1820 that had banned slavery in the region and authorizing the people living in the new territories to decide for themselves whether or not slavery would be permitted ("popular sovereignty"), the "Nebraska Act" reopened the divisive question of slavery's westward extension, sparked the rise of a Northern-based party dedicated to halting slavery's spread, and made the Union's breakup virtually inevitable. When it comes to the Civil War itself, however, I suspect there is less understanding of Nebraska's place in the story of the four-year conflict and its immediate aftermath.

Perhaps that's because what happened in Nebraska Territory between 1861 and 1867 may have seemed peripheral to the great national drama playing out on battlefields in the East and South, in the White House and the halls of Congress, and in the arena of American politics. No massive armies clashed on Nebraska's soil, no gunboats plied the Missouri River along its eastern shore, no towns were occupied or sacked within its borders, and the only Confederate soldiers to set foot here had been released from federal prison camps as Union "volunteers" to fight Indians or were deserters escaping the war. Some Nebraskans acted as though the war had never come, traipsing off to search for gold in Colorado or Montana, speculating in real estate, eking a living from the soil, or supplying travelers moving west. During the war years many "Nebraskans" were here barely long enough to leave their footprints.

Although Nebraska Territory was distant from the Civil War's major theaters, its people were not unmindful of the war's issues, uninvolved in its prosecution, or insulated from its effects. One concern was how the settlements and the lines of communication and commerce to the west were to be protected after U.S. Army garrisons at Forts Kearny, Laramie, and Randall were withdrawn to fight Confederates. As the war continued, it disrupted the territorial economy, delayed statehood, brought conflict with the indigenous peoples, and deferred the anticipated benefits of the 1862 Pacific Railroad and Homestead Acts. It also reshaped territorial politics, and its legacy was reflected in the leadership and institutions of the new state of Nebraska for decades to come.

Despite its status during the war years as a federal dependency with a modest population and a fragile economy, Nebraska Territory made a remarkable contribution to the Union war effort, furnishing more than three thousand soldiers from a pool of barely nine thousand men of military age in 1860. Unlike the states that provided the majority of Union troops, Nebraska Territory had little manpower to spare if it were to maintain and develop its fledgling agricultural and urban economy, which had barely gained a foothold when the war broke out. Nevertheless, and often contrary to the wishes of those they left behind, Nebraska's volunteer soldiers stepped forward to risk their lives and livelihoods to help save the Union.

Nebraskans fought Confederates on Tennessee and Missouri battlefields, carried on a "bushwhacker's" war with partisans in Arkansas, skirmished with Indians in Nebraska and Dakota

Territories, and garrisoned forts and tiny outposts along the Platte Valley transportation and communications corridor. They endured physical hardship and harsh discipline and ate bad food or sometimes nothing at all. Many died from disease or accidents or saw the service ruin their health. A few were killed, wounded, or taken prisoner in battle. Most served faithfully, fought bravely, and completed their enlistment; others malingered, got drunk, committed crimes, or deserted. Although they left behind a rich record in the form of letters, diaries, and official documents, their story has never been fully told.

The war also had important consequences for Nebraskans who stayed home. Economic hardship, the loss of family members to military service, and the stresses of coping with the harsh Great Plains environment all took their toll. With Nebraska's soldiers serving in distant theaters, who would protect the territory if the Native peoples resisted the increasing white encroachment upon the homelands they had occupied for generations? Even if there were no conflict with the Indians, "Jayhawkers" and other lawless bands periodically swept through southeastern Nebraska, and footloose migrants from east of the Missouri River, often suspected of being Rebels, fled to the territory to escape their war-torn firesides or conscription by the contending armies.

National debates about who was to blame for bringing on the rebellion, the policies the government should pursue to put it down, and what kind of nation should emerge once it was over were echoed here. As the fighting dragged on, journalists and politicians on both sides of the aisle, as well as citizens in the street, spoke out with passion and often with invective. Was the war being fought only to restore the Union or was it also a war to end slavery, the divisive issue that all efforts at political compromise had failed to resolve? Lincoln's Emancipation Proclamation and his decision to enlist black men in the Union army sparked particularly heated opinions. Epithets branding Lincoln's supporters as "black Republicans" or "radical abolitionists," along with those labeling his critics as "secession sympathizers," "Copperheads," or even traitors were frequently invoked.

In some ways Nebraska Territory benefited from the Civil War. Platte Valley road ranches prospered, along with several of the Missouri River towns, by serving emigrants, Mormons, military expeditions, miners, or those simply fleeing the war. Nebraska City and Omaha saw a freighting boom when the war diverted military transportation northward from Kansas. The boom increased with a gold rush to the Idaho/Montana mountains beginning in 1862. The buildup for a campaign against Indians in Dakota Territory in 1863 brought military contracts to Nebraska firms. The economic boost continued when in 1865 the army mounted an expedition into the Powder River country against Indians who had resisted the ever-increasing trespass on their prime hunting grounds brought on by the war and the gold rush to the mountains. The secession of the slave states removed from Congress representatives and senators who had long blocked the passage of acts providing for a transcontinental railroad and free homesteads, both considered keys to Nebraska's future.

The war's conclusion brought new debates about the place of the freed slaves in American society, how the broken Union should be restored, and the scope of political and social change that would validate the four-year sacrifice of blood and treasure. These issues would have a major impact upon Nebraska's transition to statehood. An examination of Nebraska politics during the years from 1865 to 1867 reveals that residents of the territory were far from oblivious to these debates and issues. Through territorial newspapers, personal correspondence, campaign rhetoric, and legislative maneuvering Nebraskans gave voice to their views on Reconstruction, loyalty, the political role of the freedmen, and the relationship between the states and the federal government. Their opinions were often propounded using language and revealing attitudes that today we find racist and offensive.

What's more, Nebraska was unique in being the only territory admitted to statehood after the war was over but before the ratification in 1870 of the Fifteenth Amendment to the U.S. Constitution, which extended black male suffrage to every state where it was still being denied. Consequently only Nebraska was required to assent to a specific congressional mandate that a "whites only" voting restriction be removed from its state constitution as a condition of its admission in 1867.

Despite the Civil War's significance to the territory of Nebraska that was and to the state of Nebraska that was to be, the years from 1861 to 1867 have been accorded uneven coverage in general state histories. The experiences and contributions of Nebraska soldiers have been mostly overlooked. Territorial politics have been more fully covered, though the early histories lack balance. Journal articles about Nebraska's military and political history and book-length studies of overland freighting or the Indian wars on the northern and central plains often omit a broader context. Nebraska is barely mentioned in surveys of the Civil War in the American West, though significantly more has been written about its role in the Reconstruction years of 1865 to 1867.

By contrast, many books and articles have addressed Nebraska's story during the 1870s and 1880s, when railroads extended across the state, thousands of Civil War veterans and European immigrants came for land, the Indians were finally defeated by overwhelming force and confined to reservations, and Nebraskans old and new focused on adapting their lives and institutions to the Great Plains environment. All this emphasis on the years of rapid settlement may prompt the notion that statehood in 1867 is really the genesis event from which Nebraska history has unfolded.

As one of the key chapters in our national narrative, the Civil War years hold an enduring fascination for many Americans. That fascination helps explain the steady stream of related books, articles, and memoirs that continue to pour forth 150 years after the war began. With the Civil War sesquicentennial having arrived in 2011, the time seems right to offer a new and more detailed look at Civil War Nebraska, the enterprising and energetic people who lived here, and the territory's transition to statehood, an era in our history that has been only vaguely understood and too little appreciated.

ACKNOWLEDGMENTS

I am grateful to the Nebraska State Historical Society, where I have spent my entire career, for providing me with the knowledge, resources, and support necessary to undertake this book. The society's decades of commitment to collecting and preserving the histories all Nebraskans share, including collections documenting the attitudes and experiences of Nebraskans during the Civil War years, have inspired me to want to tell more fully the story of this fascinating and crucial period in our past.

While the research for this book has spanned many years and has been aided throughout by the society's staff, both past and present, I particularly want to thank Director/CEO Michael J. Smith and Associate Director for Publications David Bristow for their encouragement and helpful suggestions and for allowing me time to work on Civil War Nebraska. During my research for the book, State Archivist Andrea Faling and her staff in the reference room let me check out microfilm to use in my Chadron office. As the society's first telecommuting historian, not having to make the four-hundred-mile trip (one way) to the library and archives in Lincoln to read newspapers and other microfilmed materials aided me immeasurably. That courtesy left me free to spend my Lincoln time consulting the archives' holdings of original military records, government documents, and manuscripts and benefiting in other ways from the society's skilled and helpful staff.

Had Edith Robbins of Grand Island not discovered Pvt. August Scherneckau's Civil War diary at the Oregon Historical Society while researching the history of the Grand Island German settlement of the 1850s, the story of the First Nebraska Regiment would be far less complete. The Scherneckau diary held such promise that Robbins not only urged its publication and invited me to collaborate in editing it, but she volunteered to translate it from the German. The Oregon Historical Society in Portland kindly granted permission. The result is *Marching with the First Nebraska: A Civil War Diary*, published in 2007 by the University of Oklahoma Press.

Eli Paul, formerly my colleague in the NSHS Research and Publications Division, was instrumental in arranging for the society in 1999 to purchase the Civil War letters of Pvt. Thomas Edwin Keen of the First Nebraska. These letters, too, enriched the story. Lori Cox-Paul, archivist at the National Archives–Central Plains Region in Kansas City and also a former colleague, alerted me to the Civil War records of the provost marshal general for Kansas and Nebraska in the archives there and made them available. John D. McDermott of Rapid City, South Dakota, lent his eye to those parts of the manuscript dealing with the Indian war of 1864 and 1865, about which he is an expert, and also provided several documents from his own research files. NSHS archeologist John Ludwickson, who has long studied the First Battalion, Nebraska Veteran Volunteer Cavalry, kindly shared documents and insights. James A. Hanson of the Museum of the Fur Trade, who knows what makes a good history book and how to write one, read the entire manuscript and offered helpful comments. Professor Will Thomas of the University of Nebraska–Lincoln history department, along with two anonymous readers for the University of Nebraska Press, likewise weighed in with thoughtful suggestions. Despite all this help, I take full responsibility for errors, omissions, or misinterpretations that remain.

Turning a manuscript into a book requires expertise well beyond what most authors can claim. For that, I'm grateful to the staff of the University of Nebraska Press, particularly acquisitions editor Bridget Barry, associate project editor Sabrina Stellrecht, and publicity manager Cara M. Pesek. I also thank NSHS assistant editor Patricia M. Gaster for compiling the index, former NSHS exhibits designer Steve Ryan for producing the maps, and Joy Margheim for editing the manuscript.

My wife, Gail, director of the Museum of the Fur Trade in Chadron, is so busy with her own work that I am neither surprised nor disappointed that she has not paid much attention to mine. She would freely admit that Civil War history is not among her primary interests. Nonetheless, she has always encouraged my research and writing, has indulged my passion for traveling to obscure sites in Missouri and Arkansas connected with the First Nebraska, and will be delighted to see the book completed.

Standing Firmly
by the Flag

Nebraska Territory on the Eve of War

T he Nebraska Territory, created in 1854, embraced some 355,000 square miles and extended westward from the Missouri River to the Rocky Mountains and northward from Kansas to the Canadian border. It included present Nebraska, those parts of North and South Dakota lying west of the Missouri River, large portions of Montana and Wyoming, and the northeastern section of Colorado.

Until Nebraska was admitted to statehood in 1867, its government was mainly funded, and to a significant extent controlled, by the administration holding power in Washington. Although Nebraskans elected the members of the territorial legislature and a nonvoting delegate to Congress, the president of the United States appointed the governor, secretary, Supreme Court judges, and other officials. The main qualification for a political appointment in Nebraska Territory was party loyalty; hence all Nebraska governors, secretaries, and judges from 1854 to 1861 were Democrats, appointed by President Franklin Pierce and his successor, James Buchanan. Many were young, inexperienced, and little more than political hacks. Most had backgrounds in journalism or the law. Scores of other aspirants waited in the wings for a chance at a patronage appointment.

Before 1860 Democrats also dominated the legislature, which consisted of an elected council and a house of representatives and furnished candidates in the races for the territory's delegate to Congress. In the absence of a two-party system, election success in Nebraska Territory hinged on a candidate's personality or place of residence.

Slavery became legal in Nebraska Territory when the 1854 Kansas-Nebraska Act repealed the 1820 Missouri Compromise, which had banned slavery in the lands of the original Louisiana Territory lying to Missouri's north and west, and substituted the principle of popular sovereignty. The people in the new territories could now decide for themselves whether to allow or prohibit slavery.

Few expected slavery to take root in Nebraska, and few slaves were brought there. At Nebraska City, freighting magnate Alexander Majors, merchant Stephen F. Nuckolls, lawyer Charles F. Holly, and farmer Robert M. Kirkham each owned slaves, as did several officers and the sutler at Fort Kearny on the Platte. The 1860 census recorded a total of fifteen slaves in Nebraska Territory. There had been at least two more before two named Celia and Eliza escaped from Stephen Nuckolls's household in 1859. And shortly after the 1860 census was taken in early June, the number of slaves in Nebraska decreased by five when three women and two boys belonging to Alexander Majors "left for parts unknown, supposed to have taken the underground railroad for Canada."[1]

Although the slavery issue had proved somewhat contentious in Nebraska during the 1850s, as reflected in newspaper editorials and debates in the legislature, it paled by comparison with the political turmoil, border raids, and bloody atrocities that plagued neighboring Kansas Territory, where proslavery and Free Soil forces bitterly contested for control. There, voting fraud by nonresident, proslavery Missourians monopolized political contests. While there was also irregular voting in Nebraska elections, it did not lead to political dominance by one faction or another and had little to do with slavery. It was perpetrated mostly by Iowans who sought to influence Nebraska development for their own benefit. Instead of slavery, Nebraska territorial politics focused on local or sectional issues, as residents living north and south of the Platte River jockeyed for political or economic advantage.[2]

The most divisive issue was the site of the territorial capital, fixed by gubernatorial proclamation at Omaha City in 1854, a location never conceded as permanent by boosters of rival towns such as Nebraska City and Bellevue. Capital removal bills dominated the first several sessions of the legislature. Other rivalries involved which towns would be the beneficiaries of federally funded internal improvements or gain prominence as the best outfitting points for freighting, emigrant, and military travel to the west. Sectionalism reached its peak in 1859, when politicians and journalists living south of the Platte River tried and failed to have that portion of Nebraska annexed to Kansas Territory.

By the later 1850s the Buchanan administration's proslavery policies, its decision to offer public lands in Nebraska for sale, and its resistance to a homestead act and land grants for internal improvements split the Democratic Party, both nationally and in Nebraska. Many disaffected Democrats, along with former Whigs, found a home in the new Republican Party, which mounted its first national campaign in 1856 and nominated John C. Frémont for president. The Republicans were committed to federal aid for western economic development, a homestead act, a transcontinental railroad, and most important, a halt to the westward extension of slavery. By 1859 both Democrats and Republicans had formally organized in Nebraska Territory, and their platforms and campaigns began to mirror national issues. Both parties declared in favor of immediate Nebraska statehood, but the people rejected the idea in a special March 1860 election.[3]

Although they could not vote for president, Nebraskans could hardly ignore the fiery sectional crisis reflected by and stemming from the 1860 presidential campaign. The Democrats split into Northern and Southern wings over the issue of slavery in the territories and each nominated candidates, Stephen A. Douglas and John C. Breckinridge, respectively. Abraham Lincoln was the standard-bearer of the northern-based Republicans. The Nebraska political parties, the aspirants for delegate to Congress, and the newspapers that supported them debated the election's implications and predicted that it would prove to be a referendum on slavery.[4]

The Nebraska territorial election of 1860, which preceded the presidential contest, was also bitterly partisan, and the stance of the national Democratic administration on issues important to the West helped the Republicans win a majority in the legislature. Although there were fewer than fifteen slaves in the territory, the prohibition of slavery in Nebraska was a paramount issue for the Republicans and also won support from some Douglas or "popular sovereignty" Democrats. Accordingly, the legislature in early 1861 pushed through a bill outlawing slavery and mustered the votes to override a veto by Governor Samuel Black, a lame-duck Buchanan Democrat soon to resign when the Lincoln administration took over in Washington.[5]

In the wake of Lincoln's November 4 election as the candidate of a Northern-based party pledged to resist slavery's extension, if not yet calling for its outright abolition, Nebraska newspapers weighed in on the country's future. The Democratic *Daily Nebraskian* in Omaha warned, "[T]he election of a president by what are denominated the Abolition states of this Union, on an issue and platform which forbade Southern men from giving him their support, will inevitably rouse to resistance those states with whose institutions he has declared eternal hostility."[6]

The *Nebraska City News*, which had always been an outspoken Democratic organ, blamed the country's woes on the Republicans in no uncertain terms: "Is it not the duty of the Republican party . . . if they wish to perpetuate the Union and nationalize their party, to retrace their steps, cease their unholy warfare upon the South, [and] repeal their unconstitutional, infamous, and insulting legislation, made expressly for the purpose of cheating and annoying the South?" Unless the Republican Party abandoned "its distinctive principles" the country would be hopelessly ruined, said *News* editor Milton W. Reynolds.[7]

Editor Robert W. Furnas of Brownville's *Nebraska Advertiser*, a former Douglas Democrat who had shifted his support to Lincoln, conceded that the nation was in the midst of a revolution. "We are not yet prepared to believe, however, as some express themselves, that it is to be a 'bloody revolution,' one that will send into fragments the only free government on the face of the globe." Like Republicans elsewhere, Furnas did not think Southerners were serious when they threatened to secede from the Union if Lincoln were elected. The *Advertiser's* optimistic editorial pronouncement was published on December 20, 1860, the same day South Carolina unanimously passed its ordinance of secession. Before Lincoln could be inaugurated on March 4, 1861, seven slave-holding states of the Deep South had followed suit and formed what they considered a new nation, the Confederate States of America.[8]

Despite Nebraska Territory's geographic isolation from the seat of the secession crisis, its citizens were not unmindful that the nation was breaking apart. The territorial newspapers received news of national affairs, first through mail dispatches and, by late summer of 1860, via a telegraph line that reached Brownville in August, Omaha in September, and Fort Kearny in October. The jubilant headline in the *Nebraska Advertiser* of August 30, 1860, announced the line's activation: "By Lightning, Telegraph to Brownville, Time and Space Annihilated!"[9]

Governor Black, in his last formal message to the legislature on December 4, 1860, lamented that the Union "trembles on a sea of troubles," and was "shaken to the center and vibrates with intense feeling to its farthest borders." Nebraska legislator and former Omaha mayor David D. Belden realized in January 1861 that even though no shots had yet been fired, "We are in the midst of civil war. . . . As for me, it makes me heart sick to think of it." The Republican *Falls City Broad Axe* speculated that the crisis "will show the world whether we have been living so long under a bona fide government, or the rule of a petty little conglomeration of insignificant and whimsical corporations."[10]

Even the inhabitants of remote ranches established to serve travelers along the Platte Valley trails to the west knew what was happening. Squire Lamb, proprietor of a ranche on Wood River adjacent to the military road to Fort Kearny, noted in a February 8, 1861, letter to his brother back east, "It is getting to [be] a damned pretty state of things[,] we shall have monocal [monarchial] government[,] if they [the Southern states] persist in the disunion I would like to help hang every trator."[11]

War came with the April 12 bombardment by South Carolina forces of the federal garrison at Fort Sumter in Charleston Harbor and the fort's surrender two days later. Nebraskans now had to decide where their loyalties lay. A handful left the territory to enlist in Confederate units being formed in the Southern states from whence they had come.[12] Others sat out the war in the Rocky Mountain mining camps or elsewhere in the interior. For some, the war was an inconvenience that diverted federal appropriations from Nebraska development and stalled the territory's settlement and economic growth, threatening their prospects for political or financial gain. Most Nebraskans, however, "stood firmly by the flag," and a remarkably large percentage joined the volunteer army being raised by the Lincoln administration to maintain the Union.[13]

On the eve of the Civil War Nebraska Territory was a pigmy compared with the states that would provide the bulk of the North's military and economic muscle in the struggle to come. The territory's non-Indian population tallied only 28,841 in 1860, concentrated in several modest towns and a handful of organized counties scattered along the Missouri River's western shore. The most populous towns were the territorial capital of Omaha (1,833) and Nebraska City (1,922); only six others boasted more than four hundred inhabitants. With the exception of a few soldiers, miners, and trailside entrepreneurs, Indians were the principal residents of Nebraska Territory's vast hinterland.[14]

The German colony at Grand Island, the tiny towns of Columbus and Fremont, the army garrisons at Forts Kearny, Laramie, and Randall (the latter sited on the Missouri River in today's South Dakota), and the Rocky Mountain mining camps located in the far western reaches of Nebraska Territory were the only inland white settlements of note. Both Fremont and Columbus, the latter founded by a company chartered to operate a ferry across the Loup River, sprang up primarily to serve travelers along the road from Omaha to Fort Kearny. The Germans at Grand Island also supplied emigrants and found a ready market for their agricultural products with the soldiers at Fort Kearny.[15]

A handful of whites also lived at stagecoach stations and road ranches scattered westward along the Platte Valley. The stagecoach stations came with the beginning of weekly mail service between the Missouri River and Salt Lake City in 1858; road ranches blossomed when trail traffic accelerated in the aftermath of gold discoveries the same year near Pike's Peak. The road ranches, crude log or sod structures with adjacent corrals, offered meals, merchandise, hay, grain, liquor, and sometimes blacksmithing. Many did a thriving business by exchanging trail-weary animals for fresh stock. All of them charged premium prices.[16]

On March 2, 1861, the area of the original Nebraska Territory was drastically reduced when Congress carved away the new territories of Colorado and Dakota. The reconfigured Nebraska Territory retained a long panhandle stretching all the way to today's Utah but otherwise resembled modern Nebraska. This reduction in area had little or no effect on the lives of most Nebraska residents except the miners in the Rocky Mountain goldfields; for the miners the change perhaps was for the better. Despite being part of the original Nebraska territory, the gold region's distance from the territorial capital of Omaha made it ungovernable.

Most of the Nebraskans enumerated in the 1860 census were young adults, many with children, who had come from states directly east, although a goodly number were from Missouri, Tennessee, Kentucky, and Virginia. About three-fourths of the inhabitants (22,475) had been born in the United States, the overwhelming majority (18,643) in the free states. The census recorded 6,351 Nebraskans of foreign birth, most from Germany, England, or Ireland. Many had come to Nebraska in hope of improving their political or financial status.[17]

By 1860 the territorial economy, which first took wing through rampant speculation in real estate fueled by "wildcat" banknotes and then crashed back to earth during the Panic of 1857, was showing some stability. The river towns, including Brownville, Nebraska City, Plattsmouth, Bellevue, and Omaha, had always been gateways for goods and people entering or leaving Nebraska by steamboat or overland, and several were depots and outfitting points for travel to the west. Freighting bolstered Nebraska City's economy when the government in 1858 awarded a contract to Russell, Majors, and Waddell to supply the U.S. Army in Utah and at other western posts.

Along with Nebraska City, Omaha and Brownville became important jumping-off points for emigrant travel and freighting across the plains, particularly after the gold rush began to the Rocky Mountain regions of western Kansas and Nebraska territories. Mormons bound for Utah regularly outfitted at Florence, near Omaha. The river towns also served as terminals for Nebraska agricultural products being shipped to eastern markets and goods arriving from the East. Steamboats plied the Missouri, connecting Nebraska to the commercial center that was St. Louis and to the nearest railroad, the Hannibal and St. Joseph, extending across northern Missouri.[18]

Agriculture, which had been mostly neglected during the speculative frenzy of the early territorial years, was finally becoming an economic mainstay. By the spring of 1859 Nebraska farmers had produced a surplus, and that fall the first territorial fair was held at Nebraska City. The 1860 census recorded production of 1.8 million bushels of Indian corn and more than 72,000 bushels of wheat, along with lesser amounts of other commodities such as potatoes, oats, tobacco, and buckwheat. Farmers and farm laborers numbered some 40 percent of the gainfully employed population.[19]

The remaining 60 percent of Nebraskans gainfully employed

worked in urban-type occupations, including merchants, clerks, real estate speculators, and lawyers. Skilled laborers, including carpenters, blacksmiths, masons, leatherworkers (harness and shoemakers), and teamsters made up 18 percent of the urban workforce. There was little industry worthy of the name, only 107 manufacturing establishments, mostly involved with the milling of grain and lumber and employing sixty millers.[20]

The territory's educational and religious infrastructure had barely developed. Although a free public school law had been enacted by the first territorial legislature in 1855, tax revenue to support schools was scanty, and the need for children to help with family work often precluded their attendance even when a school was available. Only 3,296 of the nearly 11,000 school-age children attended any school at all during the year preceding the 1860 census. The Methodists were the first to establish churches in Nebraska Territory; by 1860 there were sixty-three congregations, the majority being Methodist and Presbyterian, with a scattering of other denominations.[21]

By reason of their education, wealth, or prestige, urban professionals such as lawyers, merchants, bankers, editors, and physicians occupied many leadership positions in Nebraska Territory. The territory in 1860 boasted 130 lawyers and 123 physicians, and it is not surprising that many of them served in the legislature or held other territorial offices and tended to focus on economic or political issues promising to benefit both their communities and themselves.[22]

Nebraska's military history can be said to date from 1854, the year the territory was established. On August 19, 1854, thirty U.S. soldiers were killed at the so-called Grattan Massacre near Fort Laramie, Nebraska Territory. A rash Lt. John Grattan and his drunken interpreter brought the deadly outcome of this encounter on themselves by projecting force and bluster instead of diplomacy to seek restitution after a hungry resident of a massive Sioux village butchered an emigrant's cow. A year later came the most significant episode of conflict with Indians during Nebraska Territory's formative years. On September 3, 1855, Gen. William S. Harney's soldiers attacked and decimated a Brule Sioux village at Blue Water Creek (near present Lewellen) in retaliation for the deaths of Grattan and his men. The sites of the Grattan affair and Harney's retribution were both so distant from the settlements clinging to the Missouri River shore as to hardly register in the minds of most Nebraskans.[23]

Nevertheless, officials and residents of Nebraska were mindful that the Sioux, Cheyennes, Pawnees, and other tribes that had long called the Great Plains their home constituted the bulk of the vast territory's inhabitants, far outnumbering the tiny garrisons of army regulars at Forts Laramie, Kearny, and Randall. The mostly village-dwelling Pawnees, Omahas, Poncas, and Oto-Missourias had already ceded most of their lands to the government, which assigned them to reservations in eastern Nebraska Territory, yet they continued to roam during their seasonal hunts. The Upper Platte Agency at Fort Laramie monitored, but did not really control, the nomadic Northern Cheyennes, Northern Arapahos, and various bands of the Lakotas or Western Sioux. Despite the government's promise to protect the sedentary Nebraska tribes, the nomads regularly raided the Omahas, Poncas, and Pawnees, keeping white settlers wondering when a similar blow might fall on them.

As one of his early initiatives, Acting Governor Thomas B. Cuming issued a proclamation on December 23, 1854, recommending the organization of volunteer companies of militia, to be divided into two regiments, one north and one south of the Platte River, and he appointed officers to command these still phantom soldiers. The first session of the territorial legislature, on February 8, 1855, requested the governor to commission officers to raise two or more companies of mounted rangers. Unlike the federal troops at the government forts, these militiamen would be subject to the orders of the territorial governor.[24]

In late July 1855 Indians, supposed to be Sioux, killed two men near Fontanelle in Dodge County. Mark W. Izard, Cuming's successor as governor, ordered John M. Thayer, a former Massachusetts militia officer, to raise a company of forty volunteers and, with a second company previously organized, pursue the Indians. The campaign proved fruitless because the Indians had already retreated to the interior. This episode, however, sparked the formation throughout the territory of some fourteen ad hoc companies of "rangers" or "guards" in the late summer and fall of 1855.[25]

In his annual message to the legislature in December 1855 Governor Izard urged the passage of a territorial militia act. The law that resulted echoed Cuming's original proposal. It provided for two brigades, one from north of the Platte and one from south of it, each commanded by a brigadier general. The individual companies under this organization were to assemble and drill three times a year. Existing militia companies were accepted for enrollment under the act. A major general would command the whole, with the governor as commander-in-chief.[26]

The day after the act was passed the legislature chose John M. Thayer as major general and Leavitt L. Bowen and Hiram P. Downs as brigadier generals. Thayer had some military experience, and Downs had been an officer in the Mexican War. By the fall of 1857 twelve militia companies had been organized. It could hardly be expected that these companies would constitute a reliable military force in the absence of rigorous training and competent leadership. They were often little more than social organizations that mustered primarily to provide pomp and circumstance on national holidays, such as Independence Day and Washington's birthday.[27]

The need for a trained territorial militia seemed more apparent with the so-called Pawnee War in the summer of 1859. A band of wandering Pawnees passing white settlements along the Elkhorn River in eastern Nebraska became involved in a brief skirmish with the settlers and then made off with livestock and other commodities. After receiving a petition from local residents and prominent Omaha men, Territorial Secretary J. Sterling Morton (Governor Black lived in Nebraska City and was frequently absent from the capital) ordered General Thayer to call out the militia and track down the Pawnees.

Thayer assembled a force comprising nearly two hundred militiamen with one piece of artillery, later augmented by Company K of the Second U.S. Dragoons from Fort Kearny, and took up the trail. Black joined the expedition a few days later but, according to Thayer, did more harm than good because the governor was drunk when he reached camp. He sobered up only after the general had poured out the last of Black's personal stash of whiskey.[28]

At daybreak on July 13 the troops caught up with and surprised the Pawnees, encamped near present-day Battle Creek, Nebraska. The Indians promptly surrendered, giving up six young men who had allegedly taken the settlers' property and promising to tap their government annuities to compensate for the damages. The prisoners soon escaped and the settlers never received compensation. Thus ended the first organized campaign by Nebraska Territory's citizen-soldiers. The next time the militia was mobilized, the men's service would be neither brief nor bloodless.[29]

CHAPTER ONE

1861

"Civil War Is upon Us"

Word of the April 12 Confederate bombardment of Fort Sumter spread quickly to Nebraska. By 5:30 p.m. the next day the *Daily Telegraph* had an extra on the streets of the capital city and its neighbor across the river being "read and talked over by the citizens of Council Bluffs and Omaha, about two thousand miles from the scene of hostilities." As the paper's name implied, it had been established to take advantage of the technology the telegraph afforded. Nebraskans also soon learned of President Abraham Lincoln's call for the states to furnish seventy-five thousand ninety-day volunteers. The regular army then comprised fewer than sixteen thousand soldiers, most stationed west of the Mississippi, a force far too weak and scattered to deal with the crisis.[1]

"Civil war is upon us," lamented the *Nebraska Advertiser* of Brownville on April 18, and editor Robert W. Furnas delivered a ringing call to arms: "Let the tocsin now sound from every hill and valley; let patriots rally to the call of their country and 'woe be to him who shall attempt to withstand the tempest of a nation's wrath.'" It would not be a bloodless revolution, as Furnas had hoped in December 1860. The *Nebraska Republican* of Omaha opined that slavery had fortified itself behind the Constitution and the laws to such an extent that "nothing but offerings of blood can loose the shackles from the limbs of its victims."[2]

The Democratic press of the territory generally echoed the Republican papers in promising to "sustain our country's flag," while at the same time "protesting against the war as unnecessary, and holding the Black Republican party responsible to the bar of history for not having averted it by a fair and honorable compromise." This viewpoint would become increasingly strident as the war went on, making it hard for Nebraska Democrats to gain credibility as a "loyal opposition."[3]

Other Democrats, such as journalist Joseph E. Johnson, who published his *Huntsman's Echo* at his Platte Valley road ranche, thought war could never restore the broken Union and if pursued would lead the country into ruin and disgrace. "Better by far [to] partition the territory, assets and debts" and let the Southern states go. "We too, are a Union man, but let brotherly peace prevail at all hazards, at all cost, at any reasonable sacrifice." That some Nebraska residents actually favored the nation's breakup seemed evident when "a small, sickly-looking secession flag" was found floating over Gray's general store on Douglas Street in Omaha one April morning. It had been hoisted there by "some nocturnal street walker."[4]

The martial enthusiasm that gripped the North surfaced in Nebraska Territory as well, spurred on by the government's order to begin withdrawing most of the army regulars from Forts Kearny, Randall, and Laramie. On April 16 two companies of the Second U.S. Infantry and the band from Fort Kearny marched for Omaha, en route to Fort Leavenworth, leaving only a single company of dragoons at the fort on the Platte. The next day John M. Thayer, commander of the territorial militia, offered the secretary of war "sufficient volunteers" to garrison Forts Kearny and Randall. The removal of the federal troops was causing "much alarm" in Nebraska, he wrote, and "some measures should be taken to keep the Indians in check."[5]

Another argument for federalizing the territorial militia came from the concurrent mustering of Secessionist militia in St. Joseph, Missouri, not far from Nebraska's southeastern border. On April 15 M. Jeff Thompson, the Virginia-born former mayor of St. Joseph and a colonel in the Missouri state militia, advised Confederate president Jefferson Davis that he could furnish several companies of "good and true men" to the Southern cause. The Confederate War Department told Thompson to organize his forces and hold them in readiness.[6]

While a few companies of Secessionist militia were unlikely to invade Nebraska Territory or attack the important Union depot of Fort Leavenworth, located downstream on the Kansas side of the Missouri River, they could threaten communication and travel between the East and the western states and territories. There was concern that St. Joseph Secessionists would obstruct passage on the Missouri River by the U.S. troops being withdrawn from the Nebraska forts as well as block commercial steamboat traffic. St. Joseph was also the western terminus of the Hannibal and St. Joseph Railroad, the only line then connecting to the river from the east. From St. Joseph, steamers transported goods and people to upriver ports such as Brownville, Nebraska City, and Omaha.[7]

On April 20 Brig. Gen. Hiram P. Downs, commander of the second brigade of the territorial militia, ordered companies in the Nebraska communities south of the Platte River to be filled up and new ones organized where they did not already exist. He anticipated that the president would soon call into federal service at least one battalion of Nebraska troops. One of the first companies to organize under this order was at Platts-mouth, where a meeting was held that very night. One hun-dred of the "undersigned citizens . . . consider it expedient in the present distracted condition of national affairs to organize ourselves into a military company," a resolution proclaimed. Robert R. Livingston was elected captain.[8]

A week later Governor Samuel Black informed Secretary of War Simon Cameron that large numbers of Sioux and Chey-ennes had been seen in the Platte Valley and had destroyed a mail station. Nebraska, the governor said, could furnish seven or eight companies, which the federal government could equip with arms on hand at Fort Kearny. The war department's assis-tant adjutant general endorsed Black's letter, remarking that army general-in-chief Winfield Scott favored posting volun-teers at the western forts.[9]

Although Black had already submitted his resignation as ter-ritorial governor, he felt compelled to take action while await-ing his successor's arrival. On April 30 the lame-duck gover-nor called for the organization of volunteer companies, along with issuing General Order No. 1 for all such companies to re-port to Maj. Gen. John M. Thayer.[10]

Thayer promptly wrote President Lincoln, reiterating local fears of Indians and raising the specter of Missouri Secession-ists invading Nebraska to seize the government arms and stores at Fort Kearny. Thayer offered a regiment of 650 men to gar-rison Forts Kearny and Randall and protect this property or "for any duty that the Government may require in any quar-ter of the country."[11]

Huntsman's Echo editor Joseph E. Johnson at Wood River Cen-ter offered a counterpoint to the territorial officials' repeated warnings about possible Indian raids on the white settlements. Johnson noted that no one living in the central Platte Valley was worried about the Indians and they presented no threat whatever "if you let them alone." While Indians were indeed seen in the area, other observers noted that nothing unusual was afoot: they were Sioux and Cheyennes making one of their periodic forays to attack the Pawnees on their Loup River reservation west of Columbus. The former tribes had not shown any significant hostility to the whites for years, though they had long been bitter enemies of the Pawnees. The Omahas, Poncas, and Oto-Missourias, the other Nebraska reservation tribes, were considered friendly and loyal to the government.[12]

May was a pivotal month in the federal government's mobilization for war and its decisions and policies trickled down to Nebraska Territory. After realizing that the rebellion could not be suppressed with ninety-day militia, Lincoln on May 3 called for forty regiments of volunteers for three years' service. The next day the war department issued orders governing the organization of these forces. The imperative for Nebraska to provide volunteers for home defense became all the more evident when, on May 2, the steamboat *Omaha* arrived at its namesake city with 173 soldiers being withdrawn from Fort Randall.[13]

Meanwhile, Nebraska militia companies had been organizing, including the Nebraska City Guards, the Nebraska City Rangers, the Saunders Flying Artillery (Nebraska City), the Brownville Home Guards, and the Paddock Riflemen (Brownville), as well as companies in Omaha, Florence, and even in the distant German settlement at Grand Island. The Union Rifle Company at Omaha was also composed entirely of Germans. The companies already established under the prewar militia law perfected their organization. They could do little but wait, however, until the government determined how many, if any, Nebraska volunteers it would accept into the Union army.[14]

Alvin Saunders, Lincoln's appointee as territorial governor, reached Nebraska on May 13 from his former home in Mt. Pleasant, Iowa. He moved quickly to find out whether the administration would accept Nebraska troops. Saunders first asked the War Department whether the territory could furnish any of the ninety-day volunteers. Secretary of War Cameron replied that Nebraska Territory's quota would be one regiment of infantry, enlisted for three years and organized according to a May 4 general order prescribing the structure of the volunteer forces. On May 18 Saunders ordered the volunteer companies to elect officers and report their organization to the acting adjutant general, "with a view of entering the service." Omaha would be the rendezvous, where the Nebraska regiment would be mustered in.[15]

Cameron followed up with a May 21 letter that had implications for the Nebraska regiment's recruiting and would later lead to accusations of government bad faith. He announced that the Nebraska volunteers would replace the regulars at the frontier forts: "in a word, they are not intended to be marched elsewhere, but assigned for the protection of your own people and interests against hostile Indians and foes." Saunders passed Cameron's assurances along to the militia officers and the territorial newspapers. This was welcome news to those men who might be reluctant to volunteer if they had to march away from Nebraska, leaving their families and livelihoods behind.[16]

Organization of the regiment for home defense seemingly could not be completed too soon, given events transpiring within or just beyond Nebraska's borders. Three companies of the Fourth U.S. Artillery had already been evacuated from Fort Randall, as had most regular army troops from Fort Kearny. Capt. Charles Tyler, a West Pointer commanding the single company of the Second U.S. Dragoons left to garrison Fort Kearny, reported on May 10 that fear of Secessionists seizing the fort had led him to spike and disable ten howitzers stored there. This report, however, was primarily a smokescreen for Tyler's own Secessionist sympathies. Three days later he granted himself leave, left Nebraska, and soon turned up as a Confederate officer.[17]

On May 22 came word that Secessionist militia commander M. Jeff Thompson had torn down the U.S. flag flying over the St. Joseph post office, sparking a near riot. Fort Leavenworth commander Col. D. S. Miles had earlier heard rumors that Thompson's troops might cross the Missouri River to attack the fort and perhaps even make a dash to seize the government ordnance at Fort Kearny, as unrealistic as that notion probably seemed in retrospect. Many Missouri families sympathetic to the Union were said to be crossing the river at Brownville "on account of the troubles." In short, the Missouri River border was in turmoil.[18]

To calm these fears and give Nebraska Territory some breathing room to organize its volunteers, Gen. William S. Harney, commander of the Department of the West, headquartered in St. Louis, ordered two companies of the First U.S. Cavalry from Fort Wise, Colorado Territory, to Fort Kearny to protect the federal stores and, if need be, resist the Indians. By June the organization of what would become the First Nebraska Volunteer Infantry was well underway in Omaha.[19]

As they flocked to the Stars and Stripes, Nebraska's would-be soldiers and the inhabitants of the towns from which they came, like their countrymen back east, were caught up in a tide of patriotic sentiment tinged with romantic notions of war as a grand adventure. The martial rhetoric that flowed from the public gatherings organized to present the volunteers with flags or wish them Godspeed hinted that the men, and those they would leave behind, realized that the regiment might be destined for more than home defense.

That Nebraska women strongly supported the territory's volunteers is amply documented by reports in newspapers of the

VOLUNTEER!

THERE will be a meeting of the citizens of Nemaha county, at Brownville, on Saturday afternoon next, for the purpose of forming a Military Company. whose services are to be tendered the Governor of Nebraska for the three year volunteer service. Let all, from every portion of the county, who desire to volunteer in defence of their country be present, and join the company.

MANY UNION MEN.

Fig. 1. Advertisement for the organization of a volunteer military company at Brownville, Nebraska Territory. *Nebraska Advertiser*, May 23, 1861.

day. Because many of the soldiers came from farms or small towns, the pomp and circumstance associated with answering their country's call was very much a community affair. Women in Nebraska City and Plattsmouth sewed flags for their respective companies, the Plattsmouth banner made by Mrs. O. F. Johnson, who was said to own the only sewing machine in town. The women of Clarinda, Iowa, hometown of two companies slated to join the First Nebraska, also presented their soldiers with handmade flags just before their departure on "the proudest day in the history of Clarinda." Women in several Nebraska towns raised money for a "full stand of colors" to be ordered for the Nebraska Regiment from a company back east. Omaha ladies contributed the proceeds from a party they hosted at the Herndon House hotel featuring music, dancing, and a supper "just as good as the country affords." The Nemaha County committee included Elizabeth McPherson and Rachael Tipton of Brownville, wives of the town doctor and the regimental chaplain. Darah Daily, the wife of Territorial Delegate Samuel G. Daily, headed up fundraising in Peru.[20]

On June 8 citizens of Nebraska City and several home guard companies, resplendent in elaborate uniforms, turned out to honor the Nebraska City Guards, the local company that was preparing to join the First Nebraska. J. Sterling Morton, the former territorial secretary, presented the company with a flag made by the ladies while the Saunders Flying Artillery fired a thirteen-gun salute.[21]

At Brownville, four days later, the volunteer company received "a fine stand of colors made expressly for the occasion" by local women. Capt. J. D. N. Thompson responded on behalf of the company, "pledging fealty to the country and his life's blood in defense of the flag." Dignitaries gave orations and each member of the company took a solemn oath on bended knee to uphold, protect, and maintain the honor of the national emblem. Editor Robert W. Furnas of the hometown *Nebraska Advertiser* termed the ceremony "the most impressive we have ever witnessed." The company was said to be "a hardy, intelligent, robust body of men, inured to labor, acquainted with the geography of the country, and familiar with fire arms." Most were young, single men without steady occupations, which meant, said Furnas, "our agricultural, mechanical, and other business pursuits are but little interfered with."[22]

The next day the Brownville soldiers boarded a steamboat bound for Omaha to "nine loud and long cheers" by hundreds of citizens. At Nebraska City the Nebraska City Guards came aboard, and the two companies reached the territorial capital on June 15. Thirty-four Germans from St. Joseph came to

Omaha to join the Union Rifle Company, led by Prussian emigrant William Baumer. Other companies continued to arrive, and the men were quartered around the city in the capitol building, hotels, and business houses.[23]

Meanwhile, on June 11 the company from Plattsmouth and the Union Rifle Company had become the first of the expected ten companies of Nebraska's regiment to be sworn in as U.S. volunteers. The men were then drawn up in front of the Herndon House hotel, where Governor Alvin Saunders delivered from the balcony "an eloquent and appropriate address" that was "well-received by both citizens and soldiers." Before falling out the soldiers and the citizens gave the governor three rousing cheers.[24]

Although the volunteers had not yet been issued arms or uniforms by the government, drilling was the first order of business. Unless they had previously served in one of the militia companies, most of the new soldiers had no prior military experience. Learning the "merest beginning of a volunteer's life," as one man put it, tended to dispel some of their heroic fantasies of soldiering. Moreover, many of the volunteers were shocked to discover that the officers they had elected in their companies back home or whom the governor had appointed (formerly their friends or neighbors) now actually expected their orders to be obeyed as "gods of the hour," eager to exercise their authority as "temporary tyrants."[25]

On June 24 one of the companies raised in Page and adjacent counties of southwestern Iowa arrived in Omaha. Iowa's governor had granted these men permission to join the First Nebraska because no Iowa regiment then had room to accept them. By early July the First Nebraska's field officers had been sworn in and the regiment lacked only two companies to be complete. Another company of mostly Iowa men was mustered in on July 21. Governor Saunders appointed John M. Thayer, the former militia commander, as the regiment's colonel.[26]

Although the monotony of soldierly life was already settling in, the men had some diversions. Independence Day in Omaha was a "tiresome, dry, and hungry time," said one soldier, during which the troops joined in a sham battle. It must have been an odd-looking demonstration, since the men were still wearing civilian garb or their varied militia uniforms. On July 10 the city's young women, led by Caroline Estabrook, daughter of a prominent local attorney, treated the soldiers to a sumptuous dinner at the capitol building. The tables groaned with food, including ice cream for dessert. After the feast the soldiers pronounced the ladies "the ministering angels of the day, and the soldier's sunlight of the hour." A dance followed in the evening.[27]

The presumption remained widespread, on the part of both the soldiers and the citizenry, that once the regiment was full it would be stationed somewhere in Nebraska. In a report to the secretary of war, Territorial Secretary and Acting Governor Algernon S. Paddock mentioned the continued concern about Indians and "secessionists," the latter said to be in the majority in one unnamed southeastern Nebraska county. Mormons outfitting near Omaha to cross the plains were suspected of being "warm secession sympathizers" who had great influence over the Indians. Paddock urged that one or two regiments, in addition to the First Nebraska, be dispatched within the territory to meet these threats.[28]

Meanwhile, Governor Saunders had gone to Washington DC, where he asked the War Department for permission to organize two cavalry companies, to be attached to the infantry regiment. The companies had already been formed, he said, and needed only horses and equipment. The War Department agreed to take the companies, and on August 12 Paddock ordered the cavalrymen to rendezvous in Omaha. Three days later the War Department telegraphed that it would accept two additional cavalry companies.[29]

As Nebraska Territory was organizing its military establishment, the war was having other effects. Much of the territorial economy hinged on overland freighting from Nebraska City, Brownville, and Omaha to the gold-mining camps near Denver, the goods coming up the Missouri by steamboat from St. Louis or from the railroad terminus at St. Joseph. The Nebraska river towns were also important outfitting emporiums for emigrants and Mormons traveling across the plains. In the summer and fall of 1861 guerrilla activity in Missouri had seriously disrupted the lines of communication and commerce reaching Nebraska. In August the Western Stage Company relocated the starting point for its daily mail coaches from St. Joseph to Omaha because of "trouble with secessionists." At the same time telegraph service to Nebraska had briefly been cut off by sabotage to the line across northern Missouri. Only two steamboats of the Hannibal and St. Joseph Packet Line were still running between the railroad terminus at St. Joseph and the Nebraska river towns because many vessels were engaged in service for the government in the St. Louis vicinity.[30]

Unrest between Union and Secessionist factions in northwestern Missouri, particularly in Atchison and Holt Counties, threatened to spill over into Nebraska. Editor Furnas at Brownville announced in late June, "[O]ur policy here is to mind our own business . . . and protect ourselves from any invasionists, come from where they may." He had hoped Brownville and the adjacent region across the river in Missouri would be "a secluded nook . . . that would escape the excitement consequent from the unfortunate state of the country." By early July, however, so-called Rebels from Atchison County were "hooting, shooting, and howling through the settlements" at night, threatening Union men, and some were crossing over to Brownville, getting drunk, and being boisterous and offensive. Residents had been patient, he warned, but they would not submit to further outrages. In late July "some cowardly rebels on the other side of the river" threatened Furnas with "cold lead" for "keeping a close eye upon their deviltry." If they interfered with the printing office at Brownville, he retorted, "the scamps . . . had better make their wills before starting and bring their coffins along."[31]

Just as a border war seemed likely to break out in southeastern Nebraska, word came that five companies of the First Nebraska had been ordered to Fort Leavenworth. As an important Union depot, the fort was a logical place for the regiment to be outfitted with arms and equipment. With the last of the companies having been mustered in on July 21, the First Nebraska, nearly a thousand officers and men strong, was ready for service. A week later the first battalion, Companies A, B, D, E, and G under Thayer's command, boarded the steamboat *West Wind* and departed down the Missouri to St. Joseph.[32]

From there the companies proceeded to Fort Leavenworth to draw muskets and ammunition, then the battalion was sent to disperse Secessionist bands near Independence, Missouri, where they freed several Kansas Unionists from the jail. The Nebraskans returned to St. Joseph and went into quarters east of town. The Nebraska territorial newspapers speculated that the regiment might remain there for a time, but within a few days Gen. John C. Frémont, newly appointed commander of the Western Department, ordered the entire regiment to rendezvous in St. Louis. As the first five companies prepared to move south from St. Joseph, the *West Wind* returned to Omaha to pick up Companies C, F, H, I, and K.[33]

As the regiment's second battalion steamed down the Missouri, an episode at Brownville revealed that Nebraskans were not immune to the wartime passions that so often pitted brother against brother or father against son, politically and sometimes on the battlefields. As the *West Wind* touched briefly at the Brownville levee on its way downstream, Robert Thompson, the twenty-three-year-old son of Company C commander J. D. N. Thompson, stood on the shore "uttering the most fearful and obscene oaths—that he hoped the boat would blow up and destroy the whole regiment; and that if he ever met his father on the battle field, he would shoot him the first man!" A few days later young Thompson left town and enlisted in Sterling Price's Rebel army in Missouri. In March 1862 he came home and was promptly arrested for treason after his father, who had resigned from the First Nebraska due to ill health, turned him in. Robert Thompson was slated to be taken before the military authorities in St. Louis. What happened next went unrecorded in the newspaper, but Thompson was back in Brownville in 1865. Perhaps the authorities merely threw a scare into him and made him take the Union oath of allegiance.[34]

While the last five companies of the First Nebraska were en route to St. Joseph, the first battalion re-embarked aboard two steamboats at Fort Leavenworth that were already heavily laden with cannon, ammunition, and other stores and sailed down the Missouri, arriving at St. Louis on August 13. The companies from Omaha reached St. Joseph August 9 and the next day took the cars of the Hannibal and St. Joseph Railroad across northern Missouri. After two days at Hannibal, the men boarded steamboats bound for St. Louis. On August 14 the reunited regiment departed for the Union base at Pilot Knob via the St. Louis and Iron Mountain Railroad.[35]

Consternation swept Nebraska when it became clear that its regiment was destined for service outside the territory.

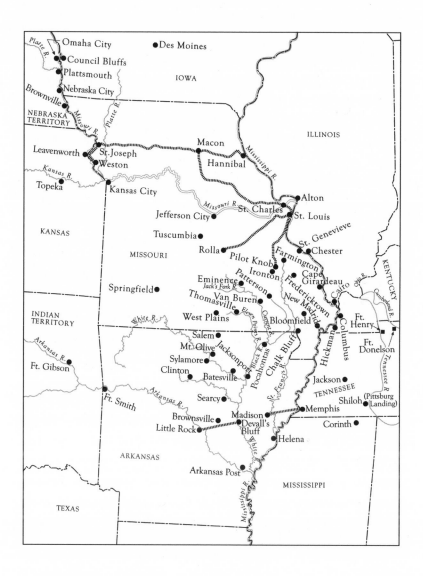

Map 1. The First Nebraska Regiment's theater of operations, 1861–64.

The *Nebraska Advertiser* reflected the sentiments. The departure of the regiment, said editor Furnas, was very unexpected and, at the very least, failed to show "a proper regard for the interest and safety of this frontier country." The secretary of war had assured Governor Saunders, "in a word, they [the Nebraska troops] are not intended to be marched elsewhere, but assigned for the protection of your own people," which made the new orders seem very much like bad faith, particularly to those men who had volunteered with the expectation that they would not have to campaign so far away from their homes and families.[36]

Some of the soldiers undoubtedly agreed with Furnas while others, still caught up in the notion of war as romantic adventure, were pleased with the prospect of engaging Rebels on the battlefield, ready to "join in fierce and bloody conflict and come off the field as conquerors covered with the halo of glory, or die under the free and starry flag of our country . . . as Spartans of a modern age." These sentiments, of course, were voiced long before any enemy came in sight or any bullets whistled overhead.[37]

Colonel Thayer, in a postwar reminiscence, recalled that leaving half the regiment behind in Omaha while the other companies went to Fort Leavenworth to get the regiment's arms was a subterfuge to reassure Nebraskans that the soldiers were not leaving for good. Once at Fort Leavenworth, however, Thayer asked Frémont to order the regiment to St. Louis. Thayer concluded his recollection by admitting that the prospect of fighting Rebels in the South seemed more attractive than garrison duty in Nebraska. He and many of the men "were tired of fighting Indians" and "wanted a try at fighting white men." Thayer had no doubt heard of the July 21 defeat of the Union army by Confederates at the first Battle of Bull Run in Virginia, signaling that the war was unlikely to be a short one.[38]

Frémont, who took charge of the Western Department on July 25, was only too glad to add the First Nebraska to his command. The border state of Missouri, which had not seceded, was expected to be a key battleground of the war, and Union forces had by no means gained the upper hand. The pro-Southern Missouri State Guard, commanded by Gen. Sterling Price, was threatening Springfield, and Confederate forces had established a foothold at New Madrid, Missouri, where they seemed poised to attack the vital Union base at Cairo, Illinois. The ninety-day enlistments of many of the troops in the Union army maneuvering against Price near Springfield were about to expire. St. Louis, the state's major Union stronghold and headquarters, also seemed vulnerable.

Moreover, guerrilla activity was rampant, particularly in northern Missouri, and Frémont's subordinates were constantly badgering him to send them more troops. The general had been authorized to accept all three-year regiments that might be offered. It was more important to have the proffered services of a fresh regiment of hardy westerners for the Missouri campaigns than to worry about Indian attacks in Nebraska Territory or a Secessionist raid on Fort Kearny that might never come. The decision turned out to be final. The men of the First Nebraska would not return home until the summer of 1864.

The departure of the First Nebraska left only poorly armed home guard militia and the as yet unarmed cavalry companies to protect Nebraska. Even the small contingent of regular army soldiers at Fort Kearny seemed under the gun. The commander there reported that the nearby civilian settlement of "Dobytown" was filled with discharged soldiers and other drifters whose only livelihood was to sell whiskey. Many claimed to be Secessionists. There was little the tiny garrison could do about it.[39]

Hopes may have risen when the Nebraska cavalry battalion

was armed, equipped, and sworn in to U.S. service in late September. Nebraskans likely expected that this force (which as yet had few horses) would remain in the territory to provide some measure of protection. These expectations were dashed, however, when the cavalrymen departed Omaha on October 12 to march across Iowa to Keokuk, where they would board steamboats for St. Louis. They encamped at Benton Barracks north of St. Louis on October 30.[40]

As they saw their husbands, sons, brothers, or fathers go off to war in 1861, Nebraska women experienced emotions that would be recognized by their counterparts today. These included a fear that their loved ones might be killed or wounded in battle, taken prisoner by the enemy, or suffer injuries or death from accidents or disease. Eliza "Lide" Patrick of Omaha, whose three brothers had enlisted in the Nebraska cavalry battalion, probably spoke for many Nebraska women when she wrote, "God knows if one of my brothers should meet the fate that has fallen to many of our dear friends, it would be more than this heart could bear." The women left behind also bore the stress of sustaining their families' lives and livelihoods in the face of uncertainty, loneliness, or financial hardship. Civil War privates were paid only thirteen dollars per month.[41]

Events in Missouri unrelated to the fate of the Nebraska soldiers sent there continued to disturb the citizens of the southeastern Nebraska border counties. In August the *Falls City Broad Axe* reported that large numbers of Missouri refugees were arriving daily with wagons and goods of every description, having been "driven off in fear for their lives and property from marauding rebels of their own neighborhoods." These people seemed to be some of Missouri's "best citizens," and by fall the paper estimated that at least a thousand Missouri families had passed through Falls City since the beginning of the war.[42]

Residents of the Nebraska-Missouri-Kansas border region feared that not only refugees but also actual "marauding rebels" might be on their way north. In early August about four hundred Union men in Atchison County, Missouri, held a two-day drill on the river bottom about halfway between Brownville and Rockport, signaling that they were prepared to defend themselves and, if necessary, "rout the last traitor" from their midst. When later reports came in that several hundred "rebel forces" from Atchison and Holt Counties in Missouri were congregating to fight two companies of federal troops sent from St. Joseph, "excitement ran high . . . on both sides of the river." On August 29 under the headline "The Difficulties in Atchison and Holt Counties, Missouri, Adjusted," the *Nebraska Advertiser* published an agreement by which the contending factions pledged not to organize military companies or molest any Union men. The "adjustment" of the difficulties proved short-lived.[43]

Secessionist militia occupied St. Joseph in late August, after federal troops were withdrawn to help counter Sterling Price's drive to capture Lexington, Missouri. This development sent St. Joseph Unionists fleeing, some to Brownville, and they reported that "large numbers of well armed rebels were between St. Joseph and the north line of Missouri moving northward and 'clearing out' Union men and property as they went." These reports, mostly rumors and no doubt exaggerated, "caused no little excitement, fear, and trembling among the weaker minds of the community," according to a local observer signing himself only as "Romulus." The rumors prompted a call for a mass meeting in Brownville on September 9 and 10.[44]

On September 10 a committee appointed the day before to assess the validity of the threats recommended the immediate organization of a militia regiment in southeastern Nebraska. Six companies of from twenty to forty men, mostly from Nemaha County, were already camped nearby. Officers were chosen, including Robert W. Furnas as colonel. If need be, this force could cooperate with Union men from Atchison County, Missouri, and from Iowa who were encamped on the east side of the river. Some Union men from Atchison County had already fled across the river to Nemaha County, including several merchants who relocated their stock to Brownville. "Romulus" was disgusted by the near panic and felt "there is no excuse for so much excitement," which had been caused by a "few sensationalists in this section."[45]

The excitement prompted the companies, including the Peru Home Guards, the Nemaha City Home Guards, the Nemaha County Cavalry, and the Paddock Guards to give "extraordinary attention to drill," though only one of the companies had been provided with arms by the territory. The others were using "ordinary shot guns and rifles." Furnas expected that the "excited state of affairs in this region" would improve the prospects for the companies to soon be fully armed.[46]

While no Secessionist invasion of Brownville materialized, men who used wartime passions as an excuse for theft and pillage kept southeastern Nebraska in turmoil. During the fall of 1861 bands of armed men, popularly called "Jayhawkers," roamed the country on both sides of the Missouri River. On October 3 the *Nebraska Advertiser* reported a skirmish in Holt County, Missouri, between a small contingent of U.S. cavalry and two hundred Rebels. Lieutenant Tyler, the cavalry commander, later captured a certain Colonel Hale, an alleged Secessionist who had fled to Brownville. Both Union and dis-Union Jayhawkers were in the field and it was hard to distinguish between them. The *Advertiser* justified the formation of Union Jayhawkers because dis-Union Jayhawkers had been driving loyal men and families out of Missouri and Kansas. "They should not complain if they get jayhawked."[47]

In early October a band of alleged Kansas Jayhawkers camped near Falls City with several horses said to have been stolen in Missouri. When pursued by Missouri men the Jayhawkers retreated into Kansas, turned the tables on the Missourians, captured the lot, and sent them home afoot. Later that month "Captain Buck's" Jayhawker company spent a week or so in the area, "visiting several of the Secessionists round about" and taking several horses and mules. Although the Jayhawkers crossed the border into Kansas, the Falls City paper later reported that several of them had been compelled to enter the Union army, which was "Good enough!" This bunch seemed to have been interested mostly in stealing horses under the pretext of punishing "secessionists."[48]

Jayhawking soon threatened to get out of hand and it was not confined to the Missouri River border region. A party of miners returning to the "states" from Colorado Territory was stopped on the trail between Beatrice, Nebraska Territory, and Marysville, Kansas, and robbed of everything, including six horses. On December 16 someone shot and wounded Samuel Long in Peru, Nemaha County, allegedly because Long had been denouncing Jayhawking. It was beginning to dawn on the residents of southeastern Nebraska that there was no way to be certain whose side a particular Jayhawker might be on, or whether he was on any side at all. Some claimed to be acting with the approval of the governor in seizing property from disloyal men. Yet many of the citizens whose property was stolen were Union supporters.[49]

This conundrum prompted the formation of military companies, such as the Union Home Guards at Falls City, and an "anti-Jayhawking" organization in Brownville. Both promised to protect the lives and property of local citizens from Jayhawkers. Men joining the Brownville group were required to take an oath to support the U.S. Constitution. Those who did not join would not be entitled to protection and, by implication, might be considered disloyal. The Brownville group also sent a delegation to Omaha to confer with the governor and the legislature about what to do about Jayhawking. The legislature was scheduled to begin its 1861–62 session on December 2.[50]

For all the First Nebraska Regiment would accomplish in Missouri during the latter months of 1861, it might as well have remained in the territory to help suppress the Jayhawkers, who turned out to be a greater threat than Indians or Rebels. On August 15, when the soldiers reached Pilot Knob, the southwestern terminus of the St. Louis and Iron Mountain Railroad and an important Union base, the regiment reported to Brig. Gen. Ulysses S. Grant. Initially the men camped in the open, "quartered in their novel style of tents, constructed of the bushes which before nearly enveloped them." Real tents and regulation uniforms were soon issued. The uniform consisted of "a blue frock coat and blue pants and a high black hat looped up on one side with an eagle, a bugle in front, and an ostrich plume on one side. We present a gay appearance," reported Pvt. Thomas Keen.[51]

For several weeks the regiment drilled, built quarters, conducted scouts, and guarded installations along the railroad. Although the regiment had seen no enemy action, it had already suffered several casualties. Pvt. John Miller of Company B died of diphtheria before the soldiers left Nebraska. Another man died of disease in St. Louis, two more were injured by accidental gunshots, and Robert Gibson of Company C was killed by a comrade, whose gun went off during a false alarm in camp. These were, reported Chaplain Thomas Tipton, "the calamities aside from battle that follow the camp and march."[52]

Although it would be nearly six months before the regiment would see any real fighting, its course in the fall and winter of 1861 was dictated by events taking place elsewhere in Missouri. On August 10 Confederate and Missouri State Guard troops defeated Union forces at the Battle of Wilson's Creek, southwest of Springfield. The victorious Rebels then marched north to the Missouri River and forced the surrender of the outnumbered Union garrison at Lexington, which Frémont had failed to reinforce, on September 21. To forestall his removal from command on account of the ineptitude he had thus far displayed in both the political and military arenas, Frémont decided to lead an army to drive the Rebels out of southwestern Missouri and secure the key town of Springfield.

The pending campaign ensnared the First Nebraska in its camp at Pilot Knob. It was ordered to St. Louis, and on the night of September 22 the regiment was transported by rail to Syracuse, located along the Pacific Railroad between Jefferson City and Sedalia. Four men riding atop the boxcars were thrown off and one, Cpl. John H. Quinn of Company E, was killed. Once the First Nebraska reached Syracuse, it encamped for a month while Frémont slowly assembled his Army of Western Missouri and began moving toward Springfield.[53]

On October 23 the men of the First Nebraska marched out of Syracuse. By November 3 the regiment had reached Springfield, only to find that President Lincoln had relieved Frémont of command of the Western Department. The general's failure to bring the Rebels to battle before they could withdraw to southwestern Missouri was the last in a series of missteps that finally exhausted the president's patience. Frémont's removal caused "terrific anger among the officers and men," wrote one Nebraska soldier.[54]

By mid-November the Nebraskans had retraced their march and gone into camp just north of Sedalia, near a small community named Georgetown. There the regiment would remain for the next several weeks. A few episodes broke the monotony

Figs. 2 and 3. Brothers John (*left*) and James Hutton, privates in Company E, First Nebraska Volunteer Infantry, about 1861. Nebraska State Historical Society RG2057-39, RG2057-40.

of camp and drill, although they did nothing to satisfy those men and officers who sought glory on the battlefield.

On December 8 an unarmed foraging party was sent out with eight wagons to gather corn and hay. A small band of "secessionists" swooped down, robbed the men of their overcoats, hats, and boots, and made off with four of the wagons. When word reached camp, the officers of the First Nebraska and other regiments camped nearby saddled up and went in pursuit (only the officers had horses in infantry regiments). They finally recovered the wagons, which had been abandoned when the mules gave out. Clearly the officers and men of the First Nebraska still had much to learn about campaigning in a guerrilla-infested country.[55]

Ten days later the First Nebraska participated in a "battle" that was their first encounter with a significant body of Rebels. Operating with other troops in Brig. Gen. John Pope's District of Central Missouri, the Nebraskans helped run to ground and capture recruits and supplies moving south from the Missouri River near Lexington to join Sterling Price's army. The Union forces in Missouri had previously suffered only defeat, and this nearly bloodless encounter, known variously as the skirmish at Milford or Blackwater Creek, seemed an important victory. More than one thousand would-be Confederates were taken prisoner, along with their arms, horses, and supplies.[56]

Following this excitement the men of the First Nebraska settled down in winter quarters at Georgetown. Sickness, attributed to the hardships of the march to Springfield and exposure during the Milford campaign, sent many soldiers to the hospital with what was termed "typhoid pneumonia."[57]

Thayer and his men soon came face-to-face with the slavery issue. A commotion in town one day brought the colonel from his tent, where he confronted two men searching for a runaway slave. The men brandished an order from division commander Brig. Gen. Frederick Steele authorizing them to recover the runaway, who had taken refuge in a nearby house. At this stage of the war Lincoln had dictated a hands-off policy toward Missouri slave owners, many of whom were Union men, to help prevent this vital border state from seceding.

Thayer quizzed the man who claimed to own the slave about his loyalty. When asked whether he would like to see Price and his army driven from Missouri the man replied, "Well, I can't say that I would." At that, Thayer ordered the men out of town and took custody of the slave. A First Nebraska soldier reported, "Never did a vacant-headed, insolent, monied lordling wilt more completely." Thayer gave the slave his freedom with directions on how to reach Kansas and later recalled meeting him in Topeka after the war.[58]

Back home, Nebraska Territory seemed vulnerable to an Indian attack, Rebel incursions from Missouri, or the more immediate prospect of being enveloped by the Jayhawking mania that gripped the southeastern counties. The territorial economy had suffered from the slowdown of Missouri River steamboat traffic caused by military demands and guerrilla activity. Prices fell, particularly when ice halted all river transportation and agricultural commodities could not be shipped to market. In the winter of 1861–62 corn was worth only eight to ten cents per bushel and hogs and cattle were priced as low as a penny per pound.[59]

At the same time, Nebraska City and Omaha benefited when some Missouri and Kansas freighters shifted their operations north to the Platte Valley. The overland mail route transited by the stagecoaches of Ben Holladay's Central Overland & Pikes Peak Express also moved to the Platte in 1861. Between August and October Edward Creighton completed building the transcontinental telegraph line along the same route from Julesburg, Colorado Territory, to Salt Lake City, linking the nation by "electricity" and ending the brief reign of the fabled Pony Express. Despite this innovation, mail and freight still had to be hauled overland to the Colorado mining camps, western military posts, and the Mormon settlements in Utah.[60]

Overland emigration was somewhat less than in prewar years, but those who could not reach the Nebraska jumping-off points by steamboat could take the Western Stage Line across Iowa from the terminus of the Iowa Railroad at Marengo and Eddyville. Both Mormon emigrants and Mormon freighters organized in the Omaha area before crossing the plains. This activity and freighting promised to sustain the economies of the river towns and the livelihoods of ranchemen living along the overland route as long as the goods and travelers could reach Nebraska Territory in the first place.[61]

On the political front, both the Democrats and the Republicans agreed to forgo partisan campaigns in the fall election. The contest was relatively unimportant, filling only the offices of territorial auditor and treasurer and a few seats in the legislative assembly vacated by members joining the army. When the legislature convened on December 2, Governor Saunders noted thankfully that the horrors of civil war had not yet visited Nebraska Territory. Much of the rest of his message was a catalog of problems, such as the territorial debt, the unfinished capitol building, and the lack of arms and munitions for the territorial militia. Also looming was where to find the money to pay Nebraska's share ($19,312) of the direct war tax recently levied by Congress. The governor's tone made it clear that the territory could not expect much in the way of financial support from the federal government, nor would settlement and the economy rebound while the war raged on.[62]

As 1861 drew to a close most Nebraskans, like other Americans, soldiers and civilians alike, realized that the war would not be over soon. The bloom of martial optimism that gripped

Fig. 4. Alvin Saunders, Republican governor of Nebraska Territory from 1861 to 1867. Nebraska State Historical Society RG2501-1.

the North in the early spring had largely wilted in the wake of Union defeats on Virginia and Missouri battlefields. Southern armies maintained a stranglehold on the Mississippi River in the western theater and menaced the nation's capital from their bivouacs in Virginia, just across the Potomac River.

Nebraska's soldiers, who had marched off with eager anticipation of soon meeting the enemy, had yet to experience an actual battle, though disease, desertion, and accidents had already thinned their ranks. In the year to come, however, the men would finally find themselves engaged on bloody battlefields, while Nebraskans at home would face fears that an Indian war might erupt on their very doorstep.

CHAPTER TWO

1862

"Nobly Did the First Nebraska Sustain Its Reputation"

While the First Nebraska Infantry whiled away the early weeks of 1862 in winter quarters at Georgetown, Missouri, nothing much happened to break the monotony of camp life. One highlight was the publication of the *First Nebraska Volunteer*. Only the January 31, 1862, issue is known, and the editor, identified only as "Provy," was probably 2nd Lt. Charles E. Provost of Company D, who had formerly worked for the *Omaha Nebraskian*. Georgetown's civilian editor had enlisted in the Union army, leaving behind the mostly intact newspaper office.[1]

Army service was taking a heavy toll on the regiment, even though it had seen no real fighting. In fewer than six months some thirty-five men had died of disease, and five or six had been killed in accidents. A significant number had deserted. The casualties from disease are not surprising; two Civil War soldiers died from that cause for each one killed in battle. Many soldiers from rural regions, unlike their city counterparts, had never been exposed to childhood diseases such as mumps or measles, which spread quickly through the crowded army camps. Despite being in a "western" regiment, many of the Nebraska volunteers were not frontiersmen and thus were not acclimated to life in the field. At Georgetown an average of three Nebraska soldiers died weekly, the deaths attributed to an "intermittent fever." One Nebraskan blamed the medical treatment: "Very few men ever come out of our hospitals alive if they are very sick unless he [sic] has an iron constitution."[2]

While the troops waited for a call to arms, the "Jayhawking war" continued back home in Nebraska. At least three such bands were said to be operating in Nemaha County, and each charged the others with being mere thieves. As the *Nebraska Advertiser* put it, "Every company of Jayhawkers in the West was organized, avowedly, to right some evil—one band of Jayhawkers has been organized to put down another, and a third band to put down the second." The Nemaha County sheriff was arrested and accused of disloyalty by one of these groups, self-styled Union Jayhawkers led by a man named Cleveland. Nebraska City citizens held a meeting to form a Union League against Jayhawking, a counterpart to the anti-Jayhawking company organized at Brownville.[3]

Activity akin to Jayhawking surfaced as far west as Fort Kearny on the Platte, where thievery plagued both the garrison and travelers along the overland trail. Post commander Capt. John A. Thompson noted that the eighty-seven enlisted men on duty at Fort Kearny could do little against groups "styling themselves Jayhawkers," whose object was to plunder and murder and whose loyalty extended only as far as their pecuniary advantage. Much of this lawlessness originated in Dobytown, a collection of shanties and adobe hovels two miles west of the fort that Thompson said housed "the greatest set of scoundrels that probably ever cursed any country, the most unscrupulous thieves and vagabonds that ever cursed humanity."[4]

The territorial legislature, meeting in Omaha early in 1862, considered an Act to Suppress Jayhawking, which passed the Council but was tabled by the lower house. The act would have authorized the summary execution of anyone found engaging in plundering or robbery, or attempting to carry away the property or livestock of others. Many legislators voted to table the act because they thought it would encourage the very activities it proposed to curtail. "All the old feuds and quarrels . . . would be settled with powder and ball, poisoning, [and] burning at the stake." The *Omaha Nebraskian* termed the act "worthy [of] the bloody days of the Spanish Inquisition."[5]

On January 2, 1862, Governor Saunders issued a proclamation commanding all "lawless bands of armed men, styling themselves 'Jayhawkers'" to disband or leave the territory under threat of severe punishment. The next day the legislature memorialized Congress to station two companies of U.S. troops in southeastern Nebraska. The memorial attributed the unrest there to Secessionists and traitors from Missouri as well as to rebellious and disloyal segments among Nebraska's own citizens. A few days later a second memorial was passed, requesting Congress to authorize raising five companies of volunteers (and to pay for their equipment), the companies to be kept within the territory for self-defense. Events in far-off Nebraska, however, seemed of minor importance in the grand scheme of putting down the rebellion; neither memorial was acted on in Washington.[6]

Despite the governor's proclamation, Jayhawking in southeastern Nebraska did not immediately subside. In late January Lowry and Watson, two men alleged to be members of the Cleveland Jayhawker band, were arrested in Johnson County and taken to Nebraska City. Rumor had it that one of the men was put under the Missouri River ice and the other was shot

dead. While no firm evidence came to light that these summary executions had occurred, the *Nebraska Advertiser* noted
that there was every reason to believe the men were guilty of
Jayhawking but there should have been positive proof "before
they were sent to perdition."[7]

Debate was particularly heated in Brownville, where some
praised and others damned the anti-Jayhawking group that
had been organized in December. The anti-Jayhawking company was necessary to prevent outrages against loyal citizens
from bands such as Cleveland's, wrote one Nemaha County resident, and even if Jayhawkers plundered only Rebels, "should
we allow them to judge our loyalty?" Another writer responded
that many loyal persons did not join the anti-Jayhawking organization because some of its members were "of secesh tenden-
cies." The Brownville paper editorialized that the best solution
would be for all such organizations, of whatever persuasion,
to heed the governor's call and disband, letting the military
and civil authorities handle lawlessness, thievery, and questions of loyalty.[8]

A Nebraska City correspondent provided another reason for
wanting Jayhawking and the related public debates to subside.
The constant publicity about unsettled conditions in southeastern Nebraska was only giving the towns north of the Platte an
advantage in promoting their route across the plains at the expense of Nebraska City and Brownville. The *Nebraska Advertiser*
echoed these sentiments. In reality, it noted, only a few hundred dollars' worth of property had been taken by so-called
Jayhawkers in Otoe and Nemaha Counties, but the difference
of opinion about how to deal with Jayhawking had divided
the residents of both counties and caused much hard feeling.[9]

Reports of the turmoil reached the Nebraska soldiers in Missouri via the territorial newspapers or in letters from home.
Martin Stowell of the Nebraska cavalry battalion reported that

the soldiers were deeply mortified by the news. Undoubtedly some were frustrated that they were not in Nebraska, where they could take a hand in restoring order.[10]

Although the newspaper debates continued for a while longer, it seemed as if the worst of the lawlessness was waning by mid-February 1862. Department of Kansas commander Gen. David Hunter's order for all armed groups in Kansas to disband and his proclamation of martial law in that state may have had some effect. Citizens, too, were growing weary of the issue, and in Brownville they held a public meeting to endorse the governor's anti-Jayhawking proclamation and condemn the roaming bands for fomenting anarchy and threatening civil liberties. As spring came to Nebraska in 1862, the excitement seemed to be dying down, and little more was said in the press about Jayhawking and Jayhawkers, at least for the moment.[11]

Perhaps in response to these activities and the seeming vulnerability of the territory now that the First Nebraska and the four cavalry companies had been sent away, the legislature toughened the existing militia law. It required all white males between the ages of eighteen and forty-five (except clergymen, postmasters, county officers, and those physically or mentally unfit) to enroll in militia companies by the first Monday in April 1862 and obligated the companies to elect officers and hold regular drills. Those who failed to enroll and enrollees who did not show up for drill were to be fined. The act also authorized the governor to appoint an adjutant general and other officers for the territorial militia.[12]

Additional war-related legislation, symbolic but with permanent implications for Nebraska history, changed the name of Shorter County to Lincoln, Greene County to Seward (for William H., Lincoln's secretary of state), Izard County to Stanton (for Edwin M., Lincoln's new secretary of war), and Calhoun County to Saunders, after the territorial governor. Some of the discarded names were those of Democrats from the now-Rebel states or, in the case of Calhoun, the late states' rights U.S. senator and former secretary of war from South Carolina. These men had been popular in Nebraska when the Democratic Party controlled the territory, but now they were viewed as traitors by the Republican legislature. As the *Nebraska Republican* noted approvingly, "It is highly proper that names which would have associated portions of our beautiful prairies with recollections of rebels have been erased from our statute books." Finally, the lower house of the legislature passed a bill appropriating $2,000 to provide relief to the families of Nebraska soldiers who were in "destitute circumstances," but the bill died in the Council when the legislature adjourned.[13]

Meanwhile the Nebraska volunteers in Missouri were thirsting for action. On December 20, 1861, the Nebraska cavalry at Benton Barracks in St. Louis had been absorbed into a regiment known as the Curtis Horse and were perfecting their training. The regiment, named for Gen. Samuel R. Curtis, commander of the St. Louis District, was a polyglot unit that also included companies from Iowa, Missouri, Minnesota, and Illinois. The four companies from Nebraska constituted the First Battalion.[14]

Just when it seemed that the First Nebraska at Georgetown and the Curtis Horse in St. Louis were destined to spend the entire winter languishing in their camps and barracks, orders came that would send them south. The regiments were to join Gen. Ulysses S. Grant's campaign against the Confederate strongholds of Fort Henry and Fort Donelson in northwestern Tennessee, the first major Union thrust in the western theater. The battles that lay ahead would satisfy the most sanguinary of the Nebraska soldiers who had been yearning to meet the enemy face-to-face.

As February 1862 dawned, Grant's army and U.S. Navy gunboats moved south on the Ohio and Tennessee Rivers from the Union base at Cairo, Illinois. On February 3 the First Nebraska marched from Georgetown to Jefferson City, where the men entrained for St. Louis. From there steamboats carried them down the Mississippi to Cairo, where the Curtis Horse had already arrived. By the time the Nebraskans reached Cairo on February 10, Fort Henry on the Tennessee River had already been blasted into submission by the Union gunboats, and Grant's army was preparing to march twelve miles east from Fort Henry to attack Fort Donelson on the Cumberland River.[15]

The First Nebraska and the Curtis Horse both reached Fort Henry on February 11, where the cavalry regiment would remain during the battle for Fort Donelson. Camped inside the devastated fort, one of the cavalrymen described his surroundings: "[D]ismounted guns—barracks shivered in pieces—ditches filled with dead—the inside of the fort bespattered with rebel blood." The horsemen were ordered to screen the surrounding countryside to prevent Confederate reinforcements from reaching Fort Donelson. Meanwhile the First Nebraska and other Union infantry regiments boarded steamboats being dispatched via the Tennessee and Cumberland Rivers to join Grant's overland-marching army.[16]

Col. John M. Thayer of the First Nebraska, whom Grant had designated as acting brigade commander, was in charge of the reinforcement-laden flotilla, consisting of five gunboats and eleven transports. It landed three miles below Fort Donelson before dawn on February 14, where the troops disembarked. Thayer's brigade, including the First Nebraska and the Fifty-eighth, Sixty-eighth, and Seventy-sixth Ohio regiments, was posted to Gen. Lew Wallace's division. The next day three Illinois regiments were also attached to Thayer's command. On the afternoon of February 14 Thayer marched his brigade into

Fig. 5. Brig. Gen. John M. Thayer, about 1865.
Nebraska State Historical Society RG2720-1A.

position opposite the Confederate breastworks surrounding the small town of Dover and near the center of Grant's army.[17]

The initial fighting at Fort Donelson on February 13 had led to stalemate, and the next day Union commanders ordered a gunboat attack against the fort's river batteries, hoping to duplicate the earlier success at Fort Henry. While the Nebraska soldiers, along with the rest of Grant's army, sat shivering in the February cold, the Union gunboats were badly riddled and soon repulsed by shot and shell from the Confederate batteries. If Fort Donelson were to be taken, the Yankee foot soldiers would have to do it.

Snow mantled the battlefield, along with the fitfully sleeping troops, on the night of February 14. The next morning Thayer's men were held in reserve as desperate fighting broke out on the Union right. The Confederate leadership had concluded that their position could not be held and ordered an attack to punch a hole in the Union lines through which the Rebel army could escape encirclement and reach the open countryside.[18]

The Confederate attack on the morning of February 15 drove back the division holding the Union army's right, sending many units into headlong retreat. As the battle reached a crisis, General Wallace, whose troops had not yet been engaged, took the initiative to order brigades from his division into the breach in the line. Thayer's brigade and the First Nebraska were in the forefront of this movement. As the First Nebraska moved past the stream of retreating Federals, the colonel posted the First Nebraska, Battery A of the First Illinois Light Artillery, and Ohio and Illinois regiments at a right angle to Wynn's Ferry Road, which arrowed through the Union lines and represented a route to freedom for the beleaguered Confederates.[19]

Almost immediately after Thayer got his men in position, four Confederate regiments attacked down the road, directly toward the First Nebraska and the battery by its side. The

Nebraskans held their fire until the enemy was within forty or fifty yards, "then such a fire—My God it was one continuous volley of musketry," recalled First Nebraska soldier Francis Cramer. The men had been ordered to keep low and fire while kneeling; thus many of the enemy bullets sailed harmlessly over their heads. Cramer was struck by a spent bullet that "scared me like thunder. There is no use talking, mother, the bravest man ever made would rather be at home than in a battle."[20]

The ebb and flow of rifle and artillery fire in the First Nebraska's front lasted for less than an hour and, by some accounts, the regiment repulsed three enemy charges. Pvt. Thomas Keen "shot at several men with as cool an aim as though they were stumps." One soldier recalled that the men in his company fired twenty-three rounds. Casualties proved surprisingly light. Thayer reported three killed and seven wounded in the First Nebraska. One private attributed some of the casualties to volleys from the Seventy-sixth Ohio, which was posted in reserve behind the First Nebraska. "They got so excited by the firing that they commenced firing over our heads and one or two were wounded in that way."[21]

Division commander Wallace reported that the First Nebraska "met the storm, no man flinching, and their fire was terrible. To say they did well is not enough. Their conduct was splendid. They alone repelled the charge." Allowing for the hyperbole that often crept into Civil War battle reports, it seems clear that the First Nebraska exceeded expectations for an untested regiment in its first major battle.[22]

The action at Wynn's Ferry Road prevented the disintegration of the Union army's right and stalled the Confederate offensive. Grant reasoned that the Rebels had weakened other parts of their lines to mount the attack and ordered an assault

Fig. 6. Counterattack of Gen. Lew Wallace's division at
the Battle of Fort Donelson, Tennessee, February 15, 1862.
Frank Leslie's Illustrated Newspaper, March 15, 1862.

on the left that penetrated the Rebel fortifications. This setback, compounded by Confederate tactical blunders as well as
the soldiers' fatigue and disorganization, sealed the Confederate army's fate. The garrison surrendered the next morning,
although several high-ranking officers and a significant number of men escaped before the capitulation took effect. When
the Nebraska soldiers entered the Confederate breastworks,
"[d]ead and wounded men lay in every direction inside and
out of the fort and horses blown to pieces by bombs [shells],
cannon knocked over, clothing scattered and trampled under
foot, tents all cut to pieces by grape shot, arms and ammunition piled up in every direction."[23]

The Union victory at Fort Donelson opened the Mississippi
River to the Tennessee border by flanking the Confederate
stronghold at Columbus, Kentucky, led to the evacuation of
Nashville (the first Confederate state capital to fall to Union

forces), and was a devastating blow to the Confederate strategic position in the western theater. It also brought Grant to
national prominence, with implications for his later ascent
to command all the Union armies. For the First Nebraska, the
battle of Fort Donelson was its first and, arguably, most important contribution to the Confederacy's eventual defeat.[24]

After Fort Donelson's fall, both the First Nebraska and the
Curtis Horse encamped near Fort Henry, awaiting further action. The Curtis Horse soon found it at Paris, Tennessee, some
twenty-five miles west of Fort Henry. There, on March 11, a
detachment of the regiment sent to break up Confederate recruiting parties was attacked and repulsed by a superior force,
suffering four killed and five wounded. One of the dead was
Sgt. Maj. Martin Stowell of Peru, Nemaha County, who had
achieved some prominence as an outspoken abolitionist and
Republican politician in territorial Nebraska.[25]

Rumor had it that the so-called Nebraska Cavalry, the four
companies of the Curtis Horse consisting mainly of Nebraska
men, would be attached to Thayer's brigade and thus share
the fate of their comrades in the First Nebraska. The transfer
was never made, however, and in June 1862 the Curtis Horse
was designated as the Fifth Iowa Volunteer Cavalry. Although
a cadre of Nebraskans remained in this regiment until it was
mustered out in 1865 and some of these soldiers reported their
experiences to the newspapers back home, the story of their
later service in Tennessee, Alabama, and Georgia became only
a sidebar in Nebraska's Civil War history.[26]

After his February victories at Forts Henry and Donelson,
Grant moved his army south via the Tennessee River to mount
an offensive against the Confederate base and railroad junction
at Corinth, Mississippi. With it went the First Nebraska. After
a brief interlude in camp at Fort Henry, the regiment boarded
a steamboat that would deposit it in mid-March, along with

the rest of Wallace's division, near Crump's Landing, about five miles north of another Tennessee river mooring called Pittsburg Landing, where the bulk of the Union army established its forward base.[27]

The three brigades of Wallace's division were scattered along the road from Crump's Landing to the small town of Adamsville. The second brigade under Thayer now comprised the First Nebraska, the Twenty-third Indiana, the Fifty-eighth Ohio, and the Fifty-sixth Ohio. Lt. Col. William D. McCord commanded the First Nebraska. Two batteries and two cavalry battalions were attached to the division.[28]

Early on Sunday morning, April 6, the troops at Crump's Landing heard the rattle of musketry and the roar of cannon in the direction of Pittsburg Landing, which Sgt. William A. Polock likened to a Nebraska storm building in intensity. Wallace prepared his division to march to the scene of what was clearly developing as a major battle. Contrary to Grant's expectations, the Confederates had moved north from Corinth to launch a surprise attack. Grant's orders for Wallace to move his troops to reinforce the Union army's right flank arrived in late morning. Bad roads, unbridged streams, and confusion about where the Union right actually lay delayed Wallace's arrival on the battlefield until nightfall. At the end of the first day's fighting in what would be known in the Union as the Battle of Shiloh, Grant's army had been pushed into a defensive perimeter clinging to the bank of the Tennessee River, teetering on the brink of defeat.[29]

With the regimental band playing the "Star-Spangled Banner," the First Nebraska led Thayer's brigade to the battlefield. The soldiers lay awake throughout the dark, rainy night of April 6, while Union gunboats on the river lobbed shells overhead into the Rebel lines and pickets exchanged fire. Other

Union reinforcements also arrived and crossed the river during the night; the weary soldiers knew the battle would resume at daybreak.[30]

At dawn on April 7 the First Nebraska and the rest of Wallace's division, posted on the extreme right of Grant's army, moved forward, along with several batteries. The battle in the First Nebraska's front consisted of a series of artillery duels, infantry advances, and firefights as the Union troops gradually pushed the exhausted and now-outnumbered Confederates over hills and through ravines. At one point the men of the First Nebraska dueled with a Confederate battery for nearly two hours, and the regiment had to briefly retire from the line to replenish its cartridge boxes. During this fight shells mortally wounded Pvt. John Roggensack and disabled Cpl. Henry Buckrau of the regimental color guard, "tearing a piece out of his thigh."[31]

According to regimental adjutant Silas Strickland, "[S]hell, cannon balls, and musketry rattled in the trees over and around our heads like an old fashioned hail storm, with a large quantity of thunderbolts thrown in." Enemy shells began hitting the First Nebraska's field hospital, but surgeon William McClelland quickly relocated it to a safer location. By about five p.m. the weary Confederates had finally been driven from the field, but Grant's soldiers were nearly as exhausted and in no condition to pursue. An eerie calm settled over the battlefield, punctuated by the cries and groans of thousands of wounded men.[32]

First Nebraska casualties included four killed and twenty-two wounded, remarkably few given the intensity of the day-long fight. As at Fort Donelson, Thayer had ordered the men to lie down when not engaged and to fire from kneeling or prone positions. Pvt. Thomas Keen reported that when they saw the flash and smoke from the Rebel guns the men would "drop as quick as though we had all been shot," and many of the enemy bullets passed harmlessly overhead. Moreover, the hilly, wooded terrain afforded natural cover.[33]

Although the Union army had very nearly been defeated on April 6, it held the field on the evening of April 7, while the dispirited Confederates retreated to their base at Corinth. More than three thousand men had been killed and sixteen thousand wounded in the Battle of Shiloh, the most horrific of the war so far. The First Nebraska again came in for its share of accolades. Division commander Wallace praised "the noble First Nebraska," and Thayer wrote, "Nobly did the First Nebraska sustain its reputation well earned on the field of Donelson." Regimental commander Lieutenant Colonel McCord reported that the First Nebraska was in action from 5:30 a.m. until 5:00 p.m. and "it steadily advanced and never receded an inch." One correspondent credited the regiment for giving "rich promise of the noble fruits the maturity of that young Territory may be expected to bear."[34]

Never again during the war would the First Nebraska join in combat between large armies on a major battlefield. Although the regiment took part in the Union advance into northern Mississippi following the battle at Shiloh, it saw no fighting during that campaign. The Confederates evacuated their base at Corinth before the slow-moving Federals could lay siege to the town. For the duration of its time in the South, the First Nebraska served mostly west of the Mississippi in one of the war's backwaters, characterized by small-scale skirmishes and guerrilla warfare.

A handful of Nebraska women had not been willing to remain behind when their husbands went off to war, and several endured the rigors of camp life, even risking the hazards of the battlefield when the regiment was stationed in Missouri and Tennessee in 1861–62. Catherine, the wife of Lt. Edward Donovan, spent eight months as the regiment's hospital matron. In February 1862 Mrs. Donovan worked behind the lines at the Battle of Fort Donelson, "rendering all the aid she could to the sick and wounded." Sarah Gillespie, the young wife of Pvt. John Gillespie, was still with her husband in the First Nebraska's camp at Crump's Landing when their daughter Emma was born, four days before the Battle of Shiloh. Emma Gillespie was known thereafter as "The Daughter of the Regiment."[35]

From Corinth the First Nebraska marched to Memphis and encamped until late July. In the meantime regimental commander McCord resigned his commission and Maj. Robert Livingston was promoted to colonel. Thayer, who had been nominated to the rank of brigadier general, continued to lead the brigade that included the First Nebraska pending his commission, which would come in October. Ironically, McCord survived the bloody battles of Fort Donelson and Shiloh and returned to Nebraska only to fall overboard from the steamboat *Omaha* and drown while traveling from Plattsmouth to Omaha for the territorial party conventions opening on August 20, 1862. Delegates from both parties were on the boat, and many were "filled up with tangle-foot," according to one observer. McCord got sick, whether from natural or other causes, and lost his balance while vomiting over the rail.[36]

On Independence Day, July 4, in Memphis the First Nebraska hosted a dinner attended by General Grant, Colonel Thayer, and several newspapermen, including Albert D. Richardson, the noted correspondent of the *New York Tribune*. Richardson toasted Thayer as "the representative of the union of Yankee shrewdness and western pluck; born in Massachusetts; reared and adopted citizen of the Great West" and announced that "the Nebraska First is indeed a first rate regiment, either to fight or celebrate with."[37]

From July 25 through October 6 the First Nebraska was posted to Helena, Arkansas, attached to the Army of the Southwest, first under Gen. Samuel R. Curtis and later under Gen. Frederick Steele. Aside from a few scouting missions along the Mississippi River, the regiment languished in camp, where Livingston put the men through a rigorous schedule of drill. The colonel was gaining a reputation as a strict disciplinarian, and Sgt. William A. Polock wrote that "the regiment has made great improvement since he has had the command."[38]

While the regiment was at Helena the Nebraska soldiers had what may have been their first direct experience with the war's effect on slavery. Beginning in 1862, under the provisions of the so-called Confiscation Acts passed by Congress, slaves who came within Union lines ("contrabands") could be seized as Rebel property and put to work as laborers, teamsters, and cooks. In August Colonel Livingston ordered his company commanders to "secure services of contraband Negroes who volunteer as follows: one Negro driver for every company team; one, two, or three Negro cooks according to the number required for a company, and all officers' waiters and cooks will be replaced by Negroes of the class above named." Company H had a black cook when the regiment was in St. Louis in October 1863. No record has been found indicating how many black men were thus employed by the First Nebraska in 1862 or 1863.[39]

While the Nebraska soldiers sat idle in their camp at Helena, disease again ran rampant through their ranks. By late September soldiers writing home reported that "raging chills and fevers" had taken the lives of ten men. At one point the regiment could muster only about two hundred men fit for duty, and even Colonel Livingston had been forced to go on sick leave. Although recruiting officers had been sent to Nebraska, there was little optimism for their success. Nebraskans at home seemed not to realize that the regiment's ranks had been so depleted. One soldier predicted that the First

Nebraska's destiny was to waste away "until annihilated" or the men's enlistments expired.[40]

Manpower was always an issue in wartime Nebraska. In addition to the drain from the troops already provided to the Union army, men were in demand for overland freighting from the river towns, which had revived somewhat in 1862. The optimism generated in Nebraska City by the July trial of Gen. Joseph R. Brown's fabled steam wagon, or "prairie motor," led to the improvement of the route from there to Fort Kearny, though the steam wagon itself proved a failure when it broke down at the edge of town. In 1862 the Byram brothers hauled some three million pounds of goods by ox team from Nebraska City to Denver, along with supplying stagecoach stations along the trail to Denver and Salt Lake City. Overall, the 1862 trade from Nebraska City exceeded 7.8 million pounds, and the freighting firms based there employed some seventeen hundred men.[41]

Emigration across the plains also picked up in 1862, and some of these migrants were undoubtedly Nebraska residents. In May one observer counted 872 wagons on the trail between Omaha and Fort Kearny and reported that nine thousand Mormons were leaving the Missouri River on their way to Salt Lake City. A Platte Valley rancheman termed the spring emigration the largest he had ever seen.[42]

Another spur to emigration to and beyond Nebraska Territory was a series of federal acts and regulations in the summer of 1862 designed to procure more men for the Union armies under quotas assigned to the several states. As with the Nebraska militia act, all able-bodied men between the ages of eighteen and forty-five in the Union states were required to enroll for potential military service. Implied was the prospect that men would be drafted if the volunteer quotas were not met. Soon after the enrollment process began, newspapers began noting an influx into Nebraska of what they termed "secesh refugees" or "Missouri draft dodgers." The provost marshal of Iowa issued an order prohibiting residents from leaving that state without a pass, and the War Department authorized federal and local law enforcement officers to arrest anyone who discouraged volunteers from enlisting. Nebraska rancheman Squire Lamb noted in late August that people were still going west to get out of the war.[43]

Protecting emigrants, draft dodgers or not, as well as the overland mail and telegraph route across Nebraska Territory, presented Union authorities with a dilemma, based in part on geographic realities. The carving away of Colorado and Dakota Territories in early 1861 left Nebraska Territory with an elongated panhandle, comprising the southern half of present Wyoming and stretching all the way to the Utah border. Through this corridor ran the emigrant trails, mail route, and telegraph lines to the West Coast.[44]

While Nebraska officials' concern for home defense was based in part on protecting travel across the territory to the west (overland freighting being a mainstay of the economy), most of their attention centered on the safety of the civilian settlements in eastern Nebraska. Periodic raids by the Brule Sioux on the Pawnees kept settlers on edge. It fell to the federal government, however, to guard the territory's far-flung western extremity, and it had few troops to spare. Most Union soldiers were engaged in a campaign and vicious battles in Virginia seeking to capture Richmond, while many more were occupied in Kentucky and Tennessee. In June 1862 only about five hundred regular and volunteer soldiers, stationed at Forts Kearny and Laramie and smaller outposts, were available to guard the trails west of the Missouri River. They included a battalion of the Sixth (later Eleventh) Ohio Volunteer Cavalry under Lt. Col. William O. Collins, whose regiment would spend its entire enlistment in service on the Great Plains. Gen. James Craig, who took his orders from the Department of Kansas at Fort Leavenworth, commanded the troops in Nebraska.[45]

Indian raids in western Nebraska Territory near Green River and Fort Laramie in the spring and early summer caused the government on July 11, 1862, to shift the mail route south from the North Platte and Sweetwater Rivers to the Medicine Bow Mountains in today's southern Wyoming, requiring Craig to further disperse his scanty forces to protect both the new mail route and the existing telegraph line. The general called for more troops, which were not forthcoming, and established a new post, Fort Halleck, as a base to guard the mail route.[46]

While no major Indian attacks broke out along the overland trails, Craig became more concerned when he learned of an uprising by Indians in Minnesota in late summer 1862. On November 2 the Department of Kansas was merged into the Department of the Missouri, and later that month Craig was assigned to command the District of Nebraska Territory, with headquarters in Omaha. By this time his forces had been augmented to some 715 men, still far too few to garrison three major posts and numerous smaller stations. But where was the manpower to come from?[47]

From the beginning of the war, Nebraska officials had based their recruitment efforts on the expectation that troops raised in the territory would be retained for home defense. Men would more readily enlist if they could serve near their families and maintain some control over their domestic affairs. This selling point faded when both the First Nebraska and the battalion of Nebraska cavalry were sent south in 1861.

Nor had the revised territorial militia law, which called for all men ages eighteen to forty-five to enroll in local companies by April 7, 1862, met with much success. A few new companies organized at Nebraska City and Brownville, but many Nebraskans ignored the law. The slow pace of enrollment prompted Governor Saunders on July 31 to issue a general order commanding all male residents of the required age not otherwise exempted to enroll forthwith. Home guard officers were ordered to report the names of those in their counties who failed to comply.[48]

A further complication came when the War Department appointed James H. Lane, U.S. senator from Kansas and Union general, as commissioner of recruiting in the military Department of Kansas, which then included Nebraska Territory. Lane sent a proclamation throughout the department urging men to enlist in regiments he was forming. Saunders, who knew officers from the First Nebraska would soon arrive home to recruit, resisted Lane's effort to siphon off Nebraska men for regiments being raised elsewhere. On August 18 the governor banned outside recruiters from working in the territory and forbade Nebraska citizens from enlisting in any unit he had not expressly authorized or leaving the territory to enlist. Saunders followed up with a letter to Secretary of War Edwin Stanton, who agreed with the governor that the first priority was to fill up the "old" regiments. Stanton, however, denied Saunders's request that Nebraska be allowed to recruit an additional regiment for home defense.[49]

Developments outside Nebraska's borders, however, would also frustrate recruiting for the First Nebraska. They included a major outbreak of Indian warfare in Minnesota and new gold discoveries along Idaho's Salmon River and in the mountains of southwestern Montana. As early as the spring of 1862 Omaha and Council Bluffs newspapers began publishing reports about gold mines on the Salmon River on the western slope of the Rockies, followed soon by news of discoveries at Bannack City and Alder Gulch on the east side of the mountains. This news prompted many young men to take off for the region, and the rush would only grow stronger in the coming years. Governor Saunders estimated that the drain of young men to the mines of the northern Rockies equaled the number who had settled in the territory since the war began. Squire Lamb at Wood River reported, "[T]he largest emiegration this Spring I ever saw for California Saumon River Oregon & Salt Lake[.] from the last day of May up till now the road has ben lined with teams."[50]

Then, in late August, word filtered down to Nebraska about a major Indian outbreak uncomfortably near the territory's borders. News that the Santee Sioux in Minnesota had gone on the rampage, killing many whites and laying waste to their settlements, brought near-panic to much of the northern and central plains. False rumors began circulating that five thousand Indians were burning and destroying everything in Dakota Territory across the Missouri River from Niobrara, Nebraska Territory. Sixteen teams were said to have left Niobrara with women and children fleeing the settlement.[51]

Concern over the Minnesota uprising and the simultaneous arrival in the territory of the First Nebraska's recruiting officers prompted sterner measures by the governor's office. On September 2, in Saunders's absence, Territorial Secretary and Acting Governor Algernon S. Paddock issued a proclamation ordering all eligible citizens to enroll under the militia act. While Paddock sought to reassure Nebraskans that they need not have "serious apprehension or alarm" about the Indians, he added that "it is our imperative duty . . . to prepare for the worst." Moreover, said Paddock, it seemed likely that the Indians were being incited by Rebel emissaries to make "a concerted movement against the loyal whites all along the frontier."[52]

Four days later Paddock sent a shrill telegram to Stanton at the War Department: "You must permit us to raise part or full regiment of militia cavalry and infantry for nine months." Stanton told Paddock to direct his plea to Gen. John Pope, who had just been appointed commander of a new military Department of the Northwest (which included Nebraska) and into whose hands had fallen the problem of the Indian war on the northern plains.[53]

Meanwhile the need remained to gather recruits for the First Nebraska. To spur on this process Paddock issued General Order No. 3, which set quotas for the number of recruits to be furnished from each organized county, based on the county's population in the census of 1860. The most populous counties, Douglas and Otoe, were each to provide fifty men. Several counties in the hinterlands west of the Missouri River were called on for only two recruits each. In all, 315 men were to be enlisted for the First Nebraska.[54]

Pope found his new department in chaos and concluded he had too few troops to deal with the Indians. After two weeks on the job he wired Stanton that the alarm evident in Nebraska Territory required raising "for immediate service, a temporary mounted force." It would be up to the federal government to furnish the arms for this regiment. On September 29 Pope issued a special order calling for the formation of a nine-month regiment of volunteer cavalry in Nebraska.[55]

Pope's order could not have come at a worse time for the First Nebraska recruiters, Capt. Sterritt Curran and Capt. Lee Gillette. The new regiment offered attractive alternatives to joining the First Nebraska. First, it was to be cavalry; no slogging through the mud for these soldiers. Second, it was to be enlisted for only nine months instead of the three years required of recruits for old regiments. Third, it offered the opportunity for enlistees to secure rank and pay beyond that of a mere private because the new regiment required the appointment of a full complement of officers, sergeants, and corporals.

Some men, said the *Nebraska Advertiser*, "will gladly brave all the hardships and dangers of the tented field in the capacity of captain, colonel, or brigadier general, but it will not be so easy to find men who will go as high privates. Patriotism and $13 per month is not near as effective [to] induce men to forego the comforts of home as patriotism and $180 per month."[56]

Perhaps most appealing was the near certainty that the nine-month regiment would remain in Nebraska during its service, protecting the territory from Indians. In fact, Isaac Coe, commander of the Second Brigade of the territorial militia, reported that one company of artillery, two companies of cavalry, and seven infantry companies had been organized in Otoe County. The companies were filled mostly with "laboring men," and "they would be somewhat discommoded by having to leave the county at present." Hence, such men would naturally prefer service in a unit that was expected to remain in the territory.[57]

First Nebraska recruiters Curran and Gillette could offer few inducements to counter these advantages. One, however, was a one-hundred-dollar government bounty for each three-year recruit who joined an existing regiment. The new recruit would receive an advance bounty payment of twenty-five dollars, plus one month's pay. A second inducement was the argument that there was more prestige associated with joining a regiment that had already earned battlefield laurels. Sgt. William A. Polock of the First Nebraska echoed this view in a letter to his hometown *Nebraska Advertiser*, noting that it was a "burning shame" that Nebraskans would join home guard and militia units instead of the First Nebraska, whose men looked with contempt on such troops.[58]

The *Nebraska City News* tried persuasion to aid Captain Gillette's recruiting efforts. "Come Up, Boys!" the notice urged. It characterized service with the First Nebraska as "parlour lounging" compared with what the nine-month men could expect. The latter would find nothing but the monotony of frontier forts and the isolation of an unsettled country, "where no hen-roosts are, and your boiled beans will be as hard and indigestible as buckshot and slugs."[59]

Gillette and Curran could not have been pleased by the radically different responses to the parallel recruiting efforts underway in Nebraska Territory. Men flocked to join the nine-month regiment, soon to be designated as the Second Nebraska Volunteer Cavalry, while enlistments languished for the First Nebraska. By mid-December 1862, nine full companies of volunteer cavalry, including previously organized companies such as Brownville's Paddock Guards, had been mustered in, with more on the way. Gillette left Nebraska in mid-November with fewer than thirty recruits for the First Nebraska, which was in camp at Patterson, Missouri. Twenty-six or twenty-seven men, "the fruit of three-months recruiting," were all that reached the regiment. No county except Hall, which provided one of the two men required, came close to fulfilling its recruiting quota.[60]

The Second Nebraska Volunteer Cavalry, still accepting companies for mustering in, came very near to being disbanded before it could be organized. On October 11, 1862, Nebraska Territory was transferred from Pope's Department of the Northwest and assigned to the Department of the Missouri under Gen. Samuel Curtis in St. Louis. Curtis had not been privy to Pope's order authorizing recruitment of the Second Nebraska, and only the personal intervention of Governor Saunders, who went to St. Louis to see the general, convinced Curtis to keep the regiment in service.[61]

Recruiting for the Second Nebraska continued through the fall and winter of 1862–63. Of the nine companies mustered in by year's end, two had been ordered to Fort Kearny. A third

Fig. 7. Pvt. Jacob Coffman of Falls City enlisted in
Company L, Second Nebraska Volunteer Cavalry, in 1863.
Nebraska State Historical Society RG2411-1025.

would soon follow. Other companies were dispersed to communities along the Missouri River. Three companies were in winter quarters at Camp Saunders, a mile and a half southwest of Omaha. General Craig wanted additional companies recruited to bring the regiment to a full complement of twelve.[62]

The fall of 1862 also brought political party conventions and the territorial elections for the legislature, delegate to Congress, and several territorial offices. After a contentious battle the Republicans renominated Samuel G. Daily of Peru as the candidate for the delegate's seat. It was not all smooth sailing, however, for many Republicans felt Daily had been ineffective in promoting Nebraska's interests in Washington and, despite being from south of the Platte, had favored Omaha instead of towns from his own section during congressional debates over the starting point for the proposed Pacific Railroad. Others charged that Daily had tried to delay the promotion of the First Nebraska's John M. Thayer to the rank of brigadier general, the legacy of a rift that had developed in 1861 over how federal patronage should be awarded.[63]

Lacking the right to vote in the House of Representatives limited a territorial delegate's effectiveness in advocating for his constituents. What's more, Daily had spent much of his time in Washington securing and then holding on to his seat. He had contested, successfully, the victory claimed by Democrat Experience Estabrook in the fall 1859 delegate election, but Daily was not awarded the seat until May 1860. After the fall 1860 delegate election seemed to give the victory to J. Sterling Morton, Daily again filed a contest. When Morton arrived in Washington DC to take his seat for the special session convening July 1, 1861, he was shocked to find Daily's credentials had already been accepted by the House. Unknown to Morton, Nebraska governor Black had given Daily an election certificate rescinding the one the governor had earlier given Morton. Not until May 1862 did the Republican-dominated U.S. House of Representatives take up what had now become Morton's contest and, to no one's surprise, Daily kept the seat that he promptly had to defend in the October 1862 election.[64]

The Democratic convention resolved its support for prosecuting the war "by the use of all constitutional and legitimate measures until the federal power shall be recognized throughout the limits of the seceded states." Despite divisions within their ranks the Democrats finally nominated John F. Kinney, formerly of Nebraska City but now serving as chief justice of Utah Territory, for delegate to Congress. Andrew J. Poppleton of Omaha also wanted to be the nominee and attacked Kinney for supporting "the black flag of Republicanism by holding an office under Abraham Lincoln." What's more, Kinney was a resident of "Mormondom," so how could he represent Nebraska Territory?[65]

The Nebraska Democrats applauded the Lincoln administration for its determination "to employ the Negro in menial, not martial service." They could not have anticipated that Lincoln would issue his preliminary Emancipation Proclamation only two days later, a development that radically altered Union war policy and would turn many Democrats in Nebraska and elsewhere strongly against the administration. Hostility to emancipation, the use of black soldiers in the Union army, and other "radical" Republican measures that struck at the institution of slavery and promised to change the status of black Americans would set the Nebraska Democrats' course for the rest of the war.[66]

In the end Daily's association with the party that had recently passed a Pacific Railroad Act and the long-awaited Homestead Act, combined with Republican charges that Kinney was an opportunistic carpetbagger and worse, enabled Daily's reelection. Dr. Frederick Renner of Nebraska City, a German emigrant and staunch Republican, took the stump for Daily. Kinney had been attacked within his own party for serving a "black Republican" administration, and Renner now demonized him as being a Secession supporter, a tactic that would become a Republican staple in subsequent campaigns: "I ask you now, is there any necessity for a Union-loving Nebraskian to step up on the 14th day of October to the polls shoulder to shoulder with a secession sympathizer or perhaps a run-a-way rebel from Missouri to vote for John F. Kinney?" If the Democrats were to prevail in the Nebraska and national elections, "it would be such a victory of the rebellion as the rebels themselves never dared to hope for." Any expectation that Kinney would support the Lincoln administration, said Renner, "has no more vitality than the Homeopathic soup made by boiling the shadow of a chicken." Ironically, when Kinney returned to Utah after his Nebraska defeat, he won election in 1863 as that territory's delegate to Congress.[67]

Although a legislature was elected in the fall of 1862, it was never to convene. During the preceding session lawmakers had debated how the territory was to pay the Direct War Tax that Congress had levied on each state and territory in 1861. Nebraska's share, based on its population, was $19,312. Considering that the territory was already $50,000 in debt and tax revenues had proven inadequate to provide for basic infrastructure, such as completing the territorial capitol building, it was unlikely that the sum could be raised by taxation. As one alternative the 1861–62 legislature asked Congress to confiscate Nebraska land owned by various Rebels, such as Eli Shorter and W. R. Cobb of Alabama, and use the proceeds from its sale to pay the war tax.[68]

There is no record that Congress responded to the confiscation memorial, but in the end Nebraska was released from payment of the war tax on the condition that no federal appropriation ($20,000) would be made to pay expenses of holding a legislative session in 1863. The diversion of the appropriation was accomplished by an amendment to the Internal Revenue Act passed in the spring of 1862. According to Governor Saunders, there was little for the legislature to do in any event, and the expense of holding a session could not be justified. A few of the legislators chosen in the fall 1862 election went to Omaha in early January 1863, but no quorum was to be had and they returned home.[69]

Toward year's end the Indian threat from within and outside Nebraska's borders seemed to have subsided; public confidence was reassured by the enlistment of the Second Nebraska Cavalry and its stationing throughout the territory. The Brownville paper was prompted to remark that "there is no more danger of an attack from the Indians than there is from the state of Ohio being overrun by Turks or Tartars." The men of the First Nebraska remained in Missouri, out of mind of many back home, although the regiment had just embarked on a winter campaign that would try the stamina and patriotism of its most dedicated soldiers.[70]

New gold discoveries in the northern Rocky Mountains had enhanced prospects for economic growth of the eastern Nebraska river ports and outfitting points, provided that the guerrilla war in Missouri did not get so bad that steamboats could not get through. The population continued to increase, the Republican Party seemed firmly in control, and statehood surely lay just ahead. The Pacific Railroad, Homestead, and Land-Grant College Acts recently passed by Congress offered bright promise for Nebraska's future.[71]

President Lincoln's September 22 announcement of the preliminary Emancipation Proclamation, five days after the Union army turned back a Confederate invasion of Maryland at the Battle of Antietam, signaled a major shift in the rationale under which the war was being fought. No longer merely a war to restore the Union, it would now decide the fate of the slaves and of slavery itself. Nebraska Territory was not immune to the debates engendered by this dramatic shift in Union policy, and Nebraskans of both political parties considered its implications for the war's outcome. As the old year gave way to the new, even the most prescient Nebraskans could not predict what that outcome might be.

CHAPTER THREE

1863

"Let Us Battle . . . for 'The Constitution As It Is, and The Union As It Was'"

For Nebraskans, both at home and in the army, 1863 would be a year of continued turmoil and uncertainty. The war seemed no closer to being over and, despite the enlistment of the Second Nebraska Cavalry, many Nebraskans remained worried about the prospect of Indians swooping down on the settlements. A tide of refugees and fortune hunters with uncertain loyalties continued to spill into Nebraska from beyond the Missouri River. Newspapers, politicians, and citizens on the street seemed constantly at each other's throats, fiercely debating administration policies and the progress of the war. Doubts about the loyalty of neighbors as well as strangers brought condemnation, arrests, and even violence. While the war brought prosperity to some, it ruined others. As long as it continued, Nebraska's future lay in limbo.

Although the future was no clearer to the men of the First Nebraska Infantry, they were likely preoccupied with what faced them each morning as they tumbled out of their bedrolls in the dark, cold dawn of the Ozark woods. New Year's Day 1863 found them huddled around campfires or in their tents at Van Buren, a small town in the highlands of south-central Missouri. Since mid-December the regiment had been criss-crossing the hills, streams, and valleys of this rugged region as part of Brig. Gen. John W. Davidson's nine-thousand-man Army of Southeastern Missouri. Davidson wanted to clear out roving guerrilla bands in southern Missouri and then move south across the border to collaborate with other Union columns in threatening the Arkansas capital of Little Rock.

The ill-fated campaign, the brainchild of Department of the Missouri commander Samuel R. Curtis, had little chance of success. The main Union effort in the west now focused on taking the Confederate stronghold of Vicksburg, Mississippi, a campaign that Gen. Ulysses S. Grant had initiated in the fall of 1862. Accordingly, few troops were available at Helena and elsewhere in Arkansas to cooperate with Davidson in a pincers movement against Little Rock. Marching an army overland from Missouri in the dead of winter seemed foolhardy.

The rugged, mostly roadless Ozarks and frequent rain and snow made supplying Davidson's army almost impossible as it marched farther away from Union bases at Pilot Knob and Rolla. The countryside afforded little in the way of forage or foodstuffs, and wagons with tents and rations often lagged so far behind the troops that the men were forced to sleep in the open and go to bed hungry. Shoes wore out quickly on the rocky ground and could not be repaired or replaced. Draft animals died by the score.[1]

The soldiers could hardly comprehend the purpose of the wearisome marches they were forced to endure, and near mutiny resulted. The men blamed Davidson, already unpopular for his tendency to be a martinet. According to Pvt. Thomas Keen of the First Nebraska, "[T]he men insulted him at every opportunity and their threats of desertion and 'shooting Davison' [*sic*] were loud and frequent." When the general later ordered the troops punished for unauthorized foraging from civilians Keen noted, "[I]f Davison [*sic*] had been there he would have been shot, so enraged were the men at him for issuing such a circular."[2]

August Scherneckau, one of the new recruits from Nebraska who joined the regiment on the eve of the campaign, also wondered what the army was up to. After marching and countermarching for days on end, waiting endlessly for the wagons to arrive with rations, and performing constant fatigue duty clearing brush, trees, and rocks from the numerous campsites, Scherneckau commented, "[W]here we were being led and what was intended remained a mystery for everyone." With a common soldier's resignation, however, he concluded, "[I]t appears to have been only one of the usual mistakes of our gentlemen officers that chased us over boulders and mountains." An Iowa soldier in the Army of Southeastern Missouri echoed the laments of his Nebraska comrades: "[I]f this army does not move with greater velocity than it has done for the past three months . . . the Southern Confederacy could be recognized by the Court of St. James and Napoleon the Third before the supply train could move fifty miles in this alluvial mud."[3]

Although the Army of Southeastern Missouri's cavalry made a brief dash to Batesville, Arkansas, and captured a few Rebel soldiers, Davidson's troops soon retraced their steps. By late February the army, including the First Nebraska, straggled back to Pilot Knob, where many of the just-paid soldiers unwound from the campaign's hardships. At a dress parade on February 26, Scherneckau observed that the First Nebraska numbered only about two hundred men—"the rest were on guard duty or scattered around, mostly drunk."[4]

On March 8 the First Nebraska marched east to the Mississippi River, where it boarded steamboats en route to the fortified Union base of Cape Girardeau, located some 140 miles south of St. Louis. Four earthen forts ringed the town of about four thousand residents. There most of the regiment would remain, with Colonel Livingston in command of the post, until late May 1863. When the six hundred officers and men of the First Nebraska reached Cape Girardeau, the regiment joined battalions of the Third and Fourth Missouri Cavalry and Company D of the Second Missouri Light Artillery to form the garrison. Although the duty was monotonous, rations were plentiful and the populace was friendly. This interlude helped the soldiers forget the hardships of the winter Ozarks campaign. Additional excitement was soon to come, however.[5]

A few days after the regiment arrived at Cape Girardeau, a detachment left for St. Louis with prisoners of war. On April 11 word came that Company H of the First Nebraska was to be detached in St. Louis indefinitely, where it would perform provost guard duty. This contingent of about fifty men, including August Scherneckau, would not rejoin the regiment until early June. The soldiers gained a whole new perspective on the war as they observed the hustle and bustle of Missouri's largest city and the headquarters of the Union's Department of the Missouri. Here were military prisons, supply depots, barracks, steamboat wharves, and navy yards for the construction of gunboats, all of which had to be guarded. The attitudes of St. Louis residents ran the gamut from loyal Unionist to unrepentant Secessionist, and Union authorities were always concerned about those who sympathized with the Confederate cause. Moreover, St. Louis had a large ethnic community, mainly Germans, and offered brothels, saloons, theaters, and other attractions to capture the attention of off-duty soldiers and the greenbacks in their pockets. All in all, the city was an eye-opener for the First Nebraska men.[6]

One noteworthy episode of their St. Louis sojourn occurred when the Company H soldiers were detailed to escort several prominent citizens to banishment within the Confederacy via a Mississippi River steamboat. The group being banished included both men and women alleged by Union authorities to have given aid and comfort to the enemy. Some of the women were the wives of Confederate officers. The two-week trek in May from St. Louis to near the Tennessee-Mississippi border gave the Nebraska soldiers a look at the devastated plantation landscape of the mid-South and the massive buildup of Union military might on the northern periphery of Grant's campaign to entrap Confederate forces in their Vicksburg stronghold to the south. The men also experienced the exiles' chilly contempt of the hated "Lincolnites" making up their escort.[7]

While Company H was in St. Louis, their comrades at Cape Girardeau faced off against the enemy in one of the more significant encounters between Union and Confederate troops in Missouri. The confrontation stemmed from Confederate cavalry commander John S. Marmaduke's April 1863 hit-and-run raid from Arkansas into southeastern Missouri. Marmaduke hoped to recruit new troops from the countryside and possibly threaten St. Louis. As the raiders crossed the border, scattered Union garrisons in southeastern Missouri withdrew into Cape Girardeau, where the defenses centered on the four earthworks.[8]

The men of the First Nebraska, now numbering about 350, along with the cannon of two Missouri light artillery batteries, took position in front of Fort B, located northwest of town. There they engaged the Confederates at about ten on the morning of April 26, 1863. While Union artillery kept the enemy off balance, the First Nebraska sent out skirmishers. After about four hours of desultory fighting during which the Confederates probed for an opening in the Union defenses, the firing ended and the Confederates began to withdraw. Casualties were light on both sides, the First Nebraska suffering only two men killed and seven wounded. Its threat more imagined than real, Marmaduke's raid caused turmoil all out of proportion to its military significance, but it earned the First Nebraska a battle streamer to sew on its flag.[9]

Union commanders hoped to cut off Marmaduke's force before it could retreat into Arkansas, and a pursuit began the next day. The Confederates were always one step ahead and slowed the pursuers by destroying bridges after the Rebels crossed the Whitewater and Castor Rivers. On April 28 the First Nebraska was ordered to join the Union troops already in the field, and some 270 Nebraska men marched out of Cape Girardeau at five the next morning. After a grueling day and night march, the Nebraskans and other Union troops caught up to the Confederate rear guard at dawn on May 1. Skirmishing continued throughout the day as the Rebels fell back across the St. Francis River at Chalk Bluff, which forms the border between Missouri and Arkansas. The Nebraska troops remained on the Missouri side as skirmishers and sharpshooters. Two First Nebraska men were wounded before the regiment was ordered back to Cape Girardeau, where it arrived on May 5. The men had marched some 190 miles in seven days. A Wisconsin officer commanding the brigade to which the First Nebraska was attached said of the regiment, "[W]e are at a loss whether to admire most its bravery in battle or its power of endurance." The name Chalk Bluff, too, would be sewn on the regiment's battle flag.[10]

While some people back home knew of the First Nebraska's adventures by way of soldiers' letters or reports in the territorial newspapers, other matters drew most local attention in Nebraska during the winter and early spring of 1863. January 1 was the operative date of two important political initiatives brought on by the war: the Homestead Act and the Emancipation Proclamation, the latter proclaiming freedom to slaves in those parts of the Confederacy not already occupied by Union troops. Although Daniel Freeman filed what was later recognized as the nation's first homestead claim just after midnight on January 1 at the Brownville land office, the act would not provide a major boost to Nebraska's settlement until the war was over. Nevertheless, 349 homestead entries claiming more than fifty thousand acres were filed in Nebraska in 1863, and those numbers would more than double in 1864.[11]

The Emancipation Proclamation, which Lincoln formally issued on January 1, 1863, sparked both praise and condemnation. It reenergized Northern Democrats, who had thus far lacked a substantive political issue on which to criticize the administration. Secession had forced them to make common cause with the Republicans, and as long as the war seemed centered on putting down the rebellion, they generally supported Lincoln's policies. Northern military successes in the early months of 1862 had raised hopes that the rebellion might end soon with both the Union and slavery intact. These hopes were dashed by Confederate counteroffensives that summer and fall. Lincoln realized that bolder measures were needed if Union victory were to be achieved.

The president's proclamation made it clear that the destruction of slavery would now be a primary focus of the Union war effort, and many Northern Democrats hated abolition only slightly less than secession. The proclamation prompted Omaha attorney and Democrat Andrew J. Hanscom to tell J. Sterling Morton, "I think it is about time to commence 'a vigorous prosecution of the war' against abolitionists in this territory."[12]

Since the war's outbreak, Democrats in the North had gradually divided into "war" and "peace" factions. War Democrats generally supported the administration's measures as necessary to restore the Union, even if they did not always give them wholehearted approval, while the Peace Democrats grew more and more vocal in their attacks on the president's policies as time went on. The latter argued that the war was justified only to preserve "the Constitution as it is" and restore "the Union as it was." They blamed abolitionists in the North for bringing on the conflict in the first place through their refusal to compromise with the South. Now Lincoln had caved in to these "radicals" by issuing the Emancipation Proclamation, an unconstitutional attack upon states' rights going far beyond any measures necessary to save the Union.

The Peace Democrats' increasingly strident criticism of Lincoln and the Republicans earned them the label of "Copperheads," an epithet likening them to poisonous snakes. While any Democrat who criticized the administration risked being branded a Copperhead, the term was most often applied to those, such as Ohio congressman Clement L. Vallandigham, who seemed to want peace at any price.

The Emancipation Proclamation sparked heated debate in Nebraska Territory as well. Editorial sparring between rival Democratic and Republican editors reflected a similar division among Nebraska citizens about the Lincoln administration's handling of the war, particularly its policies toward slavery and the enlistment of black soldiers in the Union army. Underlying the debate was the question of what freeing the slaves and giving them previously denied social, economic, and political rights might mean for the country and for Nebraska. The *Nebraska City News* saw the Emancipation Proclamation as "one more concession to the radicals. . . . To be sure, it is not so universal—does not declare niggers to be free white men—as they have demanded; but since it means emancipation, they will have to 'dry up.'"[13]

The proadministration view held that to restore the Union, the Confederacy must be utterly crushed, and attacking slavery was an effective way of doing so. Slavery supported the South's military and civilian infrastructure, making it easier to field the insurrectionary armies. Editor W. H. H. Waters of the *People's Press*, Nebraska City's Republican paper, had said as much when Lincoln issued the preliminary Emancipation Proclamation in September 1862: "The administration has determined to strike, *strike to kill*, and remove every means from them that tends to prolong the war. . . . This measure is hailed by the loyal masses as the beginning of the end of this unholy war." The Union armies also needed more manpower to wage total war, and the administration's decision to enlist black soldiers was a practical way both to provide more men and to turn slavery against the Confederacy.[14]

The Nebraska soldiers had learned of the pending Emancipation Proclamation when the president first announced it in September 1862. Many of them, such as "More Again," an anonymous correspondent to the Brownville newspaper, thought the war had not been prosecuted vigorously enough and urged, "Heaven speed the time when our generals and colonels will look upon the rebels as our sworn and bitter foes, instead of seeing brothers whom we must take by the hands and gently urge them in the way of right and reason." Sgt. Reynel Noyes of the First Nebraska said of Lincoln's decision, "Nothing has given me so much courage and I know most of the soldiers feel the same way. Indeed, I have not heard a word against it yet."[15]

The Democratic *Omaha Nebraskian* called the Emancipation Proclamation "an ill-starred, unauthorized, and indefensible document." As an expression of the administration's future conduct of the war, the proclamation dashed the hopes of Democrats who had clung to the idea that the conflict might somehow end in compromise, with the Union restored to its prewar status. Now, said the *Nebraskian*, "There is not the slightest probability, not even the remotest ghost of a chance, in our opinion, that the war will close and Peace . . . again return to this ruined, distracted land during Mr. Lincoln's presidential term." The *Nebraskian's* stance on wartime issues prompted the *Council Bluffs Nonpareil* to comment that "a stranger couldn't tell now, without looking at the dateline, whether the paper emanated from Nebraska or South Carolina."[16]

When the formal proclamation came out, the *Nebraska City People's Press* offered fulsome praise: "There can be no question that incalculable benefits to the cause of the country must result from this important measure." Of course, not everyone shared that opinion. The news that Lincoln had issued the proclamation prompted half a dozen Nebraska City men "to pour forth imprecations against the administration and its friends and supporters that would have been loudly cheered on the streets of Richmond." The *Press* editor wondered why the local citizens tolerated "such soulless blockheads, who are walking monuments of the most damning villainy."[17]

Differences of opinion translated into charges and countercharges. Those who differed with the administration (mostly Democrats) were accused of Secessionist sympathies, disloyalty, and even treason. In turn, some Democrats labeled the president and those who supported him as "black" Republicans seeking to elevate an "inferior" race to a position of equality with free white men. One of the most outspoken Democratic organs was the *Nebraska City News*, edited by Augustus Harvey, which epitomized the vehement racist and antiadministration tone of the Democratic press.[18]

As early as 1862 the *News* had urged the territorial legislature to pass a law excluding Negroes and Negro laborers from Nebraska. "Cannot this be kept sacred as a home for white men—a field for white labor?" asked Harvey. Did anyone really want the races to intermingle and amalgamate? "If yes! support the black republican party now in power and you can

Fig. 8. Augustus "Ajax" Harvey, the outspoken editor of the
Nebraska City News from 1861 to 1865, photographed about 1867.
Nebraska State Historical Society RG2411-2215b.

have your desires." As it became clear that the administration intended to make war on slavery, the Peace Democrats raised the specter of equality of the races hoping War Democrats and even moderate Republicans might turn against the administration. Many Northerners who opposed slavery did not believe black persons could or should become their political and social equals.[19]

For a time during the winter and early spring of 1863 the two Nebraska City newspapers and their editors went at each other tooth and nail. In late January four black men seeking work were driven out of town at gunpoint by a mob. Continuing in the same vein as in previous editorials, the *News* noted approvingly, "Nebraska is no place for the African, free or slave, black, yellow, or bleached." The *People's Press* denounced the mob, and by implication the *News* and its editor, as "inhuman and barbarous." A few days later *News* editor Harvey circulated a petition justifying the expulsion of the blacks, but few citizens would sign it. Gloated Waters of the *People's Press*, "O News, thou wicked and rebellious smut-machine, you may labor in the cause of treason with your harmless lies, but when you attempt to create a disturbance in the community, see how every good citizen turns from your villainous schemes in disgust."[20]

Undeterred, Harvey made "a willful and malicious attack on the respectability of the German citizens of this place," leading the Germans to call for Harvey's dismissal as editor or else they would boycott the newspaper. Harvey had used the term "Damned Dutch" in a report of a social event the German residents were hosting. *News* publisher Thomas Morton promised to rein Harvey in, but the editor was soon up to his old tricks.[21] *People's Press* editor Waters also excoriated Harvey for having the "audacity" to denounce all loyal men as abolitionists and thieves. Such men as Harvey "should not find fault if at any time a squad of soldiers should suspend their filthy carcasses between Heaven and earth; or cut out their villainous lying tongues." At the very least, the *News* editor might "be favored with provender from Uncle Samyule's cribs for three years or more, gratis."[22]

Support for emancipation and the use of black soldiers often had a brutally pragmatic basis, even among Republicans, who did not necessarily subscribe to the idea of racial equality. Black soldiers might not be moved by the same patriotism as white soldiers, said editor Waters, "but a minnie ball from a negro's gun has as good effect as if a white man fired it." Crushing the rebellion would cost many lives, and "we would much rather the negroes would fall in battle than our own kindred."[23]

On May 9, 1863, J. Sterling Morton, one of Nebraska's leading Democrats and an outspoken critic of the Lincoln administration, addressed the Democratic Club in Council Bluffs, Iowa. His views mirrored those of leading Peace Democrats such as Ohio congressman Vallandigham, with whom Morton had become close friends during the latter's 1861–62 contest to be seated as Nebraska delegate to Congress following the disputed Nebraska election of 1860. Although Morton was not seated, Vallandigham and other prominent Peace Democrats had vigorously supported him. Barely a month before Morton delivered his Council Bluffs speech, Vallandigham invited him to take over the editorship of a Dayton, Ohio, newspaper noted for criticizing the administration. Before Morton could consider the offer, Vallandigham was arrested for speaking out against the administration's policies on emancipation, the draft, and other war measures.[24]

Morton began his speech by posing the premise that "an American citizen may differ with any administration and denounce it and its measures without being disloyal." And denounce the administration he did. Morton blamed the war on

Fig. 9. J. Sterling Morton in an 1870 photograph.
Nebraska State Historical Society RG 1013-8.

the abolitionist or Radical Republicans. They had provoked war instead of seeking compromise, "because through it they saw, or thought they saw, the abolition of slavery in all the states." Although the Lincoln administration had proposed compensated emancipation for the border states that had not seceded, such a course would not only bankrupt the country, it would "make slaves [of] the free white laborers of the North in order to unslave the black laborers in the South." In this same vein, he charged that abolition would hurt the markets for commodities produced in Nebraska Territory and elsewhere in the Northwest. Without slavery the South could no longer raise cotton and would substitute corn, wheat, and pork. By abolishing slavery, "you abolish the industry and prosperity of your own people."[25]

Morton extended greetings to Vallandigham, who had been arrested only four days earlier, and praised the Ohio congressman's patriotism as being "far superior to that of [Wendell] Phillips and [U.S. Senator Charles] Sumner," both leading Abolitionists. Morton echoed themes that had led to Vallandigham's arrest, calling for the voters in 1864 to turn out of office the "Abolition rulers [and] the party who by confiscation, emancipation edicts, and their entire legislation have evidently aided rebellion." Once Lincoln and his party had been defeated, said Morton, "We propose then, perhaps, to try peace as a means of Union."[26]

In concluding his lengthy speech, which was largely a catalog of the sins of Lincoln and the Republicans, Morton returned to the Peace Democrats' mantra: "Let us battle then manfully, both in the South and in the North, against the cohorts of secession and the hordes of abolition, for 'The Constitution As It Is, and The Union As It Was.'" For Morton and many Democrats, that meant a Constitution and a Union that protected and perpetuated slavery.[27]

Morton had earlier flirted with supporting a Vallandigham proposal that the states and territories of the Old Northwest also withdraw from the Union, commenting somewhat favorably on the scheme in a letter to a Chicago newspaper. This tactic caused even some of Morton's firmest Democratic friends in Nebraska to suggest that he had gone too far. George L. Miller of Omaha, a staunch War Democrat but often critical of Lincoln, warned Morton that "[t]he idea of the Northwest declaring for separation from the Northeast, & for union with the South, will never be realized, in my opinion." If the idea were pursued, said Miller, "a reaction will be created in public opinion which will engulph [sic] its authors in a sea of odium."[28]

The hardening of viewpoints about the conduct of the war was also demonstrated by the formation of Union clubs or leagues in Nebraska Territory and elsewhere to counter the Peace Democrats. The Brownville Union Club held an organizational meeting on February 28. In May 1863 a mass meeting, said to be the largest ever held in Nemaha County, convened in Brownville to organize the Loyal National League "to bind together all loyal men, of all trades and professions." A loyalty pledge was adopted, and Republican Samuel Daily, Nebraska's congressional delegate, addressed the crowd, "excoriating the rebel sympathizers of the North and rendering it very uncomfortable for any of that persuasion who were present."[29]

Fulminations against the administration, such as Morton's speech, and editorial comments in the Democratic press lent credence to suspicions that treason might actually be afoot in Nebraska Territory. The Brownville paper reported, without providing any evidence, that local Democrats and others had been invited in January 1863 to a meeting to organize a chapter of the Knights of the Golden Circle. This organization had roots in the prewar South but now was centered in the Midwest to promote the Peace Democrats' scheme of a Northwest Confederacy. In May an individual in Nemaha County was reported to have confessed to being involved and furnished a partial list of the local members, though the newspaper offered no names or verification.[30]

Morton himself received a letter in June 1863, signed by several rural residents of Otoe County, requesting him to come and help them become members of the "nights of the Golden sircle." There is no indication that Morton replied or any evidence that he actually belonged to the Knights of the Golden Circle. Nevertheless, the invitation suggests that Morton's criticism of the Lincoln administration's policies had raised that possibility in the public mind. Morton's attacks on the president and his own friendship with, and support of, Ohio Copperhead Clement Vallandigham made it easy for Republicans to brand him as disloyal.[31]

By the summer of 1863 the opposing political views had acquired a basic simplicity. Those who criticized the Lincoln administration's handling of the war, and particularly its policies on emancipation and black enlistment, were "secession sympathizers" or "Copperheads" at best, and traitors at worst. Administration supporters were "vile abolitionists" or "black Republicans," who had brought on the war for the sole purpose of destroying the constitutional right of states and citizens to determine their own policies on questions such as slavery and suffrage. In the middle were those who cared little about the political issues and were mainly interested in avoiding being sucked into the war.[32]

While the administration's policies and the potential impact of emancipation on Nebraska's future were being debated in the newspapers and in the streets, Indians were a more immediate concern to many Nebraskans. The mustering in of the

Fig. 10. Officers of the Second Nebraska Volunteer Cavalry at Camp Cook near Sioux City in the spring of 1863. *Back row, left to right*: Maj. John Taffe, Maj. John W. Pearman, Adj. Henry M. Atkinson; *front row, left to right*: Col. Robert W. Furnas, Lt. Col. W. F. Sapp, surgeon A. Bowen, Maj. George Armstrong. Nebraska State Historical Society RG4389-19.

first nine companies of the Second Nebraska Volunteer Cavalry, however, instilled some confidence that the home front was being protected. Companies B and C were posted to Fort Kearny, while others were stationed at communities up and down the Missouri River. Part of Company K was sent to Columbus in February 1863. On March 24 Robert W. Furnas, formerly editor of the *Nebraska Advertiser* and fresh from a stint as commander of a regiment of "loyal" Indians in Kansas and Indian Territory was mustered in as the regiment's colonel. The Second Nebraska soldiers "added to those stationed at Forts Kearney, Halleck, and Laramie will constitute a force sufficient to disperse every band of hostile red-skins which may show itself on the plains," predicted Omaha's *Nebraska Republican*.[33]

The early spring of 1863 also brought prospects that emigration to the gold camps of the northern Rockies would be heavy. In fact, the gold rush led Congress on March 3 to create the new Idaho Territory, which comprised parts of present Idaho, Montana, and Wyoming. Many travelers bound for the Salmon River and Bannack City mines outfitted at Omaha, resulting in some merchants registering sales of $40,000 per month during the summer of 1863. In fact, money was flowing into the territory from several sources. The handful of Nebraska banks dealt mostly in gold dust from the western mines that arrived via the overland stagecoaches or on steamboats and mackinaw boats descending the Missouri River. Agricultural production outstripped local needs, leaving a surplus for export.[34]

Most of the military freight for western forts also left from Omaha, while Nebraska City continued to dominate private freighting to gold mining camps and stations along the stagecoach routes to the west. Dealing in government vouchers became a lucrative business. Demand for goods drove prices up. In the fall of 1863 Squire Lamb at his Wood River road ranche had to pay $200 more for his winter supplies and, in turn, doubled the prices he charged travelers, raising his price for serving a meal to stagecoach passengers from two to four dollars.[35]

The organization of the Second Nebraska Cavalry also stimulated the territorial economy when the army let hay and corn contracts to provision the troops. Omaha was designated a depot for commissary supplies. Governor Saunders, meanwhile, on February 18 reported that the secretary of war had authorized recruitment of two more companies, increasing the Second Nebraska Cavalry to a twelve-company regiment.[36]

The comforting thought that Nebraska Territory was being protected by the Second Nebraska Cavalry proved short lived. As Gen. John Pope planned for a spring and summer campaign against the Minnesota Sioux who had fled to Dakota Territory, his eye fell upon the Second Nebraska, whose recruitment he had authorized in September 1862. Soon afterward Nebraska Territory had been transferred to the Department of the Missouri, and the Second Nebraska passed beyond Pope's control. Undeterred, Pope in late February 1863 asked the War Department to order the Second Nebraska Volunteer Cavalry to Sioux City, where it would join columns slated to move up the Missouri River against the Sioux. In early March Union general-in-chief Henry W. Halleck ordered Department of the Missouri commander Samuel Curtis to assign the Second Nebraska to Pope, and Curtis complied. The order held out the prospect that the two or three companies of the regiment already stationed along the overland route might remain in Nebraska.[37]

Halleck's order drew a quick response from Nebraska's acting governor, Territorial Secretary Algernon Paddock, who urged that the order be suspended because it "will leave a large portion of the frontier settlements that have contributed half their men, unprotected." A month later Governor Saunders again asked Halleck to rescind the order that "will leave the whole frontier of Nebraska, as well as the emigrants' stage and telegraph [route] to the mountains unprotected." Halleck refused because "it was the opinion of military officers in the West that the Nebraska Cavalry could be spared to operate against hostile Indians up the Missouri River." The unnamed officers must have meant Pope, for it was he who had made the plea to have the regiment assigned to his department.[38]

The assignment of most of the Second Nebraska to the Department of the Northwest was also unwelcome news to District of Nebraska commander James Craig, who had been pleading for more troops to help guard the overland emigrant, telegraph, and mail route. In early March he had proposed his own campaign against Indians in the western reaches of the district, which Curtis denied on account of the transfer of the Second Nebraska. On April 17 Craig resigned as district commander, to be replaced in June by Brig. Gen. Thomas J. McKean.[39]

As the Second Nebraska companies rendezvoused at Omaha to prepare for the march to Sioux City, the territorial newspapers took up a hue and cry of government bad faith resembling the local reaction when the First Nebraska was sent away in 1861. The *Nebraska Republican* editorialized that sending the soldiers away would leave their wives and children "exposed to the tomahawk and scalping knife" and "will be the ruin of Nebraska and the sacrifice of the interests of the thousands of pioneers now en route for the mining regions of the west and north-west." The *Nebraska Advertiser* reported that the soldiers were surprised because they had enlisted to protect the Nebraska settlements. Even if Indians were not a threat, Confederate sympathizers were active in northern Missouri and southern Iowa, and they would surely pave the way for a raid by Confederate general Sterling Price unless soldiers were stationed near the border.[40]

Pope, however, had a different view of how troops should be used to protect outlying settlements. If the men were kept at home, he wrote, "[I]t requires five times as many troops to protect in this way a line of frontier settlements as the Indians can possibly bring against them." The small settlements not actually occupied by troops "are constantly subjected to encroachments of small parties of Indians who, having no fear of the invasion of their own country and homes, spend

Fig. 11. Headquarters of the Second Nebraska
Volunteer Cavalry at Camp Cook, near Sioux City, 1863.
Nebraska State Historical Society RG4389-53.

their time in stealing into the settlements to commit depredations." The proper course, which Pope intended to pursue,
was to send strong columns into the Indians' own country
to hunt them down. He conceded that it was difficult "to get
troops away from any frontier settlement where momentary
necessity has occasioned their being posted" on account of the
boost military expenditures brought to the local economy.[41]

By late May 1863 nine companies of the Second Nebraska
Volunteer Cavalry had reported to Camp Cook near Sioux City,
Iowa. Companies B, C, and D remained in Nebraska for their entire enlistment, assigned to Fort Kearny, Cottonwood Springs,
and the Pawnee Agency near Genoa. The Nebraskans at Camp
Cook were led by Col. Robert W. Furnas and would soon join
Gen. Alfred Sully's force representing the southern prong of
Pope's campaign against the Sioux in Dakota Territory. Sully
was to cooperate in a pincers movement to trap the Indians
between his soldiers and Gen. Henry Sibley's column that had
departed from southwestern Minnesota.[42]

On June 20 the Second Nebraska began its march from Sioux
City to Fort Randall, then up the Missouri River. Company A

was left behind at Randall. The remaining eight companies plodded upstream as part of Sully's force. The weather was hot and dry, the scanty grass had already been eaten off, and the river was low, making it difficult for steamboats to supply the weary soldiers. "To say that we have had a rough time and a rough, broken country to march through since we left Yankton is a very poor way of expressing it," wrote an anonymous Nebraska soldier. Cpl. Henry Pierce of Company K described the country as a district "that would starve a forlorn hope of caterpillars," destitute of game "save only now and then a couple of poor half starved choked Jack Rabbits."[43]

Although the men's dissatisfaction at leaving Nebraska had been moderated somewhat by the prospect of fighting Indians, outrage returned with word that Indians had attacked the family of one of the Second Nebraska's soldiers, Pvt. Henson Wiseman of St. James in Cedar County. On July 24, 1863, Wiseman's wife, Phoebe Ann, returned home from a trip to Yankton, Dakota Territory, to find that three of her children had been killed and two others mortally wounded, allegedly by Yankton or Santee Sioux. Private Wiseman was released on furlough to be reunited with his distraught wife. Corporal Pierce noted the episode in his diary, commenting bitterly, "May God forgive the man that called us hence, and console the mourner over his dead babes and insulted wife."[44]

By the time Sully's column of approximately nineteen hundred men reached Fort Pierre in mid-August, Sibley had already fought the Sioux to a stalemate and returned to Minnesota from the Missouri River, dashing hopes that the two columns could trap the Indians between them. Sully pressed on, however, and on the late afternoon of September 3 his scouts discovered a large Sioux encampment of some four hundred lodges at White Stone Hill, midway between the Missouri and James

Fig. 12. "Cavalry Charge of Sully's Brigade at the Battle of White Stone Hill, September 3, 1863." *Harper's Weekly*, October 31, 1863.

Rivers near the southern boundary of present North Dakota, southwest of present Jamestown.[45]

The eight companies of the Second Nebraska, numbering about 350 men, led the charge by Sully's forces and struck the village near nightfall, while the Sixth Iowa Volunteer Cavalry supported the Nebraska regiment's right. After several volleys were fired in the semidarkness, the Indians "melted away ... like grass before the flames," and the soldiers occupied the field. Skirmishing and scouting occupied the next two days, while the troops destroyed thousands of pounds of dried meat, tipis, and cooking utensils the Indians had abandoned. Some 150 Indians, mostly women and children, were taken prisoner, and the army, probably erroneously, estimated Indian casualties as ranging from a hundred to more than three hundred. Sully reported that the Second Nebraska ("among them probably some of the best shots in the world") fought on foot and engaged the enemy at about sixty paces with their rifles. The soldiers' casualties were light, amounting to six killed and fourteen wounded in the Second Nebraska Regiment.[46]

Following the battle Sully withdrew down the Missouri River, signaling the end of the 1863 Dakota campaign. The Second Nebraska companies proceeded to Omaha, where some were mustered out, while others returned to the towns from which they had enrolled. All had been mustered out by the end of December 1863. For many of the men, however, it would not be the end of their military service.[47]

Although the absence of most of the Second Nebraska soldiers did not have serious consequences for the settlements at home, peace and tranquility did not always reign. On June 22 soldiers of Company D of the Second Nebraska Cavalry skirmished with Brule Sioux warriors raiding the Pawnee Agency near Genoa, the first real fighting between Indians and the military in Nebraska since 1855. One observer reported that the Brules were "very much offended" that the soldiers had interfered with their raid on the Pawnees. He noted that the Platte River Sioux had gone south to the Republican River and predicted that a major Indian outbreak was likely, a prediction that would come true in little more than a year. The Brules returned to attack the Pawnees again that September.[48]

By fall 1863 the heavy emigration to the Bannack mining camps prompted a warning from Upper Platte Indian Agent John Loree at Fort Laramie. The government should immediately make treaties with the Crows and the Sioux, "as the whites are now overrunning their whole country." Ben Connor, a soldier in the Eleventh Ohio Cavalry on his way to Fort Laramie in late summer 1863, ascribed another reason for the increasing tension between the whites and the Indians: "Every sort of crime or misdemeanor committed by stage robbers or horse thieves was laid to the Indians."[49]

In late July came the attack on Henson Wiseman's family near St. James. Letters continued to flow from Nebraska to the War Department calling for protection from the Indians. Finally, the government gave in and ordered the Seventh Iowa Volunteer Cavalry to take station in Nebraska. That regiment began its organization soon after the 1862 Minnesota uprising, but it was not complete in time to participate in the Sully campaign. On July 27 six companies of the Seventh Iowa began a march from Davenport to Omaha, where they arrived in September to join the troops assigned to the District of Nebraska. From Omaha the companies were dispatched to various locations, including Fort Kearny and Cottonwood Springs, where at the latter place in October the Iowans would begin constructing a new military post first named Cantonment McKean. The location was chosen to interdict a north-south Indian trail that passed through the Platte Valley breaks at Cottonwood Canyon.[50]

The Seventh Iowa would figure in an episode later that year that called into question whether the soldiers being sent to the plains could or would distinguish between the so-called hostile Indians who might threaten settlements, commerce, and travel and the friendly tribes, whom the soldiers were supposed to protect. The latter included the Omahas, Oto-Missourias, Pawnees, and Poncas, who had ceded most of their lands in return for designated reservations, government annuities, and the expectation that the government would protect them from their enemies, particularly the Brule Sioux. The June 22 skirmish at the Pawnee Agency represented the army at least making the effort to do so, while the brutal killing of several Ponca women and children near Niobrara in early December 1863 was nothing less than a case of soldiers committing cold-blooded murder.

A detachment of Company B of the Seventh Iowa had been stationed at Niobrara, ostensibly to guard that settlement against incursions of Sioux from north of the Missouri River. In the middle of the night of December 3–4 several soldiers stumbled into a camp of fifteen Ponca men, women, and children returning to their agency from a visit to the Omahas. The soldiers, drunk from a payday spree, began to plunder the Indian camp and tried to rape the women, whereupon the Indians fled. In the morning they returned to the campsite, gathered what possessions they could, and started off. The soldiers soon reappeared, shot dead three women and a girl, and fired on the survivors, some wounded, as they fled across the icebound Niobrara River.[51]

After Ponca Agent John B. Hoffman reported the killings, the army conducted an investigation. Capt. George Armstrong of Company A, First Battalion of Nebraska Cavalry, interviewed the soldiers involved and several local civilians. He concluded that "[w]hat really did take place . . . is only known to the soldiers on the one side and the Indians on the other," notwithstanding that Armstrong apparently did not even bother to talk to the Poncas. Hoffman and the commissioner of Indian affairs kept the pressure on, however, and in June 1864 the secretary of war ordered Department of Kansas commander Curtis to bring the soldiers before a court-martial. Before that could happen, Lt. Francis J. Comstock, who had commanded the Seventh Iowa detachment at Niobrara, resigned from the service, and the enlisted men were transferred to Fort Kearny. No one was ever charged with the murders, and it is unclear whether the government eventually paid the Ponca Tribe any restitution.[52]

The surge of emigration to Nebraska Territory, along with a revival of thievery and violence reminiscent of the Jayhawking days of 1862, added to Nebraskans' uneasiness during 1863. In addition to prospective gold miners, some of the migrants were escaping the bitter internecine fighting in Missouri or avoiding possible conscription into the contending armies. Some were undoubtedly army deserters and others were escaped slaves, termed "contrabands." In June the *Nebraska Advertiser* reported that "a sable stream of contrabands has been flowing into this city and neighborhood for the last few weeks." They were said to be from Missouri's hemp- and tobacco-growing counties adjacent to the Missouri River in the central part of the state. Still other emigrants were attracted by the opportunity to claim land in Nebraska under the Homestead Act or by possible employment due to the resurgence of overland freighting from the Missouri River towns.[53]

A major cause of the increase in Nebraska Territory's population in 1863 was the federal government's efforts to build up the Union armies. The initial rush of volunteering that marked the first year of the war had lost momentum by the fall of 1862. Under the oversight of the state and territorial governors many of the early volunteer regiments had been enlisted for only nine months or two years. Such short terms could hardly sustain the Union war effort. The Enrollment Act of March 3, 1863, was designed to help overcome these drawbacks by making every able-bodied man between the ages of twenty and forty-five (and aliens who had declared their intention to become citizens) eligible for a draft. The act gave the Provost Marshal General's Bureau in Washington ostensible control over recruiting, acting in concert with the governors. Seemingly a conscription law, the Enrollment Act was primarily an effort to stimulate volunteering by threatening a draft if recruiting quotas assigned to each congressional district were not met.[54]

Although Nebraska Territory was exempted from a draft because it had already furnished such a large percentage of its eligible men to the Union army and the governor had previously issued an enrollment order, in July 1862, to help organize home defense forces, the territory was assigned a provost marshal. His job was to track down men who fled to Nebraska to avoid enrollment or conscription in their home states and to capture army deserters. As a border region exempt from the draft, Nebraska Territory was a favored haven for those trying to escape the war's dangers and obligations.[55]

While the provost marshal and his deputies were also empowered to arrest civilians who aided or counseled desertion or evasion of the Enrollment Act, they were not authorized to arrest civilians for other kinds of "disloyal" conduct. That task, however, was performed by military officers, as when Maj. John Pearman of the Second Nebraska Cavalry arrested five Nebraska City men for "having hurrahed for Jeff Davis, drank to the Southern Confederacy, and of having threatened the lives of U.S. soldiers." Three of the men were sent to Omaha for further investigation, and two were released after taking the Union oath of allegiance. The newspaper said nothing more about the fate of the arrested men.[56]

After observing streets thronged with "pilgrims" waiting to cross the river into Nebraska in the spring of 1863, the *Council Bluffs Nonpareil* attributed the emigration, in part, to "Uncle Sam's" tendency "to 'draw' them unto his 'arms,'" that is, the Enrollment Act. Other attractions included the "filthy lucre" promised by the gold rush to Idaho and Montana. A local provost marshal in Colorado Territory reported "hundreds who are arriving here from the Border States weekly are nearly all Southern sympathizers." In fact, said the Council Bluffs paper, the emigration was larger than that of any year since 1855.[57]

Many Nebraskans, particularly some of the newspaper editors, ascribed the basest motives to the new arrivals. T. R. Fisher of the *Nebraska Advertiser* editorialized that strangers should not be allowed to settle in Nebraska unless they could produce evidence of loyalty to the Union. "Hundreds of secessionists have abandoned or been banished from Missouri. . . . The proper place for all such is the land of Dixie, and the sooner they go there, the better for them and us."[58]

In early June 1863 a former Confederate soldier by the name of Nathan Handley was murdered in Brownville by a mob, apparently Union men from across the river in Atchison County, Missouri. Although Handley had taken the Union Oath of Allegiance, he moved to Brownville after getting into several fights with Union supporters on the Missouri side. Some of these men were suspected of being the murderers. Although editor Fisher condemned the murder, he also noted that it had the effect of ridding the Brownville vicinity of former "rebels or rebel sympathizers," who began to leave about the time of Handley's murder.[59]

Another murder took place in Salem, Richardson County, in late June. Lafayette Shamblin, a deserter from the Sixth Kansas Volunteer Cavalry, had threatened to kill a man. The citizen had Shamblin arrested and arraigned. When he could not post bond, Shamblin was kept under guard in a vacant building. During an escape attempt on the night of June 27 he was shot to death by the guards. Some said that Shamblin had been killed by "secesh," but the guards all claimed to be Union men. The violence in southeastern Nebraska continued when in late October Felix Von Eaton Jr., U.S. marshal of Fremont County, Iowa, was killed near Nebraska City while attempting to arrest alleged Missouri "bushwhackers." Although the Nebraska provost marshal sent a posse after the bushwhackers, the men returned empty-handed after a three-day hunt.[60]

This latter episode is likely what prompted District of Nebraska commander McKean to order two companies of the Second Nebraska Cavalry not yet mustered out to Nebraska City and Falls City, respectively. Reports about organized bands of horse thieves had also been coming in. As had been the case during the Jayhawking outbreak in 1861–62, the perpetrators passed themselves off as Rebel sympathizers or loyal Unionists depending on the circumstances. In reality, opined Waters of the *Nebraska City People's Press*, "It is simply an organization of thieves and cutthroats for the purpose of preying on the public."[61]

Unfortunately, calm would not soon return. The population would continue in flux as wartime issues or economic opportunities prompted more and more people to come to Nebraska Territory. Some were certainly settlers or gold-seekers seeking a better life, while others had less admirable motives. When the Seventh Iowa Cavalry reached Omaha in September 1863, en route to build the military post at Cottonwood Springs, Lt. Eugene Ware observed that "the city was full of deserters from the Confederate Army." Of the men in the wagon trains passing the new post that fall, he noted that they did not care who won the war. "They were deserters from the army, North or South, or were out for cash only."[62]

Evidently some of the men Ware saw *did* care about how the war was going. Emigrant Peter Winne traveled along the Platte Valley in May 1863 and noted in his diary that "there were a great many Confederates on the road." On May 17 a man Winne described as "a great tall slim Missourian" came up to Winne's wagon and asked, "Say Mr., any news from the fight?" At Fort Kearny a few days earlier Winne had learned of the Union army's recent defeat at the May 1–4 Battle of Chancellorsville in Virginia and replied, "Yes, there had been a great battle and our troops have been badly beaten." That prompted the Missourian to respond, "Say Mister, who do you mean by our troops?"[63]

While unrest plagued Nebraskans at home and the men of the Second Nebraska Volunteer Cavalry spent the summer plodding up the Missouri River into Dakota Territory, mid-1863 proved less eventful for the men of the First Nebraska Volunteer Infantry. After the excitement of the Confederate raid on Cape Girardeau in late April and early May, the Nebraskans briefly resumed garrison duty in the town that had been their home since March.

On May 27 orders came that sent the regiment marching off to the familiar environs of Pilot Knob Mountain and the small towns of Arcadia, Pilot Knob, and Ironton that lay at its base. On July 4 Vicksburg surrendered to Ulysses Grant's army, freeing troops for campaigns west of the Mississippi, including an effort to take the Arkansas capital of Little Rock. Consequently, many of the soldiers in southeastern Missouri were sent south of the border, leaving behind small garrisons, including the First Nebraska.[64]

Concern that the Union base at Pilot Knob remained vulnerable to guerrilla raids from Arkansas led to construction of an earthen fortification. The earthwork was subsequently named Fort Davidson for Brig. Gen. John W. Davidson, the First Nebraska's nemesis during the grueling campaign of the previous winter. For much of July and August 1863 the Nebraska soldiers, along with local citizens and contrabands, labored on the star-shaped fort, though some soldiers seemed mystified why the army was expending so much effort and expense on this "unimportant location." They could not know, of course, that Fort Davidson would figure prominently in a small but bloody battle a year later, in September 1864, long after the Nebraskans had departed.[65]

Nebraska Territory's exemption from conscription did not solve the problem of how to fill up the ranks of the First Nebraska, which by the summer of 1863 was again short of men.

Two recruiting officers sent home in July had limited success, in part because of competition from recruiters for Kansas regiments working in Nebraska. Nor had the First Nebraska's officers forgotten what they considered a slap in the face by territorial officials who had endorsed forming the Second Nebraska Cavalry the year before. The pending muster out of the Second Nebraska, branded by the First Nebraska's Col. Robert Livingston in August 1863 as a "useless organization now . . . about to be disbanded," offered hope that some of those men might be willing to reenlist in the First Nebraska. Livingston implored Governor Saunders not to support organizing new bodies of troops in the territory "while your soldiers of the old 1st are crying to you for more men."[66]

Unfortunately for Livingston and his soldiers in Missouri, his plea to the governor went unheeded. The War Department had recently issued an order making veterans eligible for cash "bounties," along with the promise of a furlough, if they were willing to reenlist. With the original enlistments of many Union soldiers about to expire, the government was compelled to offer incentives to keep men in the ranks. Otherwise the Northern armies might simply melt away.[67]

When he became aware of the new regulations, Saunders ordered Nebraska's adjutant general to open recruiting for what would be known as the First Battalion, Nebraska Veteran Volunteer Cavalry. The governor realized that the terms of the Second Nebraska soldiers were about to expire, and those men would qualify for the reenlistment bonus. Here was a way to keep experienced soldiers on duty in Nebraska for home defense and also provide them with some cash they might spend locally. In a scenario reminiscent of the parallel recruiting in the summer and fall of 1862, Nebraska newspapers in September 1863 published simultaneous advertisements from the recruiting officers for both the First Nebraska regiment and the

First Battalion. Both recruiters could promise bounties, but the likelihood that the First Battalion would remain in the territory outstripped the incentives for recruits to join the First Nebraska.[68]

The First Nebraska did have one thing to offer new recruits that had not been available the year before: the former infantrymen were soon to become horse soldiers. By the time the regiment was ordered from Pilot Knob to St. Louis at the end of August 1863, Colonel Livingston had already received word of this prospect from Department of the Missouri commander John Schofield. Several other former infantry regiments were also slated to become cavalry. Mounted troops were far more effective in countering local guerrillas during the brief, hit-and-run raids that were now the main threat from weakened Confederate forces. Word of the change had also reached Nebraska, and the *Nebraska Advertiser* was optimistic that it would help recruiting for the First Nebraska. The editor noted that more than a thousand men had enlisted from the surrounding district during the last year, but nearly all had joined cavalry regiments instead of the First Nebraska, "objecting to it as infantry."[69]

When the First Nebraska soldiers were ordered from Pilot Knob to St. Louis in August 1863 the companies were dispersed to guard prisons, barracks, and the navy yard at Carondelet where Union gunboats were being constructed. The men of Company H drew this latter assignment and were fascinated by the technology involved in building these "armor-plated monsters," as Private Scherneckau called them. The St. Louis sojourn was interrupted when some 150 men of the regiment were quickly dispatched by rail to Jefferson City in early October as part of the Union response to Confederate Gen. Joseph Shelby's fast-moving cavalry raid that reached the Missouri

River before he retreated into Arkansas. The Nebraska soldiers did no fighting and were back in St. Louis by October 22.[70]

Meanwhile, on October 10 the Department of the Missouri issued the order to mount the First Nebraska. Over a three-week period the men received horses, cavalry uniforms, sabers, and revolvers and learned how to set up camp in a new way. Because no cavalry carbines were available, the men kept their long infantry rifles, complete with bayonets, causing Scherneckau to grump, "Oh how we cursed these old heavy things." While most of the men had ridden in civilian life, the cavalry mounts were young horses, virtually unbroken. "Falling off is the order of the day," wrote Scherneckau, and several men were seriously injured before the men learned the ways of the cavalryman.[71]

On November 4 the First Nebraska officers began reenlisting men for three years under the government's bounty program, which also promised a furlough as a bonus for reenlisting. At the same time Colonel Livingston got bad news from Lt. Edward Donovan, his recruiting officer in Omaha. Recruits for the First Nebraska were hard to come by, reported Donovan, "as labor here is so well rewarded." The First Nebraska officers were also irritated by competition from the former Second Nebraska officers now enlisting men for the First Battalion of Nebraska Cavalry. In fact, said Donovan, the First Battalion recruiters "have done all they could to injure our regt."[72]

Livingston finally despaired of getting enough men from Nebraska to bolster his under-strength companies and requested permission to recruit new soldiers in Missouri. Although the regiment had enlisted Missouri men beginning with its arrival there in 1861, the Enrollment Act of 1863 had assigned quotas to each state and congressional district, which the states had to meet to avoid a draft. Thus Livingston needed permission to recruit in Missouri in the fall of 1863. Permission was granted by the Department of the Missouri and the Missouri adjutant general's office on November 20. Livingston was required to furnish muster rolls of Missouri residents who had formerly joined the First Nebraska as well as for those who might enlist in the future. These men would then be credited to Missouri's quota under the Enrollment Act. In the end this initiative added some ninety soldiers to the ranks of the First Nebraska.[73]

There was a good reason for wanting the regiment at as nearly full strength as possible. On November 12 Brig. Gen. Clinton B. Fisk, commanding the District of Southeastern Missouri, wrote Schofield that the whole country from Pilot Knob south to DeVall's Bluff in Arkansas was open to the enemy. To prevent "rebel organizations in Arkansas" from threatening southeastern Missouri and navigation on the Mississippi, Fisk urged that a regiment of cavalry commanded by "a vigorous and discreet officer" be stationed in northeastern Arkansas without delay. While Fisk may or may not have had Livingston in mind, clearly the First Nebraska's colonel met those qualifications.[74]

General Schofield alerted Livingston that the assignment was in the wind and, on November 30, sent orders for Livingston to take command of the District of Northeastern Arkansas, with his headquarters at Batesville. His force would include the First Nebraska Cavalry, a battalion of the Eleventh Missouri Cavalry, and one section of Battery D of the Second Missouri Light Artillery. The troops were to rendezvous at the Union base at Rolla, Missouri, and march to Batesville "as soon as practicable."[75]

Schofield admonished Livingston that his "chief object" in northeastern Arkansas was "to destroy, drive out, or capture the guerrilla bands which now infest the district" and to organize loyal Arkansans for Union service. If this goal were accomplished, said the general, Union forces in southern Missouri could be reduced. In carrying out these responsibilities, Livingston was to be as lenient as possible to disloyal persons, letting "their future rather than their past conduct determine the treatment they are to receive."[76]

Having been forewarned of his pending assignment, Livingston ordered four companies of the regiment to Rolla by rail on November 26. Horses for some of the other companies were still being shod. Early on the morning of November 30 the remaining companies of the First Nebraska, along with the company supply wagons, entrained at St. Louis for the ride to Rolla, where they arrived the next day.[77]

There preparations continued for the expedition to Arkansas. More than two hundred half-broken mules were acquired from the government corral to pull the regiment's supply wagons. Livingston inspected the troops, and each man drew forty rifle and forty-eight revolver cartridges. Each company wagon was loaded with five thousand cartridges of each kind. On the evening of December 9 the troops were ordered to be ready to march at noon the next day. They would be accompanied by the battalion of the Eleventh Missouri Cavalry and two six-pounder cannon of the Second Missouri Artillery.[78]

On December 10 Livingston's little army marched away from Rolla with the regimental band playing and the company guidons flapping in the wind. On Christmas Day it arrived in Batesville, Arkansas, the seat of Independence County, located on the north bank of the White River. The trip was not uneventful. En route the men skirmished with guerrillas and made "short work" of several prisoners they captured, which was Private Scherneckau's euphemism for summary execution. Livingston's official report, written upon his arrival in Batesville, tallied fifteen guerrillas killed and seventeen captured, with the loss of one of his own men. His plan for the future was to "drive the freebooters out of Northern Arkansas without delay," a task that would be easier said than done.[79]

Back home in Nebraska, the year 1863 began winding down with an election for members of the legislature that would convene in January 1864. No session had been held since 1862, because the federal appropriation for an 1863 session had been diverted to pay the territory's Direct War Tax. Not only does the government take but sometimes it gives, and in December it awarded Nebraska a prize of immense value. The 1862 Pacific Railroad Act required the president to select the eastern and western points from which a transcontinental line would be built. On December 2 the news reached Nebraska that President Lincoln had fixed the eastern terminus on Iowa's western border at Council Bluffs. With no bridge spanning the Missouri River, everyone realized that Omaha would be the real starting point for the Union Pacific.

Groundbreaking for the railroad was held that very day. Cannons boomed, an American flag measuring thirty-eight by eighteen feet was "thrown to the breeze," speeches were made, and a thousand people cheered as dignitaries including Governor Saunders and the mayors of Omaha and Council Bluffs turned the first shovelfuls of earth. Telegrams from President Lincoln and Secretary of State William H. Seward were read. Speakers opined that under the influence of the Pacific railroad, Nebraska, the former Great American Desert, "will . . . be revealed to the world as the great American Garden." This revelation, however, would have to wait until the war was over. No rails would be laid west from Omaha until the summer of 1865.[80]

The designation of the transcontinental railroad terminus spurred hopes that statehood for Nebraska might soon be realized. On December 23 congressional delegate Samuel Daily wrote Colonel Livingston predicting that "the present session of Congress will pass an enabling act to let us come into the Union as a state by time to vote for the next president." Congress in 1861 and 1863 had already configured the future state of Nebraska by carving away the territories of Colorado, Dakota, and Idaho from the original Nebraska Territory of 1854. Although Daily's prediction would come true in part during 1864, statehood itself would be delayed for several years and prove far more complicated than he or anyone else could have imagined.[81]

CHAPTER FOUR

1864

"You May Expect a General Indian Outbreak in All This Western Country"

Wh
hen Governor Alvin Saunders rose to address the ninth session of the territorial legislature on January 8, 1864, his message was cautiously optimistic. "The pursuits of our people have rarely been interrupted," said the governor, the territory's population was increasing, harvests had been abundant, and trade had prospered. "The hostile Indians on our frontier have been restrained." During the two years since the legislature had last assembled, the Union armies had made significant gains. Vicksburg had fallen, opening the Mississippi River, Robert E. Lee's invasion of the North had been turned back at Gettysburg, and the Confederates had been driven out of Tennessee. A few months more of "vigorous and persistent efforts" and the war might be over. Then the benefits of the Homestead and Pacific Railroad Acts could be realized, and "none can hesitate to predict for Nebraska gigantic strides in the attainment of wealth and power."[1]

Saunders also praised Nebraska's soldiers, urged the legislature to grant them the right to vote, "whether in the field, camp or hospital," and outlined issues important to the territory's governance and finances. It was time, said the governor, for the legislature to revisit the question of whether Nebraska should apply for statehood. He reminded the legislators that during the session of Congress that met from December 1862 to March 1863, bills had been introduced to authorize statehood for Nebraska, Colorado, and Nevada. "These bills would probably have become laws had they been introduced at an earlier period in the session," but they failed "for want of time to act upon them." The current session of Congress would undoubtedly reconsider statehood for Nebraska and the other two territories. The legislature, therefore, "should make some expression of opinion upon this subject." Would statehood's benefits, including federal land grants for schools, railroads, and internal improvements, along with voting representation in Congress, outweigh the drawback of higher taxes to support a state government? If the legislature so decided, it should promptly memorialize Congress to pass a statehood enabling act.[2]

The Republican governor concluded his message with his views on "our duty to support the federal government." His admonition was aimed at administration critics, particularly those Nebraska Democrats and Democratic newspapers who had vehemently and persistently criticized Lincoln for issuing the Emancipation Proclamation and for his decision to enlist black soldiers. It was also meant for those who counseled resistance to the federal Enrollment Act and sought to undermine recruiting efforts. "When this opposition to the measures of the government is made in the interest of the rebels, it is far from innocent," said Saunders. It helped sustain "men who have conspired to sever the Union and whose hands are dripping with the blood of the nation's defenders, . . . who have levied war on the stars and stripes—the emblem of our power and glory—and are fighting and toiling to destroy the best government that ever blessed the world." The only means of "securing a permanent peace with such a people, is a vigorous prosecution of the war." Those in rebellion against the government had "forfeited all right to the protection of the Constitution and laws" and did not deserve the "tender regard" that seemed to motivate many of Lincoln's critics in the North.[3]

While Saunders did not identify any of those critics by name, the governor may well have been thinking of J. Sterling Morton, who had never wavered in the belief that making peace with the Rebels was the only means by which the Union could be restored. Morton's friendship with the North's leading Peace Democrat, Clement Vallandigham, was no secret, nor had the Nebraskan been shy about expressing his view that if Lincoln and the Republicans could be turned out of office in the fall 1864 elections, the Democrats should "try peace as a means of Union." Fellow Nebraska Democrat George Miller cautioned Morton "that if Abolition deserves your hatred, you have no cause for sympathy with that other heresy, its diabolical twin, secession."[4]

As the year 1864 opened, the territorial Republican press also did its part to assess how things were going and bolster public support for Lincoln and the Union war effort. On January 29 Edward B. Taylor, editor of Omaha's *Nebraska Republican*, encapsulated his views, which were exactly the opposite of those held by the Peace Democrats. The gains made thus far toward ending the rebellion had been important but not decisive. The Rebel armies "must be met and vanquished in an open struggle upon the field before we can begin to talk of Peace." Although "Copperheads and rebel sympathizers may sing the siren song of Peace," the American people would accept nothing less than unconditional submission to the rightful authority of the federal government and "restoration of the time-honored and revered Union of our fathers." It was also clear to Taylor that the war would decide the fate of slavery. "The contest is no longer one of good government against mediated anarchy—the South has forced upon us the issue of Freedom for all or Slavery for all," and this issue would decide the coming presidential election.[5]

Before adjourning in mid-February the legislature passed a bill authorizing Nebraska soldiers serving away from home to vote in territorial elections. One member of the Council argued that he would not trust soldiers with the right of suffrage, prompting the *Nebraska Republican* to credit his stance to fears that the soldier vote would help elect loyal men instead of Copperheads. "The experiment may be distasteful to the Copperheads, but we have an abiding faith that *liberty* will survive the shock."[6] Over opposition by several Democrats, the Republican majority adopted resolutions praising the Emancipation Proclamation and the enlistment of black men in the Union army and endorsed the president's reelection. The legislature voted a resolution of thanks to the Nebraska soldiers in the field. Finally, as the governor had suggested, the members memorialized Congress to pass a statehood enabling act, hoping that perhaps Nebraska could achieve statehood in time to vote in the fall elections for president and members of Congress.[7]

While the legislature was meeting in Omaha, an outbreak of violence revealed that wartime passions still motivated some Nebraskans' conduct and personal relationships. A mob severely beat an elderly man on the street in Brownville because he was a "secession sympathizer" who had publicly wished that Indians would cut out the hearts of Union soldiers (he called them "Lincoln's nigger thieves"). After the man was granted refuge in the Brownville hotel owned by Dr. John McPherson, a letter signed "Union League" appeared in the newspaper expressing "unmitigated contempt" for McPherson's harboring of a Rebel. Dr. McPherson, one of the town's leading citizens, fired back with his own letter. If the man he had sheltered was guilty of a crime then he should be punished by the proper authorities, "but not persecuted or murdered by men who act in open defiance of all law." The hometown *Nebraska Advertiser* editor agreed, noting that those who took the law into their own hands hurt the Union cause "by atrocities committed in their insane zeal for its welfare." Not long afterward two men invaded a farmer's house near Falls City, abused his wife, and made off with household goods. On February 4 "midnight assassins" went to Rulo, destroyed the contents of two grocery stores, robbed a Mr. Poteet of horses and nearly $200, and beat him before leaving.[8]

Some of these episodes, like others that had plagued Nebraska since 1861, may have been mere thievery or the settling of old scores cloaked in the guise of suppressing so-called Jayhawkers or "secession sympathizers." On the other hand, Nebraska Territory had become a refuge for military deserters or men evading conscription, and many citizens felt action should be taken to suppress outspoken critics of the government or those who publicly praised the Rebels and their leaders. While military provost marshals had been appointed in Nebraska to deal with desertion and to enforce the Enrollment Act, only troops seemed able to deal with mob violence or pillage by roaming armed bands.

Accordingly, as had been the case in 1863, soldiers were dispatched to southeastern Nebraska, first to Nebraska City and later to Brownville and Falls City. Company C of the Seventh Iowa Cavalry, ninety officers and enlisted men, was ordered to Nebraska City on January 14. While the Brownville newspaper had editorially hoped the local outbreak of violence would not "make it necessary to have a military force quartered here to teach us loyalty," a lieutenant and ten soldiers from the Seventh Iowa arrived there on February 21.[9]

By late February 1864 the military held some thirty prisoners under arrest in Nebraska City, with thirty more in Brownville. They were alleged "horse thieves" and deserters from Missouri. District of Nebraska commander Gen. Robert B. Mitchell issued an order calculated to put on notice "lawless individuals engaged in robbing and murder." Those who claimed they were acting from patriotic motives against the enemies of the government should join the army, the order instructed. The general promised to take vigorous measures "to suppress robbery and other disgraceful crimes."[10]

A military commission was seated at Nebraska City to try alleged offenders, though it was soon disbanded because department commander Curtis told Mitchell that he did not think the military had jurisdiction over civil disorders. The commission's findings were never made public, but the Brownville paper reported that most of the prisoners had been acquitted. If nothing else, the orders, arrests, and investigations seemed to bring at least temporary calm. The *People's Press* of Nebraska City reported on April 29, "Everything quiet in the lower part of the Territory." At about the same time, the troops were withdrawn from the southeastern Nebraska towns.[11]

The officers in charge of military jurisdictions west of the Missouri River were constantly shifting their limited forces wherever the need seemed greatest. On January 1, 1864, Nebraska Territory became part of a new military Department of Kansas in charge of Gen. Samuel R. Curtis; in late February command of the District of Nebraska Territory had passed from Brig. Gen. Thomas McKean to Mitchell. The district, which stretched all the way from the Missouri River into today's central Wyoming and parts of northern Colorado, could muster fewer than six hundred officers and men for duty.[12]

In March Gen. John Pope, commanding the Department of the Northwest, asked Curtis to send him a battalion of the Seventh Iowa or the newly forming First Battalion, Nebraska Veteran Volunteer Cavalry to bolster his pending summer campaign against Indians along the Upper Missouri and its tributaries. Curtis replied that he "could not spare a man" because of "an immense emigration . . . concentrating in the Platte Valley, en route for the Bannack mines." He also informed District of Nebraska commander Mitchell that he could not promise him any more troops because of the existing "great demands" elsewhere. Union forces west of the Mississippi were beginning the Red River Campaign to capture Shreveport, Louisiana, as a jumping-off point for an invasion of Texas. In the east newly appointed army commander-in-chief Grant was coordinating a major spring offensive against Lee's Confederate Army of Northern Virginia, while William Tecumseh Sherman's Union armies began grinding their way through Georgia toward Atlanta.[13]

Not only gold miners but Mormons bound for Salt Lake City and freighters supplying the mining camps, road ranches, and military outposts swelled spring travel along the Platte. Both Omaha and Nebraska City continued to be major outfitting points. Steamboat arrivals at Nebraska City were double that of previous years, with five steamboats owned by the Hannibal and St. Joseph Railroad operating upriver from the town. By early May there had been fifty-one steamboat arrivals at Nebraska City, including vessels owned by the Merchants Line of St. Louis and by independent operators. An estimated eighteen to twenty-three million pounds of freight went west from Nebraska City in 1864.[14]

From his ranche on Wood River Squire Lamb reported the passing of "one constant train from March first and from all parts of the world." By early June Lamb characterized traffic along the north side of the Platte as heavy enough to form a continuous dust cloud from morning to night; he had heard that eighty thousand teams had crossed the Missouri River at Omaha. The traffic was also immense along the trails south of the Platte. Observers at Fort Laramie recorded 6,161 wagons, some twenty-five thousand animals, and more than nineteen thousand emigrants passing that point from mid-March through July 9.[15]

Some observers revealed that many of the "emigrants" going west in 1864, as in earlier years, were not mere home seekers, fortune hunters, Mormons, or freighters. The editor of the *Council Bluffs Nonpareil* suspected they were leaving "the states" to avoid military conscription, "asking at the same time, that the arms of the country shall guard them as they go." Eugene Ware of the Seventh Iowa Cavalry noted that "the Civil War was loosening up whole blocks of society and giving them an impulse to the West." They might be Union supporters or Rebel sympathizers, depending on the majority sentiment in the communities from whence they came. In early August a deputy provost marshal in Brownville arrested a man suspected of being a Missouri bushwhacker. The man admitted he had been in the Rebel army and was now "trying to escape to the Plains" to avoid being conscripted into either army. George Forman, traveling from St. Louis to the Montana gold mines in June, encountered three wagon trains on the Little Blue River, "all Secesh from Missouri leaving there to avoid the troubles of the war."[16]

Travelers reported that Indians had grown "very bold" in the western reaches of the Platte Valley. Military pressure being applied by Pope's forces in Dakota Territory had forced many tribesmen south, where they encountered the massive numbers of whites. Inevitably miners and supply trains proceeding overland to the Idaho/Montana goldfields began to trespass on Indian hunting grounds. In April Fort Laramie's Col. William O. Collins of the Eleventh Ohio Volunteer Cavalry reported that a large party from Denver was heading north to the Idaho mines along a new route through the heart of Indian country laid out in 1863 by John M. Bozeman, which would become known as the Bozeman Trail by 1865. Several civilian wagon trains followed the trail in the summer of 1864.[17]

By late May 1864 reports were reaching Department of Kansas headquarters of "powerful combinations of Indian tribes who are pledged to sustain each other and drive the white people from this country." The Indians were concentrating in northern Kansas on the Smoky Hill and Republican Rivers and near the forks of the Platte. In April and again on June 8 General Mitchell counseled at Cottonwood Springs with Spotted Tail, Whistler, Two Strike, Bad Wound, and other representatives of the Brule and Oglala Sioux. These leaders had been, and pledged they would continue to be, in favor of peace. They were concerned, however, about their bands being attacked by Southern Cheyennes and allied Arapahos, Kiowas, and Comanches. The friendly chiefs told the general about Cheyenne depredations in Kansas and along the South Platte route to Denver and warned that the Cheyennes had promised to kill all the whites on the Platte Valley and Santa Fe trails.[18]

On July 4 Mitchell summarized his views on the Indian situation in a letter to John Evans, governor of Colorado Territory. The general was fully aware of "the existing troubles" affecting the Platte Valley routes to Denver and elsewhere. Most attacks had been made by Indians from northern Kansas, which was not in his district. And without more soldiers the general could do little to control the Indians within his own district. Mitchell predicted, however, that any future Indian problems "will be confined to petty depredations committed by strolling bands, and not by any combined efforts of the Indians in

this district." As subsequent events would reveal, his prediction could not have been more wrong.[19]

While opposing forces seemed to be girding for actual warfare in Nebraska Territory's western reaches, Nebraska Democrats and Republicans continued to skirmish on the political
front. On April 19, responding to the legislature's memorial,
Congress passed a Nebraska statehood enabling act. It authorized the governor to order an election to be held June 6 for
delegates to a constitutional convention, followed by the convention itself on July 4. If a constitution were drafted, then it
would be submitted to the voters for approval at the October
11 territorial election.[20]

The Democratic and Republican newspapers had distinctly
different views regarding statehood for Nebraska. Democratic
organs, such as the *Omaha Nebraskian*, saw it merely as a ploy
to support Lincoln's reelection and supply extra Republican
votes in Congress to pass the pending Thirteenth Amendment
abolishing slavery. In return, "numberless fat offices shall be
bestowed upon the faithful leaders of the [Nebraska Republi-
can] party as a reward for services, sufferings, and wear and
tear of conscience in singing hallelujahs to an administration
the most imbecile, reckless, profligate, and corrupt that has
ever existed." Underlying the Democrats' inflammatory rhetoric was the realization that if statehood came soon, their party
was unlikely to reap its political benefits.[21]

The Republican papers touted statehood in more moderate
terms, emphasizing its promise for Nebraska's future growth
and development. Not only would statehood gain Nebraska
voting representation in Congress (two senators and a congressman), but vast tracts of public land would be granted
as subsidies for schools and railroads. The population would
quickly increase because statehood would signal new oppor-

tunities for would-be settlers. That Nebraska had been a territory for ten long years cast it in an unfavorable light to the
outside world: "[I]n these storm and lightning days, a territory
that cannot support itself after that length of national foster-
ing may reasonably be deemed a land of barrens and of barren men," wrote the *Nebraska Republican*.[22]

Moreover, said the *Republican*, the Democrats were being dis-
ingenuous. While they cloaked their antistate arguments in
terms of higher taxes and the prospect that statehood might
result in the removal of the capital from Omaha, "their hostility is based upon their devotion to the 'peculiar institution.'"
Because Democrats thought slavery should be forever perpetuated by constitutional sanction and protection, "we find them,
before any discussion has been had as to the merits of the question of admission, arrayed as one man in opposition to it."[23]

Whether a smokescreen or not, the Democrats' main argument against statehood, higher taxes, proved effective. If Nebraska became a state, they said, its people would have to bear
the entire cost of a state government. If Nebraska remained
a territory, Washington would continue to pay most of the
bills. Most delegates elected to the constitutional convention,
whether Republican or Democrat, were pledged against statehood; when the convention assembled on July 4, it promptly
adjourned on a vote of thirty-seven to seven without drafting
a state constitution.[24]

Had the convention convened and drafted a constitution,
and had the voters subsequently approved it, Nebraska would
have become a state in 1864. Congress had passed identical enabling acts for Nebraska, Nevada, and Colorado in March and
April. Each act provided that if a constitution conforming to
the required conditions was formed and approved by the voters
and certified to the president, "it shall be the duty of the President of the United States to issue his proclamation declaring

the state admitted into the Union . . . without any further action whatever on the part of Congress." Colorado held a convention and produced a constitution, but the voters rejected it. Nevada also held a convention, and the voters approved the ensuing constitution, enabling Lincoln to proclaim Nevada statehood before the fall presidential election.[25]

The Nebraska Democrats' elation over the setback to the statehood drive gave the Republican papers another opportunity to upbraid the rival party. Although the Democrats knew the federal government needed every dollar "to whip out the rebellion," they were "mean enough" to expect it to continue subsidizing the territory. Yet "the same class would call loudly for a regiment if a few strange Indians appear on our border."[26]

Some Democrats also made it easy for the Republicans to continue to brand them as rebellion sympathizers. No critic of the administration demonstrated more outrageous behavior than *Nebraska City News* editor Augustus Harvey, or "Ajax," as he signed himself, who had earlier stirred up a firestorm with his denunciations of President Lincoln's policies on slavery and black soldiers. On July 5, 1864, Harvey, evidently intoxicated, paraded through town dragging a small U.S. flag in the mud and occasionally stamping it underfoot. "He declared himself a d——d Secessionist, which no sane man doubted." Nevertheless, said the *Nebraska Advertiser*, Harvey had the merit of candor in expressing his true sentiments while intoxicated, which other Democrats "are too cowardly to do when sober." Harvey was arrested and hauled off to Omaha for an investigation of his loyalty and was soon released after signing the federal oath of allegiance and giving bond that he would observe it.[27]

In far-off Arkansas the officers and men of the First Nebraska Cavalry, stationed at Batesville since Christmas Day 1863, knew little or nothing about what was happening back home. The first mail from Nebraska did not reach the regiment until late February, more than two months after it had marched away from Missouri to Arkansas. The Union supply line to Batesville via the White River had proved undependable, with either floods or low water often preventing steamboats from reaching the town with rations, ammunition, and mail. Bands of armed guerrillas with no affiliation to any army, commonly called "bushwhackers," as well as small Confederate army units, disrupted travel throughout the countryside.[28]

When they arrived in Batesville, Livingston and his soldiers hoped that most of the region's inhabitants might be ready to concede that the Southern cause was lost. Federal forces had captured Little Rock the previous September and occupied most of the larger towns in the northern half of the state. President Lincoln had laid the groundwork for the reestablishment of loyal governments in Arkansas and other Rebel states via his December 8, 1863, Proclamation of Amnesty and Reconstruction. It offered a full pardon to those who would swear an oath of allegiance to the United States and obey all laws and proclamations relating to slavery.[29]

For his part, Colonel Livingston on December 25 issued his own proclamation to the citizens of northern Arkansas, offering protection and security to those who had always been loyal, to those who had renounced allegiance to the Confederacy, and to those who would subsequently lay down their arms. "Return to your firesides and the bosoms of your families, and as far as in my power lies, I will protect you and yours from harm." Guerrillas and bushwhackers who did not "forego the course of bootless warfare you have carried on . . . against the government" would suffer death wherever they might be found. People in these categories, however, were not necessarily fighting for the Southern cause but often only for plunder or to settle old scores and were unlikely to respond to offers of amnesty.[30]

Bringing peace to northeastern Arkansas, therefore, would require continued warfare. Some citizens had remained loyal, if silent, Unionists when the state seceded in 1861, and when federal forces occupied northern Arkansas some of them came forward for protection, to take the president's oath of allegiance, and sometimes to enlist. When the First Nebraska and the Eleventh Missouri reached Batesville, organization of the Fourth Arkansas (Union) Mounted Infantry was already underway, with 131 men on the rolls, soon to exceed 350. The Fourth Arkansas was attached to Livingston's command.[31]

Also augmenting Livingston's forces at Batesville were several black men, probably former slaves, who enlisted in the First Nebraska as "undercooks." This designation was in accordance with a provision in the Enrollment Act of 1863 that authorized companies to enlist two "undercooks of African descent." They would be paid ten dollars a month, plus one ration per day, and accounted for as other soldiers.

The undercooks included Peter Holliday and Anderson Henderson in Company A; Washington Grigsby and Harrison Johnson in Company H; and William Dougherty and Alfred Smith in Company K. Holliday and Henderson deserted in Arkansas and Grigsby deserted at St. Louis in June 1864, when the veteran portion of the regiment was there en route to being furloughed. Johnson, Dougherty, and Smith came to Nebraska with the veterans, where Dougherty and Smith later deserted. Smith evidently rejoined the regiment, because he was mustered out with the rest of the soldiers in early July 1866. Of the six, only Harrison Johnson served with the First Nebraska continuously from his enlistment until the regiment was discharged.[32]

Livingston and his little army would spend the next five months trying to gain control over the District of Northeastern Arkansas by capturing, killing, or driving out roaming guerrillas and remnant Confederate forces. At the same time they sought to secure their supply lines and help keep the river routes open to other Union enclaves. The job required frequent patrols over a rugged landscape in all kinds of weather, duty that wore down both the soldiers and their horses. Physical fatigue was exacerbated by the mental strain of being constantly on alert for ambushes or brief firefights that might erupt at any farmstead, hamlet, or stream crossing.

Contesting with Livingston's forces were several hundred Confederate troops under the overall command of Gen. Dandridge McRae, with small units led by Col. Thomas R. Freeman and Capt. George Rutherford. Other combatants, whom Livingston termed "pestiferous hybrids," acknowledged no formal military command and often donned captured Union uniforms or civilian garb. Union authorities considered such men "brigands and guerrillas," subject to execution under martial law. Men fitting this description caught wearing Union uniforms were to be shot on the spot, as Livingston's proclamation had warned.[33]

Throughout the winter and early spring of 1864 the men of the First Nebraska and Livingston's other regiments played a deadly game of "cat and mouse" with guerrillas and with Rutherford's and Freeman's soldiers. On January 23 Private Scherneckau and his comrades clattered through the streets of the small town of Mount Olive, where the advance guard shot down a man who ran away when hailed. He turned out to be a Confederate soldier on leave and for Scherneckau, "The first man I have seen killed in this war!"[34]

Aside from sharp skirmishes at Sylamore Mountain on January 26, Morgan's Mill on February 9, Waugh's farm on February 19, and Jacksonport on April 20 that involved a few hundred men each time, most engagements were like the Mount

Olive affair, accidental encounters between Livingston's scouting and foraging parties and guerrillas or Confederates. At Sylamore Mountain Scherneckau fired his rifle "very calmly and quite deliberately" at a guerrilla, "the first human being at whom I had shot" during his fifteen months in the army. Men on both sides were killed, wounded, or captured, wagon trains were burned, and so-called bushwhackers were summarily executed. Civilians caught in the middle saw their farmsteads plundered, their crops and livestock "requisitioned," and their loyalties questioned.[35]

When the White River proved undependable for timely steamboat delivery of supplies for Livingston's troops at Batesville, the colonel was forced to send frequent expeditions to scour the countryside within a fifty-mile radius for food, forage, and horses. Gathering supplies proved a daunting task in a region where three years of war had already consumed or destroyed crops and livestock and disrupted planting and harvesting. The extensive scouting and foraging further exhausted the men and horses, so much so that by mid-April Livingston reported, "[M]y stock is dying daily for want of food," with fewer than half his men still having serviceable mounts. Private Scherneckau of Company H noted that "my horse is nothing but skin and bones" and because the immediate area was "completely drained" of forage, "our wagons must go out three to four days' march in order to get corn."[36]

In his April report the colonel cataloged a grim outlook for the civilian population in his district. In late January 1864 he had appointed First Nebraska chaplain Thomas Tipton as "superintendent of destitute and deserving loyal Arkansians." By March 31 the chaplain had issued rations to 408 persons. But when supplies could not be delivered or secured by foraging, both soldiers and civilians suffered. Twenty-one hundred families sent in reports of the amount of grain and forage they had on hand, along with the acreage under cultivation, and Chaplain Tipton noted, "[T]he result is destitution."[37]

Accordingly, Livingston on April 16 ordered most of his force to withdraw from Batesville and retire downstream to the Union base at Jacksonport, located just below the confluence of the Black River with the White River. The combined flow of the two rivers meant Jacksonport could more easily be supplied by steamboats coming upstream on White River from the Mississippi. The last elements of the Union garrison at Batesville departed for Jacksonport in mid-May 1864. Accompanying them were several hundred refugees, mostly dependents of the men in the Fourth Arkansas Mounted Infantry, who could not remain behind in the absence of Union troops to protect them.[38]

Livingston's command would not stay long at Jacksonport. Aside from continuing supply problems, another reason for evacuating Batesville and subsequently Jacksonport was the resumption of Confederate offensive operations in northern Arkansas as a prelude to a planned invasion of Missouri. The disastrous failure of the Union's Red River Expedition, including the defeat and retreat of the Arkansas column under Gen. Frederick Steele, revived Confederate military prospects. Gen. Joseph O. Shelby and twelve hundred tough Confederate cavalrymen were sent into Livingston's district to organize men and resources for the Missouri raid. Shelby's command was a much more formidable opponent than the scattered soldiers and guerrillas with which the Union troops had previously been contending. On May 22 the Department of Arkansas ordered Livingston to withdraw farther south to DeVall's Bluff on the White River, at the eastern end of a railroad extending to Little Rock. Shelby and his Confederates promptly occupied both Batesville and Jacksonport, signaling the end of Colonel Livingston and the First Nebraska's brief reign over the District of Northeastern Arkansas.[39]

Unofficial statistics reflect some of the accomplishments Livingston claimed for the time he commanded the district. They included the killing or capture of more than eight hundred Rebels, guerrillas included, and the breaking up of numerous Rebel bands. From two to three thousand citizens had taken the Union oath of allegiance, and some 1,614 people in the district had voted in March elections for a provisional Union state constitution for Arkansas and a slate of state officers, as provided by Lincoln's amnesty proclamation. Nevertheless, at the end of Livingston's tenure as district commander, regular Confederate forces and guerrillas still operated throughout most of the region, the population remained destitute, and the countryside remained a virtual wasteland. For the people of northeastern Arkansas, the first half of 1864 brought no respite or conclusion to their long Civil War nightmare.[40]

Worse, perhaps, was that Arkansas had long since ceased to play a significant role in the war's military outcome. Both sides had channeled most men and resources east of the Mississippi River, where they would be employed in titanic battles between Grant's and Lee's armies in Virginia and during Gen. William Tecumseh Sherman's campaign against Confederate forces in Georgia. Yet the ongoing guerrilla war in Arkansas and elsewhere supported the Confederacy's broader strategic goals. Many Southerners hoped that prolonging resistance to federal authority might contribute to Lincoln's defeat by a "peace" candidate in the fall 1864 presidential election, who would then negotiate for Confederate independence.[41]

On June 1, 1864, the Department of Arkansas issued orders to furlough the First Nebraska veterans who had reenlisted in the fall of 1863 under the government's incentive plan. These men would have thirty days of freedom before beginning their second enlistment. On June 10 the veterans (and a few wounded men being sent home on medical furloughs) left DeVall's Bluff on the steamer *Westmoreland*. Beforehand, Colonel Livingston made it clear that this was to be a triumphal return: "The regiment is going home where hearts and eyes await them and the col. commanding looks to his officers that the men may be presented in such a manner as will gratify the highest hopes of those who love them."[42]

The veterans, numbering about 330 officers and men, reached St. Louis on June 16, where they were treated to a welcoming banquet hosted by the mayor. There the men were released, many to visit family and friends in the states where they had lived before settling in Nebraska. The remnant that arrived in Omaha on June 28, numbering fewer than eighty men, was welcomed with flags, cannon salutes, and a banquet at the capitol building. It had been almost three years since the First Nebraska sailed down the Missouri en route to the war. When the furloughs expired, the regiment would reassemble and return to Arkansas, or so everyone expected.[43]

Colonel Livingston wasted no time in launching efforts to recruit new soldiers for the First Nebraska. On July 4 he issued a lengthy call for "the able-bodied yeomanry of Nebraska" to join the "Old First" and "cover the standards we bear with glory." He urged the "warm-hearted women of the territory" to use their influence to "break down the selfish and sordid motives behind which men entrench themselves" and much more in the same vein. Recruiting offices were opened in several of the river towns.[44]

As had so often been the case, the times were not propitious for gathering recruits. The Nebraska cavalry battalion authorized in the fall of 1863 had already enlisted three companies, mostly former Second Nebraska men, and the last company would be ready for mustering in by August. As before, these cavalrymen were slated to remain in the territory, while men joining the First Nebraska could expect to go to Arkansas.

Moreover, the gold rushes and overland freighting continued to siphon men from the pool of prospective enlistees. Chaplain Tipton, who surveyed recruiting prospects in his hometown of Brownville, was not optimistic: "The very high prices [i.e., wages] for teamsters interferes with our chances." Teamsters engaged in overland freighting could earn from sixty to seventy-five dollars per month, which contrasted with army pay, now sixteen dollars a month for privates.[45]

The First Nebraska men and officers who had not reenlisted, and those whose original enlistments had not yet expired, stayed behind in Arkansas. Four days after the veterans departed, Lieutenants William Polock and Edward Donovan reached De-Vall's Bluff with sixty-four new recruits from Nebraska, bringing the number of Nebraska soldiers in Arkansas to about 270 men. Some of these men were soon to engage in battle and suffer the terror and hardship of becoming prisoners of war, while others would find themselves snared in a web of military bureaucracy for which their World War II counterparts coined an acronym: snafu (situation normal, all f——d up!).[46]

Companies A, B, and D had not achieved the three-quarters reenlistment rate qualifying them to maintain their company organization in the First Nebraska Veteran Volunteer Cavalry. Consequently the three companies would be mustered out as units, save for a few men from each whose enlistments had not expired and who would be assigned to other companies. The three companies retained their records in Arkansas, pending their imminent mustering out.

The records of the other seven companies went to Nebraska with the officers. When the veterans returned to Arkansas after the furloughs expired, Polock and Donovan's recruits would then be assigned to companies. At least that was the plan. In the meantime the First Nebraska detachment, both the new recruits and "old" soldiers whose terms had not yet expired, was posted to the Third Brigade of the Second Corps, commanded by Maj. Gen. Eugene A. Carr.[47]

In late June and July the Nebraska soldiers patrolled the railroad linking DeVall's Bluff with Little Rock and joined in several sharp skirmishes with Shelby's Confederate cavalry and guerrillas. On June 27 ninety men of the First Nebraska led by Capt. John Potts encountered some six hundred Rebel cavalrymen and charged them so fiercely that the Confederates turned tail and fled.[48]

The nonveterans of Companies A, B, and D left for home on July 21, where they were mustered out in August. Also in July the three-year enlistments of the nonveterans of companies C, E, F, G, H, I, and K expired. These men, who had been mustered in at Omaha in the summer of 1861, soon found themselves victimized by a bureaucratic foul-up beyond their control and one for which the army, with all its rules and regulations, had no solution.[49]

Because the furloughed officers had taken the company muster rolls and descriptive books of the seven "veteran" companies to Nebraska, no one in Arkansas had documentation to "assume the responsibility of settling company accounts, furnishing necessary transfer papers, or preparing muster out rolls." On August 4, 1864, the seventy or more men whose enlistments expired on July 21 refused to perform duty. Although they were fully entitled to discharge they were still in the army until formally released, and the Department of Arkansas considered their refusal as a mutiny. The men were accordingly confined under arrest at DeVall's Bluff.[50]

The outraged soldiers blamed the officers for their dilemma and were very angry at Colonel Livingston, "being backed up by some of the officers left behind . . . one in particular that was disappointed in going to the territory." Leaving the men "down in that God forsaken country" was "punishment for refusing to reenlist," claimed one Nebraska soldier in a post-war reminiscence.[51]

The men's plight moved territorial officials to intercede. Acting Governor Algernon Paddock wrote Maj. Gen. Frederick Steele, Union commander in Arkansas, requesting their release. By this time an outbreak of Indian raids in Nebraska Territory and elsewhere along the overland routes made it clear that the First Nebraska Veteran Cavalry would never return to Steele's department. On October 7 the Department of Arkansas finally relieved the First Nebraska detachment and ordered it to report to the regiment in Nebraska, now under the jurisdiction of the Department of Kansas. The nonveterans of the seven "veteran" companies, whose terms had expired on July 21, were finally mustered out of service in Omaha on November 10.[52]

These men were not the only Nebraska soldiers in Arkansas to suffer an excessive dose of war's misfortunes after their comrades left on furlough. On August 24 some seventy First Nebraska men, mostly new recruits but including several of the "old" soldiers, were scooped up as prisoners of war by Shelby's Confederates during an attack on federal hay-cutting parties on the Grand Prairie, adjacent to the railroad line between DeVall's Bluff and Little Rock. Several small forts or stations guarding the hay cutters, constructed in part of hay bales, were garrisoned by Illinois and First Nebraska soldiers, the latter commanded by Lieutenant Polock.

Shelby's much larger force quickly overwhelmed the stations, shelling them with artillery and setting the bales ablaze. The Nebraska and Illinois soldiers defending station number four broke for the timber bordering the prairie, only to be run down by the Rebels and forced to surrender. Shelby's men confiscated their coats, boots, shoes, and personal effects, "then hurried us north and marched us all night and the next day without any rest or food," recalled Polock. Cpl. Merritt Slocum was sick and had trouble keeping up. "The rebels abused and cursed him until he got desperate and angry and then they shot him to death." Shelby's men also executed another First Nebraska soldier named Hedrick, who had enlisted in Arkansas; the Rebels claimed that the man was a deserter from the Confederate army. On September 1, near the Missouri-Arkansas border, the weary Yankees were "paroled" by their captors and released. A week later, still hobbling along barefooted, Polock and his men straggled in to the Union base at Pilot Knob, where the First Nebraska had spent much of the summer of 1863. They then took a train to St. Louis, arriving on September 10, and were sent to the "paroled prisoners' barracks" to await exchange.[53]

Polock and his men, like their comrades still under arrest at DeVall's Bluff, also presented the army with a conundrum. The Rebels had confiscated or destroyed the men's personal papers; any other records documenting their military status were in Nebraska with the regiment. Lacking records, the men could not be paid, nor would the army issue them new clothing and mess equipment. The men had no money to buy essential personal items, and the army would not let them work. Several soldiers whose enlistments had expired since their capture could not be discharged.[54]

Polock's frustration was obvious in letters to the regimental officers in Nebraska and to the territorial newspapers: "The government has furnished the men with nothing. . . . They need tin cups, plates, knives and forks, . . . They drink their coffee out of a few oyster cans that they have picked up and take their bread and meat in their fingers." He appealed to the people of Nebraska for aid, prompting a subscription that raised nearly $350. Unfortunately, in another blow to the morale of the long-suffering soldiers, someone misdirected the money to regimental headquarters at Fort Kearny, and the donations did not reach St. Louis until November. Near year's end Polock and his charges were finally released from their lengthy incarceration as virtual prisoners of their own army.[55]

By January 1865 the last of the First Nebraska soldiers who had been left in Arkansas finally reached Omaha and were discharged or sent to join the regiment at Fort Kearny. By then the First Nebraska Veteran Volunteer Cavalry had been engaged for several months in a radically different phase of the war. Now the enemy was Cheyenne, Arapaho, and Sioux warriors who seemingly threatened the very hearths and firesides the veterans had originally enlisted to defend. The Platte Valley and its adjacent Great Plains landscape would provide the setting for the final chapter in the First Nebraska's Civil War story.

The Indian war that began full force along the Platte Valley overland routes in early August 1864 was not unexpected. Mid-July raids on emigrant parties, road ranches, and telegraph stations, particularly on the road west of Fort Cottonwood to Denver, had already forced General Mitchell to retreat from his earlier prediction that Indian trouble would be confined to "strolling bands." On July 27 he conceded that the difficulties were "much more than I anticipated" and alerted department commander Curtis that "you may expect a general Indian outbreak in all this western country."[56]

To meet the threat Mitchell had about fifteen hundred soldiers in his District of Nebraska, including portions of the Seventh Iowa Volunteer Cavalry and Eleventh Ohio Volunteer Cavalry and two companies of the First Battalion, Nebraska Veteran Volunteer Cavalry. These troops were scattered from Omaha and Dakota City in eastern Nebraska all the way to Camp Collins in Colorado Territory and to the Sweetwater River in Idaho Territory (present Wyoming).[57]

Governor Saunders and Colonel Livingston had also gotten wind of the Indian outbreak and offered Mitchell the First Nebraska Veteran Cavalry when its furlough expired, or even earlier if need be. Saunders told Curtis that the regiment had no horses but "these boys have had a three-years' service against the rebels and I would like to see them try their hands on the savage Indians." The governor also offered to call out the territorial militia.[58]

The plan to retain the First Nebraska in Curtis's department had to wait for authorization from the War Department in Washington. On July 30 army chief of staff Halleck wrote Curtis that "if absolutely necessary" the First Nebraska could be assigned to temporary duty in the Department of Kansas. This somewhat grudging concession was made even though the last thing the Union army command wanted to do was to deploy more troops west of the Missouri at a time when the war's outcome hinged on the success of the Union Army of the Potomac, then besieging Lee's Confederate Army of Northern Virginia at Petersburg, and on Sherman's Union army maneuvering to capture Atlanta, one of the South's key railroad junctions and manufacturing centers.[59]

From the war's onset, Union military authorities had allocated few resources to the region west of the Missouri River. The region had been shortchanged, noted one observer, because "the thunder of the Southern war silenced the casual and fugitive rattle of Indian hostilities, though the latter have been going on from the very outbreak of the Rebellion." Only when Indians seemed poised to actually halt overland travel and the U.S. mail coaches and disrupt telegraph service did the authorities respond.[60]

Even then, the army high command seemed to begrudge the modest forces assigned and used the region as a dumping ground for general officers such as Samuel Curtis, whose military and administrative abilities had been found wanting when he commanded elsewhere. Halleck, however, reminded Union army chief Ulysses S. Grant of the "absolute necessity" of retaining troops in the Indian country. It was not so much because of real damage the Indians might do, claimed Halleck, but because "the military authorities will be very seriously blamed if they withdraw the troops now there." Like their modern-day counterparts, Washington bureaucrats had only a hazy grasp of conditions in a distant hinterland almost the size of the Confederacy, which most of them had never laid eyes on.[61]

President Lincoln saw the importance of the overland communication routes more clearly than did his generals. As early as 1862 Lincoln had informed agents of Ben Holladay's stagecoach line that the overland mail must go through at all hazards, though the president admitted that few troops could be spared to protect it. When Holladay visited Washington DC in 1864, an anxious Lincoln reiterated that maintaining overland telegraph and mail connections with the loyal western states and territories was crucial to the Union war effort. It was also crucial to the Republicans' political agenda. Only by telegraphing Nevada's new state constitution to Washington DC at a cost of $4,303 had that territory been admitted to statehood in time to participate in the fall presidential election. Its new senators helped Congress pass the Thirteenth Amendment, abolishing slavery, and Nevada subsequently ratified it. Lincoln was also mindful of the need to keep gold and silver from California, Nevada, and Montana flowing into the U.S. treasury to help pay the war's staggering costs, estimating that in 1864 "the product of the mines . . . reached, if not exceeded $100,000,000 in value."[62]

Although it was already clear to politicians and military officers on the ground that a full-scale Indian war was in the offing, the extent and coordination of the attacks that swept Nebraska's Platte and Little Blue River valleys on August 7–8 were stunning. Virtually every stagecoach station and road ranche between Fort Kearny and Julesburg to the west and from Fort Kearny to Big Sandy Creek on the east was attacked, along with the freighting and emigrant trains that happened to be moving through this region. Thomas Morton's wagon train was wiped out near Plum Creek, with eleven or twelve men killed and Mrs. Nancy Morton carried off as a prisoner. Six months later she was ransomed from the Indians. Another wagon train was attacked on the Little Blue, and Indian raiders killed seven members of the Eubanks family at Oak Grove, making captives of Laura Roper, Lucinda Eubanks, and Lucinda's daughter Isabelle. Soldiers in Kansas rescued Laura Roper and Isabelle a month later, but Lucinda Eubanks was not set free until May 1865.[63]

Survivors of the raids and other civilians living in the scattered settlements and ranches along the Platte and Little Blue fled to Fort Kearny or the Missouri River towns. One exception was the German settlers at Grand Island, who threw up sod fortifications and prepared for their own defense. Squire and Caroline Lamb left their ranche on Wood River but soon returned unharmed, reporting that soldiers moving to the scene of action, rather than the Indians, had stolen bedding, clothing, and "everything" from many of the abandoned civilian enclaves. William Stolley reported that a detachment of Company E of the Seventh Iowa Volunteer Cavalry temporarily stationed at the Grand Island settlement "acquired grain by swindle and theft and took cattle whenever they found them. . . . In a word, they carried on as if they were in enemy territory." Squire Lamb, an experienced frontiersman, was pessimistic about the future: "[T]he thing is rather dark for this winter, the country is desolate, the government is seising horses[,]

Fig. 13. Nancy Jane Fletcher Morton was captured by Indians in early August 1864 when her husband, Thomas Morton's, wagon train was attacked by Indians west of Fort Kearny. She was released a few months later. Nebraska State Historical Society RG3310-54.

men, mowing machine[s] and its [a] damned site worse here than in Dixie."[64]

While some civilians feared the Indians might even swoop down on the larger settlements in eastern Nebraska (a few straggling Santee Sioux raided the Omaha Reservation on August 24, unrelated to the attacks along the Platte), the press took a more realistic view. The outbreak's worst effect was its potential to halt "trade with the West," the mainstay of the territorial economy, particularly in the Missouri River towns. The *Nebraska Advertiser* in Brownville looked beyond the raids' direct impact on the region west of the Missouri River to put them in a larger context. By requiring the services of soldiers that might otherwise be made available on the war's main fighting fronts, "This Indian war is a God-send to the rebels."[65]

It was widely believed and reported that Rebels had incited the raids and "guerrillas and bushwhackers" were leading the warriors on the attack. Most seasoned observers discounted this notion. One editor noted that the raids were rendering insecure and dangerous the very route by which "secesh" could hope to escape the draft. Colonel Livingston laid the cause to "the natural antipathy between the Indian and Anglo-Saxon races," exacerbated by the "annually increasing current of white emigration toward his once quiet and bountifully supplied hunting grounds."[66]

Mitchell and those of his troops already stationed in the Platte Valley were ill-prepared to respond quickly. Fort Kearny had only a single company of mounted cavalrymen from the Seventh Iowa, some fifty men under Capt. Edward B. Murphy. Murphy's company was promptly dispatched to the Little Blue River, where some of the greatest loss of life had occurred. There the soldiers encountered locally organized militia from Beatrice, and on August 15 the combined force moved south and skirmished with what was said to be some five hundred

Indians, losing two men killed. By this time the Indians were melting across the Republican River into Kansas. The efforts of the Beatrice militia and Murphy's troopers represented the first organized military response to the early August outbreak.[67]

Aside from the modest expedition to the Little Blue, about all the authorities could do until more soldiers reached the Platte was to prevent the Indians from overwhelming the existing military outposts weakly garrisoned by mostly unmounted troops. Accordingly, Col. Samuel Summers of the Seventh Iowa, commanding at Fort Kearny, ordered the construction of a stockade and earthworks to be an ultimate refuge in case the tribesmen actually had the audacity to attack the fort.[68]

The raids' ferocity pried department commander Curtis away from his Fort Leavenworth headquarters to take personal charge in the field, and he reached Omaha aboard the steamboat *Colorado* on August 16. Per the War Department's authorization, General Mitchell on August 11 had assigned the First Nebraska Veteran Cavalry to duty in his District of Nebraska, but it would take time before the regiment could contribute much to the territory's defense. The men were only then straggling in from their furloughs, and they lacked horses, guns, and other equipment, those necessities having been turned in when the veterans left Arkansas. Colonel Livingston designated Omaha as the rendezvous where the regiment would outfit for the plains.[69]

Also on August 11 Governor Saunders and Territorial Adjutant General W. W. Hughes issued a proclamation and order calling for the organization of twelve companies of mounted militiamen. The call elicited little response. According to Edward Rosewater, then a telegrapher for Edward Creighton's Pacific Telegraph Company, an August 15 "war meeting" in Omaha "amounts to nothing[,] people cant see it to volunteer for [the] Indian War." Only four companies were subsequently mustered in, for terms ranging from two to four months. The first of them reported at Fort Kearny on August 30 and another arrived there September 12.[70]

On August 18 about three hundred of the First Nebraska veterans left Omaha for Fort Kearny. The detachment had only sixty horses, the balance of the men marching or riding in the supply wagons. Department commander Curtis accompanied the expedition, which reached the fort on August 24. En route, the soldiers delivered some old muskets and a six-pounder cannon sent out by Governor Saunders to help the Grand Island settlers defend themselves.[71]

Curtis and district commander Mitchell immediately began dispatching small contingents of soldiers to provide at least limited security along the trails. A company of the Seventh Iowa Cavalry went to the Pawnee Agency, and part of Company A of the First Battalion, Nebraska Veteran Volunteer Cavalry, was sent to Fort Cottonwood to augment the Iowa cavalrymen already there. A company of the Eleventh Ohio Cavalry was sent from Fort Laramie to establish a new military post just west of Scott's Bluff. First known as Camp Shuman for the captain in charge, the adobe structure was later renamed Fort Mitchell. Seventy-six Pawnees under command of Joseph McFadden were accepted as scouts, to receive the same pay as white soldiers.[72]

Curtis and Mitchell decided that an expedition against the Indians in the field offered a better prospect of protecting the Platte route than merely posting a handful of soldiers to the scattered stagecoach stations and road ranches. Like most U.S army commanders then and later, they did not reckon on the mobility and elusiveness of the Plains warriors, who rarely offered a stand-up fight and who could easily outdistance army horses, which weakened rapidly when forced to subsist on the prairie grasses instead of grain.

Fig. 14. Fort Mitchell, near Scotts Bluff, built by the Eleventh Ohio Volunteer Cavalry in 1864, as painted by William Henry Jackson. National Park Service, Scotts Bluff National Monument.

On September 1 Curtis and Mitchell, with several companies of the First Nebraska Veteran Volunteers, a company of Nebraska militia, two companies of the Seventh Iowa Volunteer Cavalry, a detachment of the Sixteenth Kansas Volunteer Cavalry, and the company of Pawnee Scouts, marched out of Fort Kearny. By September 8 the expedition had crossed the Republican River, Beaver Creek, and Prairie Dog Creek to encamp on the Solomon River in north-central Kansas. No Indians were encountered or even sighted during the week-long march.

There the expedition divided, with Curtis, Livingston, and the First Nebraska troopers proceeding east to Fort Riley, while Mitchell and the other soldiers moved west. The eastern battalion then circled back to Fort Kearny, where it arrived on September 26. Mitchell's force returned to Fort Cottonwood, then marched northwestward up the Platte to Ash Hollow. By September 24 Mitchell was back at Cottonwood; since leaving there on September 17, his command had traveled 212 miles, "seeing no hostile Indians save an occasional scout." The grand expedition had accomplished nothing except for wearing out its horses and men.[73]

Although Mitchell saw no Indians, some of his troops at Fort Cottonwood did. On September 8 Indians killed a soldier near the post, and ten days later they killed four more Seventh Iowa soldiers while the men were out gathering wild plums for comrades lying in the post hospital with scurvy. This attack demonstrated how small bands of Indians could easily elude ponderous columns such as those led by Curtis and Mitchell and strike elsewhere with relative impunity.[74]

The failure of the expedition to strike a blow at the Indians in their Kansas strongholds and the small number of troops available in a military district spanning some six hundred miles forced the military commanders to adopt a defensive strategy to keep open the overland route. It was unlikely that more soldiers would be forthcoming while the war's outcome hinged on Grant and Sherman's campaigns in the East. An additional complication was provided by Confederate general Sterling Price's raid from Arkansas into Missouri, which began on September 19 and kept Union troops in Missouri and eastern Kansas tied down until the Rebels were finally routed at the Battle of Westport near Kansas City on October 23.

To maximize command and control of the troops that were available, the District of Nebraska was divided on September 29, 1864. The East Subdistrict comprised the region from the Missouri River to Fort Kearny, through which passed the overland roads from Omaha, Nebraska City, and Fort Leavenworth, and the main Platte Valley trail extending from Fort Kearny to Julesburg, Colorado Territory. Colonel Livingston of the First Nebraska was assigned the command, with his headquarters at Fort Kearny. The West Subdistrict extended from Julesburg to South Pass and was commanded from Fort Laramie by Lt. Col. William O. Collins of the Eleventh Ohio Volunteer Cavalry. Omaha remained the district's headquarters.[75]

Livingston had 971 men in his subdistrict, including the First Nebraska, one battalion of the Seventh Iowa Cavalry, the battalion of Nebraska Veteran Volunteer Cavalry, and four militia companies. The soldiers were dispersed to sixteen locations along the trail, with the smallest garrison being 23 men at Mullally's Ranche (southeast of present Cozad) and the largest, 112 men, at Fort Kearny. The object was to protect the stagecoach and telegraph stations, along with wagon trains of emigrants and freighters. By October 5 Mitchell reported to Curtis that troops were located every fifteen miles from Plum Creek to Julesburg and "coaches can run." The resumption of stagecoach service along the Platte was confirmed by rancheman Squire Lamb a few days later.[76]

With the exception of Forts Kearny and Cottonwood, most of these enclaves were nothing more than road ranches abandoned by their owners when the war broke out in August. Some were already adequate to house their assigned garrisons and others were readily adapted by constructing additional log or sod buildings. A few were fortified with earthworks but most were already defensible, "the sod buildings being deemed sufficiently secure against any Indian attack," according to Colonel Livingston.[77]

That the posts themselves were relatively secure was well and good, but the Indians were not inclined to attack them, preferring instead to pounce on stagecoaches and small parties of soldiers sent out to cut hay or gather wood. Livingston and his subordinates understood that the soldiers' primary task was to escort the coaches, protect the wood and forage details, and conduct reconnaissance to forestall the buildup of large, well-organized war parties. Civilians traveling the

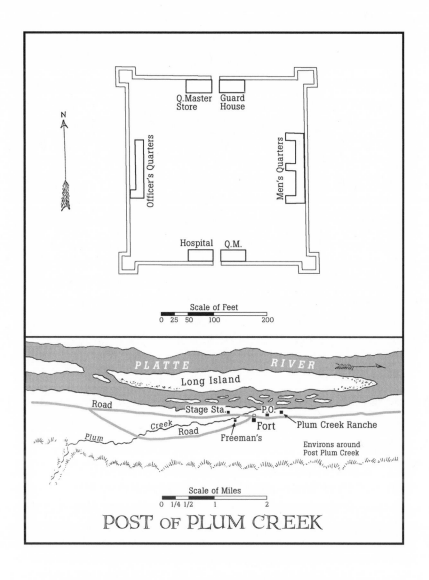

Map 2. A plat of the Post of Plum Creek, ca. 1865, located on the
south side of the Platte River near present Lexington, Nebraska.
Adapted from *Post of Plum Creek, No. 8*, Fort File, RG 77, Records
of the Office of the Chief of Engineers, National Archives.

trail during the fall of 1864 were largely responsible for their own defense. Livingston tried to impress this fact on them by ordering his post commanders to prevent wagon trains from proceeding unless, in the commander's judgment, "there are enough men with it to defend it against Indian attack." The colonel set this number at not less than fifty to sixty "well-armed men."[78]

This was prudent advice considering that the Indians persisted in their efforts to disrupt trail traffic all throughout the fall of 1864. In October and November bands of Indians numbering from a dozen to more than a hundred attacked stagecoaches, emigrant trains, and hay cutters as far east as the Little Blue River but most often west of Fort Kearny in the corridor between Plum Creek Station and Fort Cottonwood. On October 13 Indians killed Privates Jackson and Kelly of Company I, First Nebraska, and cut off six of their comrades, all of whom had sortied from Mullally's Ranche after the tribesmen had attacked a stagecoach. The six men finally drove off their attackers without further loss, prompting Colonel Livingston to cite them to the regiment as an example of how "coolness and determination such as evinced on that occasion will nearly always be successful."[79]

Many of the raids began just before dark, limiting pursuit by the soldiers. During the two-month period the Indians managed to kill one militia officer, Jackson and Kelly, and several civilians and wound other civilians and soldiers. The military reports tallied some fifteen Indians killed. Despite the small number of casualties, the raids succeeded in disrupting if not actually halting trail traffic and kept the soldiers on constant alert.[80]

A major reason for the inability of the District of Nebraska troops to do more than react to Indian forays lay in the contrast between the two forces, one highly mobile and used to living off the land and the other tied to fixed positions by its mission and hampered by the inadequate numbers and miserable quality of the horses with which it was supplied. Historian John D. McDermott has aptly termed the lack of good horse-flesh as "the army's Achilles' heel" in the plains campaigns. Jim Bridger, the former mountain man turned army scout, gave Iowa cavalryman Eugene Ware a succinct summary of the Indian mode of campaigning: "[E]ach one of them [is] riding a spare pony. They whistle up their dogs and start off. The dogs can keep up with the horses, and when they camp, the horses can eat grass and the Injuns eat the dogs. . . . They don't have to have any corn for their horses, nor any bacon and hard-tack, and that is the reason that they can always run away from our people, and we never can chase them down . . . and catch them unless we can travel like they do."[81]

The First Nebraska was largely dismounted when it marched away from Omaha in mid-August and, by month's end, General Curtis reported from Fort Kearny that "[o]ver half my cavalry in this region is without horses." Complicating the procurement issue was the War Department's requirement that all army horses be purchased by the quartermaster's department, leaving the field commanders dependent on a ponderous bureaucracy to meet their needs.[82]

As a result, getting all the volunteer cavalrymen in the East Subdistrict of Nebraska on horseback took time, and the horses already issued to the troops were, in the words of one officer, "compelled to do a vast amount of duty and are thin and somewhat exhausted." The American horses, unlike the Indian ponies, could not maintain their stamina by grazing alone. The officers' reports reveal their frustration: "I started out [after Indians] with twenty-seven horses, every one that was fit to travel out of forty-five horses. . . . Two gave out in the first five miles and I sent back four that could not travel faster than a walk." Indians who attacked Alkali Station on October 21, 1864, were repulsed by the soldiers on duty "but not pursued on account of exhausted condition of horses at the post." The condition of the available horses was so poor that Colonel Livingston on October 17 prohibited any enlisted man from riding his horse, "except when detailed to duty."[83]

On December 2 First Nebraska quartermaster Lt. Charles Thompson reported that eighty cavalry horses recently purchased in Omaha had been received at Fort Kearny. Although the horses had never been used in the service, the company commanders refused to accept them. A Board of Survey was convened and condemned the lot. The herd had been driven the 215 miles from Omaha to Fort Kearny by slow marches, yet "the animals are so poor that a number actually died on the road."[84]

Many officers, including Colonel Livingston, believed the only solution to relieving the trail from constant guerrilla-style raids was to seek out and attack the Indians in their winter camps in Kansas, south of the Republican River. Such a campaign was out of the question in the fall of 1864, so the army decided to strike at the Indians' commissary, the prairie grasses that sustained their ponies and their game. Accordingly, General Curtis on October 17 ordered Livingston to set a massive prairie fire south of the Platte Valley as soon as the grass was dry enough and the wind was out of the north.[85]

The favorable wind arrived on October 22, and Livingston sent word to his post commanders to have the soldiers set the prairie on fire simultaneously from ten miles east of Fort Kearny to twenty miles west of Julesburg, Colorado Territory, a distance of some two hundred miles. According to Livingston, the fire burned as far south as the Republican River. Detachments were sent out afterward to rekindle the grass on the tablelands and in the stream valleys where the fire had gone out. The uplands between the Little Blue and Republican Rivers from east of Fort Kearny to Little Blue Station were not burned, so the Pawnees could make a fall hunt in that region, their summer hunt having been halted by Sioux attacks. The Pawnees promised to warn the soldiers at Little Blue Station and Pawnee Ranche if they encountered hostile Indians. When the wind later shifted to the south, the prairie on the north side of the Platte Valley was also set ablaze from a point opposite Mullally's Ranche to twenty-five miles west of Julesburg, the scorched earth extending 150 miles north in some places by Livingston's reckoning.[86]

Although Livingston boasted that "this burning of the prairie has produced a marked effect on the Indian tribes along the road," he reached that conclusion before the warriors mounted raids in November and December on emigrant trains and mail coaches in the Platte Valley. Although the number and severity of attacks declined in December, Livingston by then had a more realistic attribution for the relative calm. It was the severely cold weather and the efforts of his troops that "seem to have discouraged the Indians in their attempts to murder and plunder travelers on the road." He did not mention the prairie fire, nor did he mention a November 29 attack on a peaceful Southern Cheyenne camp at Sand Creek in Colorado Territory by Colorado troops led by a former Nebraska clergyman, now Col. John M. Chivington. The indiscriminate slaughter of men, women, and children in the "Sand Creek Massacre" would spark a renewal of deadly Indian warfare in the districts of Nebraska and Colorado as the year 1865 dawned.

The hostilities that began in the summer of 1864 also had an adverse effect on Nebraska's reservation Indians. Although the Pawnees, Oto-Missourias, and Omahas were practicing agriculture with varying degrees of diligence and success, they continued to rely on buffalo hunting for a major part of their subsistence. In 1864 (and in several of the previous years) drought and swarms of grasshoppers caused what the superintendent of Indian affairs in St. Joseph termed a total crop failure among most tribes in the Central Superintendency. Most of them were unable to secure a supply of meat on account of the Indian war.[87]

The Omahas raised a fair corn crop, but their summer buffalo hunt had to be aborted. The same circumstances cut off the Oto-Missourias and Pawnees from their expected meat supply. The Poncas had a successful buffalo hunt but raised no corn, so the entire Ponca tribe traveled to the Omaha Reservation in September to trade meat for corn. If that weren't problem enough for Omaha agent Robert W. Furnas, twelve hundred Winnebagos were temporarily living with the Omahas, and the preceding June soldiers stationed at Dakota City had murdered one Omaha woman and seriously wounded another. Furnas was able to get the approval of the commissioner of Indian affairs to pay the aggrieved relatives $150.[88]

While many Nebraska citizens were preoccupied with the Indian war raging within the territory's borders during the summer and fall of 1864, others realized that the coming elections would be crucial to the Civil War's outcome and, indeed, to Nebraska's future. Should Lincoln win reelection and the Republicans retain their congressional majority, the effort to utterly defeat the South, restore the Union, and abolish slavery would continue unabated. The party would retain control over Nebraska Territory's appointive offices, ranging from governor to lesser officials such as land office registrars and postmasters. A Republican victory in the territorial election for delegate and members of the legislature would keep the Nebraska party positioned to oversee the territory's transition to statehood, an event that would surely come soon.

On May 26 the Republicans met at Plattsmouth to choose

delegates to the national convention. They met under the banner of the Union Party, hoping to attract War Democrats who could not otherwise abide affiliation with the Republicans. The convention instructed six delegates to cast their votes for Lincoln's renomination. The convention also adopted resolutions favoring the complete crushing of the rebellion and endorsing the Emancipation Proclamation, the use of black soldiers in the Union army, and a constitutional amendment abolishing slavery. The Nebraska resolutions anticipated the national Union Party Platform adopted at the Baltimore convention in early June, where Lincoln was nominated for a second term.[89]

One of Nebraska's Union delegates was W. H. H. Waters, editor of the *Nebraska City People's Press*, who took the opportunity to visit the nation's capital en route to the convention. While he was there, Waters and Nebraska delegate to Congress Samuel Daily visited the White House and "called on 'Uncle Abraham,' who we found in excellent humor and as familiar as one of our western farmers." Lincoln gave the Nebraskans the latest war news and "conversed fully on the questions of the day." Waters's description of the president matched the stereotype: "He is long, lean, and presents rather a homely phiz, but it bears the impress of honesty and superior intelligence." Waters and Daily also enjoyed a concert on the White House grounds by a navy band and looked on as Lincoln met with a delegation of Indians from New Mexico. The president acknowledged the Indians' grievances and "explained the necessity of patience and forbearance on their part, while our country is engaged in this struggle for its existence."[90]

The Nebraska Democrats met in Plattsmouth on June 22 to select their national convention delegates. J. Sterling Morton was among those named and he drafted the Nebraska party's resolutions, which were silent about the war. Instead, they commended voters for having elected an "anti-state" majority pledged to adjourn the pending constitutional convention without drafting a document. Although the resolutions avoided mentioning the war, the *Nebraska Advertiser* detected "the unmistakable evidence of the copperhead in this convention" and characterized the delegates chosen for the national convention as "unadulterated Vallandighammers."[91]

At this juncture, the Democrats had some reason for optimism. Republican victory in the presidential election seemed problematic. War weariness in the North stemming from stalemate on the battlefields and enormous casualty lists had reached its zenith, causing even President Lincoln to doubt his reelection. In July the Confederates were able to threaten the nation's capital with an offensive in Virginia's Shenandoah Valley. These developments energized the Peace Democrats, who saw an opportunity to control the party, elect a president, and possibly realize their hope of a negotiated peace and preservation of "the Constitution as it is and the Union as it was," with slavery left intact.

Accordingly, when the Democrats gathered in Chicago on August 29, a divided party adopted a platform written by the Peace wing but nominated former Union general George B. McClellan, a War Democrat, for president. The key plank in the platform declared the war a failure and called for an immediate cessation of hostilities and a convention of the states to restore the Union by negotiation. Despite his opposition to emancipation, McClellan believed the Union could be restored only by military victory. He accepted the nomination, but with the proviso that no peace negotiations would be held until the Confederates agreed to accept reunion.[92]

Locally, the recent defeat of the statehood proposition encouraged Nebraska Democrats to think they had a chance to capture the legislature and win the delegate's seat, from which incumbent Republican Samuel Daily was stepping down. Some Democratic leaders, such as T. W. Bedford of Nemaha County,

advised the continued avoidance of direct reference to war issues in the party platform for the fall elections. A platform
based on "Union and Constitution" that avoided attacking the
administration would be best, said Bedford in a letter to J. Sterling Morton. Bedford understood what the Peace Democrats
seemingly did not: "The public mind is not prepared to endorse any party that favors at this time, a speedy and unconditional compromise." And because Nebraska, as a territory,
had no voice in the presidential election, urging a change in
administration "would completely destroy our chance of success in the territorial election."[93]

When the Democrats met in Nebraska City on September 16
they nominated Dr. George L. Miller of Omaha as their candidate for delegate. Miller was a longtime party warhorse who
had served several terms in the territorial legislature during
the 1850s and from 1861 to 1864 had been the post sutler at
Fort Kearny. The Democrats approved a platform similar to
the "reunion first, peace second" approach McClellan had adopted in his letter accepting the presidential nomination: "We
shall encourage all efforts towards a peaceful solution of our
national difficulties as soon as the armed forces of the states
in rebellion shall lay down their arms and acknowledge the
supremacy of the Constitution and the laws, with territorial
integrity preserved intact." Unfortunately, it was not enough
to insulate the Nebraska Democrats from the firestorm of neg-
ative public opinion generated by the national party's "peace"
platform.[94]

The delegates to the Nebraska Union convention, who had
met in Nebraska City on August 17 and nominated Phineas
W. Hitchcock as their candidate for delegate, had no need for
such gymnastics in drafting their platform. It was an unqual-
ified endorsement of the election of Lincoln and vice-presi-
dential candidate Andrew Johnson and of the principles ar-

Fig. 15. George L. Miller, Nebraska Democratic Party
stalwart and founder of the *Omaha Herald*.
Nebraska State Historical Society RG2411-3767c.

ticulated in the national platform, along with a pledge to do "everything in our power" to aid the government in quelling the rebellion by force of arms.[95]

The platforms adopted by the Democrats nationally and in Nebraska, combined with recent Union victories at Mobile Bay, Atlanta, and in Virginia, dashed any prospects for their electoral success. Nebraska Republicans and their political organs had a field day castigating Dr. Miller, the Democratic nominee for delegate, as "positively a Copperhead" who was "trying to run on *Peace* and *War* both." When word came that Sherman's army had occupied Atlanta on September 2, only three days after the Democrats had nominated McClellan for president, the *Nebraska Republican* editorialized gleefully, "What an auspicious moment in which to ratify the nomination of McClellan on a *Peace* platform!! Surely 'there is a God in Israel'!" In September and October Union forces swept the Confederates from Virginia's Shenandoah Valley. The *Daily Press* of Nebraska City gloated that Miller's prospects for election "are growing 'beautifully less' as each day rolls by, chronicling some new Union Victory."[96]

Nebraska Advertiser editor William H. Miller was quick to point out inconsistencies in the territorial Democratic platform, "which means—if it means anything at all—that if the peace doctrine does not win and we fight the war out, they will 'encourage efforts towards a peaceful solution of our difficulties' after they have been settled by war, and accept peace when there is nothing more to fight for. It is a very weak attempt to get on both sides of the question, and so transparent that it is repulsive."[97]

Something of the attitudes of other Nebraska citizens was revealed by William Lamb, son of the Wood River rancheman, in a letter to his uncle in New York State: "Please write how the [Democrats'] Chicago platform takes there. It does not take well out here." First Nebraska soldier Lt. William A. Polock wrote that "any loyal man who has had the opportunity to hear the rebels talk that I have had will never affiliate with the Democrats, or as we call it, the Copperhead party." The Rebels, said Polock, were convinced that Democratic victory in the Northern elections would end the war and bring the Confederacy's independence.[98]

Miller and Hitchcock sniped at each other through letters published in the Nebraska newspapers and held a series of face-to-face debates before the October 11 territorial election. At several locales in the South Platte region it was alleged that Miller was practically mobbed and that his friends were prevented from cheering for him under threat of personal violence. Republicans at Pawnee City denied that Miller faced any danger there "unless he undertook to talk *treason*" and held that the reason there had been no cheering was because "he had not a friend in the audience."[99]

There was never much doubt about the election's outcome. Hitchcock won the delegate's seat in Congress by a 1,087 vote majority of the 5,885 votes cast, and the Republicans retained control of the legislature. For the first time Nebraska soldiers serving away from home were eligible to vote, and although the figures are incomplete, it is clear they voted overwhelmingly for Hitchcock and the Republicans. Some disgruntled Nebraska Democrats claimed the First Nebraska's soldiers gave Hitchcock a majority because they were "threatened with the guard house for going for Miller," but they offered nothing in the way of evidence. A more likely explanation for the men's support of the Republican candidate was offered by a First Nebraska soldier at Fort Kearny: "It would be strange, indeed, if after more than three years of hard service to sustain the unity and integrity of the government, they had turned square about and said, 'We are wrong, and this war is a failure.'"[100]

Similar sentiments held by thousands of Union soldiers who cast votes in the presidential election of November 8 helped return Lincoln to the White House and gave the Republicans an overwhelming victory in the congressional elections. Although soldiers whose legal residence was Nebraska Territory were ineligible to vote for president, Iowa soldiers serving in Nebraska contributed to the Republican landslide. The *Nebraska Republican* reported that Iowa men at Fort Kearny (including those in the First Nebraska and Seventh Iowa regiments) cast sixty-one votes for Lincoln and none for McClellan. At Julesburg, in Eugene Ware's Company F of the Seventh Iowa, about half the men declined to vote, but those who did tallied twenty-six for the president and only fourteen for McClellan. In late September Lt. William Polock had taken a straw poll among First Nebraska men at the paroled prisoners' barracks in St. Louis and found that forty-five favored Lincoln's reelection and only nine preferred McClellan.[101]

On October 15 and again on October 30, George Miller wrote his friend and political associate J. Sterling Morton to reflect on the debacle that had befallen the Democrats in the territorial election. "I believe it to be generally understood that somebody has been pretty handsomely threshed out in a race against P. W. Hitchcock for the position of delegate to Congress," said Miller. He blamed his own defeat and the looming fate of the national party on "the bad policy of Democratic leaders," particularly Clement Vallandigham and the Peace Democrats. While Miller could praise Vallandigham for his defense of the principles of private and public liberty, his course on the war "has certainly weakened the great [Democratic] party by running counter to the public judgment of the country and instead of moulding itself to the currents of popular opinion, it has fatally undertaken to resist them." While Miller knew Morton would not agree with his assessment (Morton had long

Fig. 16. Ohio Peace Democrat Clement L. Vallandigham in an 1865 portrait preserved by his Nebraska confidante J. Sterling Morton. Nebraska State Historical Society RG1013-34-49.

been Vallandigham's confidante and supporter), "I shall always think you ought to do so."[102]

Morton took the comments personally, concluding that Miller blamed him, at least in part, for the Democrats' defeat, and relations between the two men became strained for a time. Morton's specific reactions are unrecorded, but his disillusionment with the outcome of the 1864 elections was signaled when he advertised his Nebraska City farm for sale soon afterward. Although Morton did not sell the farm and leave Nebraska as threatened, the Nebraska Democratic Party and its leaders entered a period of dormancy that would not be broken until the war was over.[103]

Lincoln's reelection and the dramatic Union victories of the fall and winter, including Confederate defeat at Nashville and Sherman's capture of the port of Savannah on the Atlantic coast, after marching his army through the heart of Georgia, signaled that the war might be nearing its end. With Lincoln and the Republicans in charge, there would be no respite for the beleaguered Confederacy and its dwindling armies and resources. The Indian war along the Platte also seemed to be waning as 1864 drew to a close. The Republicans held firm control in territorial politics. Though nothing was certain, Nebraskans could be forgiven for thinking that the coming year might give them a chance to focus on the long-sought goals of achieving statehood, building the Pacific railroad, and settling the land.

CHAPTER FIVE

1865

"Peace Will Soon Again Bless the Land"

Chivington's brutal massacre of a village of Southern Cheyennes and Arapahos at Sand Creek, Colorado Territory, in late November 1864 signaled even those Indians not inclined to go to war that they were no longer safe in their camps south of the Platte and Republican Rivers. The Cheyennes and Arapahos decided to retaliate. Enlisting the aid of the Brules and Oglalas, they began a series of raids on whites and white settlements that took them eventually to the haven of the Powder River country of Wyoming and Montana. There they briefly reunited with their northern kinsmen and the more populous Sioux. While en route, they exacted revenge for Sand Creek.

On the morning of January 7, the same day Governor Saunders opened the tenth legislative session in Omaha by congratulating the members "on the termination of the Indian war on our own frontier," a thousand or more warriors swept out of the bluffs south of Julesburg, Colorado Territory. Their first goal was to wipe out Camp Rankin, the sod-walled military post nearby, and they almost succeeded. The Indians decoyed

Capt. Nicholas O'Brien and thirty-seven men of the Seventh Iowa Volunteer Cavalry out of the post, but impetuous warriors gave the ambush away before the trap could be sprung. The troops employed a mountain howitzer to help hold off the attackers and retreated to the fort, but not before fourteen soldiers had been killed. The warriors then looted the telegraph office, stagecoach station, and other buildings in the Julesburg settlement before withdrawing in the afternoon. Five civilians also lost their lives in the raid. Estimates of more than fifty Indian casualties could not be substantiated.[1]

The Julesburg raid and simultaneous attacks on ranches and stage stations along the road west to Denver prompted a new effort by the army to strike the warriors in their camps, still thought to be located on the Republican River and its tributaries in the border regions of Nebraska Territory, Kansas, and Colorado Territory. On January 15 District of Nebraska commander Gen. Robert B. Mitchell led some 640 cavalrymen of the First Nebraska, the Seventh Iowa, and the Nebraska militia out of Fort Cottonwood. For the next twelve days, often in subzero weather, the soldiers scoured southwestern Nebraska and sent scouts across the border into Kansas before circling back to Fort Cottonwood. All they found were abandoned Indian camps; the foray's main result was to disable numerous men and horses from the bitter cold. In frustration, Mitchell ordered the grass burned for a hundred miles along the Republican and its tributaries. While the expedition was out, small parties of Indians returned to the Platte Valley to attack and burn ranches, stagecoach stations, and telegraph stations along the Denver road.[2]

During the last week of January more raids extending eighty miles west of Julesburg devastated previously untouched ranches and stations, culminating in a second overwhelming attack at Julesburg itself on February 2. Again, soldiers and civilians

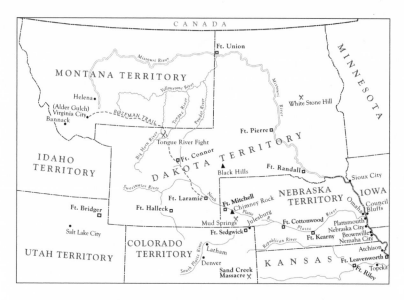

Map 3. The central and northern Plains in 1865.

holed up at Camp Rankin could only watch as hundreds of warriors sacked and burned the stage station, telegraph office, and other buildings. They ran off livestock, burned stockpiles of flour, hay, and corn, chopped down and set ablaze telegraph poles, and otherwise destroyed the line for ten miles west along the Denver road and more than thirty miles westnorthwest along the road to Fort Laramie.[3]

The empty encampments Mitchell had seen during his excursion and the raids on the trail enclaves that resumed as January gave way to February made credible the general's conclusion that the camps' former inhabitants were moving to the Powder River country to join their brethren in that stronghold. After sacking Julesburg, the Indians on February 4 besieged the sod and log telegraph station at Mud Springs on the high divide about halfway between the Lodge Pole Creek valley and Courthouse Rock, which was occupied only by the operator and nine soldiers. The line from Mud Springs to the west was still functioning, and the operator managed to send word of the attack to Col. William O. Collins at Fort Laramie, who dispatched reinforcements from the Seventh Iowa and Eleventh Ohio Cavalry. A detachment from Fort Mitchell arrived first on February 5, followed by troops with Collins the next day. Skirmishing at Mud Springs continued until the Indians finally withdrew on the afternoon of February 6.[4]

After first sending out scouts on February 7, Collins led his 185 soldiers northeastward on February 8 to the spot where Rush Creek flowed into the Platte. Beyond the bluffs north of the river lay a vast Indian encampment, and warriors, whose numbers Collins estimated at two thousand, soon swarmed across the icebound stream to fight. By digging rifle pits the greatly outnumbered soldiers, fortunately armed with Spencer breech-loaders, managed to hold off the assault with the loss of two men killed and nine wounded. By the morning of February 9 most of the Indians had resumed their northward trek; Collins began his return march to Fort Laramie the next day. Army casualties for the campaign were three killed, sixteen wounded, and seven men disabled by frostbite. With the exception of the September 3, 1855, Battle of Blue Water Creek near Ash Hollow, Mud Springs/Rush Creek was the largest pitched battle between soldiers and Indians on Nebraska soil.[5]

In the meantime, word of the attacks on the ranches and stations west of Julesburg had prompted Colonel Livingston to start west from Fort Kearny with two companies of the First Nebraska Veteran Volunteer Cavalry, gathering other troops along the way. Although Livingston learned of the February 2 Julesburg raid while en route, his 360-man detachment did not reach there until after the Indians sacked the settlement. He promptly informed his superiors that "this is no trifling Indian war" and that communications to the west had been completely cut off. No stagecoaches were running west of Fort

Cottonwood and because the telegraph line was down between Mud Springs and Julesburg, the colonel did not learn about the fighting at Mud Springs and Rush Creek until February 11.[6]

Livingston and his men promptly set to work repairing the telegraph line, a daunting task in a country lacking timber. The Indians had cut off the poles close to the ground and burned many, while the wire that had not been carried away "was twisted and entangled in the most inextricable manner." By February 10, 315 poles reached Julesburg after having been hauled more than a hundred miles from the vicinity of Fort Cottonwood, and wire was requisitioned from Fort Mitchell. By dividing his men into three parties and working them night and day, Livingston had the circuit restored on the Denver line by February 12 and on the Fort Laramie line by February 17. He commended his men for their endurance and zeal repairing the "mischief done by the worthless savages" and ordered that when the line was found damaged in the future, the stagecoach escorts were to "halt the coaches and repair the line as they proceed."[7]

Well before the January and February raids so dramatically refuted Governor Saunders's rosy pronouncement that "the Indian war on our own frontier" was over, military and civilian leaders had become convinced that merely defending tiny outposts and escorting stagecoaches and travelers along the various routes to the west offered no solution to ending the frequent raids. B. M. Hughes of the Overland Stage Line, General Mitchell, and Colonel Livingston, among others, argued that military columns should seek out and "exterminate" the Indians in their winter camps before the grass was up in the spring and while the Indian ponies were in poor condition. Such campaigns, said Livingston, would take pressure off the overland road by compelling every warrior "to defend his own wigwam instead of leaving it in security while engaged in plundering and murdering our citizens." Along with these proposals came a plea for more soldiers, particularly after Mitchell's January expedition to the Republican Valley with more than six hundred cavalrymen failed to catch up with a single warrior.[8]

Capt. Charles F. Porter of Company A, First Battalion, Nebraska Veteran Volunteer Cavalry, summed up a soldier's view of the situation. With the troops available in the District of Nebraska, it was impossible to seek out the Indians in their camps and also "protect the line of travel up this valley." How much longer, wondered Porter, "will the 'powers that be' close their eyes to these solemn facts? Will they wait till the children of Colorado cry for bread, till starvation stares the hardy pioneer in the face?" At least two more "well mounted" regiments of cavalry were needed to keep open the trail.[9]

From the perspective of army commander Grant and other representatives of the "powers that be," the plains jurisdictions already had more than their share of troops and supplies, and the Indian war rated low on the list of military priorities. Regardless of the threat the roving warriors posed to overland commerce and communications beyond the Missouri, this problem paled in comparison with the need to keep pressure on the Confederacy, which still showed surprising resiliency. Confederate invasions of Missouri by Sterling Price in September 1864 and of Tennessee by John Bell Hood in November and December had tied down many Union troops, not to mention the large numbers required to sustain Grant's campaign against Lee's encircled army at Petersburg in Virginia and Sherman's march through the heart of Georgia to the sea. Few resources remained for the distant plains, the Civil War's backwater of backwaters.

Residents of the trans-Missouri region felt that the "knowing disciples of the quill" were as ignorant of the true conditions on the plains as were the "powers that be" in the War Department. Neither group appreciated or understood the difficulty of trying to protect the vast landscapes embraced within the District of Nebraska and other western military jurisdictions. One Nebraska observer thought General Mitchell had done everything he could with the fourteen hundred soldiers in his district, scattered from the Missouri River to South Pass, but "[n]o man that God ever put breath in can suppress such a wide-spread and gigantic Indian war with a handful of men, the statements of all enlightened Eastern Editors to the contrary notwithstanding."[10]

Efforts to convince the military and civilian authorities in Washington that the concerns emanating from constituencies in the West were both legitimate and deserving of attention were made even more difficult because the commanders of the Departments of the Missouri (William S. Rosecrans) and Kansas (Samuel R. Curtis) had already lost the confidence of Lincoln, Grant, and army chief of staff Halleck. These generals had been shunted off to these assignments because of previous failures, and once there they seemed to fare no better. Weary of the generals' constant calls for more troops and supplies that he believed were needed elsewhere, Grant decided that reorganizing the western commands offered the best prospect of achieving both "subordination and intelligence of administration."[11]

Accordingly, on December 2, 1864, Gen. Grenville M. Dodge was ordered to relieve Rosecrans at the Department of the Missouri in St. Louis. On January 30, 1865, the Department of Kansas (including Nebraska Territory) was assimilated into Dodge's department, and Curtis was transferred to the Department of the Northwest. A new Military Division of the Missouri was created to oversee the Departments of the Missouri and the Northwest, with Gen. John Pope in charge. Although Pope, too, had been reassigned to the trans-Mississippi after his

August 1862 defeat at Second Bull Run in Virginia, he had since commanded the Department of the Northwest effectively.[12]

Both Pope and Dodge shared their subordinates' view that the best solution to the Indian "problem" was offensive action. In Pope's case this theory harkened back to his approach to the summer 1863 campaign in Dakota Territory: cut the troops loose from guarding fixed points and send them into the heart of the Indian country. The two commanders began formulating a similar plan for offensives into the Natives' strongholds on the southern plains and in Dakota, as well as in the Powder River country. Now that the Civil War seemed near its end, surely more troops and resources would be available for service west of the Missouri River.[13]

In the meantime the governors, legislatures, and prominent citizens of Kansas, Nebraska, and Colorado had also been calling for more resources and a more centralized command structure to deal with the Indian war. On January 18 the Nebraska legislature memorialized Secretary of War Edwin Stanton to create a Department of the Plains, encompassing Nebraska, Colorado, Montana, and Utah Territories "under the control of one competent officer." In a subsequent letter Governor Saunders asked Stanton to send out an additional regiment of cavalry.[14]

The "competent officer" turned out to be Brig. Gen. Patrick Edward Connor, who had dealt firmly and sometimes brutally with Indians and Mormons while he commanded the District of Utah. As early as October 1864 stagecoach king Ben Holladay had suggested Connor "as the man for the work of punishing these marauders," and Pope and the army high command decided he was the best choice to take over the new District of the Plains when it was created on March 28, 1865, within Dodge's Department of the Missouri. Mitchell was relieved as District of Nebraska commander and sent to Kansas. The former districts of Nebraska, Colorado, and Utah were revamped to create four subdistricts within the District of the Plains, Colonel Livingston retaining command of the East Subdistrict.[15]

Before his reassignment Mitchell had hoped to make a winter campaign against the Indian camps on Powder River, "regardless of snow." "All I want is troops and supplies." Aware that not enough troops and supplies were then available for a major thrust, Dodge gave Mitchell permission to "make a quick dash at them, using pack mules from Laramie." As it turned out, neither Mitchell nor Connor would be able to launch a significant offensive against the Indians in the Powder River country for more than five months.[16]

The first priority for making such a campaign was to assemble the needed soldiers and supplies at Fort Laramie, a task already begun. In early February the secretary of war authorized the enlistment into Union service of two regiments of Confederate prisoners of war confined at the Rock Island Arsenal in Illinois. These "U.S. Volunteers," popularly known as "Galvanized Yankees," would be sent to the plains. Other volunteer regiments that could be spared in the wake of recent Union victories and whose enlistment still had months to run were also to be sent west. Before his transfer Mitchell had gained War Department authority to enlist a company of Pawnee Scouts, this time led by Capt. Frank North, a unit whose intermittent service as U.S. Army auxiliaries would span more than a decade during the plains Indian wars.[17]

The second priority for the beleaguered plains command was to reestablish the overland mail service, which had again ground to a halt during the January and February raids. On February 10 Dodge ordered all wagon trains moving west of Forts Kearny and Riley to be organized with at least a hundred armed men before being allowed to proceed. All government trains and the overland mail coaches were to be escorted by soldiers. All mail stations were to be sited within protecting distance of military posts. A similar system was to apply to trains returning east from Denver.[18]

Accordingly, Colonel Livingston dispatched soldiers from the garrisons at Fort Kearny, Plum Creek, Fort Cottonwood, and Camp Rankin to occupy Gilman's, Midway, O'Fallon's, Beauvais, and Alkali Stations on the trail west of Fort Kearny. With the troops thus dispersed, the escorts required to accompany every eastbound and westbound stagecoach had to travel fewer than twenty miles, reducing the fatigue on both men and horses. By February 24 the *Nebraska Republican* reported that the first through mail from Denver had arrived in Omaha. By March 10 General Mitchell at Fort Kearny informed Dodge that "stages are running regularly westward."[19]

When the soldiers stationed at these tiny posts were not escorting stagecoaches, their time was occupied with cutting and hauling firewood, building stables and quarters, grooming horses, making hay, or taking an occasional hunting or scouting trip. At Midway Station at Penniston and Miller's ranche, where Company H of the First Nebraska was quartered, men were sent out daily with the two company wagons to cut firewood in ravines twelve miles away. Periodically the wagons went to Fort Kearny or Fort Cottonwood for supplies, including corn for the horses. Company clerk Pvt. August Scherneckau noted that each man on duty kept his horse picketed near his quarters, ready to escort stagecoaches or to make a quick dash when Indians were reported nearby. All in all, said Scherneckau, "life here is terribly boring."[20]

Consequently many soldiers "blew in most of their pay at the bar," which was bad for discipline and order but good for the pocketbooks of the ranchemen who ran these trailside saloons. Freighter C. B. Hadley recalled that the ranche owner "at the upper junction" (i.e., the Upper California Crossing of the South Platte River, near today's village of Brule) "told me in November 1865 that he had made about $25,000 that year." According to Hadley, whiskey sold for fifty cents per glass "during the Indian War." August Scherneckau on September 3 at Midway Station noted that the men there owed Penniston and Miller more than $3,000 for whiskey.[21]

The problems of too few horses and their poor quality that had plagued the First Nebraska soldiers at the Platte Valley outposts in 1864 had not been solved by the spring of 1865. Capt. William H. Ivory, Scherneckau's company commander, inquired on March 25 about the prospect of getting more and better horses. Otherwise, said Ivory, keeping his company at Midway Station was a useless expense to the government. With his "mostly broken down" horses, "it would be impossible for me to send a scout of a dozen men fifty miles, or to successfully follow Indians any distance."[22]

While the soldiers served out their lonely existence along the Platte, other routines of Nebraska life continued. The tenth legislature assembled in Omaha on January 5 for its forty-day session. In contrast to his premature declaration that the Indian war was over, Governor Saunders in his opening address made a more accurate prediction that "this war for the preservation of our National Life . . . is at length happily drawing to a close." Given the rejection of the statehood movement via the aborted constitutional convention of July 1864, the governor did not urge the legislature to revisit statehood during the session. In case the legislature should be so inclined, however, Saunders could not resist suggesting a patriotic justification: "All loyal and Union-loving people . . . should not longer insist upon drawing from the General Government that which we might provide for ourselves," a reference to the federal appropriations that had sustained the territorial government since 1854.[23]

Aside from the usual bills incorporating ferries, defining roads, regulating livestock, or organizing counties, several bills and resolutions related to the war and wartime issues. Saunders asked the legislature to devise some method of compensating the four companies of Nebraska militiamen he had called out in August 1864 to fight the Indians. These men had recently been discharged without ever having been paid because the territory lacked the funds. Accordingly, the legislators approved issuing $35,000 worth of territorial bonds for this purpose, along with a resolution asking Congress for reimbursement. On February 1 Saunders left Omaha for the national capital to urge Congress to make the appropriation. He also planned to make a personal appeal for more troops to help suppress the Indians.[24]

Reminiscent of a similar outcome during previous legislative sessions, a bill for an appropriation to relieve destitute families of Nebraska's long-serving volunteers was tabled. This time the bill failed, said Republican councilman A. S. Holladay, because it had been consigned to a committee temporarily controlled by the soldiers' "avowed political enemies," that is, the Democrats. When a legislator offered a substitute bill for the same purpose Democratic members, "true to their hostility against the Government and the soldiers voted to a man that the bill should not be introduced." The legislature approved a resolution asking President Lincoln to reappoint Governor Saunders and Territorial Secretary Algernon S. Paddock, along with another promising ratification of Congress's recently passed constitutional amendment abolishing slavery as soon as Nebraska, by admission to the Union, "shall acquire the right to be heard on the question."[25]

The legislature's failure to make an appropriation for the relief of soldiers and their families was partly offset by the humanitarian efforts of Nebraska civilians, primarily women.

In the spring of 1862 women in the small town of Florence, north of Omaha, had rolled cotton and linen bandages for the First Nebraska Regiment. In December 1863 well-known raconteur and speculator George Francis Train lectured in Omaha to benefit the Ladies' Soldiers' Aid Society. Secretary Sarah Davis reported that the proceeds would afford "speeding relief to many of the suffering wives and children [of men] who are dying in our glorious cause of the Union." In early 1865 Brownville ladies organized a society to provide relief to sick and wounded Nebraska soldiers wherever they might be serving and "to destitute families in Nemaha County having father, husband, or sons in the Union army." Mrs. Rebecca S. Chivington was elected president, with dues set at twenty-five cents per month.[26]

Nebraska women also worked on behalf of the U.S. and Western Sanitary Commissions and their local affiliates. The commissions' most notable projects were the mammoth sanitary fairs held in St. Louis, Chicago, and other cites to raise money to provide hospital care for wounded soldiers and help support their families. Committees in several Nebraska towns raised funds for the fairs in St. Louis in 1864 and Chicago in 1865. By early May 1864, $212 had been subscribed in Brownville. The St. Louis fair was held later that month and garnered profits in excess of $550,000.[27]

The governor's wife, Marathena Saunders, Emma (Mrs. Algernon) Paddock, Caroline (Mrs. Andrew) Poppleton, and other prominent Omaha women were among the leaders of that city's sanitary committee. The committee held two concerts featuring piano and violin performances at the Herndon House hotel in February 1865 that raised $242. Several of the committeewomen personally contributed $25 each; combined with other subscriptions and a donation from the territorial legislature,

the receipts came to $450. By May 18, 1865, the Omaha com-
mittee had received cash donations of $883 and merchandise
valued at $175. Items "manufactured" by the ladies of Omaha
were valued at $278, bringing the grand total to $1,336. Isabella Spurlock of the Plattsmouth Sanitary Committee reported
that her group had already forwarded cash and goods valued
at $300 to Mrs. Mary Livermore of the Northwestern Sanitary
Commission in Chicago. The Omaha committee sent $475 to
Mrs. Livermore in April.[28]

Other communities also participated. Nebraska City collected
$740 and Cuming City $45. The sanitary committee in Decatur
raised $114.50 in cash from various localities in northeastern
Nebraska, plus a donation of "four pairs Moccasins" and "bow
and arrows & c." valued at $12.75 from the Omaha Indian Res-
ervation. Altogether, cash and goods collected in Omaha and
elsewhere in Nebraska for the 1865 Northwestern Sanitary
Fair in Chicago totaled some $25,000.[29]

The war news reaching Nebraska by telegraph in late winter 1865 signaled that final Union victory was in sight and
was cause for celebration. Reports of the February 18 capture
of Charleston, the "cess-pool of treason," prompted the illumination of the capitol building in Omaha, which "looked like
a huge ball of fire" and brought celebratory editorials in the
newspapers. On March 4, Inauguration Day, a large gathering
at Omaha's Congregational Church offered prayers "for the
President this day inaugurated, for the success of the national
arms, for an early reunion of the states, and for an enduring
peace." Several papers reprinted Lincoln's inaugural address,
which the *Nebraska Advertiser* termed "inferior to none" while
praising the president's "calm reliance upon the Ruler of the
Universe and the justice of the cause of Freedom."[30]

Even more exciting news soon followed. Grant's breakthrough
of the Confederate lines at Petersburg and the subsequent oc-

cupation of Richmond by Union troops on April 3, followed by Lee's surrender at Appomattox six days later, touched off celebrations throughout Nebraska. In Nebraska City on April 10 some two thousand people assembled downtown, fireworks were set off, Main Street was "a blaze of light" for half a mile from the river, and many private dwellings were "brilliantly illuminated." The *Daily News* remarked that "abolitionists and copperheads had dropped all partizan feeling and met on the common ground of exultation that peace will soon again bless the land."[31]

Upon receiving news of Richmond's capture and Lee's surrender Omaha experienced another "grand illumination," although the symphony of celebration included a few sour notes. The provost marshal's office arrested William Vanderwater for "persisting in drinking to the health of Jeff Davis, after the news of the fall of Richmond" and J. B. Allen and Alexander Ritchie for "drinking the health of Gen. Lee." While Vanderwater's fate went unrecorded, Allen broke jail and Ritchie was soon released after taking the oath of allegiance and posting a $1,000 bond that he would observe it.[32]

Omaha's Democratic paper, the *Nebraskian*, criticized the arrests as arbitrary and unwarranted. Post of Omaha commander Lt. Thomas Griffin of the First Nebraska responded in a letter published in the *Republican*. The *Nebraskian* was wrong to defend a person's right to praise the enemies of the free form of government under which that individual lived and thrived. Such a person, said Griffin, was like "a viper on its [the government's] bosom, being warmed up to life, assaying to sting his benefactor to death."[33]

Brownville celebrated "the capture of Gen. Lee and his army" on April 7, two days before the surrender became a reality. "The big gun was brought out and fired; all, with a few exceptions wore smiling countenances, and those that didn't kept mainly indoors." *Nebraska Advertiser* editor John Colhapp sheepishly admitted that the reports of the capture of "Gen. Lee" sparking the premature celebration had referred to Gen. Fitzhugh Lee, not to his uncle Robert E. Lee. Nonplussed, the Brownville celebrants decided that "we had illuminated for the fall of Richmond & c." Confirmation of the actual surrender arrived on April 10, which Colhapp thought warranted another "grand jubilee."[34]

The troops serving along the Platte learned of Robert E. Lee's capitulation via a telegram from Secretary of War Stanton and President Lincoln. Private Scherneckau heard the news on April 10 when he was at Fort Cottonwood, whereupon "general cheerfulness prevailed." A two-hundred-gun salute was ordered fired at Fort Kearny by First Nebraska cavalrymen delegated as artillerists. Unfortunately, a premature discharge from one of the cannons mortally wounded two of the temporary cannoneers, casting gloom over the celebration. More gloom was to follow.[35]

Elation over Union victory barely had time to sink in before stunning dispatches reached Nebraska reporting Lincoln's assassination at Ford's Theater on the evening of April 14. Scherneckau and his comrades at Midway Station heard the "very depressing" news late the next day from a passerby on the stagecoach. Telegrams bearing the grim reports arrived in Brownville about noon on April 15, just a few hours after the president died. "Instead of gathering in crowds in the streets to discuss the horrible tragedy, all seemed desirous of privacy, all seemed to feel the loss as one of their own. The church bells were tolled, and the community seemed hushed, as in a stupor." The mayor requested citizens to abstain from business on April 17 and assemble at the Presbyterian Church for a memorial service, which was "conducted with a fervor and devotion creditable to the loyal hearts engaged in it." The choir sang a special hymn composed for the occasion by a local woman. During the day of mourning the Brownville cannon was fired every half hour and a large flag sewn by "a few patriotic women" was suspended over Main Street.[36]

Omaha residents reacted similarly. Military offices, business houses, and many private homes were draped in mourning. Acting Governor Paddock issued a proclamation designating a thirty-day period of mourning and requesting every city, village, and neighborhood in the territory to hold memorial services on the day of Lincoln's funeral. Accordingly, the Omaha clergy conducted "Union services" in the capitol building on April 19 at the hour the funeral began in Washington DC. *Nebraska Republican* editor Edward B. Taylor opined that perhaps some of the "Northern journals" and "bitter partisan speakers" might not be blameless for the tragedy. "Have we not heard of Lincoln the tyrant, the despot, etc. for four years? . . . It is difficult to say that those things may not have begotten and festered a spirit which has culminated as we chronicle this hour." Taylor characterized the assassination as "the best illustration of the barbarism of slavery. It is one of its legitimate fruits."[37]

At Fort Kearny an officer of the First Nebraska recorded "the unutterable woe of our brave and noble patriots here" upon learning of the death of "our beloved and lamented Abraham Lincoln." The soldiers assembled to hear a eulogy by Chaplain Thomas Tipton and "solemn music" by the First Nebraska band. Even at the tiny trail outposts the men honored the dead president. At noon on April 19, the day of Lincoln's funeral, the soldiers of Company H at Midway Station drew up in ranks and fired twenty-one shots from their carbines.[38]

No doubt many Nebraskans kept their thoughts to themselves or reflected on the president's murder in the company of a few close friends. Private Scherneckau reported "many debates about the value of Lincoln" among his comrades. "Several put him even higher than Washington." J. Sterling Morton,

Fig. 17. Downtown Omaha, about 1865, looking northwest from Thirteenth and Farnham Streets, with the territorial capitol building on the horizon. Douglas County Historical Society Collections, Omaha, Nebraska.

one of Lincoln's severest critics, confided in his diary that the assassination was "a sad and portentous crime which greatly imperilled life, liberty and the Union." Even Augustus Harvey, the *Nebraska City News* editor who had made some of the most vehement attacks on the president and his administration, urged a contemplative response to "the terrible intelligence of to-day." "It becomes all good citizens to abstain from the use of intemperate language and by example, as far as possible, allay undue excitement.... Long thought and short talk should be the mood of every American in this portentous and fearful hour."[39]

From late April through May the death throes of the Confederacy and the flight and capture of President Jefferson Davis; the manhunt for Lincoln's assassin, John Wilkes Booth; and the activities of the new president, Andrew Johnson, dom-

inated headlines in the territorial newspapers. Many Nebraskans, especially Republicans, were gratified to learn of Governor Alvin Saunders's reappointment, later determined to have
been one of President Lincoln's last official acts. In response
to congratulations, the governor noted that Southern sympathizers, bushwhackers, guerrillas, and Indians "have all had
their share in rendering the office a difficult one to fill satis-
factorily." Now that the war was over, Saunders hoped "more
of our time can be given to the building up of our territory and
to the interests of our own people." These interests included
ending the Indian war, the prospect that the Union Pacific
would soon begin laying rails west from Omaha, and the issue of whether statehood should be revisited.[40]

Before the District of the Plains was created in late March and
before the dramatic events of April and May 1865 unfolded,
Generals Pope and Dodge had started assembling troops and
supplies for a general offensive against Indians, both in the
Powder River country and elsewhere. The Third U.S. Volunteer
Infantry, commanded by Col. Christopher McNally and comprising 820 ex-Confederates enlisted from Union prison pens,
reached Fort Kearny April 8, preceded by the Sixteenth Kansas
Cavalry en route to Fort Laramie. The Galvanized Yankees of the
Third U.S. Volunteer Infantry were assigned to guard stage stations, twelve to fifteen men at each, where their lack of mobility would be least serious, while others were posted to the major forts. Regimental headquarters was at Camp Rankin near
Julesburg. Scherneckau welcomed the former Rebels, whom
he thought were good soldiers with "many decent men among
them."[41]

On May 3 a company of Winnebago Indian scouts was mustered in for one year to serve with Connor's command in the
field. The company, led by Capt. Edwin Nash, formerly the miller

on the Omaha Reservation, would be known as the "Omaha Scouts" even though, the *Nebraska Republican* reported, "there is not one of the Omaha tribe in the ranks." The misnomer was probably applied because the Winnebagos were then living with the Omahas on the latter's reservation.[42]

On May 22 Dodge informed the adjutant general's office that he wanted to mount the Second Missouri Light Artillery and use it as cavalry. This regiment was a strong one, and many of the men still had two years to serve on their enlistments. Commander-in-chief Grant approved the request and also told Pope that he was sending a brigade of Michigan cavalry to the plains from Washington DC. Had the Missouri and Michigan soldiers known what was in store for them, many would have mutinied or deserted on the spot.[43]

The end of the Civil War, a milestone achieved with the May 26 surrender of all Confederate troops west of the Mississippi, would have significant implications for the pending Indian campaigns and for many of the soldiers being transferred to or already serving on the plains. Dodge and Connor had counted on reinforcements to provide enough men to protect some twenty-six hundred miles of overland mail and telegraph route while at the same time delivering a punishing blow against the warriors in their wilderness camps. They had not anticipated how rapidly the government, in the interest of economy and to satisfy demands coming from the volunteers, would demobilize the vast Union armies. On April 28 the War Department issued General Orders No. 77 "for reducing expenses of the military establishment." This directive halted all procurement and enlistments and provided for "the immediate reduction" of the armed forces.[44]

Nor had the generals in the western jurisdictions planned on the revival of initiatives from Congress and the Interior Department to make peace with the Indians in lieu of their punitive subjugation by the army. The peace proposals were being heavily promoted by U.S. Senator James R. Doolittle, who was heading a committee investigating the Sand Creek Massacre, and by Dakota territorial governor Newton Edmunds. Accordingly, military offensives on the southern and northern plains were called off and replaced by commissions appointed to hold peace talks with tribes in those regions, just as Connor and Dodge were initiating their campaign into the Powder River country. These peace initiatives were generally condemned by newspaper editors and residents living in the West.[45]

Gathering the troops for a major Indian campaign was one thing, supplying them with horses and subsistence was another. On April 14 Connor wrote Dodge that there were not four hundred horses in the District of the Plains in fit condition for a campaign and not enough corn on hand to remedy the problem. Later in the month he noted that "[w]e are nearly out of supplies at some points" and the pack mules that had been sent out to Fort Laramie "are scarcely able to carry their saddles." A month later Dodge reported that Connor needed eight hundred horses and lamented that the War Department's order that would muster out several hundred cavalrymen then serving on the plains had just arrived. Dodge was later able to get the order temporarily suspended as it applied to the District of the Plains.[46]

Both Dodge and Connor were highly critical of the pace at which supplies and troops were being delivered for the Powder River Expedition, whose departure from Fort Laramie was delayed repeatedly. The quartermaster general's department did not even let contracts for the supplies until May 1 and then incorporated no provisions requiring their prompt delivery. Although by late May Dodge reported that "trains are going out daily with stores for all points on the Plains," it was too little and too late for an Indian campaign that had been proposed to start "before grass was up." Many of the cavalry regiments being transferred from the East did not reach Fort Leavenworth until June 1, and only some of their men had horses. Then the regiments moved west at a snail's pace. As late as July 21 Connor wrote from Fort Laramie that "I am losing much precious time now; cause, contractors."[47]

The failure of timely deliveries of supplies for Connor's Indian campaign was not because of a lack of freighting firms, wagons, and ox teams to carry them west. Platte Valley commercial traffic during the spring and summer of 1865 was tremendous. Although estimates vary, as many as four thousand wagons per month passed Fort Kearny going west during the peak travel season, carrying supplies for both civilian and military enclaves. To take better advantage of the old military road from Omaha, both for freighting and for the movement of troops, Dodge requested that two wood and canvas pontoon bridges constructed under his supervision in Tennessee be shipped to Nebraska for installation on the Loup near Columbus and on the Platte at Fort Kearny. By early July he reported to Connor, "[W]ill have the Loup Fork and Platte River bridged in a few days."[48]

The two major Nebraska depots for overland freighting in 1865 were Nebraska City and Plattsmouth. Nebraska City firms hauled goods for the army as well as for the Colorado mining camps and road ranches. Plattsmouth became a major depot primarily for military shipments. Together the two towns may have been responsible for dispatching some eighty-eight million pounds of freight west from the Missouri River. Freighting from Nebraska City alone in 1865 employed more than four thousand wagons, three thousand men, and almost thirty-six thousand oxen. The goods were shipped to the Missouri River ports from St. Joseph, St. Louis, or New Orleans on board five steamboats of the Hannibal and St. Joseph Packet Line, eleven

Fig. 18. Freight wagons on the main street of Nebraska City, about 1865.
Nebraska State Historical Society RG2294-37.

boats operated by St. Louis or New Orleans merchants, and several other independently operated vessels. Altogether, 207 boats stopped at the Nebraska City levee during the 1865 navigation season to discharge freight and passengers.[49]

The almost hourly passage of emigrants, miners, stagecoaches, soldiers, and freight wagons through the Platte Valley provided some diversion for the soldiers at the lonely trail outposts, but it also made their lives miserable. Except when it was raining, billowing clouds of dust kicked up by the hundreds of wagons and thousands of oxen, horses, and mules filled the sky and were then blown around by the prairie wind. Iowa soldier Eugene Ware reported standing with his field glass atop Sioux Lookout, a high hill near Fort Cottonwood, observing an ox train with a "vast prism of dust rising either to the north or south, and the dust would be in the air mile after mile until the dust and teams both reached the vanishing-point on the horizon." At Midway, said Private Scherneckau, "one sees nothing but an immense dust cloud in the entire area when a large train is moving," a problem he mentioned almost daily.[50]

Freighters and military columns were not the only trail travelers during the summer of 1865. As had been the case earlier, many were fortune hunters or escapees from the war's economic, political, or social disruptions. Pvt. Daniel Goodman of the First Nebraska thought many of those passing Fort Kearny were "them old copperheads that is getting ashamed of them selves." General Pope believed many travelers to the mining regions of Colorado, Idaho, or Montana were "disloyal and vagrant elements set loose by the termination of the war." After Capt. Edwin Nash and his company of Winnebago Indian scouts escorted a wagon train of "secesh pilgrims from Missouri" to Fort Laramie, Nash concluded that the Missourians had gone west "because they could live there [Missouri] no longer and to rid themselves of the army blue."[51]

A reverse migration was also underway. Squire Lamb at Wood River wrote his brother that "the road is lined all day with returned Pilgrims. The war is over and [they] think they can live in the states." Iowa cavalryman Eugene Ware summed it up: "The East demanded an outlet West and a reflex tide much weaker was always seeking the East. An open road between the Missouri River and the Pacific Ocean was a constant necessity."[52]

That significant numbers of the fighting Indians had gathered in the Powder River country did not halt attacks by other warriors in the travel and communications corridors to the south. In the East Subdistrict of the Plains, officers and men of the First Nebraska Regiment; the First Battalion, Nebraska Veteran Volunteer Cavalry; the Seventh Iowa; and the Third U.S. Volunteers had to cope with a revival of spring raids on Platte Valley outposts and travelers. May 5 brought an attack on a wagon train near Mullally's Ranche, followed by the expected flight of the Indians across the Platte and the equally expected inability of the soldiers to cross the river in pursuit due to the broken-down condition of their horses. On May 12 thirty Indians attacked several soldiers just west of Smith's Ranche, killing Sgt. Hiram Creighton of Company A, First Battalion, wounding three Galvanized Yankees from Company D, Third U.S. Volunteers, and driving off thirty head of cattle. The losses might have been worse except for the spirited defense put up by Pvt. Francis Lohnes of Company H of the First Nebraska Regiment, who stumbled into the fight while on a wood-cutting detail. His resolute action that day, despite being wounded by an arrow in the hip, would make him the only member of a Nebraska-named regiment to receive the Medal of Honor. Three months later the medal was pinned on Lohnes's blouse at Fort Kearny while Governor Alvin Saunders, General Dodge, and other dignitaries looked on.[53]

On May 18 fifteen soldiers of the Third U.S. Volunteers left behind at Fort Leavenworth to recover from illness were on their way to join their comrades when they were attacked by Indians on the Little Blue River east of Fort Kearny. They had been sent off unarmed. Two soldiers were killed, six wounded, and their supply wagon was looted. The surviving soldiers blamed the Pawnees, who had been hunting buffalo in the area. An army investigation that included taking the survivors to the Pawnee Reservation failed to identify any of the culprits or locate any of the plundered livestock or supplies. Although he had initially been convinced that the Pawnees were guilty, Colonel Livingston subsequently concluded that they were blameless. Suspicion then centered on the Cheyennes, but the actual perpetrators remained a matter of speculation.[54]

Also in May Col. Thomas Moonlight, who replaced Col. William O. Collins in command of the North Subdistrict of the Plains, launched an expedition from Fort Laramie to track down Cheyenne raiders. His five hundred cavalrymen, including men from the First Nebraska and the First Battalion, Nebraska Veteran Volunteer Cavalry temporarily assigned to Fort

Laramie after Collins and part of his Eleventh Ohio were mustered out, reached the Wind River Mountains before returning to the fort empty-handed. Moonlight's report reinforced the belief that only a major army expedition into the heart of the Powder River Indian stronghold would produce positive results.[55]

As the combatants girded for Connor's long-delayed foray to the Powder River, fighting escalated along the trail both east and west of Fort Laramie. Some of the bloodshed came as a surprise. Although several hundred Brules and Oglalas, the so-called Laramie Loafers, had been living quietly near Fort Laramie for decades, the army command decided to send them and their intermarried white and mixed-blood "squaw men" to Fort Kearny to get them out of the way. Four officers and 135 enlisted men of the Seventh Iowa Cavalry left Fort Laramie on June 11 in charge of an estimated fifteen hundred to two thousand Indians. Not only did the Laramie Loafers not want to go the country of their bitter enemies, the Pawnees, but en route some of the soldiers began to mistreat their charges, which made them even more furious. While the column was breaking camp on the morning of June 14 at Horse Creek, forty miles east of the fort, the still-armed Indians killed Capt. William Fouts and three enlisted men and wounded four soldiers. The remaining troops tried to regain control, but the Indians forced them to retreat, then escaped across the Platte and headed north toward the Black Hills. Despite this confrontation, these Sioux did not want to join their brethren on the Powder River in making war on the whites. A few weeks later the runaways returned to Fort Laramie and surrendered.[56]

Colonel Moonlight led out a column from Fort Laramie to corral the fugitives, but the incompetent officer let his stock be turned out to graze one night and lurking warriors made off with seventy-five of the best horses in his command. For this and other transgressions Connor soon sent Moonlight packing. Worse was to come in late July when a large war party swarmed down on Platte Bridge Station some 120 miles west of Fort Laramie, killing twenty-eight Kansas and Ohio soldiers there and at nearby Red Buttes. The most notable casualty was Lt. Caspar Collins, son of the former Eleventh Ohio Cavalry commander of Mud Springs/Rush Creek fame.[57]

Cheyennes thought to be from the same group that attacked Platte Bridge moved south to raid the overland mail route near Fort Halleck, near which Company C of the First Nebraska was temporarily posted. There the Indians killed several civilians, carried away a woman and a child, and ran off livestock. Ed Smith of Brownville, a sergeant in Company C, saw some of the bodies and expressed his outrage in a letter to his hometown paper. The members of the government commission who had recently censured John M. Chivington for his conduct at Sand Creek in 1864 "should be made to hold an inquest over these butchered women. . . . This war must be stopped, and treaties will never do it, nor does censuring a good officer help the matter. Men well equipped and generals who fight to whip, are the only effective arguments to these devils."[58]

Attitudes about Indians like those expressed by Sergeant Smith were prevalent among the soldiers serving on the plains, leading to atrocities like the Sand Creek Massacre and the killing of the Poncas near Niobrara in 1863. Some Indian agents, including Vital Jarrot of the Upper Platte Agency at Fort Laramie, recognized that stereotyping all Indians as brutal savages only made the problem worse and admitted to being "frequently shocked at the barbarity advocated by our soldiers." Many of the Sioux and Arapahos were disposed to be friendly, said Jarrot, but they were afraid to come to the military posts on account of threats by soldiers and officers that "none should be spared; all ought to be killed, men, women, and children, and no quarter given."[59]

The May orders to discharge troops, not only on the plains but throughout the nation's military jurisdictions, marked the beginning of the rapid demobilization of the Civil War volunteers. Well before the end of the war was clearly in sight, however, Union authorities had taken steps to streamline the army and cut expenses. The Enrollment Act of 1863 included a provision to consolidate under-strength regiments from the same state or territory, which would also reduce the number of officers. By the time the First Nebraska veterans were furloughed in the summer of 1864, the regiment tallied fewer than five hundred men, while the First Battalion of home defense cavalry mustered about four hundred. Once the decision had been made to keep the First Nebraska home to fight the Indians, the prospect of consolidating the two units came to the fore.[60]

Colonel Livingston, always mindful of protecting the lofty reputation he believed his regiment had earned and justly deserved, tried without much success to fill up the First Nebraska by recruiting at home in the summer and fall of 1864. His efforts garnered only about 110 men, not nearly enough to replace those whose enlistments had expired. At the same time, the War Department denied his request to muster in replacement officers for those left behind in Arkansas. As early as September 1864 Lt. John Wilcox, the territory's mustering officer, advised his superiors that consolidating the First Nebraska and the First Battalion "would make it a strong and effective regiment."[61]

On January 31, 1865, the War Department ordered the consolidation, although nearly six months would pass before it was finalized. Responding to Indian raids and protecting overland communications and travel took priority. Despite the pending consolidation, Livingston in the spring of 1865 persisted in seeking permission to recruit, arguing that his regiment still had two years left to serve on its second enlistment. The colonel's hopes of filling up his regiment were dashed when Department of Missouri commander Dodge bluntly and negatively endorsed his April 3, 1865, request: "The Secretary of War directs that no more recruiting be allowed." By month's end the provost marshal general had ordered that all salaried employees and deputy provost marshals in the bureau's recruiting districts be discharged and all rented offices given up, soon followed by the discharge of the district provost marshals themselves.[62]

Colonel Livingston's fervent desire to bring new soldiers into his regiment did have its limits, however. When an examining board determined that recruit John Miller was "of African descent" because his mother was a mulatto, the board censured the mustering officer for "highly reprehensible" conduct, "Col. Livingston preferring to accept none but white men into the regiment." The board recommended that Miller be transferred to an all-black unit. The episode showed that even Union soldiers and officers who favored the abolition of slavery were unwilling to grant African Americans the same rights and opportunities as white soldiers. Black men were welcome to serve the Union cause and suffer all the dangers and hardships of military life, but only in segregated regiments or as teamsters and "undercooks" for white regiments.[63]

Livingston claimed that consolidation of the regiment and the battalion had been his idea. If true, it was probably because the colonel expected he would command the reorganized regiment and finally be able assert his authority over the "home guards" he had looked down on for so long. In March he had written the assistant adjutant general of the District of Nebraska stating, "I am anxious to remain in the service." Army regulations, however, provided that consolidated regiments would not be entitled to a colonel or to the same number of company officers (captains and lieutenants) that the separate units had previously been authorized.[64]

This realization did not sit well with Livingston and some of the First Nebraska's officers, who had never really respected their First Battalion counterparts for choosing service at home instead of joining the "gallant First" in the South. Most of the First Battalion's officers had previously served in the Second Nebraska Volunteer Cavalry, which Livingston in the summer of 1863 had branded "a useless organization." "I will not serve an hour," blustered Capt. Thomas Griffin of the First Nebraska, if the consolidation brought into his company a battalion officer with greater seniority than Griffin had. Lt. John Seaton of Company G hoped he would be mustered out when the units merged, not only to reunite with his family but also to avoid the "broils" he predicted would make life miserable for the officers remaining.[65]

The "holier than thou" attitude on the part of some First Nebraska officers irritated their counterparts from the former Second Nebraska Cavalry. In June 1864 Henry M. Atkinson, the Second Nebraska's former adjutant, happened to be in Omaha when the furloughed First Nebraska veterans arrived from Arkansas, and he attended the reception for them at the capitol. Writing to Robert W. Furnas, who had commanded the Second Nebraska, Atkinson reported, "One of the officers [of the First Nebraska] took occasion to speak in rather sneering terms of the 2nd Nebraska and it made me *mad* and the gentleman hauled in his horns." The editor of the *Nebraska Republican* was aware of the friction that had characterized relations between the two Nebraska regiments: "It is perhaps natural for an old regiment, with a good reputation for fighting, to act in an imperious manner toward those whom they regard as military 'freshmen,' and it is quite as natural for the latter to resent such treatment."[66]

Regardless of the officers' feelings and preferences, the consolidation could not be prevented now that the war was over. Even though Governor Saunders, General Connor, and many of the First Nebraska's officers pleaded for Livingston to be retained (otherwise "a positive injury will be inflicted upon the service and Nebraska"), he was mustered out on July 10, 1865, and the consolidation of the First Nebraska Regiment and the First Battalion was consummated. The regiment also lost Chaplain Thomas Tipton, two lieutenants in charge of the quartermaster and commissary departments, an assistant surgeon, and several noncommissioned officers. The battalion saw two captains discharged, along with noncommissioned officers from each of its four companies. Unlike the First Nebraska, however, the First Battalion also lost its identity. A July 18 order from regimental headquarters at Fort Kearny provided that "from and after this date, the organization heretofore known as the First Battalion Nebraska Veteran Cavalry Volunteers ceases to exist." The consolidated regiment would continue to be known as the First Nebraska Veteran Volunteer Cavalry, even though some of its new soldiers had never before served in the "gallant First." Lt. Col. William E. Baumer, whose credentials as a First Nebraska man dated to the June 1861 muster in, took over the command.[67]

As a sop to Livingston's feelings and also because he deserved it, upon his discharge the colonel was promoted to the rank of brevet brigadier general for "faithful and meritorious services during the war," a promotion that pleased his fellow officers at Fort Kearny. They tendered Livingston "our sincere regrets at this separation, with the purest desires and brightest hopes that the same qualities of head and heart which have won our esteem will preeminently serve him in civil life." The enlisted men, too, regretted losing the colonel and praised his "last act of kindness" in seeking to have the entire regiment mustered out when it became clear that Livingston would not be retained.[68]

The attitudes expressed by officers and enlisted men who had not been discharged at the consolidation did not bode well for the future effectiveness of the First Nebraska Veteran Volunteer Cavalry. Capt. Thomas Weatherwax of Company G congratulated Livingston upon his discharge while noting, "I whish I was in the same fixt for I am tired of the survis the grand struggle is over and I want to quit." A soldier correspondent at Fort Kearny summed up the enlisted men's feelings: "[W]hile conscripts, drafted men, and negroes are allowed to go home and boast of their deeds of valor and heroism, we feel it is an injustice to us as veterans, who have done our duty faithfully and honorably during the past four years of arduous struggle and bloody battles . . . not to be permitted, now that the war is over and the object for which we enlisted is obtained, to go to our homes once more and enjoy the blessings of that peace we have so bravely conquered."[69]

These feelings led to an incipient mutiny at Fort Kearny when First Nebraska men in Companies K and F demanded their discharges. General Connor authorized Bvt. Brig. Gen. Herman Heath of the Seventh Iowa Cavalry, the new commander of the East Subdistrict of the Plains, to suppress the mutiny "with grape and canister" if necessary. Instead, Heath issued a general order reminding the men that their service could expire only at the will of the government and appealing to their sense of patriotism and honor: "You are therefore ordered to remain true to your past fame and leave unsullied the name of your regiment." Heath soon reported that the mutiny had subsided and that "Colonel Livingston was the cause of it."[70]

It is doubtful that the July 30 presentation to the First Nebraska of new and "elegant" regimental colors made by the women of Nebraska did much to salve the men's feelings. The Fort Kearny ceremony did give Lt. Col. Baumer an opportunity

Fig. 19. The flag of the First Nebraska Veteran Volunteer Cavalry, about 1866. Nebraska State Historical Society Museum Collections 24272.

to try to stoke the waning fires of patriotism: "I feel proud to accept this eloquent tribute to us all and to say that I but express the common sentiment of each and every one of you; that it shall wave in triumph over our heads or lie in glory in our graves . . . ; for our highest aim shall be to flaunt it defiantly in the midst of the foes of our country, whether at home or abroad."[71]

While consolidation was taking place at the small unit level, there was another major restructuring of the army's trans-Mississippi commands. A new Military Division of the Mississippi was created on July 10 to oversee the Departments of the Missouri, the Ohio, and Arkansas, which embraced ten Midwestern states plus the territories of Nebraska and Dakota and Indian Territory. William Tecumseh Sherman of Marching through Georgia fame was put in charge. Pope took command of the enlarged Department of the Missouri, which now included Wisconsin, Minnesota, Iowa, Missouri, and Kansas, along with Nebraska and Dakota territories. Former department commander Dodge was assigned responsibility for "U.S. forces serving in Kansas, Colorado, Nebraska, Montana, and that portion of Dakota lying west and south of the Missouri River; headquarters in the field." For the time being, Connor's District of the Plains remained intact.[72]

By midsummer Dodge and Connor's plans to punish the Indians were in shambles due to slow delivery of supplies, conflicting views by government departments about whether warfare or negotiation was the best approach, and the constant shuffling of volunteer units being transferred into the District of the Plains, then being mustered out before they could be deployed. At the same time, the volunteers in the regiments already there had begun deserting in droves.[73]

These conundrums were exacerbated by tremendous pressure being applied by Grant and the War Department to slash expenses and the number of troops west of the Missouri. The most persistent admonitions along this line descended on Pope, Dodge, and Connor in June and July, just as the latter was finally ready to launch some twenty-five hundred men on a three-pronged campaign against the Indians in the Powder River country. At the same time, the generals got wind of the new peace initiatives being pushed by Congress and the Indian bureau that doomed the comprehensive, multifront offensive they had conceived back in February.[74]

By the time Connor finally began his march from Fort Laramie on July 30, the eastern column of his Powder River Expedition was already floundering through the trackless expanse of the Nebraska Sandhills, en route from Omaha to the Black Hills. Elements of the Second Missouri Light Artillery, mounted as cavalry, and the Twelfth Missouri Cavalry, both under Lt. Col. Nelson Cole, left Omaha on July 1. After waiting there some ten days for promised supplies that failed to arrive by steamboat, the frustrated Cole was forced to purchase rations, harness, and wagon parts locally to the tune of some $15,000. It was a welcome boost to the Omaha economy but another blow to the army's efforts to cut expenses.[75]

Connor himself led the left column of his expedition, including the Pawnee and Omaha Scouts, which trekked northwestward along the eastern slope of the Big Horn Mountains. Some of the Kansas troops in Lt. Col. Samuel Walker's center column, which was to link up with Cole northwest of the Black Hills, refused to leave Fort Laramie on the grounds that their term of service would soon expire. According to one of Connor's aides, "they had not enlisted to fight Indians—had not lost any red devils and were not disposed to hunt for any." The Kansans capitulated when Connor sent other troops with orders to suppress the mutiny with artillery fire, if necessary.[76]

Walker's command marched out of Fort Laramie on August 6 and moved directly north, passing the Black Hills on the west and joining forces with Cole's column on the Little Missouri River. The united force then proceeded toward Powder River for an intended rendezvous with Connor, expecting to trap the Indians by a pincers movement. The plan soon went terribly awry due to poor guides, garbled orders, and failure to account for the vast distances and rugged terrain through which the soldiers had to march, not to mention the stiff resistance the Indians put up.[77]

Connor's column reached Powder River on August 11, having fought several skirmishes, and began constructing a log post named Fort Connor. The Pawnee Scouts jumped a party of twenty-four Cheyennes on August 17 and killed them all. On August 28 Captain North and his Pawnees discovered an Arapaho village on the Tongue River, which Connor attacked and destroyed the next day. Meanwhile, Cole and Walker were still floundering to the north, running a steady gauntlet of Indian attacks. On September 1 they lost six men in a skirmish and on September 8 fought a desperate battle with an estimated three thousand warriors, repelling repeated attacks with skillful use of artillery. A storm of freezing rain that night killed 414 horses and mules, forcing the exhausted command to limp south and finally straggle into Fort Connor on September 20.[78]

Before Connor could regroup his forces and mount another expedition against the Indians, he learned to his chagrin that his District of the Plains had been abolished by an order issued August 22 and his campaign had been terminated. The Powder River Expedition's effort to deal the Indians a crushing defeat had thus far been a failure and now had no hope for redemption. Pope's orders to Connor's successor, Frank Wheaton, were explicit: "[I]t is the purpose to return to a purely defensive arrangement for the security of overland routes to Salt Lake."[79]

Fort Connor established a military presence in the Powder River country and became a beacon for travelers heading overland from the Platte Valley to the gold-mining regions in Montana. By the end of 1865 the road that Connor had used to move against the Sioux and their allies, known as the Bozeman Trail, had become the standard route. Despite Connor's limited accomplishments, his campaign increased awareness and use of the trail by whites and signaled the Indians that they were not immune to military strikes even in this remote region, motivating them to fight even harder to save one of their last, best hunting grounds.[80]

Both the Pawnees and the Winnebagos performed well during the campaign, losing a few men and many horses. On September 25 Omaha Scouts commander Nash reported, "I have had one man killed, seven men wounded, and used up and left dead on the road 108 horses. I am worn out, exhausted, *gone in.* . . . My men are neither naked nor by no means clad, but principally barefoot." Nash and his Winnebagos, along with two companies of Galvanized Yankees from the Fifth Regiment of U.S. Volunteers, would remain at Fort Connor throughout the winter of 1865–66. Nash's top sergeant, Little Priest, "made himself notorious on the plains as a daring scout and brave man," particularly for an incident in which the scout, though wounded, held off an attack by twenty Sioux, killing four of them. The Pawnee Scouts returned to Nebraska in the fall of 1865 and were sent to guard the Pawnee Agency at Genoa until mustered out on April 1, 1866. The Omaha Scouts were discharged on July 16, 1866.[81]

The Indian War of 1865 petered out slowly rather than ending with the army dealing the Indians a decisive blow. The *Omaha Weekly Herald* offered a gloomy assessment of the summer campaign's results: "[P]lans modified, forces reduced, dissatisfied troops, supplies short, and every other hindrance, succeeded by positive orders to withdraw the troops, have left things in a deplorable condition." Outrage over the November 1864 Sand Creek Massacre, the heavy expense of military operations in remote regions, and a yearning for peace after four years of civil war had tipped political and public opinion toward negotiating with the Indians rather than fighting them. Although military leaders in the West continued to believe that the Indians must be punished before negotiations would succeed, they were forced to bow to the reality imposed by troop cutbacks and the loss of support for their plans by superiors in Washington. Never again would the army be able to mount an offensive against Indians on the scale of the Powder River Expedition.[82]

During the next decade and beyond, the "Indian problem" would persist; trying to solve it would sometimes fall to the Interior Department and sometimes to the War Department, which battled over who should have primary management of Indian affairs. Gen. Grenville Dodge, in his November 1, 1865, report, foresaw difficulties with this divided approach, difficulties he had already experienced: "[W]hile all departments of the Government are disposed to do justice to the Indian, and aiming to make him friendly, each has its separate and distinct aim, and while the military has been fighting them in one section of the country the representatives of other departments have been negotiating for or making peace with the same Indians in other sections of country."[83]

Of all the western commanders, perhaps General Pope had the best grasp of the shortcomings of the nation's Indian policy, including what he believed was a treaty system that promoted wholesale fraud and actually encouraged Indians to make war. Another problem was the government's practice of treating both the "semi-civilized" and "wild" tribes the same and placing Indian reservations where their inhabitants would be constantly exposed to "white debauchers" and "unscrupulous frontiersmen." While many of Pope's suggested reforms held promise, according to Historian Richard N. Ellis, they came at an inopportune time and gained little traction.[84]

Even as Connor and his men retraced their steps to Fort Laramie in late September 1865, Indian raiders resumed "their devilish work of pillage, plunder, and massacre" in Nebraska's Platte Valley, dooming the weary Nebraska volunteers to several more months of service. On September 30 warriors killed J. H. Temple and wounded three others in an attack on two Quartermaster Department wagons seven miles west of

O'Fallon's Station. Less than a month later, on October 22, Indians struck again, this time at Alkali Station (southwest of present-day Paxton), where they killed Corporals James Gruwell, DeWitt Chase, and Frances Stanley of Company C, First Nebraska.[85]

Six days later an estimated one to three hundred warriors attacked a civilian wagon train four miles west of Alkali Station, cut off ten wagons, and killed Albert Gaskill, George W. Selby, and father and son H. B. and Elijah Garton. Selby's body was said to have been "burnt to a crisp." The next day Capt. Henry Krumme, with thirty-six First Nebraska and Seventh Iowa soldiers, trailed the Indians toward the headwaters of Whiteman's Fork of the Republican River (now called Frenchman Creek). On October 30 Krumme and his men engaged in a running skirmish lasting several hours, claiming to have killed twenty-one Indians with one soldier wounded.[86]

In the meantime Gen. Herman Heath, commanding the East Subdistrict of Nebraska, led another hundred men from Alkali Station to rendezvous with Krumme's detachment. About midnight on October 31, Indians attacked Heath's camp near the mouth of Stinking Water Creek. The soldiers sprang from their bedrolls and repulsed the attackers after a half-hour fight under the bright light of the moon, but the army horses were too exhausted to allow pursuit. A trail discovered at dawn indicated that the warriors had retreated toward Kansas, and the troops returned to their stations. Heath claimed that another thirty to forty Indians had been dispatched to their celestial hunting grounds during the midnight skirmish.[87]

While Heath and his men were out, Indians on November 3 ran off eighty-seven oxen from Henry T. Clarke's freighting outfit camped near Sand Hill Station (east of present Ogallala). A few days later warriors simultaneously attacked Pole Creek Station northwest of Julesburg and soldiers who were escorting the mail coach about a mile away. Sgt. Fred Elwood of Company H, First Nebraska, led seven privates and company cook Harrison Johnson out of the station and drove off the Indians. Johnson, a former slave who joined the regiment as an "undercook" when it served in Arkansas, "behaved very well, fired several shots."[88]

Except that the calendar now read "1865" instead of "1864," life for the soldiers had changed little during the year they had been guarding Nebraska's Platte Valley trails. Indian raiders still threatened stagecoaches and the passing wagons of emigrants and freighters, while tiresome escort duty, heavy labor, and the occasional scout occupied most of the men's time. The most significant change was in their morale. The war for which they had enlisted had been over for several months, the government had seemingly forgotten them, and they desperately wanted to go home.

By late summer of 1865 the volunteers in the Department of the Missouri had become so dissatisfied that General Pope feared "disintegration of the organized forces in this department." The men believed "unjust discrimination has been shown in retaining them for service on the plains, whilst so many other regiments, enlisted under the same circumstances and with the same conditions, have been mustered out of service." These feelings infected regiments such as the First Nebraska that had been on the plains for months, as well as those recently sent from the East for the Indian campaigns. The long-serving volunteers, said one observer, "very much prefer digging gold to fighting Indians."[89]

In September 1865 alone some fifty men deserted from the First Nebraska, prompting outraged demands from the adjutant general's office in far-off Washington for an explanation for the loss of $8,000 worth of government property. Sometimes a soldier absconded with his entire outfit, horse included, which cost the government a total of $241. On October 4 August Scherneckau noted in his diary that Company H deserters had made off with fourteen horses and three mules during September, stock the still poorly mounted company could ill afford to lose. Eighteen men had deserted from Company H the same month. Five more deserted on October 13.[90]

One reason the desertion rate spiked in Company H was the September 22 order that sent it to Julesburg, abruptly abandoning the almost-finished quarters at Midway Station that the men had labored all summer to build. Five soldiers, including Medal of Honor recipient Frances Lohnes, deserted while the company was on the march. In December Company H was permanently assigned to escort stagecoaches along the windswept trail between Lodgepole Creek and Mud Springs. Twice a week the troopers had to ride the forty-mile route, which lacked any water or shelter for men or livestock.[91]

Though company commander William W. Ivory obeyed the order to send his men out along the trail to Mud Springs, he vented his feelings in an angry letter to the regimental adjutant: "I hope the col. comd. the regiment fully appreciates the injustice done my company in sending them out here in the middle of winter. . . . I venture the assertion that no negro company in the service has been worse treated. After building quarters all summer, besides doing very severe escort and other duties . . . the quarters they built and were promised they should remain in all winter were given to another company." On the back Ivory penned an aside alleging that "an infernal system of favoritism" existed within the regiment.[92]

Although army commander-in-chief Grant desperately wanted to muster out all the volunteers on the plains and assigned eight regiments of regular infantry to Pope's Department of the Missouri, getting the regulars to their stations before winter set in proved problematic. On October 26 Pope told

Grant, "It would not be possible to relieve troops farther west than [Forts] Kearny and Lyon without enormous cost for forage and other trains, and great suffering to men." This conclusion sealed the fate of the First Nebraska and other volunteer regiments until the spring of 1866. Only a handful of regulars made it to the plains, such as the headquarters staff and a battalion of the Eighteenth U.S. Infantry that reached Fort Kearny in November, too few to replace all the volunteers. Some soldiers, such as August Scherneckau, were fortunate enough to be discharged in the fall of 1865 when their enlistments expired, while others simply deserted. Still others, whose fortitude or patriotism proved stronger than their dissatisfaction, hunkered down in their log or adobe quarters to endure another Great Plains winter.[93]

Well before the chill winter winds whistled across the prairie, another kind of whistle was being heard in the Missouri River bottoms and then echoing through Omaha's hills and hollows. It was the steam whistle of the Major General Sherman, the first Union Pacific locomotive seen in Nebraska, which arrived in early July on board the steamboat *Colorado*. By July 28 a mile of track had been laid and the Major General Sherman was "puffing and dashing away continually," carrying ties and rails being delivered at the river landing to build the transcontinental railway, "the great idea of the age."[94]

Preliminary steps had already been taken. In early May, grading the rail bed from the Missouri to the Elkhorn River had been completed, and the first rails reached Omaha from Pennsylvania foundries on May 22. A sawmill in Washington County had been running for nearly a year, producing some forty thousand hardwood railroad ties. Parts for another sawmill already lay on the levee, with two more soon to arrive. Also visible was a fifty-five-ton iron cylinder called a "Burnetizer,"

in which cottonwood logs would be soaked in a chemical solution to make them durable enough to use as ties. The construction of machine shops and engine houses, which would
consume some two million bricks, would soon be underway.[95]

On October 10 the locomotive's namesake, Maj. Gen. William Tecumseh Sherman himself, stepped off a steamboat at
Omaha. The commander of the Division of the Mississippi was
on an inspection trip of his vast military jurisdiction. After
being feted at an October 11 reception at the Herndon House,
Sherman joined other dignitaries the next day for what may
have been the first passenger trip on the Union Pacific. The Major General Sherman, heavily draped in the national colors, including the "tattered banner of the First Nebraska Regiment,"
pulled several luminary-laden cars to Papillion Creek and back
along the fifteen miles of track that had been laid since July.[96]

Although nearly four years would pass before the rails were
joined at Promontory Summit in Utah and the transcontinental line completed, the modest accomplishments of 1865 bolstered the optimism many Omahans felt now that construction was actually underway. "As we look out from the inner
sanctum of the [Omaha] *Herald* office upon the Missouri River
bottom-lands," wrote editor George L. Miller on November 17,
"rising above the earth at a place which, ten years since, we
knew as a favorite resort of rattlesnakes and prairie wolves, we
see huge brick buildings . . . covering a large tract of ground.
. . . Today we speak of these rich ornaments, signs of our ap-
proaching greatness, as things actually accomplished and existing." At the same time, Squire Lamb informed his brother
that the roadbed had been graded within forty-five miles of
his Wood River ranche and "the cars will be here next fall."[97]

While Nebraska's physical landscape was being reshaped by
grading and track laying for the Union Pacific, the figurative

landscape of territorial politics and journalism was also chang-ing. In June W. H. H. Waters, the longtime editor of the Repub-lican *People's Press* in Nebraska City sold his interest in the pa-per. Barely two months later Waters's Democratic antagonist, Augustus "Ajax" Harvey of the *Nebraska City News*, also stepped down from the tripod. It is not clear whether either man's de-cision related to a recent physical altercation between them. The editors had exchanged personal and political barbs in print for years before their verbal sparring finally escalated to the real thing.[98]

Other Nebraska newspapers picked up the story about Har-vey being fined five dollars and costs for assault and battery against Waters. "Ajax" pronounced the fine "moderate for kick-ing a purp" and justified his fisticuffs by claiming that Waters had "upon every occasion lugged in some matter of our private affairs or personal habits" whenever he alluded to Harvey in the *People's Press*. For example, on September 22, 1864, Waters had referred to Harvey as *Nebraska City News* publisher Thomas Morton's "filthy squirt gun. . . . He is regarded as a calumnia-tor and low-lived dog by almost everybody who has ever met him." Finally, said Harvey, "We had to visit him [Waters] in his office and inflict corporeal punishment upon him." Waters, of course, saw things differently: "The filthy victim of tangle leg did come staggering into our office, and proclaimed the intention of thrashing us, but was so beastly drunk that he was helpless as a child."[99]

Shortly before Harvey left his post as editor of the *Nebraska City News*, he fired parting shots on several issues that would dominate territorial politics for months to come, the most im-portant being black suffrage and Nebraska statehood. Both re-lated to a developing, and soon to grow bitter, battle between President Andrew Johnson and Congress over the conditions by which former Confederate states would be restored to full

Fig. 20. *Nebraska City People's Press* editor
William H. H. Waters in a postwar photograph.
Nebraska State Historical Society RG2411-5899.

participation in the federal union. Related developments in Missouri, which had not seceded, prompted Harvey's initial outburst.

On June 6, 1865, Missouri adopted a new state constitution that abolished slavery and disenfranchised anyone who had expressed sympathy for or aided the rebellion in any way. Less than a month later Harvey invited Missouri residents who had been deprived of citizenship privileges by "the abolition rulers of the state" to move to Nebraska. He also extended the invitation to "the old population—the families who were brought up under and to believe in the slave labor regime,—but who have maintained a status of loyalty and therefore have not come under the proscription rule of the abolitionists." Missouri residents in those categories "we are sure will prefer living where freedom is voluntary rather than where it has been forced."[100]

It did not take long for Republican editors such as John Colhapp of the *Nebraska Advertiser* to come down hard on Ajax: "[L]anguage fails to express our contempt for the depraved political lickspittle, toady and fool who will invite this treason cursed, disorganizing and damnable element to settle in our midst." Colhapp acknowledged that newcomers from Missouri could not legally vote in the fall Nebraska election but "the copperheads hope next winter to defeat any legislation which would disfranchise them." In the end, "[i]t is not emigrants they want, but Demo-copperhead voters."[101]

Throughout the summer and fall of 1865 most of those who had elected Lincoln and Johnson in 1864 seemed to think the new president's policy toward the South was right. Johnson had laid down certain conditions for the return of the wayward states, which included drafting new constitutions abolishing slavery, nullifying secession, and repudiating Confederate debts. Because the president was a War Democrat and former slaveholder who believed in white supremacy, he prescribed that only white men could take part in this process. While the omission of any grant of suffrage to the former slaves outraged Radical Republicans, moderates in the party did not consider it a fatal flaw in the reconstruction process. They had faith that Johnson would eventually take steps to enfranchise black men to a limited degree while at the same time preventing "the lash to descend again" on their backs. Most Northern states then denied the vote to black men, and state constitutional amendments to grant black suffrage would go down to defeat in Connecticut, Wisconsin, and Minnesota at the fall 1865 elections.[102]

Although suffrage for former slaves had no immediate implications for Nebraska Territory, the issue became a topic of discussion during Independence Day observances at Nebraska City. The committee on arrangements had invited Omaha attorney Experience Estabrook, a Democrat turned Republican, to be orator of the day. His comments did not sit well with editor Harvey, whose article reporting the speech was headed, "The 4th and Sambo." Harvey blasted Estabrook for favoring universal suffrage: "The nigger was praised, glorified—deified almost—until we were nearly brought to the conclusion that Ethiopia was Paradise, ignorance and bestiality were bliss, and educated white men the menial race." Harvey also pilloried the speaker for suggesting that a justification for Nebraska becoming a state was that it could join in ratifying the Thirteenth Amendment abolishing slavery.[103]

The *Nebraska City People's Press*, now edited by William Miller, former editor of the Brownville paper, praised Estabrook for speaking of "the struggle we have been so lately engaged in with treason and slavery in such a manner as to make every one . . . realize the importance of the issue at stake." Estabrook further admonished his audience, "We have work before us, so let us buckle on our armor and join in the conflict determined to prove ourselves worthy of the ancestry we boast and never falter until the glorious cause of liberty shall be won and every man, whether white or black, made *free* in the most absolute meaning of the term."[104]

There were many shades of opinion, both nationally and in Nebraska, regarding the fate of the freedmen, but few went as far as Estabrook in advocating universal male suffrage. Many Republicans thought suffrage for the freedmen should not be a "condition precedent" for the political restoration of the former Rebel states and that neither Congress nor President Johnson had the power to grant it. Suffrage was, and had always been, a state matter. Nebraska Territory's leading Republican organs endorsed this view. The *Nebraska Republican* advised friends of universal suffrage to "labor for the education and improvement of the freedmen." Suffrage might be considered once that goal had been achieved. Brownville editor Colhapp argued, "[I]f the government will guarantee and assist him in his new sphere in living as a freeman, we think enough will have been done for the present." Even better, said Colhapp, "We would willingly pay our proportion of a tax to defray the expense of colonizing the negroes of this country in Africa or anywhere outside this Government."[105]

Most Democrats, as epitomized by Harvey, did not think the former slaves, or the free blacks of the North for that matter, should be granted any civil, economic, or political rights. As early as 1862 Harvey had attacked the administration and Congress ("Abolitionists and black-Republican violators of the Constitution") for their "nigger elevating policy." Once the war was over, the Democrats continued to exploit the racial prejudice of many Northern whites by linking the Republican Party, black suffrage, and the granting of civil rights with the specter of hordes of freedmen flooding the North to compete for jobs with white laborers and mingle with their wives and daughters.[106]

In fact, this motive became clear when the *Nebraska City News,* now edited by J. Sterling Morton, in mid-September charged the "Radicals of Nebraska," that is, the Republican (Union) Party, with making plans to grant black suffrage during the next legislative session. Afterward, said the *News,* from two to five thousand black laborers would be hired to help build the Union Pacific Railroad, "and then Radicals and niggers expect to govern Nebraska. Every man who votes against the Democracy this fall, votes for a nigger regency in the territory."[107]

This editorial showed that if "Ajax's" departure from the *Nebraska City News* had produced any deficit in the territory's budget of inflammatory and racist journalism, Morton promptly made it good after assuming the editor's chair on August 5. Taking the job signaled the end of his temporary retirement from politics after the Democrats' disastrous defeat in the 1864 elections. Morton had always been outspoken about his views on race and his fidelity to his party's conservative, states' rights view of government. During his former stint as *News* editor from 1855 to 1857, he had also demonstrated his understanding that newspapers were the primary vehicle for parties and politicians to get their message out to potential voters. His current editorship would prove no exception.[108]

Morton was soon joined on Nebraska's journalistic front lines by George L. Miller. After Omaha's longest lived Democratic paper, the *Nebraskian,* fell on hard times and ceased publication in June, its standard was picked up by Miller, whose daily and weekly *Omaha Herald* first hit the streets on October 2. Miller, too, had seemingly recovered from his crushing defeat in the 1864 delegate's race. Morton and Miller and their respective Democratic papers would prove formidable adversaries for the Republicans and their leading journals, the *Nebraska Advertiser*

215

Fig. 21. The *Daily Herald* building in Omaha, 1868.
Nebraska State Historical Society RG2341-195.

in Brownville, the *Nebraska Republican* in Omaha, and the *Nebraska Herald* in Plattsmouth, particularly as the issues of Reconstruction, statehood, and suffrage came to dominate Nebraska politics in the coming months.[109]

The fall 1865 territorial election was important primarily because it would determine who sat in the legislature's lower house during the coming session. Council members elected for two years in 1864 would carry over, and the only territorial officers subject to the ballot were the auditor and treasurer. Both parties understood that the legislature convening in January 1866 would revisit the statehood issue, and each laid plans for how best to address that question within the context of the forthcoming election.

When statehood had been put before the people in the 1864 election for delegates to a constitutional convention, most Democrats, along with many Republicans, opposed it as too costly.

Most of the delegates then chosen were pledged to adjourn the convention without forming a constitution, and they had done so promptly when the convention convened on July 4, 1864. By the fall of 1865, however, the Civil War was over, the Union Pacific Railroad was under construction, and a large emigration was bolstering the territory's population. Nevada had already become a state, and Colorado seemed poised to become one soon. Neither had been territories as long as had Nebraska. Hence, said the *Nebraska Republican*, "the time has now arrived when this subject should receive the serious consideration of our people." Unstated was the understanding that achieving statehood while the Republicans were firmly in control augured well for the party's future.[110]

Despite perceptions stemming from their antistate stance in 1864 and more recent statements by important party leaders, Nebraska Democrats in the fall of 1865 were not united in opposing statehood. As one scholar put it, "[N]either party was against statehood, per se. . . . The art lay in timing this happy consummation in order to get the maximum profit." George L. Miller, for example, favored statehood if the Democrats were to win the legislature in 1865 and "Omaha could thereby secure the services of two senators and a rep. next session [of Congress] in sustaining our old railroad line [the Union Pacific]." The problem was that prospects for Democratic victory in the fall election did not look particularly bright.[111]

In the weeks before their convention, Democratic leaders dithered over the stance the party should take. Omaha attorney E. B. Chandler noted that leading Democrats in his city would not "strenuously" oppose statehood, probably for the same reasons Miller expressed. However, because the party had been strongly against "state" in 1864, and some Democrats such as Morton continued to be so, party leaders advised against taking a stance on the issue in the platform. Thomas Bedford of

Brownville urged this course on the grounds that if the Democrats advocated statehood and it came to pass, the Republicans then in power would derive all the benefits. If statehood failed and the Democrats had remained silent, the "odium" would attach to the Republicans, who were "almost insane" on the subject and willing to do almost anything to get Democratic cooperation.[112]

Two things complicated Democratic decision making. One was the progress being made toward Colorado statehood, whose people ratified a state constitution in a September 5 election. Miller had noted earlier that if Colorado were admitted, "I tell you opinion [in Nebraska Territory] will rapidly change in favor of our own speedy admission." Colorado's fate now rested on action by Congress and the president during the forthcoming session.[113]

The second complicating factor was Andrew Johnson's reconstruction policy. Since assuming office Johnson had softened his stance on punishing the South and proposed lenient terms for the seceded states' readmission to full political equality, a policy that moved him closer to the Democratic Party's views. In early September Johnson met with Southern leaders and, through them, reminded the people of the South, "I love them and will do all in my power to restore them to that state of happiness and prosperity which they enjoyed before the madness of misguided men . . . led them astray."[114]

Nebraska Democrats were mindful of these developments and had begun praising the president's "life-long service in the Democratic party and his many bitter denunciations of abolition fanaticism." Johnson's conservative approach seemed to offer hope that Nebraska might attain statehood without being forced to adopt radical provisions such as black suffrage. As Omaha Democratic stalwart James M. Woolworth put it, "It appears as if Johnson was going to take Democratic ground . . .

as if he was about to turn the gov't over to our party to receive the cordial approval of the south and the support of the democrats in the north." Therefore, Nebraska Democrats should be noncommittal about statehood. "We may, in the course of a few months, see reasons for coming in as a state which are not now apparent." Woolworth felt so strongly about the need for his party to remain silent on the statehood issue that he sent two lengthy letters to Morton just before the party convention in Plattsmouth on September 21.[115]

As the Democrats' most committed "antistate" leader, Morton was not inclined to waffle, which he made clear in his role as chairman of the platform committee. The platform that the convention adopted had four planks. The first praised President Johnson's reconstruction policies as "wise, safe, humane, and patriotic." The president's recent comments to the Southern delegation to Washington DC "are an emphatic rebuke and repudiation" to the reconstruction policy of the Republican Party. The second plank stated that Republican efforts to force the South to enfranchise blacks were an unwarranted infringement on states' rights. The third resolved "[t]hat negroes are neither by nature nor by education entitled to political or social equality with the white race," and that the Nebraska Democrats opposed their voting or holding office in Nebraska. Finally, the statehood plank emphasized that the party considered the 1864 election for a constitutional convention, which had produced a majority against statehood, "as decisive of that question." The issue should be revived only when and if the people of Nebraska voted to hold another constitutional convention.[116]

The Republican (Union) convention had met in Plattsmouth on September 19, two days before the Democrats gathered there. Their platform also praised the "policy and patriotism" of President Johnson and expressed confidence in his pending reconstruction agenda. (The Republicans had not yet learned of Johnson's conciliatory comments to the delegation from the Southern states, and many of them were then moderates on Reconstruction.) A second plank declared that the benefits derived from the sacrifices made to win the war could be secured only by "excluding from office the disloyal." A third plank praised Nebraska soldiers for their years of patriotic toil and sacrifice, and the last invited "all loyal men," regardless of present or past party affiliation, to join the Union Party.[117]

Of course the party organs made derogatory comments about the proceedings at the rival party's convention. The Democratic *Plattsmouth Sentinel*, speaking of the Union convention, reported, "The negro show what met here on Thursday last failed to exhibit Sambo in his full manhood, but they succeeded in making him visible in their political programme. Great and glorious negro-elevating party." Not to be outdone, the *Nebraska Advertiser* began its report of the Democratic convention with a catalog of Morton's sins since his appointment as territorial secretary in 1858 by "that toad of treason James Buchanan." As for the Democratic platform, "[T]hey cannot finish up one decent resolution, but wind up each with falsehood and sneaking innuendo, unbecoming to the lowest pothouse caucus, let alone men pretending to be gentlemen assembled to frame a set of principles for a party."[118]

The two conventions nominated Democrats John S. Seaton and St. John Goodrich and Republicans John Gillespie and Augustus Kountze, respectively, for auditor and treasurer. The more important nominations of the candidates for seats in the territorial legislative assembly were made in each party's county conventions. Although the two territory-wide races were not for offices exercising much political power, a loss would tarnish the respective parties' images, so their organs kept up a drumfire of derogatory innuendo. Morton's *Nebraska City*

News claimed that Republican Kountze (a German Lutheran) was "a distant relative of the man who killed Christ," that is, Jewish. The *Plattsmouth Herald* alleged that Democratic nominee Seaton, a lieutenant in the First Nebraska regiment, was a turncoat for accepting the Copperheads' nomination, which was a blatant attempt "to 'honey' the soldiers, whose utter contempt they have so well earned."[119]

The October 10 election for the offices of auditor and treasurer favored the Republican (Union) candidates, Gillespie and Kountze, who racked up majorities of 590 and 922 votes, respectively. Gillespie had been a First Nebraska officer until the consolidation mustered him out, and his opponent was still serving in the regiment. This and voter confusion about whether Seaton was a Republican or a Democrat explained Gillespie's rather modest victory, said the *Daily Republican*. Seaton actually won the soldier vote, taking 131 of the 158 ballots cast. The paper went on to blame lack of interest for the light tally of only 6,088 total votes cast in the auditor's race. A "live issue" could be expected to poll at least 10,000 votes.[120]

The outcome of the election as it related to the races for the lower house for the upcoming session of the territorial legislature was something of a wash. Douglas and Otoe Counties, both Democratic strongholds, filled nine of their ten seats with Democrats, while Nemaha and Cass Counties elected eight Republicans, all of the seats they were apportioned. Of the thirty-eight representatives actually seated when the 1866 session opened, nineteen were Democrats and nineteen were Republicans. The Territorial Council of thirteen members had a one-vote Democratic majority.[121]

Neither party was happy with the results of the legislative election, since it failed to provide a clear mandate, one way or the other, on the statehood issue, which was bound to come up during the next session. The *Daily Republican* lamented that "the Copperheads have carried Douglas County," while the *Nebraska Advertiser* charged that the Democratic victory in Otoe County demonstrated that "Nebraska City is the greatest stronghold of Rebels and traitors west of the Missouri River." The paper also claimed that J. Sterling Morton had taken "Ajax" Harvey's invitation to disenfranchised Missourians to a whole new level in calling "for [former Missouri Confederate general Sterling] Price's men to come forward and help vote down the *blue-coated, brass-buttoned* Abolitionists." As Democratic counterpoint, *Omaha Herald* editor Miller grumped to Morton that "Cass [County] could have been as well carried as not, couldn't it? Of course it could. Men's indifference has lost to us the legislature. That damnable Nemaha plays hell with us."[122]

In the interim between the election and the opening of the eleventh legislature, set for January 4, 1866, the party newspapers continued desultory sparring over the statehood question. The *Daily Republican* blasted Morton and Miller for their "political speculation" on the issue. If the Democrats had carried the territorial election, then Morton and Miller planned "to come out fiercely for state" and subsequently seek the U.S. Senate seats that statehood would bring. If the election went against them, "they could continue to harp on 'high taxes' and 'financial ruin' as substantial reasons against . . . that measure." Now that the election was over and "the bubble had burst," said the *Republican*, Morton and Miller "have ridiculed the idea of state organization as a bold absurdity."[123]

It is true that Miller maintained at least the façade of resistance to the idea of statehood, and his *Herald* aimed barbs at "the plans and the machinations of the myriad political acrobats and harlequins who are silently pressing with unseemly importunity the subject of early state organization." Nevertheless, he was also a pragmatist. If rumors that the Union Pacific line might be relocated from the Platte Valley to the Smoky

Hill in Kansas were to become credible, said Miller, "[W]e . . . should yield our unreserved support" for statehood in order to gain congressional representation and protect Omaha's railroad interests.[124]

The *Nebraska Advertiser* sought to play on Nebraska Democrats' antipathy to black voting as a reason they should drop their resistance to statehood. It reminded readers that Congress had begun discussing whether or not to make "equal rights" a condition for the admission of all states in the future. "Will Democrats retard the present movement for State Government and thereby place themselves on record for Negro Suffrage by the delay which will bring it upon us?"[125]

Pro-state politicians, a group dominated by Republican territorial officers, devised a plan to generate a public groundswell in favor of an accelerated method for achieving statehood. They distributed printed petitions praying for the legislature to draft a state constitution during its forthcoming session. This method was justified as a money-saving measure because it would avert the need for a delegate election, followed by a constitutional convention. The petitions also mentioned "the recent action of the people of Colorado in forming a state government" as an incentive for Nebraska to move forward without delay. That the petitions did not represent a true "grass roots" push for statehood was beside the point.[126]

As Nebraskans reflected on the momentous year of 1865, they took notice that the Indian war seemed to have moderated, the Union Pacific was finally under construction, and immigration by farmers and stock raisers taking advantage of the Homestead Act was bolstering the territory's population. What that population actually was remained uncertain; estimates ranged from thirty-five thousand and upward. Crops in Nebraska had been bountiful, and the territorial economy, particularly that of Omaha, was bound to benefit as the rails threaded their way west across the plains.

Some, if not most, Nebraskans surely knew that the great issue sparking the Civil War just ended had finally been laid to rest. With the December 13, 1865, ratification of the Thirteenth Amendment, slavery was no more. A former Nebraskan living in Washington DC informed readers of the Plattsmouth newspaper about the "glorious announcement" that the amendment was now part of the U.S. Constitution. Now that all men had been secured in their equal natural rights, the remaining "great and pressing question" was whether all men would be entitled to equal civil rights, "in other words, whether artificial distinctions merely on account of the texture of the skin or *cuticle* shall be removed." Nebraskans would have an important role in answering that question during the year ahead.[127]

CHAPTER SIX

1866

"A Change of Government . . . Is Being Freely Discussed"

No matter what else might transpire in Nebraska Territory during 1866, statehood would be the dominant
issue. Parties or splinter groups thereof, public officials, newspaper editors, and individuals determined their
support for or opposition to statehood on the basis of political,
economic, or sectional self-interest. Confounding everything,
and with significant implications for Nebraska's future, were
the thorny questions of race and whether the reconstruction
plans of the president or Congress would ultimately prevail.

The major political consideration was statehood's benefits
or liabilities for the local parties and their aspirants to office.
If statehood came soon the Republicans, still under the banner of the Union Party, were likely to "hold possession of the
territory," particularly in view of the widening rift between
President Johnson and the Radical Republicans in Congress.
Many of the prominent Nebraska Republicans increasingly
sided with Congress but, as appointed territorial officials, they
risked removal by the president. The prospect of winning election to a state office beyond presidential control was therefore

appealing. Statehood would also bring Nebraska two U.S. senators and a congressman, providing additional opportunities for party stalwarts to gain elective office or to dispense patronage. While the Democrats were as interested in reaping statehood's political benefits as were their rivals, the significant setbacks they had suffered in recent elections prompted them to resist a change in government until prospects for their party's ascendancy seemed more favorable.[1]

Both parties disguised their political motives with economic or financial arguments. The Republicans continued to proclaim that statehood's expected entitlements, including large grants of public land for educational and economic endowments plus 5 percent of the revenue from public land sales, trumped concerns that state government's cost would overburden the citizens. Looking to the future, they claimed that capitalists from elsewhere would never invest in Nebraska until it "put off the territorial badge of penury." For their part, the Democrats continued to harp on the territory's still modest population and its inability to bear the heavy taxation required to support a state government, essentially recycling the argument they had used with success in 1864. While the population was certainly well below the number technically required for a representative in Congress (some 127,000 as of 1863), Nevada had already been admitted to statehood with a population that even by 1870 had barely reached 42,000, suggesting that the mere number of inhabitants would not be an overriding factor.[2]

Newspaper commentary about statehood, which had declined in volume somewhat in the immediate aftermath of the fall 1865 election, intensified as the legislature prepared to meet at the capitol in Omaha for its eleventh session. The Omaha *Daily Republican*, in an editorial titled "Spirit of the Press," summed up "the lively discussion going on in the territorial papers in relation to the state question" and admonished fellow journalists not to use the excuse that "their party was opposed to the measure" as a reason to avoid airing all viewpoints.[3]

The *Daily Republican* went on to characterize its exchanges' views. The *Nebraska City News* and the *Omaha Herald*, both Democratic organs, considered statehood as a ploy to benefit "office holders," that is, the Republican territorial officials. (In fact, the principal proponents of statehood *were* men such as Governor Saunders, Chief Justice William Kellogg, and other federal appointees.) The *Southern Nebraskian* of Falls City favored statehood, but not on the basis of having the legislature draft a constitution. Bellevue's *Nebraska Times* was flatly opposed. The December 26 issue of the *Nebraska City People's Press*, a longtime Republican paper, editorialized that state government would be "a blessing to Nebraska" but citizens should reserve judgment until they could fully evaluate the constitution that was expected to emerge from the coming legislative session. The *Daily Republican*'s editor was shocked that the *Nebraska Herald* of Plattsmouth saw the statehood movement in terms reminiscent of the sectionalism that had plagued antebellum Nebraska, that is, as an effort by those living north of the Platte, Omaha residents in particular, to protect their railroad interests at the expense of South Platters, who did not yet have a railroad. Finally, the *Nebraska Advertiser* of Brownville wholeheartedly favored statehood on grounds that Missouri, Kansas, and Colorado would profit from immigration and railroad promotion at Nebraska's expense as long as the latter remained "utterly powerless" for lack of representation in Congress.[4]

The legislature convened on January 4, and Governor Saunders delivered his annual address on January 9. Much of it was devoted to Nebraska Territory's finances and his reflections on "the return of peace and its concomitant blessings." He noted that "the subject of a change of government . . . is being freely discussed by our people" and offered a rather rosy assessment of new revenue streams that would come with statehood. The federal government was currently expending $20,000–$29,000 annually to support the territory, said the governor. Statehood would bring a donation of public lands to support schools, along with other endowments that would more than cover the costs of education and "go far towards defraying the whole expense of an economical state government."[5]

After thus calling the legislature's attention "to a few of the advantages which I believe would grow out of a change of government," the governor proclaimed, "I would in no wise wish to be understood as urging this subject upon you." Notwithstanding that disclaimer, Saunders could not help expressing "my candid opinion that the resources of Nebraska would be sooner developed and her wealth and population increased by becoming a state." The governor, of course, was well aware that pro-statehood petitions sent out of his office were already being circulated and, as the *Nebraska City Daily Press* noted in late December, it was no secret that the legislature would likely draft a state constitution before adjourning. Evidence suggests that the governor and other pro-state politicians had already been meeting behind closed doors to discuss and perhaps even draft such a document. They adopted this course to avoid the prospect that voters would reject any plan for holding a convention to draft a constitution, as they had done in 1864.[6]

The Omaha *Daily Republican* clearly favored statehood, although it tried to soft pedal its enthusiasm with editorials giving both the pros and cons. As to the cost of a state government, the *Republican* used the governor's figure of the current cost of the territorial government as a point of departure to estimate what a state government "would probably cost the people" if biennial, rather than annual, legislative sessions

were held. The bottom line came out at $20,500, even "allow-
ing liberally for salaries" of $2,000 for the governor, $1,500
for the other elected officers, and $1,800 for the chief justice.[7]

Omaha Herald editor George L. Miller, who had already signaled some ambivalence on the issue, kept the anti-statehood
flag flying while at the same time crafting a rationale by which
he might later endorse statehood. The method of achieving it
was the key, said Miller. Another convention should be called
to frame a constitution, which should then be submitted to a
vote of the people. "Let them have the naked state issue, and to
their decision we shall most humbly and cheerfully submit."[8]

Some Democrats elected to the legislature, such as Councilman J. B. Bennett of Otoe County, made no excuses for their
pro-statehood stance. Bennett wrote J. Sterling Morton that he
thought statehood was in Nebraska's best interest, as well as
that of the Democratic Party, and "now is the most favorable
time we ever have had or ever will have." Democrats should
not make it a party issue. This pronouncement must have irked
Morton, who had never wavered in his hostility to statehood,
and he could not have been pleased with the obvious division
developing within his party's ranks.[9]

By late January "state" had risen to the top of the legislature's agenda. Antistate Democrats introduced several resolutions calling for the body to foreswear taking action on a
constitution, all of which were handily defeated. On February 3 Council File 32, a resolution bundled with a state constitution to be submitted to a vote of the people, was introduced in the Council by a Democrat, John R. Porter of Omaha,
and given a first and second reading. Two days later the bill
passed the Council seven to six and was sent on to the House,
which passed it February 8 on a twenty-two to sixteen vote.
Three Democrats in the Council and four in the House provided crucial "yes" votes. The constitution that had surfaced

so suddenly was alleged to have been drafted in secret by Governor Saunders, Secretary Paddock, and Chief Justice Kellogg, among others, never printed for a reading in the legislature, and never referred to committee in the lower house. An election was set for June 2 to adopt or reject the constitution and to elect a slate of state officers.[10]

The constitution was a bare-bones document, providing the merest outline of a state government and penurious salaries for the elected officials. The governor was to receive $1,000 annually, the auditor $800, with other officers' salaries even lower. These figures undoubtedly represented an effort to undercut the claim that state government would burden the taxpayers. The *Daily Press* of Nebraska City thought the salaries meant state officers would be "expected to steal a living, the compensation offered them not being sufficient to buy their bread." The constitution's suffrage provision, which limited the franchise to white male citizens, was typical of most such documents of the day, including those operative in many Northern states. It likely also represented an effort to forestall an argument that Democrats opposed to black suffrage would otherwise be sure to use against the constitution. Hints soon surfaced that the "whites only" clause would not long remain as an unremarkable feature of Nebraska's proposed state constitution.[11]

The organs of the Democrats promptly pulled out all the stops to blast a crescendo of condemnation at the constitution and its makers. The *Omaha Weekly Herald* called it "among the most offensive political abortions of which our Territorial history furnishes any record. The mode of begetting it stamped it with odium." Morton's *Nebraska City News* asked, "Is this constitution the child of patriotism or the bastard of demagoguism? Who made it? Who authorized it to be made?" Morton returned to this theme by publishing a letter referring to "the bastard constitution of Kellogg & Co."[12]

Events transpiring in the nation's capital signaled that even if the constitution gained voter approval locally, Nebraska statehood would not merely be rubber stamped by Congress and the president. At the same time the Nebraska legislature was perfecting its constitution making, President Johnson and Congress were grappling with the issue of statehood for Colorado. Congress had passed an enabling act for that territory in 1864, as it had for Nebraska, but Coloradans rejected the first constitution. A second convention in late summer 1865 brought forth a new charter, which voters adopted. That document, also containing a "whites only" suffrage clause, was now being considered in Washington.[13]

Senator Charles Sumner of Massachusetts tried to amend the Colorado admission bill to require the "whites only" clause be stricken from the Colorado constitution. Among Nebraska newspapers, perhaps only the *Nebraska City Press* may have seen merit in Sumner's proposal at this juncture. Editor William Miller had supported equal suffrage as early as 1865, when he reported on Experience Estabrook's Independence Day speech at Nebraska City. Miller had also criticized the Nebraska constitution's bar to black men voting: "We regard this word 'white' as a compromise with treason and slavery."[14]

The Sumner amendment drew the ire of most other Nebraska editors, regardless of their party affiliation, and gave them to realize that suffrage could represent a major obstruction on Nebraska's road to statehood. Predictably, Democrats such as Morton and Miller damned the "Negro-Indian suffrage party" and the "radical zanies . . . in legislating for the degradation of the white and the exaltation of the black race." Said Morton, editorially, "It will be more manly to accept negro suffrage from Congress by legal enforcement than to humiliate ourselves by its voluntary adoption as the price of admission to the Union." Personally, "[w]e take nigger only when forced to it by Congress and therefore are for remaining at present a territory."[15]

The Republican *Nebraska Advertiser* had previously gone on record as favoring black suffrage as a political but not as a natural right. Nevertheless, said editor John Colhapp, "We . . . will kick against all attempts of Congress to force it upon us as a condition to our admission." Herman Heath, an army officer and Union Democrat who then also edited the *Nebraska Republican*, saw Sumner's amendment as "an outrage upon the independence and rights of the people of Colorado with whom we are bound to sympathize, since the chalice which the Senator from Massachusetts would press to their lips may ere long be held to ours, filled with a like draught." Heath was more prescient than he knew.[16]

The rift between Johnson and congressional Republicans over suffrage and Reconstruction promised to become a chasm with the president's February 19 veto of a bill to extend and expand the jurisdiction of the Freedmen's Bureau. That bill and an accompanying civil rights bill were both designed to protect freedmen in the former Rebel states from a "new slavery." Among other reasons, the president vetoed the bill on grounds that the states primarily affected by it were not represented in Congress. In his view the wayward states of the South had never left the Union and could, in the words of one Nebraska politician, "at any time come back with their carpet sack, deposit their hats, gloves and overcoats in the anteroom, march to their seats, and answer at roll call the same as before the rebellion." Many Republicans in Congress and elsewhere, however, contended that the seceded states were now like territories over which Congress had control, and they had not yet demonstrated sufficient political and social change (i.e., "loyalty") to qualify them for readmission.[17]

The president's stance moved him closer to the Democratic

Party, both nationally and in Nebraska. Local party stalwarts were positively giddy in the veto's aftermath. A "grand ratification meeting of the Democracy" at the Omaha courthouse was reported under the headline "Andrew Johnson Indorsed by the Unterrified Democracy of Douglas." The *Herald*'s Miller lost all restraint, proclaiming, "Nebraska is henceforth and, we hope, forever a Democratic Territory." The president's "bold and vigorous espousal of Democratic theories and doctrines . . . imparts a moral force to, and constitutes a vindication so complete of the positions assumed by the Democracy that their power to wrest the nation from Radical rule is admitted."[18]

Nor had conservative Republicans and Union Democrats given up on Johnson. Although there had been erosion of the Republicans' support, as recently as February 10 the legislature had passed a resolution that endorsed the president's overall policy. Herman Heath urged a "wait and see" approach in one of his last editorials for the *Daily Republican*. Johnson was still a "great patriot" deserving of support, though Heath was not surprised "that Congress refuses admission to representatives from such disloyal constituencies." Colhapp of the *Nebraska Advertiser* remained foursquare for Johnson, warning Copperheads not to claim him as a kindred spirit: "His every act and deed is pregnant with true radicalism, which must work in harmony with the Constitution, with honest conviction of duty, and with the true Union party which seeks a united, prosperous, and permanent union of all the States." At this stage conservative members of the Republican (Union) Party were still standing by the president, while other Republicans remained silent.[19]

It was not long, however, before the more radical Nebraska Republicans began to echo their contemporaries in Congress by denouncing the president's reconstruction policy and his veto of the Freedmen's Bureau bill. After Heath left the editorial chair of the *Nebraska Republican* in late February, the paper returned to its more liberal stance. It skewered the new love fest between Johnson and the Democrats, noting that "Democrats formerly elected presidents; now they are willing to kidnap one." Plattsmouth's *Nebraska Herald* damned the president's veto and its endorsement by the Democrats. Unlike the Democrats of the North, "the gallant black . . . shouldered a musket and fought for our common nationality." The veto "is calculated to throw four millions of people [former slaves] . . . upon the mercy of unrepentant rebels—who proclaim unblushingly that they are 'only whipped, not conquered.'" Many of the federally appointed officials kept their mouth shut for the time being to avoid complicating prospects for the state constitution's acceptance at the June 2 election and statehood's subsequent approval in Washington.[20]

These issues would continue to fester and intensify as the Nebraska parties geared up for their conventions and the campaign leading up to the June 2 election. Because the election would also choose state officers-in-waiting, pending voter approval of the constitution and Nebraska's expected admission, the parties had to choose candidates or, in the case of the Democrats, decide whether they would present any at all. Just before the parties were to convene, news reached Nebraska of new developments in the nation's capital. On March 27 Johnson vetoed a civil rights bill that declared all persons born in the United States to be citizens and generally provided black Americans the equal protection of the law, though not suffrage or the right to serve on juries. On April 9 Congress overrode the veto, though the episode's main effect was to convince congressional Republicans that only a constitutional amendment would finally safeguard the rights and security of the former slaves. Hence, on June 13 Congress adopted the Fourteenth Amendment for ratification by the states.[21]

The Republicans, still labeling themselves as the Union Party, met in Plattsmouth on April 12. They nominated David Butler as their candidate for governor. Thomas P. Kennard, John Gillespie, and Augustus Kountze were tapped for secretary of state, auditor, and treasurer, respectively. Turner M. Marquett was the nominee for the seat in Congress. The platform was largely a catalog of the advantages to be gained from statehood. Many Republicans were still ambivalent about the president's policies or, if they were appointed officials, did not want to risk the prospect that he might replace them. The platform did not directly mention either Congress or the chief executive, noting only that the party "owes it to itself, to its cherished principles and to humanity to secure liberty and equality before the law to all men." Brownville editor Colhapp felt "[t]he Convention did wisely in asserting the principle of equal rights; and would have acted very unwisely to have condemned or lauded either Congress or the President." Morton of the *Nebraska City News* pointed out the inconsistency between the "equal rights" Republican platform and the "whites only" constitution that was to be the Republicans' passport to statehood.[22]

The Democrats remained divided over statehood and unsure whether the party should or should not nominate candidates for state offices. Doing so would be tantamount to endorsing the idea of a state government, while declining to make nominations would shut the Democrats out if the voters adopted the constitution at the June election and Congress then admitted Nebraska. In a letter to Morton, the most uncompromising antistate Democrat, George Miller argued that the party could not afford to risk everything on defeating the constitution and should make nominations. Several of the county delegations, including the one from Douglas County, were "pledged to state and the nomination of a ticket."[23]

"Ajax" Harvey was another Democrat who strongly favored

statehood. In the spring of 1866 he began publishing the pro-
statehood *Nebraska Statesman* at Nebraska City, ending his brief
hiatus from journalism. Harvey saw the local benefits of statehood as overriding all other considerations, even the potential election of "radicals" to Nebraska's new seats in Congress.
While such an outcome might be considered as "a calamity in
our national politics, . . . [i]t is of infinitely more importance to
us to have two men in the senate and one in the house—three
votes in Congress—with an influence that can be felt in carrying forward railroad enterprises for us and helping to sustain
in Washington the power that the Great West has, or ought to
have, in the nation, than to reject the attainment of such influence because forsooth, Governor Saunders, Judge Kellogg,
Secretary Paddock, O. H. Irish, or James Sweet, esq. might be
a senator."[24]

Surprisingly, Morton did not strongly resist the nomination
of a state ticket at the party's April 19 convention in Nebraska
City and even allowed himself to be anointed the candidate
for governor. As chairman of the platform committee, he was
able to keep out any direct favorable reference to statehood
and emphasized "states rights" and "fundamental doctrines
and tenets of democracy" by using language drawn verbatim
from Thomas Jefferson's first inaugural address as the pream-
ble and first plank of the platform. The remaining planks endorsed President Johnson's "legitimate endeavors to restore,
under the constitution, the several states to their legal status
in the American Union," condemned "the destructive policies of the Stevens, Sumner, and Fred Douglass directory," and
asked all Nebraskans to aid in verifying the "historic saying" of
Andrew Johnson: "This is and shall be a government of white
men and for white men."[25]

The lack of any specific allusion to statehood in the Democratic platform made it hard for the Republicans to exploit the

split over that issue in the rival party's ranks. The *Nebraska Advertiser* called the platform "the greatest medley of sense and nonsense, treason and a stagger at loyalty, copperheadism and Democracy that could be hatched up by even so gifted a cuss as J. S. Morton." Because he had so urged Morton before the convention, George Miller was privately pleased that his party had put up a ticket. Editorially, he kept up the antistate façade, noting that, "while this [nomination of a ticket] was contrary to our own views, we hail the result with satisfaction."[26]

Just before the formal campaign kicked off, word came that Congress had passed the Colorado admission bill without requiring the "whites only" voting clause to be stricken out, but the president had vetoed the bill nevertheless. Nebraska observers ascribed the veto to Colorado Territory's small population, probably no more than thirty thousand now that the Colorado gold rush had waned in favor of the more recent discoveries in Idaho and Montana. That the "white" restriction in Colorado's constitution had made it through Congress encouraged Nebraska's pro-state forces that the same requirement in theirs might not, after all, be a bar to admission, provided the voters approved the document in the coming election.[27]

After the territory-wide conventions nominated candidates for state offices, county conventions selected nominees for seats in the first state legislature, which would meet on July 4 if the constitution were approved. Although the campaign for "state" had been ongoing in some sense since before the fall 1865 election, the formal political canvass leading up to the June 2 election occupied barely a month. The newspapers were filled with charges and countercharges. Prominent men of both parties flooded the territory, sometimes speaking independently and at other times debating their rivals on a range of issues, including statehood, the reconstruction policies of the president and Congress, and equal suffrage. Gubernatorial candidates Morton and Butler debated several times, initially in a correspondence "war" to arrange the debate schedule, each charging the other with dodging the issues, misrepresenting each other's position, or broaching irrelevant subjects. Their letters were published in the newspapers.[28]

Reportage of the debates themselves in the partisan journals of the day made up in color what it lacked in objectivity. George Miller's Democratic *Omaha Weekly Herald* published a letter by "Farmer," who had taken in the Morton-Butler clash in Brownville:

> The greatest triumph ever achieved in this Territory was last night by J. S. Morton over a galaxy of Radicals consisting of Hon. D. Butler, candidate for governor, Jno. I. Redick of Omaha and Jno. Chapman. . . . He handled the Radicals without gloves, especially David, whom he demolished even to exciting sympathy from me (if I had any for a Rad). . . . [T]he entire Radical party will be out as curs yelping on the track of Morton ere he arrives at your place, but you need give yourself no trouble, he is enough for the entire outfit.[29]

The *Omaha Daily Republican* reported a debate in the capital city between Morton and Republican Party stalwart John M. Thayer, commander of the First Nebraska Regiment at the beginning of the war: "The debate took the course which everyone who has been long acquainted with Morton supposed it would. He dodged all of the questions before the people of the Territory, and went off at a tangent on miscegenation and general blackguardism. These are both 'sacred rights' of their southern democratic brethren and we are not surprised that the doughface Morton, their golden circle champion at the north, should insist upon these glorious privileges with such pertinacity."[30]

The campaign was enlivened by the participation of George Francis Train, entrepreneur, world traveler, author, orator, Union

Pacific promoter-financier, and a man once characterized as a "genius of eccentricity" rather than as an eccentric genius. He was also a Democrat who supported statehood because he thought his own financial interests in the Union Pacific and Omaha would benefit thereby. Train also endorsed the president and opposed equal suffrage. Some Republicans thought Train was simply providing cover so Morton did not have to take a position on "state" when they made their joint campaign appearances.[31]

Nebraska's long-serving volunteer soldiers, still garrisoning trail outposts from Fort Kearny westward to Mud Springs, were distant observers, if at all, of the political battles leading up to the June 2 election. From the onset of their last six months in Uncle Sam's army, concerns about Indians and a persistent longing for their discharge to civilian life occupied the soldiers' minds much more than territorial politics.

In January and February the First Nebraska men joined in yet another exhausting winter campaign, reminiscent of the one General Mitchell led from Fort Cottonwood a year earlier. The 1866 expedition had a similar goal, to hunt down Indians in southwestern Nebraska and northwestern Kansas, and a similar result. It was in charge of Lt. Col. R. H. Brown of the Twelfth Missouri Cavalry, whose unit was still on the plains following the aborted Powder River campaign of the previous summer and fall. The troop complement comprised five companies of the First Nebraska, six companies of the Seventh Iowa, seven companies of the Twelfth Missouri, a company from the Sixth regiment of Galvanized Yankees, and smaller detachments from the Second U.S. Cavalry and the Eighteenth U.S. Infantry. Also along were Captain Frank North's company of Pawnee Scouts and two mountain howitzers.[32]

The troops left Fort Cottonwood on January 6 and established a base camp six days later on the north side of the Republican River, five miles east of the mouth of Medicine Creek. A temporary storehouse and hospital were constructed at Camp Wheaton, named for the District of Nebraska commander. Several men, including four First Nebraska soldiers, were sent out on January 23 to scout for Indians. They found a few, and one Seventh Iowa soldier named Rowley was killed in a brief skirmish. The main command left Camp Wheaton on January 30 en route to the south fork of the Solomon River in Kansas, where a buffalo charged into camp and gored a horse to death before the Pawnee Scouts killed the beast. By February 19 the troops were back at Fort McPherson (formerly Fort Cottonwood), concluding a forty-four-day trek covering some three hundred miles. One officer's journal summed up the frustrating results: "Every effort was made to find and punish the Indians, but without success, . . . having lost one man killed, three horses lost on the road by deserting them, one horse killed by a buffalo, and five horses died of overwork and disease." The officer forgot to count the buffalo among the casualties.[33]

The Nebraska volunteers had not been totally forgotten by territorial officials. On January 23, while many of the troops were out on their expedition, Governor Saunders urged the legislature to pass a joint resolution requesting the secretary of war to order the regiment's discharge. The legislature duly passed the resolution, which was forwarded to the War Department. On March 15 the adjutant general's office notified Territorial Secretary Paddock that the First Nebraska would be mustered out as soon as it could be relieved by regular army troops slated to leave Fort Leavenworth on May 1.[34]

The vanguard of the regular army relief force, in the shape of the headquarters staff and the second battalion of the Eighteenth U.S. Infantry, had already reached Fort Kearny in November 1865. While awaiting the arrival of more troops come spring, regimental commander Henry Carrington employed his men and others, including men of the First Nebraska, in sprucing up Fort Kearny, which had fallen into significant disrepair. Carrington also planned to finally span the quicksands of the Platte River with a timber bridge to be built by the troops and sent parties to scour the countryside for sturdy oak and cedar. Before the bridge scheme could be accomplished, the Eighteenth U.S Infantry left Fort Kearny en route to build and occupy new posts along the Bozeman Trail in the Powder River country.[35]

Carrington's force arrived at Fort Laramie on June 13, just in time to disrupt a treaty council underway there. The council was part of the government's peace initiative in the wake of the 1865 Powder River Expedition. Following the pattern set by the Edmunds and Doolittle negotiations the previous fall with tribes on the southern plains and in Dakota, the president appointed a commission to treat with the northern bands of Sioux, Cheyennes, and Arapahos who had resisted General Connor's offensive. In March, three months after emissaries were dispatched to the Indian camps to announce the pending council, word came that the Indians would come in to talk. The council, chaired by Edward B. Taylor of Omaha, head of the Northern Superintendency and former editor of the *Omaha Republican*, opened in early June. In addition to friendly chiefs such as Spotted Tail of the Brules and the leaders of the "Laramie Loafers," Red Cloud and other Oglala war leaders were present, along with a few Northern Cheyennes and Arapahos.[36]

Taylor's representations of the government's desire for peace and what he could promise the Indians to achieve it apparently omitted any acknowledgment that a plan was afoot to station troops and build more forts along the Bozeman Trail. The arrival of Carrington's command at Fort Laramie on June 13 made this omission patently obvious, prompting Red Cloud and other leaders of the northern Indians to withdraw from the council in protest, at the same time promising resistance if soldiers were sent into their hunting grounds. Taylor and his commission proceeded to "sign up" the friendly chiefs who had no stake in the Powder River region, then blithely reported that the Indians "acquiesced in our request [for a road through their hunting grounds] . . . after a full expression of sentiment had taken place on both sides." Taylor characterized the negotiations as "a treaty entirely concluded with the Ogallala and Brule Sioux" and "thoroughly understood by every Indian who signed it." He dismissed Red Cloud and his followers as nothing more than a small minority of "refractory and desperate characters of the tribe."[37]

The resulting treaty, which the *Omaha Herald* branded the "Laramie Abortion," was hardly worth the effort involved in its negotiation, and it certainly did not bring peace to the northern plains. No one could doubt its failure after Red Cloud and his allies wiped out a substantial portion of Carrington's command near Fort Phil Kearny at the base of the Bighorn Mountains in the so-called Fetterman Massacre on December 21, 1866.[38]

Meanwhile, the men of the First Nebraska lived out their monotonous existence at the Platte Valley outposts, still waiting for orders that would send them home. On Election Day, June 2, polls were opened for several companies of the regiment stationed at Fort Kearny. Other companies located at small trail enclaves, such as Scherneckau's Company H, evidently did not have the opportunity to vote. The votes cast by the soldiers at Fort Kearny would figure prominently in the election's outcome, giving the men an unexpected role in Nebraska's statehood struggle.

The question of statehood for Nebraska should have provided the "live issue" the *Nebraska Republican* predicted would poll ten thousand votes when it reflected on the modest turn-out following the fall 1865 election. Based on that prediction, the returns from the June 2 statehood election must have been disappointing. Barely eight thousand votes were cast in the race for governor and even fewer, pro and con, for the constitution. The tallies trickled in from around the territory for several days, and not until near month's end did the official vote become known. It showed the constitution passing by a 100-vote majority and David Butler elected governor over J. Sterling Morton by 145 votes. All the major state offices except one were in the hands of Republicans. The outcome was decided by what became known as the Rock Bluffs contest.[39]

As one of the early state histories put it, "The disgraceful record of elections and election contests in the territory finds a fitting climax in the exclusion of the vote of Rock Bluffs, a precinct of Cass County." The county canvassing board headed by County Clerk Burwell Spurlock threw out all the votes cast in Rock Bluffs precinct on a technicality, costing Butler 50 votes and Morton 107. Not counting the Rock Bluffs vote also made Republicans the winners in six Cass County legislative races, for which Spurlock awarded certificates of election. Predictably, the Republican papers approved of the decision and the Democratic editors were apoplectic, particularly George Miller of the *Omaha Herald*. He was so exercised, said Plattsmouth editor H. D. Hathaway, "Our up-river contemporary of the *Omaha Herald* . . . will probably succeed in moistening his under-garments before he gets entirely over it."[40]

The territorial canvassing board consisting of Governor Saunders, Chief Justice William Kellogg, and Territorial District Attorney Daniel Gantt, all Republicans, accepted the Cass County canvassing board's decision and also the votes cast by First Nebraska soldiers at Fort Kearny that went heavily for Butler and for the constitution. Some of the soldiers there had enlisted from Iowa in 1861 and still claimed that state as their legal residence, making them ineligible to vote in a Nebraska election. Capt. John P. Murphy of Company I, who had enlisted from Page County, Iowa, in 1861 and knew most of the Iowa men in the First Nebraska, signed an affidavit listing sixteen Iowa soldiers who voted on June 2. The same men, said Murphy, had voted in the 1865 Iowa election. One soldier whose name appeared in the poll books at Fort Kearny had been mustered out of the regiment two years earlier. As Morton of the *Nebraska City News* put it, "[M]any a 'loyal' voter at the election of June 2, 1866, in Nebraska was depositing his vote far, far away from his home and the 'girl he left behind him.'"[41]

The *Nebraska Republican*, on the other hand, praised "this gallant regiment, the pride of Nebraska, [which] has again spoken through the ballot box and the result is truly cheering to all loyal men. . . . The legislature is undoubtedly Republican; this secures to the Union party two U.S. Senators, and without the aid of the Nebraska 1st, we might have failed." A total of 193 soldiers voted in the race for governor and 166 on the state constitution. The Democrats alleged that some forty soldiers who voted were not Nebraska residents. While records are too sketchy to provide reliable statistics on this question or on how the presumed illegal votes were divided in the important races, the *Nebraska Republican* was right about one thing: the territorial canvassing board's acceptance of the soldiers' votes helped carry the election for the Republicans.[42]

Had the Rock Bluffs vote been counted and the entire soldier vote been disallowed, Morton and the other Democrats would have been elected and the constitution defeated, leaving a slate of state officers without a document under which they might take office. On behalf of outraged Democrats, Omaha attorney James M. Woolworth drafted a scathing "Address to the Public" that detailed "the history of the last scheme to force a state government upon you against your will." Published in pamphlet form, the address reviewed the statehood issue beginning with the 1864 enabling act and tracing it through the June 2 election and the subsequent canvass of the votes. Woolworth boldly stated that the constitution "was represented to have received the approval of, when in fact it was rejected by, the people." The Democrats would cling to this position even after statehood became a fact. Twenty-one Democratic members of the first "state" legislature endorsed Woolworth's treatise.[43]

There was no certainty that Democratic votes were free of taint. Republicans remained convinced that disenfranchised Missourians had voted illegally in Otoe County in 1865 and again in this election. One Republican newspaper printed a deposition claiming that a Democrat serving as a judge of election in Rock Bluffs precinct was not a Nebraska resident. In fact this was one of the grounds upon which the Rock Bluffs vote had been disallowed. James R. Porter of Plattsmouth wrote Morton after the election that "there are many no doubt that voted irregularly on each side, and were the truth all told which side would have the adds [additional votes] I could not say." George L. Miller, who had privately harbored the view that statehood would benefit Omaha, accepted the election's outcome, fraudulent or not, with a degree of realism that belied the Plattsmouth paper's claim of his outrage: "We receive the verdict of our people and bow to it as rendered."[44]

On the heels of the election came June 10 orders that the First Nebraska Veteran Volunteers were to turn over all public property and proceed to Omaha for discharge. By June 18 the veterans were encamped on the outskirts of the capital city. Having been retained in the service for more than a year after the Civil War proper had ended and almost forgotten in Nebraskans' rush to put the war behind them, the soldiers were denied a joyful homecoming with waving flags and cheering crowds. Englishman Joseph Barker Jr., who had made Omaha his home, saw the veterans arrive: "They were a dirty stained, battered lot of men, just like the old stampeeders we used to see coming in 7 years ago. The mules and horses seemed worn out. And the men with their long hair and burnt appearance looked more like Indians. There was no Glorious Pomp of war to be seen. However, they will do good to the town. They are to be paid off here and will have plenty of money to spend."[45]

The Democratic press, including the *Omaha Herald* and the *Nebraska City News*, welcomed the veterans but could not resist giving the homecoming a political cast connected with the recent election. A *News* correspondent claimed that when three of the companies were finally mustered out, the men "threw up their hats, pulled off their jackets, and actually danced for joy, exclaiming, 'we are free at last, we can now vote as we like.'" The *Herald* praised the "gallant Democrats" of the returning regiment, who "stand by Andrew Johnson's policy of restoring that Union in defense of which so much blood and treasure have been expended." Several of the officers and soldiers demonstrated that the *Herald*'s mention of their Democratic Party bona fides was not entirely wishful thinking. Three captains and an unstated number of enlisted men held a meeting and adopted resolutions endorsing the president and his policies.[46]

Politics aside, the regimental officers gave a complimentary dinner to the men on June 29, attended by Governor Saunders and leading citizens of Omaha and the territory. The occasion was tempered with regrets on the "eve of the sundering of the relations which had so long existed between the participants. ... The soldiers of the Nebraska First will ever remember this last social reunion of its members as one of the green spots in their lives." More than a year after the guns fell silent at Appomattox Courthouse, the five-year saga of Nebraska's preeminent Civil War regiment came to an end. Of the complement of nearly a thousand First Nebraska officers and men who left Omaha in late July 1861, only about 150 still remained in the regiment when it was finally mustered out. This tiny remnant had truly stood "firmly by the flag" as the rest of their comrades experienced the attrition of war. A few died in battle, many more from accidents or disease, while most melted from the ranks due to disability, desertion, or discharge.[47]

By this time the companies of the Seventh Iowa Volunteer Cavalry had already marched from their scattered stations to be mustered out at Fort Leavenworth on May 17. The last of the volunteer soldiers still on the plains were the Galvanized Yankees, and the army brass decided that they, too, could now be discharged. Seven companies of the Fifth U.S. Volunteers serving along the Platte assembled at Fort Kearny on October 11, and there they were released from the service. Many of them undoubtedly stayed in the West rather than returning to the war-ravaged South from whence they had come. Two who did so were John Colby Griggs, a Nebraska resident until 1892, when he moved to South Dakota, and George W. Colhoff, who clerked for Red Cloud Agency trader Frank Yates in the 1870s.[48]

As the new constitution provided, the initial session of the state legislature convened on July 4 to elect two U.S. senators who could take their seats once Congress and the president actually admitted Nebraska. Although state governor–elect David Butler had no lawful authority, he nonetheless delivered an "inaugural" address. Most of it was laced with the bright prospects Butler could foresee for the new state-to-be. He estimated the population at seventy thousand and opined that the "vexed question" of the elective franchise was "about to be placed beyond the reach of agitation by an amendment to the Constitution of the United States." The pending Fourteenth

Amendment to which Butler referred "will in due course of time permanently settle the political status of the African." In fact, said the governor-elect, the legislature should act on it "during your present session." Perhaps he thought a positive expression on the amendment would curry some favor with Congress to move quickly on Nebraska's admission.[49]

Before the legislature could elect U.S. senators, it had to dispose of the contest filed by Cass County Democrats who felt they had been defrauded of their seats in the legislature. The Republicans who had been awarded election certificates by the county canvassing board had already occupied the seats. The Committee on Privileges and Elections refused to consider depositions that claimed to prove the Democratic contestants had won, and the legislature allowed the Republicans from Cass County "to vote for themselves on the resolutions of . . . the election committee, and thus gave the House [and Senate] permanently to the Republicans." The Republicans took the view that, at most, there could be nothing more than honest doubt about the legality of the transactions surrounding the Rock Bluffs vote. "Believing this, they proceeded to give themselves the benefit of the doubt rather than to give it to their political enemies." Subsequently, the two houses defeated resolutions coming from the Democratic side praising President Johnson and calling for an investigation of Republican officials. The legislature passed a resolution introduced by the Republicans asking Congress to grant statehood.[50]

On July 11 the legislature, in joint session, accepted nominations for U. S. senators, one seat to be filled from south of the Platte River and one from north of it. House member Charles H. Gere reported that "there were 15 actual candidates for the U.S. Senate, all electioneering among the 51 legislators." The Republicans nominated John M. Thayer of Omaha and Thomas W. Tipton of Brownville, both of whom had strong ties to the

Fig. 22. Thomas W. Tipton, chaplain of the First Nebraska
Regiment from 1861 to 1865, served as one of Nebraska's first
two U.S. senators once statehood was achieved in 1867.
Nebraska State Historical Society RG2411-5631.

Civil War service of the First Nebraska regiment, while the Democrats put forth J. Sterling Morton of Nebraska City and A. J. Poppleton of Omaha. To no one's surprise Thayer and Tipton were elected. Because this transitional period from territory to state presented so many opportunities to snag a public office, Nebraska was overrun with aspirants, said Gere. With the Senate seats decided, "there are 13 patriots left willing to stand their chance for Congress next fall."[51]

Notwithstanding the brevity of their session and their status as "state legislators-in-waiting," the members experienced a perk of office in the form of a July 7 junket to the Union Pacific's end of track. Most representatives and several senators, along with territorial and state officers and dignitaries from both parties, took advantage of railroad vice president Thomas Durant's invitation. Three elegant passenger coaches and a baggage car, drawn by the locomotive Omaha, chugged out of town at twenty-five miles per hour and reached Columbus by noon. After a lunch washed down with champagne and enlivened by speeches, the train proceeded to a site some forty miles west of Columbus where the rails were then being laid. The rapidity of the work astonished one observer who claimed that while he was looking at the track, "it passed out of sight." The excursionists were back in Omaha by 10:00 p.m., pleased with the railroad's "almost prodigal hospitality."[52]

Completion of the Union Pacific to Columbus had a significant effect on overland freighting in Nebraska Territory and marked the beginning of the end for that important industry. Considerable savings could be gained if the government and private contractors shipped their goods from Omaha to Columbus on the railroad. As the rails continued their inexorable reach westward, the distance freight had to be hauled by wagon to its final destination steadily decreased. This reduction became especially important as the government fortified the Bozeman Trail in 1867, and these changes greatly benefited Omaha at the expense of Nebraska City, Plattsmouth, and depots in Kansas. In the summer and fall of 1866 some six million pounds of government freight was shipped from Omaha by rail to the end of track. Another boost came with Omaha's selection in March 1866 as headquarters of the army's Department of the Platte.[53]

Much of the 1866 trade consisted of grain, which also benefited Nebraska producers. By August the Union Pacific had attained its goal of building to a point opposite Fort Kearny and pushed on to just beyond North Platte before winter set in. Distances that had once taken freighters and their ponderous ox or mule trains two weeks to traverse could now be spanned by rail in a matter of hours. While a few freighters still set off from Nebraska City and other river towns in the spring of 1867, the railroad had now superseded an industry that had dominated the Nebraska economy for most of the decade. While Omaha boomed, Nebraska City declined from a near rival in size and activity to become "a rather quiet little river town."[54]

Just after the state legislature adjourned and Senators-Elect Thayer and Tipton left for the national capital to urge Nebraska's admission, word came that President Johnson on July 16 had vetoed a new Freedmen's Bureau bill, a veto that Congress promptly overrode. The veto was the last straw for many of the president's supporters in Nebraska's Republican (Union) Party. The *Nebraska Advertiser* blasted Johnson for "now playing for the benefit of rebels." Editor Colhapp cataloged a host of laws the former Rebel states had enacted that, absent the Freedmen's Bureau, would be used to keep the former slaves "shackled into the hands of the tyrant." "Let who will stick to Andrew Johnson; if our readers will forgive us for our past course in sustaining him for his *past patriotic record*, we will try not to be dazed by it in future." By contrast, the president's course further endeared him to Nebraska Democrats and conservative Republicans.[55]

News of more direct significance to Nebraska, both good and bad, soon arrived. On July 23 Senator Benjamin Wade of Ohio introduced the Nebraska admission bill, which passed both the Senate and the House on July 27, the day before the first session of the Thirty-Ninth Congress adjourned. What's more, neither house saw fit to include Senator Sumner's amendment to strike out the "whites only" clause, though Sumner had proposed it. The bad news was that President Johnson left the admission bill on his desk without signing it, and there it died once Congress adjourned.[56]

The vetoes widened a split that had been forming in Nebraska's Union Party ranks. Republicans currently holding appointive office and others favoring statehood no longer saw a reason to avoid risking Johnson's ire and sided with Congress. The president had already signaled that he would be going after Radicals and replacing them with his supporters, yet it seemed clear his power was waning. Some conservative Republicans, however, who were generally in agreement with the president's reconstruction policy or who wanted to curry presidential favor to protect an existing office or possibly to gain appointment to one, shifted further toward the president. They included Chief Justice William Kellogg, Superintendent of Indian Affairs Edward B. Taylor, and Secretary Algernon S. Paddock. Johnson's Nebraska supporters, both Democrats and conservative Republicans, began organizing "Johnson Clubs" to select delegates to a so-called National Union Convention scheduled to convene in Philadelphia on August 14. A national coalition of pro-Johnson conservatives favoring the immediate readmission of the former Confederate states without strings attached had organized the convention. Perhaps a new conservative party might even grow from this nucleus.[57]

One of the conservative movement's principal spokesmen in Nebraska was Herman H. Heath, a War Democrat who came to the territory in 1863 as an officer in the Seventh Iowa Volunteer Cavalry. After Colonel Livingston was mustered out, Heath commanded the East Subdistrict of Nebraska and, while still in the army in the fall of 1865, purchased an interest in Omaha's *Nebraska Republican*. Heath used the paper to support the president and won election to the 1866 territorial legislature from Kearney County on the Union ticket. After he was denied his seat on grounds that he was ineligible because he had been elected while in the army, Heath sold out his interest in the newspaper. He then went off to Washington DC to pull strings to gain his own patronage appointment. His role in the Nebraska Johnson coalition was part of that agenda.[58]

Heath first sent a long letter to the president outlining the anti-Johnson transgressions of Nebraska officials ranging from Governor Alvin Saunders and Superintendent of Indian Affairs Edward B. Taylor on down to Indian agents and land office receivers. Their main fault, according to Heath, was not that they had overtly criticized the president but that they had damned him with faint praise by not endorsing his policies. He went on to list conservatives whom the president should appoint to replace the sitting officials. Heath offered no specific candidate to replace Governor Saunders, but the appointee should be "some man in whose judgment the President can have entire confidence," obviously meaning himself. Heath's real goal and that of other Johnson loyalists of whatever political stripe was a political office, said the *Nebraska Herald*: "[E]very office holder has a pack of these purps with empty maws snarling and snapping at his heels. The whole crowd of the 'outs' can be summed up in their desire to be 'ins.'" Little more than a year before, these men "likened Andrew Johnson to Caligula's horse, giving the latter the preference. But a small post office or the prospect of it appears to have turned this 'beast' into a saint."[59]

Heath returned to Nebraska in late July to organize a convention to select the Nebraska delegates to the August 14 convention in Philadelphia. The August 1 meeting chose Heath himself and three others and passed a resolution calling for the dismissal of "disloyal" territorial officials. In the end three separate factions of the Nebraska "Johnsonites" sent delegates to the Philadelphia convention. The disparate groups making up the Johnson coalition had trouble submerging their former rivalries in working toward a common goal. As recently as January Heath had been "abusing the copperheads" such as Morton during Heath's battle for his legislative seat. For his part, Morton in an October 1865 editorial had pilloried Heath as an "artful dodger" who could not be trusted.[60]

Despite the accession of several prominent Republicans, including Territorial Secretary Algernon S. Paddock (one of the "renegades . . . who think more of trying to get some little office than they do of the great principles of Truth, Liberty, and Justice," said the *Nebraska Herald*), the Johnson party in Nebraska as well as nationally ended up being dominated by Democrats, who had become the president's staunchest supporters once they realized he shared their views on race and Reconstruction. J. Sterling Morton and George L. Miller, the latter by proxy, both attended the Philadelphia convention and while en route made a side trip to pay their respects to Johnson at the White House. After introductions by former Nebraska governor William A. Richardson, Miller and Morton chatted with the president about statehood and the Nebraska admission bill, which Johnson noted was still lying on his desk. At that, Morton responded, "If the bill lied there as well as its friends lied for it, it would continue there for some time."[61]

The death of the Nebraska admission bill by pocket veto meant that statehood would not be revisited until the short session of the Thirty-Ninth Congress convened in December. Accordingly, the regularly scheduled Nebraska election set for the first Tuesday in October would be held as usual to fill seats for the twelfth session of the territorial legislature opening in January. It would also choose members of a provisional state legislature because the terms of the senators and representatives elected on June 2, 1866, expired on the first Monday in January 1867. The state officers elected in June held two-year terms expiring in January 1869 and remained eligible to assume their offices whenever statehood came. Both a territorial delegate and a congressman would also be elected, one or the other to take his seat in Congress depending on the statehood outcome.[62]

The Republicans held their joint territorial and state nominating convention at Brownville on September 6. John Taffe of Omaha was the nominee for representative in Congress and Turner Marquett of Plattsmouth was the nominee for territorial delegate. The sitting territorial auditor and treasurer, John Gillespie and Augustus Kountze, were renominated. The two men had already been elected to two-year terms in the comparable state offices at the June election and thus could serve under statehood without further action. The Republican platform was the complete text of the pending Fourteenth Amendment to the U.S. Constitution, with added resolutions commending the Union soldiers and proclaiming "[t]hat loyalty shall direct and control the destinies of this nation." The follow-up county conventions nominated the same individuals to run for seats in both the territorial and state legislatures.[63]

The Democrats and Johnson Republicans met September

11 on different floors of the same building in Plattsmouth to pick their candidates for territorial and state offices. The Democrats nominated J. Sterling Morton for delegate to Congress, Frank Murphy for auditor, and Andrew Dellone for treasurer. The conservative Republicans were allowed to name the candidate for representative in Congress and for territorial librarian, and they chose Territorial Secretary Algernon Paddock and Robert C. Jordan, respectively. Both conventions embraced the resolutions from the August National Union Party convention in Philadelphia as their platforms. The key planks stated that Congress had no authority to deny the former Rebel states immediate readmission; that the U.S. Constitution gave the states, not Congress, authority to set suffrage qualifications; that the Constitution could be amended only if all the states had an equal voice and vote; and that President Johnson's reconstruction policy was proper and deserved respect and sincere support. The Radical Republican press in Nebraska had a field day branding the amalgamated convention as the "great Plattsmouth muddle" and nominees Morton and Paddock as "the premature offspring" of the marriage between the Democratic Party and "the what-is-it party."[64]

As the most prominent Johnson Republican, Paddock's "apostasy" drew broadsides from the Republican press. The *Nebraska Republican* devoted a full-page supplement to the territorial secretary's sins. Paddock had "jumped into the awful vortex of Copperheadism and rebellion." He was "a traitor to his party and his own former principles, and political traitors ought to be politically shot down." The paper conceded that Paddock had made great efforts for "state" and to elect a Republican legislature back in June. These efforts, however, were only calculated to help him win one of the Nebraska seats in the U.S. Senate. When he failed to do so, he "went with unseemly haste to Washington and secured his reappointment to the secre-

Fig. 23. Territorial Secretary Algernon S. Paddock
also served periodically as acting governor.
Nebraska State Historical Society RG2411-4214.

taryship of the Territory. . . . Immediately upon his return he heads a movement with the expressed intention of disorganizing his old party, and today he is a nominee on the same ticket with J. Sterling Morton, a bitter, uncompromising Vallandigham Democrat."[65]

Paddock was probably aware that Johnson's Nebraska supporters, particularly J. Sterling Morton and George L. Miller, along with Herman Heath, were trying to help their party's cause by encouraging the president to "cut off the heads" of Republican officials such as Governor Saunders and Superintendent of Indian Affairs and former *Nebraska Republican* editor Edward B. Taylor and replacing them with conservatives. In June Morton's friend and mentor William A. Richardson wrote that the president was determined to remove all Radicals from office and appoint his friends in their places.[66]

In the relatively short time since the June 2 state election, developments nationally and in Nebraska Territory had shifted the political landscape. The economics of statehood may have seemed paramount in June, but the outcome of the pending fall campaign and election would have more to do with national issues, particularly Reconstruction and the struggle between the president and Congress, and with political patronage within the territory. The conservative coalition's dominance by Democrats seemed to confirm that Johnson, who had been elected in 1864 on a ticket he shared with the Great Emancipator, had now been captured, heart and soul, by a party tainted with treason and rebellion. What the South could not win by secession and war, it now seemed poised to win politically.

More evidence of a recalcitrant South was provided by riots in Memphis and New Orleans in May and July that killed scores of blacks and several of their white supporters. Then, during an August–September speaking tour through the Midwest, Johnson blamed Republicans for provoking the New Orleans riot and praised the "loyal" South, while indicting congressional Radicals as disunionists and traitors. Radical territorial papers termed the president's actions "Our National Disgrace" and his speeches "a drunken harangue and a promiscuous bandying of epithets with the crowd."[67]

The canvass leading up to the October 9 Nebraska election followed that of previous campaigns in both its prosecution and its partisanship. Joseph Barker Jr., writing to his parents in England just before the election, observed that "[p]olitics in a Democracy like this is a very dirty and unpleasant profession." Candidates took to the stump in joint debates, party stalwarts fanned out to speak at rallies, and party organs sniped relentlessly at rival journalists and candidates. This time the Republicans' fire had the better chance of inflicting serious damage on targets ranging from the president on down to local Democratic and conservative Republican candidates. The *Omaha Daily Republican* invoked what became known as "waving the bloody shirt" in its admonition to "vote in the direction our brave soldiers shot." The election promised to confirm "the most disastrous overthrow ever inflicted upon the rebel-loving, Union-hating, muddle-headed Democracy of Nebraska."[68]

The *Nebraska Advertiser* branded the president a "demagogue" who deserved rebuke. Because most Republicans reacted to Morton's name like a bull to a red flag, the paper lost no opportunity to link the "sop-hungry Paddock" to the "rebel Morton." As a Republican turncoat Algernon Sidney Paddock was beneath contempt, which editor Colhapp conveyed with a clever play on the territorial secretary's initials: "Are you prepared to nourish to political life the ASP that was nurtured in the sunshine of your favor but to strike its fangs at your vitals? . . . If such a change has come over the spirit of your dreams, then vote for Morton, Paddock and the copper-Johnson ticket."[69]

For their part, Morton and the Democratic newspapers fell

back on their standard arguments that the only test for read-mission of the conquered states should be "loyalty to the Constitution and the government of the United States" and that support of the president "is the support of the Constitution and laws." As for the Radicals, "the whole scope and beat of their policy and efforts aim at giving three millions of unlettered, ignorant, chattering negroes the full right of the ballot in the Southern states."[70]

By the fall of 1866 these arguments had worn thin, and the outcome of the fall elections in Nebraska and across the nation was reminiscent of the Republican landslide of 1864. In both instances the Democrats (and the conservative Republicans in 1866) had failed to correctly gauge public opinion that saw politics as threatening the fruits of wartime sacrifices. In 1866 the Republicans maintained their three-to-one majority in Congress and captured every Northern state. Republican majorities in Nebraska ranged from 770 in the race for delegate to Congress to slightly over 500 for territorial librarian. While the Republicans' margin of victory was not as great as in the 1864 delegate race between Miller and Hitchcock, it was sweeping nonetheless. For the third time in the same year J. Sterling Morton was denied election to public office (governor, U.S. senator, and delegate to Congress).[71]

Even before the final returns came in, Morton conceded the depth of the defeat: "In Nebraska we have met the enemy and, up to date, appear to be theirs. They have 'gone for us' and seemingly have reached us and gone through us with celerity, certainty and security. . . . We are vanquished for the present but not disheartened." In the *Omaha Herald* Miller noted matter-of-factly, "The Democracy and Conservatives of Nebraska have experienced an overwhelming defeat in the present contest. We are badly beaten." A few days later he unburdened himself much more darkly in a letter to Morton, calling Omaha "a town I wish even in this hour of its greatness I have never seen. . . . I work very hard and fight my enemies like the devil. Vide Saunders vs. Miller. It doesn't pay yet. We get beaten in elections and beaten in everything. Damn things generally, I say. If A. Johnson had stayed at home we would have done better."[72]

After the election was over a few Radical heads did roll, but the president's action was too little and too late to have any effect on Nebraska's political landscape. Even if Johnson had replaced the prominent Nebraska officials with conservatives before the fall elections, there was too little time for a shift in patronage to have weakened the Radical landslide. Since Governor Saunders was popular among voters of all political persuasions for his steady service during four years of war, his removal probably would have increased the magnitude of the Democratic–Conservative Republican defeat, and Johnson's confidantes had so advised the president. Herman Heath's machinations to be awarded the Nebraska governorship fell apart when prominent Democrats such as former U.S. Senator Augustus C. Dodge of Iowa, a leading member of the conservative coalition, damned Heath as "an adventurer in politics who attaches himself without scruple or principle to any cause which he thinks will pay." Local Democratic stalwart J. W. Paddock warned the president that a Heath appointment "could not be endorsed by gentlemen wishing, in good faith, to strengthen and give character to the National Union Party."[73]

The most prominent Republican to lose his job was Superintendent of Indian Affairs Edward B. Taylor, the former owner and editor of the *Nebraska Republican*. Taylor had helped arrange the "radical" Union Party convention at Plattsmouth in April 1866 and had been critical of President Johnson editorially before selling his remaining interest in the newspaper to St. A. D. Balcombe in July 1866. Taylor became a "Johnsonite," probably in an effort to make amends for his earlier transgressions against the president and his policy and to save his job. Nonetheless, Taylor's perceived connection to the *Nebraska Republican* during the fall campaign was given as the reason for his dismissal. Republican congressman-elect John Taffe gloated that Taylor's "summersault hardly paid. He certainly didn't alight square enough on his pins. A good joke on him to be hoisted by his own petard." Aside from Taylor, a few Indian agents, including Omaha agent Robert W. Furnas, and several Republican postmasters and land office officials were also removed, but most of Johnson's replacements were rejected by the Senate. Morton had coveted Taylor's Indian superintendency, but it went to a Kansan.[74]

For some conservative politicians and journalists, the sting of the October election debacle may have been moderated somewhat by another grand Union Pacific excursion that followed soon afterward. Newspapermen, members of Congress, territorial officials, eastern financiers, and a scattering of European nobility mingled during a four-day trip to the end of track. *Herald* editor George Miller and Secretary Algernon Paddock perhaps found it somewhat awkward to rub shoulders with Nebraska senators-elect Thayer and Tipton, Governor Saunders, and *Nebraska Republican* editor St. A. D. Balcombe, all of the latter responsible in part for the recent drubbing the conservatives had received. Nevertheless, everyone could appreciate how the excursion showcased the railroad's intimate connection to the future of Omaha and Nebraska.[75]

Joseph Barker Jr., who with his family had speculated in Omaha real estate for years, reported with delight that the visiting dignitaries "had expected to see a rough little logg village & they found the finest carriages & horses & people and one of the most prosperous and well built & beautiful towns west of the Mississippi River." Moreover, during the previous three years, some 3,037 homestead entries totaling almost 434,000

Fig. 24. Union Pacific Railroad directors pose at the 100th meridian signpost, 247 miles west of Omaha, during an October 1866 excursion to the end of the track. Union Pacific Museum, Council Bluffs, Iowa.

acres had been filed in Nebraska, surely only the beginning now that the war was over and the railroad was becoming a reality. Several members of Congress would see firsthand that Nebraska was far from being the Great American Desert of the early maps and guidebooks. Said the *Daily Republican*, "We trust that every one of them may feel that it is to the interest of the Union and of Nebraska that she should become a state immediately."[76]

One of the excursionists was Ohio U.S. senator Benjamin Wade. Although Wade in 1854 had damned the Kansas-Nebraska Act for opening the territory to slavery, he outlived both its architect, Stephen A. Douglas, and the civil war the act helped spark. Ironically, Wade was now positioned to help realize the goal for which Douglas had conceived his act in the first place: the occupation and settlement by white Americans of the region between the Missouri River and the West Coast.

With visible evidence of both the railroad's progress and a "vast tide of immigration" pouring in, Nebraska had become "of too great importance to remain longer in a territorial condition." On December 5, during the second session of the Thirty-Ninth Congress, Wade introduced Senate Bill 456, providing for Nebraska's admission to statehood. The long-sought and much-debated "change of government" at last seemed imminent.[77]

CHAPTER SEVEN

1867

"Nebraska Has a Singularly Bright and Prosperous Future"

W ade's newly introduced Nebraska statehood bill was debated in the Senate during December 1866 and early January 1867. This time there was even more discussion of the "white" restriction in the Nebraska constitution. Senator Wade and other so-called practical Radicals were primarily interested in adding Nebraska's Republican delegation to their forces in Congress. They saw the suffrage restriction as a technicality far outweighed by the contribution another Republican state would make in their fight with the president over Reconstruction. "Doctrinaire" Radicals, as exemplified by Senator Sumner, were adamant that Nebraska's admission should set an "equal suffrage" precedent that could be applied to the readmission of the Southern states.[1]

As the debate got underway, Senator B. Gratz Brown of Missouri offered a variation of the amendment Sumner had wanted incorporated in the Colorado and Nebraska statehood bills of the previous summer, bills that had died from the president's vetoes. Like the Sumner version, Brown's amendment required Nebraska's assent, via a vote of the people, to the "fundamental condition" that neither suffrage nor any other right would be denied on account of race or color. Senator George Edmunds of Vermont offered a substitute amendment whereby the fundamental condition would simply be imposed on Nebraska. The Edmunds substitute was finally adopted, and the bill passed the Senate on January 9 and was then sent on to the House.[2]

Because Nebraska's admission was tied up in Congress, the territorial legislature elected the previous October had no choice but to convene for its twelfth session on the appointed day of January 10, 1867. The Republicans enjoyed a majority in both houses. Governor Saunders had gone to Washington DC, perhaps to help keep statehood moving forward and also to settle the territory's military claims against the government. Acting Governor Paddock, fresh from his defeat as the "Johnson Republican" candidate for Congress on the state ticket, gave the opening address, which included remarks some Nebraskans found offensive.[3]

Most of the message was the standard recitation of territorial finances, prospects for immigration, the progress of the Union Pacific Railroad, and of course, the pending state government. Railroad development, in particular, would ensure that "Nebraska has a singularly bright and prosperous future open before her." In his conclusion, titled "Peace and Union," Paddock criticized the proposed Fourteenth Amendment to the U.S. Constitution for "what are considered impossible requirements by those most deeply interested." He referred to the Southern states that Congress was depriving of representation until they ratified the amendment. If the amendment "threatens to perpetuate hatreds, strife, and discord," said Paddock, "it should be abandoned at once, whatever sacrifices of cherished political dogmas or partisan prejudices are involved." In short, he still thought the president's reconstruction policy, and not that of Congress, was the right one.[4]

The *Nebraska Republican* blasted Paddock for daring to "promulgate Copperhead sentiments in an official document" while speaking on behalf of the absent governor, a "truly loyal and freedom-loving man." At the same time that an "accidental president" was assuming dictatorial powers, "an accidental governor for the time being apes the offensive precedent set in Washington." George Miller's *Omaha Herald* mildly pronounced the address "equal to any similar document that has been presented to our legislature" and felt the acting governor "presents sound views and recommendations with singular clearness, brevity, and force." Both houses of the Republican-dominated legislature passed resolutions "dissenting" from the "Peace and Union" section of Paddock's address and requiring the resolutions be appended to the printed versions of the address that were made available to the public.[5]

Even though everyone understood that this session of the territorial legislature would likely be the last and controversial subjects might therefore be put off until the state legislature met, controversy based on political and sectional issues surfaced nonetheless. The most significant of the former was a bill eliminating "distinctions on account of race and color" from the Nebraska school law. It was introduced by former *Nebraska City News* editor Augustus Harvey, and the bill's title seemed to suggest its goal was integration, even though Harvey was well known as no supporter of rights for black Americans. While the bill did remove the word "white" from the existing school law, its main purpose was to provide that black and white children be educated in separate schools.[6]

By the time the bill came out of committee, the Republican majority had amended it to strike out the "separate schools" provision; now it simply removed the "white" restriction from the statute. To this Harvey protested, "This is reaching too far in advance of the age. The people of Nebraska are not yet ready to send white boys and white girls to school to sit on the same seats with negroes . . . especially are they yet far from ready to degrade their offspring to a level with so inferior a race." The committee amendments were retained nonetheless, and the bill passed both the House and Council. Paddock, still sitting in the governor's chair, vetoed the bill on grounds that legislation could not eradicate "the fact that a strong prejudice exists in the public mind against the intimate association of the two races in the same public schools." Although Governor Saunders returned to the territory late on the same day Paddock issued his veto, Saunders declined the legislature's request to intervene on grounds that he had not resumed his official duties until the following day. Therefore the veto stood.[7]

A bill that attracted only modest attention was one that amended the territorial election law by striking out the words "free white" in the section enumerating who was entitled to vote. As amended, the statute granted the franchise to "every male citizen of the United States." It was approved by Governor Saunders on February 18 and took effect immediately.[8]

Two days before the legislature adjourned, a sectional controversy sparked a near riot in the House. Legislators from counties south of the Platte cooked up a reapportionment scheme that promised to give that section an advantage at the expense of Omaha and counties lying to the river's north. In an effort to force the reapportionment through, the bill's supporters and the Speaker, who was from Cass County, blocked all other legislation, including a bill authorizing an Omaha tax levy to raise funds for a railroad bridge across the Missouri. Representatives from both parties finally voted to depose the Speaker. He did not go quietly, brandishing a revolver at the sergeant at arms and quickly adjourning the House before leaving the chamber. A compromise was reached the next day whereby the Speaker was restored to the chair, the apportionment bill was tabled, and the Omaha levy bill was passed. On February 18 the last Nebraska territorial legislature adjourned sine die, never to reconvene.[9]

While the legislature was in session, Congress had not been idle on the issues of Nebraska statehood and universal male suffrage. On January 10, the same day the legislature opened, the U.S. House of Representatives took up the Senate's admission bill as passed with the Edmunds amendment. Some members argued the incongruity of Congress authorizing "the people" to make a constitution and then, once they had made it, imposing a condition on them that denied one of its provisions. Congressman Henry Dawes and others wanted to let Nebraskans vote on the "fundamental condition." As a compromise between dictating the condition by congressional fiat and submitting it to a popular vote, Congressman George Boutwell of Massachusetts offered a substitute to the Edmunds amendment. His version retained the "fundamental condition" and provided that the Nebraska State Legislature should accept it "by a solemn public act." The Boutwell substitute was adopted and the bill then passed on January 15 by a vote of 103 to 55. The Senate concurred in the house amendments the next day by a vote of 28 to 14. The Nebraska bill, as well as a Colorado admission bill containing the same "fundamental condition," was sent on to President Andrew Johnson's desk.[10]

When word of the admission bill's passage reached Nebraska, the reaction was predictable. Democrats, as reflected by the *Omaha Weekly Herald*, thought Congress had "taken a mighty stride in usurping the power that belongs to the people and crushing out their right to local or self government." Republican journalists, such as St. A. D. Balcombe of the *Nebraska Republican*, were convinced that universal suffrage was the only remedy for "the contumacy of the lately rebellious South." The former Rebel states had rejected "magnanimous measures" offered as a basis for the restoration of their political rights. The only loyalty in those states "lay in the breast of the black man. It has become a necessity to confer upon him the ballot as the method of putting to effective service that loyal weapon. . . . This is the political necessity that compels the nation to the adoption of negro suffrage."[11]

Balcombe's argument about the necessity of black suffrage in the South was echoed in a letter from U.S. Senator J. S. Fowler of Tennessee to U.S. Senator-Elect Thomas Tipton of Nebraska, which was published in the *Nebraska Advertiser*. Tennessee had already ratified the Fourteenth Amendment and its representatives had been admitted to Congress in July 1866. Said Fowler, "I press upon your legislature the importance of their action. . . . Without the principle of suffrage as laid down in the condition of the admission of Nebraska, the Union men of the South can hope for no adequate protection." To this, *Advertiser* editor Colhapp added, "Nebraska—whose infancy was wracked with the devil which slavery attempted to cast into her—will be the first to welcome Universal Suffrage and re-light the flickering light of Liberty to burn unceasing but with time."[12]

Congress took another step along the road to universal suffrage when it granted the elective franchise to all male citizens of U.S. territories by a bill that became law on January 25 after the president had declined either to sign or veto it. The territorial suffrage bill's adoption meant that if Nebraska remained a territory, black men living there would be empowered to vote. Three Republican members of a committee appointed in the Nebraska legislature to consider the issue of impartial suffrage praised the territorial suffrage bill in a majority report, while the committee's Democratic minority argued that the bill was "a gross usurpation of the most sacred rights of the people." The majority report was readily adopted by the legislature. The *Nebraska Herald* noted that Nebraska should accept the Edmunds-Boutwell amendment to the statehood admission bill to further "show to the world that we are fully up to the forward movement in behalf of liberty and human rights."[13]

The *Nebraska Republican* on January 25 reprinted an editorial from the *Chicago Journal* that effectively summed up the contrasts between the "Nebraska Bill" of 1854 and the pending admission act that would finally transform Nebraska Territory into a state. The editorial also assessed the significance of the Territorial Suffrage Act:

> The first Nebraska bill had for its object the extension of slavery; the second, as amended by Senator Edmunds of Vermont, will have the effect of extending the elective franchise to all its citizens, regardless of race or color.
>
> The popular sovereignty which the former pretended to respect but really aimed to prevent, the latter will fully establish. The term "Nebraska Bill" is therefore relieved of the odium under which it rested. . . .
>
> [The territorial suffrage bill] marks an important era in the history of our legislation. It appears from the Senate's passing a general bill providing that in none of the territories there shall be any distinction in suffrage on account of color that the principle involved in the Edmunds amendment is to become a part of settled territorial policy. . . .
>
> In like manner, as we may hope, the full guarantee of a republican form of government in all the territories will be followed, at no very distant day, by the erasure from all our state constitutions of the word "white."[14]

President Johnson vetoed the Nebraska admission bill on January 29, citing as his reasons that Congress had no constitutional authority to regulate suffrage in a state, the people of Nebraska had not requested the modification of their state constitution as required by the "fundamental condition," and they were not being given an opportunity to vote on said condition. The Nebraska enabling act of 1864 had not made universal suffrage a requirement for admission to statehood. Congress should, therefore, let Nebraskans vote on whether or not to accept the terms being imposed. Johnson vetoed the Colorado bill on the same grounds, plus the additional reason that Colorado had insufficient population to justify statehood. Colorado would thus be denied statehood until 1876.[15]

When word of the veto reached the territorial legislature, which was still in session, Augustus Harvey introduced a resolution praising Johnson's veto message as "a high compliment to the people of Nebraska" and extending him thanks "for his appreciation and statement of the rights of the people." A Republican member immediately moved to lay Harvey's resolution on the table, a motion that passed easily on a vote of twenty-one to thirteen.[16]

Meanwhile, the U.S. Senate and House overrode the Nebraska admission bill veto by wide margins on February 8 and 9, respectively. D. M. Kelsey, a former Plattsmouth resident employed in the Treasury Department, was present in the house gallery on February 9, as were other Nebraskans. When the override motion passed 120 to 44, "tokens of gratitude and applause were heard on the floor and in the galleries." Kelsey looked around and saw Edward B. Taylor, the former Indian superintendent and former *Nebraska Republican* editor, also rejoicing. On the house floor he saw the outgoing territorial delegate Phineas W. Hitchcock, Delegate-Elect/Congressman-Elect Turner Marquett, Senator-Elect Thayer, and Congressman-Elect Taffe "surrounded and congratulated not only by Representatives but by Senators who had taken great interest in the admission of Nebraska, foremost among whom were 'Old Ben Wade,' Howe, Grimes, Yates, Kirkwood, Sherman, Lane, and Ramsey."[17]

Boutwell's amendment provided a thirty-day window for the state legislature to convene in special session to act on the "fundamental condition." If the legislature accepted the condition by "a solemn public act," the president was required to issue his proclamation of Nebraska's statehood upon receiving an authentic copy of the act. Accordingly, on February 14 Governor Saunders issued his proclamation calling for the state legislature to meet on February 20 at 2:00 p.m. The sole item of business would be "taking action upon the conditions as proposed by Congress."[18]

The Democratic papers returned to their argument that the "condition" was arbitrary and unconstitutional. "Let the state legislature assemble and accept the 'conditions precedent' imposed by Congress if it dare," wrote Miller of the *Omaha Herald*. The people had ratified a state constitution limiting suffrage to white men, and "Congress has no more right to go behind that act, nor to in any way interfere with it than has the Czar of Russia or the Parliament of Great Britain." The editor of the *Nebraska Advertiser* did not consider Congress's mandate much of an issue: "Negro suffrage now exists in Nebraska by the law of Congress [the Territorial Suffrage Act], so that the change demanded is really no change at all."[19]

When the state legislature met on February 20, Governor Saunders reminded the members why they were there and mildly lamented that Congress had not presented the "fundamental condition" directly to the people of Nebraska. "We must now meet the question as we find it. . . . That a great revolution or change in the minds of the people of our whole country, in regard to granting equal and exact justice to all men, irrespective or race or color, is in proof before us. . . . My opinion is, that this liberal spirit is rapidly on the increase among the people of our own Territory, and if such would be your belief, it would cause you to have much less hesitancy about accepting the conditions proposed than you otherwise might have."[20]

Bills accepting the conditions were promptly introduced. In the House, Democratic member George N. Crawford of Sarpy County vented his ire with a frivolous amendment: "And be it further enacted that the governor of this territory be authorized to procure a coffin to be constructed of the material of which this document is composed in which to enclose the remains of the sovereign rights of the people of the territory." Of course his motion lost. Before the first day's session ended the Senate had approved Senate File 1 accepting the conditions; the House concurred by passing the senate bill the next day. Both bodies then approved a joint resolution transmitting engrossed and enrolled copies of the act as signed by state governor-elect David Butler to the president and Congress. U.S. Senator-Elect Thayer would personally convey the documents to Washington, and he duly delivered them there on February 28.[21]

Douglas County senator Isaac Hascall was the only Democrat voting yes on the bill, for which he expected and received criticism from the party faithful. Perhaps as a preemptive measure, Hascall gave a dramatic speech on the Senate floor that the Republicans were only too happy to reprint and distribute. The speech was an indictment of his party's approach to the whole statehood issue, and Hascall's charges were hard to refute. He began with the premise that the party leaders would not have opposed statehood in the first place "if Democrats could get the offices." What's more, they had provided no good reasons why Nebraska should not become a state.[22]

Hascall's most damning argument was that the Democratic leadership was really responsible for Nebraska now being forced to accept impartial suffrage as a condition of statehood. It was they who advised the president in July 1866 to veto the first admission bill, a bill that had ignored the "whites only" voting restriction in Nebraska's constitution. Although most Nebraska Republican leaders and many Republicans in Congress favored universal suffrage, they had not insisted on its being included in the first Nebraska bill. "That [Negroes] have secured the right to vote in Nebraska so soon is attributable to the fact that the President pocketed the bill for our admission into the Union, after Congress had passed the same without any conditions annexed." Since then, of course, circumstances had changed as relations between the president and Congress over Reconstruction deteriorated further and the South proved ever more recalcitrant.[23]

Nebraska's Democratic leaders had committed political suicide on the state question, said Hascall, and deserved their monuments in the political graveyard. The monuments would be inscribed with the names of the decedents and with "the causes that led to the final catastrophe, as follows: Anti-state, Negro suffrage, Anti-Nebraska, Anti-Ballot-Box, Demagogue, Congress-on-the-Brain, Governor-on-the-Brain, Office, Old Fogy, For-Self-and-Against-the-People." One of the principal decedents was *Omaha Herald* editor George L. Miller, who had straddled the fence on the state issue according to his own political prospects and even now did not seem to accept that Congress had settled statehood and the suffrage question once and for all.[24]

As every Nebraska fourth-grade student knows or should know, President Andrew Johnson proclaimed Nebraska as the thirty-seventh state on March 1, 1867. Word of the proclamation first reached Nebraska by telegraph, prompting a mixed response in the newspapers. From J. Sterling Morton's pen came a brief announcement in the *Nebraska City News* dripping with the sarcasm for which Morton was famous: "According to the promises made to her inhabitants by the advocates of State, they will now enter upon a career of unexampled prosperity. Taxes will be low. The prices of labor will be high. Flush times will drive out lean times, wealth will be the rule and poverty the exception among our people." Miller's *Omaha Weekly Herald* professed shame at "the fraud and wrongs through which this result has been reached" but promised to "advance the prospects which invite us forward upon our new career." The *Nebraska Republican* waxed ecstatic. The people of Nebraska had "added another star to the flag of our country." They had "sanctified the act with another of equal justice to all men. . . . The people of Nebraska are now their own masters, the peers of their fellow American citizens—free themselves and conferring freedom on all within her limits. It is a glorious consummation. Let us be glad."[25]

Notwithstanding the president's March 1 proclamation, statehood did not become effective for nearly a month. Not until March 27 did Territorial Governor Alvin Saunders announce to the people of Nebraska, "I have this day received official notice from the State Department at Washington of the President's Proclamation . . . declaring the fact that Nebraska is admitted as one of the independent States of the Union." Accordingly, "my duties as the Chief Executive of the Territory this day cease." David Butler took his seat as the first governor of the state of Nebraska the same day. Saunders had held office for nearly six years, longer than any other Nebraska governor, territorial or state, until the 1930s.[26]

Although Saunders had been a frequent target of partisan attacks by the Democratic press, *Omaha Herald* editor Miller conceded, "We have had a good deal of respect for the steady, prudent, and capable manner in which [Saunders] served Nebraska Territory as its Chief Executive." Miller was also well aware that the governor "has been and is, an influential and respected citizen of Omaha," whose stature might be important to the city's future. This expectation would be realized when Saunders took a leading part in later negotiations with the Union Pacific that confirmed Omaha as the site for the Missouri River bridge and solidified the city's status as the railroad terminus. While newspaper editors and other leading men exhibited intense and often rancorous partisanship during political campaigns, they also understood their roles as boosters of their communities and of Nebraska itself. Given the modest population of even the larger towns and of the territory as a whole, prominent citizens of whatever political persuasion had to work together from time to time on projects that promised to benefit their community and their own economic self-interest. On such occasions most of the epithets hurled in the heat of political battles seemed to be forgiven or forgotten, at least until the next election.[27]

During the hiatus between March 1 and March 27 came the first test of whether black men in Nebraska could exercise the elective franchise. The occasion was the Omaha municipal election of March 4, 1867. The number of black men who tried to cast ballots is unknown, as is the number who may actually have voted, the latter presumed to be none. Newspaper reports of the day's proceedings are highly colored by both partisanship and racism. The *Omaha Weekly Republican* charged that on election morning "slips of manuscript" were found posted around the city threatening "[t]he first Black Man that takes his Stand at the Polles to Vote he will get his head Skinned to the Bone from his Enemy." Moreover, said the *Republican*, a mob of four hundred "rioters" led by two of the "most notorious bullies of the Democracy in the city" gathered at the second ward polling place at the courthouse and declared "no colored man should vote." The election was, therefore, a "gross outrage" on citizens attempting to exercise their right to suffrage for the first time in their lives.[28]

The Democrats' organ, the *Omaha Weekly Herald*, claimed the Republicans were to blame for the controversy by urging

Fig. 25. African Americans loading wagons in Brownville,
about 1864, the earliest known photograph of black Nebraskans.
Nebraska State Historical Society RG3190-283.

black men to vote "against their known wishes" and by marching them to the polls "in a body, itself a menace of force, mar-
shaled under leaders and armed." According to the *Herald* it
was leading Democrats, including the winning mayoral candidate Charles H. Brown, who had counseled nonviolence. Not
only had the Republicans been desperate for the black men's
votes, but "nothing would have suited them better than riot
and bloodshed." The *Herald* saw the election, with its heavy
Democratic majorities, as firm repudiation of universal male
suffrage by Omaha voters, and the paper proclaimed, "The verdict has not been doubtful." The *Herald* even published a mock
obituary for "Mr. Radical Negro Suffrage Esq."[29]

While some Democrats continued to deny that Congress
had authority under the U.S. Constitution to impose universal suffrage on Nebraska after the people themselves had approved a state constitution limiting the franchise to white
men, the Republican press pointed out that the Omaha election was being held under territorial law. Official notice of

statehood had not yet reached Nebraska, and the territorial officers were still serving. What's more, in January Congress had enacted a law imposing equal suffrage in all federal territories, and the territorial legislature in February had stricken the words "free white" from the Nebraska election law, extending the franchise to "every male citizen of the United States." The Omaha election made it painfully clear, however, that statutory or even constitutional rights remained abstractions without enforcement.[30]

Omaha had rejected the opportunity to be remembered as the place where the first ballot was cast by an African American in Nebraska. That honor would fall to Plattsmouth on April Fool's Day 1867, a month to the day after Nebraska statehood was proclaimed. It was the city election, and victory perched on the Republicans' banner. Even more noteworthy, according to the Plattsmouth paper, "[t]he laws were respected and the colored man named James Walker was allowed to deposit his ballot without opposition—being the first colored citizen to exercise that right in the State of Nebraska."[31]

Statehood's coming and James Walker's ballot marked the end of a beginning. Six years earlier President Abraham Lincoln had been inaugurated on the steps of an unfinished Capitol building to assume the leadership of an unfinished experiment in popular government, an experiment that then seemed doomed to fail in the face of the secession crisis and pending civil war. Slavery had divided the nation politically for decades and, as Americans overspread the continent, had confounded all efforts to confine it geographically, which the 1854 creation of Nebraska Territory seemed to make clear. The so-called Kansas-Nebraska Act exacerbated the contentious debate that, in 1861, finally tore the nation apart.

Nebraska had been in the forefront of granting rights to

Fig. 26. The Great Seal of the state of Nebraska, with its Equality before the Law motto, adopted in June 1867. This painted glass seal once formed part of the skylight ceiling in the House chamber at the U.S. Capitol building. Nebraska State Historical Society Museum Collections 7434-2.

black Americans since before the war. Its legislature had used the "popular sovereignty" that permitted slavery's existence there to abolish it within its borders in January 1861. Its people had contributed men and resources to winning a civil war that ended slavery in the United States forever. At war's end, when Nebraska was poised to be the next territory admitted to statehood, its legislature agreed to Congress's mandate to open suffrage to all male citizens, including black men. The territory that became a state in 1867 thus had a significant role in the grim story of slavery and war and in shaping the postwar legacy of Reconstruction and civil rights.

That legacy included the Fourteenth and Fifteenth Amendments, which finally made color-blind fundamental rights enumerated in the Constitution. The amendments could not, in and of themselves, however, sweep away the pernicious racism that for decades would find legal loopholes to relegate black Americans in Nebraska and elsewhere to the status of second class citizens ("Jim Crow"). Half a century after Nebraska joined the Union and adopted its state motto proclaiming Equality before the Law, a vicious Omaha race riot in which a black man was lynched revealed just how much remained to be done if the motto's promise were to be fulfilled.

The territorial system was designed to give the people in new territories a chance to learn self-government and to build an economic and political infrastructure qualifying them to assume the responsibilities of statehood. Congress had not envisioned this process taking place while the nation was being torn apart by civil war. Nebraskans nevertheless rose to the challenge and persevered during an extended territorial apprenticeship of thirteen years. Finally, after March 1, 1867, they could turn their attention to building the state that had been so long in the making.

The New State and the Old Soldiers

By the time Nebraska achieved statehood on March 1, 1867, its physical configuration resembled that of modern Nebraska. The creation of Idaho Territory in 1863 had reduced the panhandle to its present extent and left the state with a land area of nearly 76,000 square miles, augmented to 77,350 square miles in 1890 by annexation of a tract of former Sioux Reservation land to form Boyd County. The resident non-Indian population was estimated at about fifty thousand. Disruptions brought on by the war years had forestalled much white settlement beyond that which in 1860 had been concentrated in the towns and counties bordering the Missouri River.[1]

By 1867 settlement had pushed westward only about a hundred miles, forming a thin but almost continuous line from Fairbury on the south to Columbus on the north. Farther north, settlements were springing up along the Elkhorn River, extending to the locality of soon-to-be-founded Norfolk and westward from Sioux City to the mouth of the Niobrara River. Other settlements were concentrated in the Platte Valley as far west as Grand Island. There were twelve organized counties in this region, with several more "paper" counties defined by the legislature beyond this line, but having no organized government and practically no residents.[2]

Many basic issues and problems stemming from the territorial period remained unresolved, concluded historian James B. Potts, who studied Nebraska Territory's political history. "Territorial" attitudes that carried over into the early statehood years continued to foster economic and financial instability, along with inefficient and ineffective government. These attitudes included a highly personal and factional style of politics practiced by officials still largely motivated by local or personal economic self-interest. The hastily written constitution of 1866 provided only the barest outline for a state government and contained few safeguards against corruption. The result was waste, extravagance, and fraud.[3]

Sectional rivalry that had persisted throughout the territorial years finally wrested the seat of government away from Omaha in 1867 and relocated it south of the Platte River as a virtual "paper" town named Lincoln. Governor David Butler's manipulations to create a viable capital city out of what was then only a ramshackle prairie village, an effort that sometimes ignored the letter of the law, was a "bald, and therefore of necessity a very bold speculative adventure." The governor's laxity in the handling of the state's financial affairs led to his impeachment and removal from office in 1871.[4]

Despite a population that tallied some 452,000 by 1880, an increase bolstered by the Homestead Act and by other land laws and railroad land grants that attracted new settlers from the eastern United States and from Europe, the Nebraska economy in the 1870s was plagued by drought, grasshopper swarms, rising production costs, and national financial panics. These factors, combined with a state government that was only marginally effective, hindered progress toward the bright future predicted by statehood's adherents during the contentious debates of 1866–67. Although a new constitution adopted in 1875 helped bring some stability, Nebraskans' continued reliance on bare-bones government and the growing influence of so-called oppressors such as railroads, financial institutions, and distant corporations helped mold what Nebraska historian Addison E. Sheldon called "the Soul of Nebraska—characteristic mind, vision, and form of action."[5]

The dispossession of Nebraska's Native peoples was rapidly completed in the years after statehood, an outcome signaled decades earlier and formally initiated in 1854 with the creation of Nebraska Territory. During the Civil War years gold discoveries, passage of the Homestead Act, and the inception of a transcontinental railroad ensured that the prewar trickle of white settlers to Nebraska would become a flood once the war was over. Even the relatively modest immigration of the 1850s and 1860s had prompted the Indians to resist invasion of their homelands, but to little or no avail. By the 1870s settlers began coveting the Nebraska Indians' last remaining hunting grounds and reservations, leading to their forced removal to distant and often barren enclaves outside the state. Of the several tribes living in the territory in 1854, only the Omahas could still call Nebraska home by the 1880s. Along with the loss of their land, Nebraska's Indians lost much of their culture.[6]

Another legacy of Nebraska Territory's Civil War years that persisted into statehood was Republican political dominance. The Democrats' stance on wartime issues and on the questions of statehood and suffrage at war's end, combined with a large postwar emigration of thousands of Union veterans ready to "vote as they shot," doomed the Democrats to Nebraska's political wilderness for nearly a quarter century. Not until 1890 would that party finally win a significant statewide office. The post-statehood Republican hegemony was overseen largely by men who had served in the victorious Union army or who had been party leaders during the war years.

This group included former officers of the First and Second Nebraska Regiments. The First Nebraska's colonel, John M. Thayer, and its chaplain, Thomas W. Tipton, were elected Nebraska's first two U.S. senators in 1866, taking office in 1867. Thayer went on to receive appointment as territorial governor of Wyoming from his old commander, now President Ulysses S. Grant, and was elected governor of Nebraska in 1886. Robert R. Livingston, who led the First Nebraska during most of the war, resumed his Plattsmouth medical practice until 1869, when Grant appointed him U.S. surveyor general for Nebraska and Iowa. Robert W. Furnas, who commanded the Second Nebraska Cavalry at the Battle of White Stone Hill in 1863, was agent for the Omaha Tribe from 1864 to 1866 and was elected Nebraska's second state governor in 1872, serving a single, two-year term.

Among other First Nebraska officers, Maj. Thomas J. Majors was elected a state legislator, Nebraska congressman (1878–79), and lieutenant governor (1891–95). He was also a founder of Mt. Vernon Academy at Peru, which became Nebraska's first state college. Former First Nebraska quartermaster Lt. John Gillespie was elected as the first state auditor, an office he also held in the last years of the territory. State Auditor Gillespie was one of the three commissioners who chose Lancaster (now Lincoln) as the site for the new state capital in 1867. John Taffe, Nebraska congressman from 1867 to 1873, had been a major in the Second Nebraska. Lt. William A. Polock of the First Nebraska, captured with his men at the Arkansas Grand Prairie skirmish in 1864, served in the state legislature and was speaker of the house. Many other former Nebraska soldiers also filled legislative seats.

The tiny band of soldiers from Nebraska Territory was soon

joined by thousands of other Union veterans who came to start new lives. Many of these men, too, would leave their mark on the new state. Four became governor (Silas Garber, Albinus Nance, Lorenzo Crounse, and John Mickey), four were elected U.S. senator (Charles Van Wyck, Charles Manderson, William V. Allen, and John M. Thurston), and six served as congressmen. Gilbert L. Laws of McCook, who represented Nebraska's Second District in Congress from 1889 to 1891 and is barely known today, made a significant wartime sacrifice, losing part of his left leg in the May 5, 1862, Battle of Williamsburg while serving in a Wisconsin regiment. Othman A. Abbott, an Illinois cavalryman, came to Nebraska in 1867 and was elected Nebraska's first lieutenant governor in 1876. Lorenzo Crounse, a New York artillery captain, perhaps had the most varied political career after moving to Nebraska in 1864. He was elected a Nebraska Supreme Court judge in 1866, congressman in 1872 and 1874, governor in 1892, and state senator in 1900.

Belgian immigrant Victor Vifquain, who settled on Nebraska's Big Blue River in the 1850s, led an Illinois regiment during the war and was awarded the Medal of Honor for gallantry at the Battle of Fort Blakely, Alabama, in 1865. Vifquain was the first person with Nebraska ties to receive the medal. He returned home to his farm at war's end and in 1891 was appointed adjutant general of Nebraska when the Democrats finally captured the governorship. During the Spanish-American War of 1898 Vifquain commanded the Third Nebraska Volunteer Infantry in Georgia and Cuba.

Territorial leaders from both parties who did not serve in the army also remained prominent in early state politics. They included Governor Alvin Saunders, Secretary Algernon S. Paddock, and Delegate Phineas W. Hitchcock (later surveyor general), all Republicans and all elected as U.S. senators in the 1870s. Although Democrats had no significant electoral success until the 1890s, J. Sterling Morton was his party's candidate for governor in 1882, 1884, and 1892, with the same result he had experienced in his first campaign for state office in 1866. He finally gained a prominent office with his appointment in 1893 as secretary of agriculture in the second Cleveland administration.

Morton is most often remembered, of course, as the father of Arbor Day, first observed in Nebraska in 1872, proclaimed by Governor Robert W. Furnas in 1874, and designated an official state holiday by the legislature in 1885. Morton and Furnas were political rivals from the early territorial days and beyond, but they enjoyed a cordial personal relationship when it came to promoting Nebraska's agricultural and horticultural resources and preserving its history. Both have been elected to the Nebraska Hall of Fame.[7]

Several of those who figured prominently in Nebraska's Civil War history were among the founders and early leaders of the Nebraska State Historical Society, established in 1878. They included Furnas and Morton, former territorial governor Alvin Saunders, former territorial secretary Algernon Paddock, former First Nebraska colonel Robert Livingston, former U.S. senator Thomas W. Tipton, and Omaha newspaperman George L. Miller. These men were in demand as speakers at the society's annual meetings or served as society officers or board members. By the later years of the nineteenth century their often bitter partisanship of the 1850s and 1860s had mellowed and been replaced by the shared goal of revisiting personal experiences from those stirring days and recording them for the benefit of generations to come.

Enlisted men from Nebraska's Civil War units and those from other states who came after the war also left their marks, although we know little about the later lives of most of them. Many veterans who had been common soldiers likely became farmers, small-town merchants, or tradesmen. One of them was Robert Ball Anderson, a former slave who enlisted in the 125th U.S. Colored Infantry near war's end and moved to Nebraska in 1870. He went on to become the largest African American landowner in the state by 1910 as a ranchman and farmer in Box Butte County. George P. Belden, who served in both the First and Second Nebraska Regiments, gained modest fame as a self-promoting frontiersman and scout, the subject of an 1870 biography, *Belden, the White Chief; or, Twelve Years among the Wild Indians of the Plains*. In 1871 he was found lying dead on the prairie, supposedly killed by Indians. Francis Lohnes, the First Nebraska Regiment's only Medal of Honor recipient, who deserted in 1865 when the burden of four years of army service finally became too great, returned to his farm in Richardson County. In 1889 he was scalded to death in a steam tractor accident, never knowing that Congress had granted amnesty to him and other Union volunteers who had deserted following the Confederate surrender in 1865.[8]

Luther North, first a private in the Second Nebraska, went on to help his brother, Frank, lead the famous Pawnee Scouts during the 1870s Indian wars. Luther in his old age became a venerated symbol of Nebraska's frontier and Indian-fighting days, frequently in demand as a speaker. August Scherneckau, the only First Nebraska soldier from the Grand Island German settlement, moved to Oregon in 1870. He prospered there and lies buried at Astoria, far from both his German homeland and the state from which he answered his adopted country's call in 1862. Harrison Johnson, the First Nebraska's black "undercook" from Arkansas, lived out his life in the capital city named for the president who helped set him free. Johnson rests under a Union veteran's headstone at Lincoln's Wyuka Cemetery. Hettie K. Painter, a Union army nurse with a medical doctor's degree from Penn Medical College, opened a Lincoln infirmary

in the 1870s and was active in the Women's Relief Corps auxiliary of the Grand Army of the Republic (GAR) veterans' society. She is also buried at Wyuka.[9]

As they were about to be mustered out of the service in 1866,
the officers of the First Nebraska Regiment met at the capitol
building in Omaha to organize a monument association "for
the purpose of perpetuating the valorous deeds of deceased Nebraska soldiers." No such monument was ever erected. As the
Civil War sesquicentennial opened in 2011, the only known
monuments specific to the First Nebraska's Civil War service
were a state historical marker in Plattsmouth commemorating the 1861 enlistment of Company A under Capt. Robert R.
Livingston and a plaque in Brownville's Boettner Park mark-
ing the site where Company C was organized prior to joining
the regiment. Aside from a marker in Falls City's Steele Cemetery commemorating three soldiers killed in the 1863 Battle
of White Stone Hill and their surviving comrades of Companies G and L, there was no known monument or memorial in
the state to the Second Nebraska Volunteer Cavalry.[10]

The soldiers of the First Nebraska, the Second Nebraska,
the First Battalion, the Nebraska Battalion of the Curtis Horse
(Fifth Iowa Cavalry), the Pawnee and Omaha Scouts, and their
Union comrades from across the land who settled here stood
"firmly by the flag" throughout the Civil War. Some lost their
lives in battle, died from disease and accidents, or otherwise
did not live to reap the rewards coming with peace and a reunited nation. Most never achieved wealth or fame after leaving the army but, nevertheless, contributed in countless ways
to building the state that came to be on March 1, 1867.

The Union veterans from Nebraska and elsewhere formed
more than 350 GAR posts in communities all across the state
and took an active part in local and state politics, with many
serving in the legislature, explaining why Nebraska counties or-

ganized in the immediate postwar years often bear the names of Union generals. By 1890 the U.S. Census recorded nearly twenty-three thousand surviving Union soldiers, sailors, and marines in Nebraska. For as long as they lived, the aging Boys in Blue were fixtures of the annual Decoration Day observances in scores of towns and cemeteries. In 1948 the last Union Civil War veteran in Nebraska died, joining the thousands of his comrades already sleeping in "the bivouac of the dead."[11]

For most of these veterans, their grave markers and the GAR memorials dotting the cemeteries in which they lie are the only physical reminders of their service and their sacrifice. Their intangible monument is all around us, represented by the opportunities, the institutions, and the principles encompassed in the nation they helped to save and the state they helped to build.

NOTES

Abbreviations

ARCIA	*Annual Report of the Commissioner of Indian Affairs*
Compiled Service Records	Compiled Service Records, First Nebraska Volunteer Infantry/Cavalry
GO	General Orders
SO	Special Orders
NSHS	Nebraska State Historical Society, Lincoln
OR	*The War of the Rebellion: A Compilation of the Official Records of the Union and Confederate Armies*
Territorial papers	Territorial Papers: Nebraska, 1854–1867, Records of the U.S. State Department

Introduction

1. Population Schedules, Eighth Census of the United States: Nebraska Territory, 1860, National Archives Microfilm Publication M653, roll 665; *Nebraska City People's Press*, Dec. 22, 1859, July 5, 1860.

2. For analysis of the differences and similarities of Nebraska and Kansas politics during this period see Etcheson, "Where Popular Sovereignty Worked."

3. The foregoing discussion of territorial politics is based on Potts, "North of 'Bleeding Kansas,'" 116–17. Though lacking objectivity by modern standards, Morton-Watkins, *Illustrated History*, vol. 1, provides a detailed survey of territorial politics and cites many primary sources. This work was proposed in 1897 by J. Sterling Morton, who engaged former journalist Albert Watkins to help with editorial work. Morton died in 1902 before much had been done and Watkins assumed responsibility for the "conception and execution" of the text (1:xv).

4. *Nebraska Advertiser* (Brownville), July 26, 1860. Although many territorial newspapers are not extant for this period, two that covered the

election were the *Omaha Nebraskian*, which supported the Democrats, and the *Nebraska Advertiser*, formerly favoring Stephen A. Douglas, which threw its support to Lincoln and the Republicans before the election.

5. *Laws of Nebraska*, Seventh (Ter.) Session, 43–44. Black, a former chief justice of Nebraska Territory, had vetoed a similar bill passed in 1860, but then his veto stood. His two veto messages rejected the bills largely on constitutional grounds, arguing that the people of a territory had no authority to decide the slavery question until they drafted a constitution and were admitted to statehood. He also cited the 1857 Dred Scott ruling by the U.S. Supreme Court. The messages appear in Lewis, *Messages and Proclamations*, 1:130–35, 136–41. As with many Northern Democrats, Black was not an advocate for slavery's extension but held a hands-off policy with respect to the South. When the war began Black returned to his native Pennsylvania, raised the Sixty-second Regiment of Pennsylvania Volunteers for the Union army, and was killed leading his regiment at the Battle of Gaines Mill on June 27, 1862. Morton-Watkins, *Illustrated History*, 1:450.

6. *Daily Omaha Nebraskian*, Nov. 14, 1860.

7. *Nebraska City News*, Dec. 29, 1860.

8. McPherson, *Ordeal by Fire*, 127, 137.

9. *Nebraska Advertiser*, Aug. 30, Sept. 6, Oct. 25, 1860.

10. Lewis, *Messages and Proclamations*, 1:125; D. D. Belden to George E. Barker, Jan. 18, 1861, in Snoddy, Combs, Marks, and Weber, *Their Man in Omaha*, 18; *Falls City Broad Axe*, Feb. 5, 1861.

11. Squire Lamb to Hiram Lamb, Feb. 8, 1861, Lamb papers, NSHS. Lamb's establishment was approximately eight miles west of Grand Island in the vicinity of today's village of Alda.

12. They included Tennessee native and slave owner George H. Nixon, former register of the U.S. Land Office in Brownville; Asa M. Acton, a former Nebraska legislator, said to have been killed in action as a Confederate soldier; Edwin A. Deslondes, a Louisiana native and register of the Nebraska City land office, whose brother-in-law was Confederate general P. G. T. Beauregard; and Philip K. Reily, who had lived in Nebraska City before the war. Reily's brother, John, served as a Union army surgeon. See Morton-Watkins, *Illustrated History*, 1:337, 443, 459; and Dale, "Otoe County Pioneers," 10:2137–38.

13. Although Nebraska Territory is credited officially with contributing 3,157 men to the Union army, the actual number is certainly higher. The official count did not include the four companies of Nebraskans in the Curtis Horse (Fifth Iowa Cavalry). Some men, such as early Saline County settler Victor Vifquain, left Nebraska for service in other states'

regiments and returned after the war. The *Nebraska Advertiser* mentioned Nebraska men serving in Kansas and Missouri regiments, such as "sixty-seven Nebraska boys" in the Eighth Kansas. In the issue of June 5, 1862, the paper's editor concluded, "[T]here are not less than five thousand of the hardy veterans of Nebraska now fighting in the armies of their country." *Report of the Adjutant General of Kansas* lists five cavalry and two infantry regiments having soldiers from Nebraska. On the other hand, some men from Arkansas or Missouri who enlisted in the First Nebraska never set foot in Nebraska before, during, or after the war.

14. Addison E. Sheldon compiled population statistics from the 1860 census in *Nebraska: Land and People*, 1:379–80.

15. Danker, "Columbus," 277–88; Stolley, "History of the First Settlement of Hall County," 17–18.

16. Mattes, *Great Platte River Road*, 217, 270–71. Massachusetts newspaperman Samuel Bowles provided a vivid description of these trailside establishments in *Across the Continent*, 20–22.

17. Wishart, "Age and Sex Composition," 109; Luebke, "Time, Place, and Culture," 154; data from the 1860 census of Nemaha County, Nebraska Territory, compiled by the author. According to the 1860 census more than a third of Nebraska residents (10,934) were children of school age. Data about nativity is compiled in Sheldon, *Nebraska: Land and People*, 1:368–72.

18. The most accessible review of Nebraska territorial history appears in Olson and Naugle, *History of Nebraska*.

19. Kennedy, *Preliminary Report*, 176–77, 190, 200–201; U.S. Department of the Interior, Bureau of the Census, *Manufactures*, 665; Sheldon, *Nebraska: Land and People*, 1:374–75. The *Nebraska Advertiser* of September 1, 1859, reported that Theodore Hill had shipped the first wheat ever sent from Nebraska Territory on the steamer *Omaha*, and in Nemaha County there would be a surplus of fifteen hundred to two thousand bushels.

20. Luebke, "Time, Place, and Culture," 154; Sheldon, *Nebraska: Land and People*, 1:374–75.

21. Olson and Naugle, *History of Nebraska*, 98–100.

22. Sheldon, *Nebraska: Land and People*, 1:374–75. While the conclusions in this paragraph do not result from detailed analysis, one need only consult the numerous biographies of territorial leaders appearing in early state histories to get a sense of the role of urban professionals during this era.

23. See Paul, *Blue Water Creek*, for a cogent analysis of the Grattan affair and the resulting Harney campaign.

24. Lewis, *Messages and Proclamations*, 1:19–20; Dudley, "Notes on Military History," 173.

25. Dudley, "Notes on Military History," 175, 189–90; Lewis, *Messages and Proclamations*, 1:36–37.

26. Dudley, "Notes on Military History," 177–78.

27. Dudley, "Notes on Military History," 177–78, 192–93. The *Nebraska City News*, June 29, 1861, noted Downs's military background.

28. Thayer, "Pawnee War"; Ludwickson, "Roster."

29. Dudley, "Notes on Military History," 182–84.

1. 1861

1. *Omaha Daily Telegraph*, Apr. 13, 14, 1861; McPherson, *Ordeal by Fire*, 149, 163.

2. *Nebraska Republican* (Omaha), May 15, 1861.

3. *Nebraska City News*, Apr. 27, 1861.

4. *Huntsman's Echo* (Wood River Center), Apr. 25, 1861; *Omaha Daily Telegraph*, Apr. 30, 1861. Wood River Center was located at the site of modern Shelton, Nebraska.

5. *Nebraska City Daily Bulletin*, Apr. 16, 1861; Thayer to Simon Cameron, Apr. 17, 1861, *OR*, ser. 3, vol. 1, p. 83.

6. Thompson to Davis, Apr. 15, 1861, and John Tyler Jr. to Thompson, Apr. 29, 1861, *OR*, ser. 1, vol. 1, pp. 684, 689. The history of St. Joseph during the war and its divided loyalties in this period is found in Filbert, *The Half Not Told*.

7. On April 30, 1861, Col. D. S. Miles reported that his troops from Fort Kearny had reached Fort Leavenworth, despite reports that St. Joseph Secessionists would resist their passing on the Missouri River. Miles to HQ, U.S. Army, Apr. 30, 1861, *OR*, ser. 1, vol. 1, p. 676.

8. Circular, Nebraska City, Apr. 20, 1861, *Nebraska Advertiser*, May 2, 1861; Robert R. Livingston to Gov. Samuel Black, Apr. 25, 1861, enclosing resolution and muster roll, RG18, box 1, Records of the Nebraska Military Department, NSHS.

9. Black to Simon Cameron, Apr. 27, 1861, *OR*, ser. 3, vol. 1, p. 123.

10. Lewis, *Messages and Proclamations*, 1:154; *Nebraska Advertiser*, May 9, 1861.

11. Thayer to Lincoln and Morton to Lincoln, May 1, 1861, *OR*, ser. 3, vol. 1, pp. 141–42.

12. *Huntsman's Echo*, reprinted in *Nebraska Republican*, May 8, 1861; Squire Lamb to Hiram Lamb, June 27, 1861, Lamb papers, NSHS; *ARCIA*, 1861, p. 50.

13. Shannon, *Organization and Administration*, 1:35; *OR*, ser. 3, vol. 1, pp. 151–52; *Omaha Daily Telegraph*, May 3, 1861.

14. *Nebraska City News*, May 4, 11, 1861; *Nebraska Advertiser*, May 16, 23, 1861; *Nebraska Republican*, May 22, 1861; muster roll of Grand Island Company, RG18, box 1, NSHS.

15. Alvin Saunders to Cameron, May 15, 1861, and Cameron to governors of Minnesota, Kansas, and Nebraska, May 15, 1861, *OR*, ser. 3, vol. 1, p. 204.

16. Cameron to Saunders, May 21, 1861, *OR*, ser. 3, vol. 1, pp. 222–23; *Nebraska Advertiser*, June 6, 1861.

17. *Nebraska Republican*, May 8, 1861; Tyler to Col. E. B. Alexander, HQ, Dept. of the West, St. Louis, reprinted in *Nebraska Republican*, May 22, 1861; Lt. Brockholst Livingston to Capt. Seth Williams, HQ, Dept. of the West, St. Louis, May 17, 1861, Fort Kearny letterbook, RG505, roll 6, NSHS; Heitman, *Historical Register*, 1:976. Tyler was dismissed from the U.S. Army on June 6, 1861.

18. Telegram, St. Joseph MO, to F. P. Blair, May 23, 1861, *OR*, ser. 1, vol. 3, p. 378; Miles to HQ, U.S. Army, May 10, 1861, *OR*, ser. 1, vol. 3, p. 369; *Nebraska Advertiser*, May 23, 1861.

19. Harney to HQ, U.S. Army, May 29, 1861, *OR*, ser. 1, vol. 3, p. 377; Capt. E. W. B. Newby, Fourth U.S. Cavalry, to AAG, Fort Leavenworth, June 24, 1861, Fort Kearny letterbook, NSHS.

20. Johnson reminiscence, NSHS; *Page County Herald* (Clarinda IA), June 21, 1861; *Omaha Daily Telegraph*, Aug. 2, 1861; *Nebraska Advertiser*, June 13, July 18, 1861.

21. *Nebraska City News*, June 15, 1861. A year later, almost to the day, the *People's Press* of June 12, 1862, reported that the flag had been returned to the Nebraska City Guards remaining at home by Capt. Allen Blacker of the First Nebraska. "After passing through the battles of Fort Donelson and Shiloh the old flag returns—being discharged from any further duty." The flag exhibited several bullet holes.

22. *Nebraska Advertiser*, June 13, 1861.

23. *Nebraska Advertiser*, June 20, 1861; *Omaha Daily Telegraph*, June 5, 1861; Rhoades diary, NSHS.

24. *Omaha Daily Telegraph*, June 12, 1861.

25. "G" [John Gillespie] to editor, June 27, 1861, *Nebraska Advertiser*, July 4, 1861.

26. Rhoades diary, NSHS; *Page County Herald*, June 21, 28, 1861; Dudley, *Roster of Nebraska Volunteers*, 104–5; Gillespie letter, July 4, 1861, *Nebraska Advertiser*, July 11, 1861.

27. Gillespie letter, July 12, 1861, *Nebraska Advertiser*, July 18, 1861; *Omaha Daily Telegraph*, July 6, 1861; Rhoades diary, NSHS.

28. Paddock to Cameron, June 24, 1861, *OR*, ser. 3, vol. 1, p. 294.

29. Saunders to Cameron, July 25, 1861, and War Dept. to Saunders, July 30, 1861, *OR*, ser. 3, vol. 1, pp. 351, 368; Paddock proclamation, in Lewis, *Messages and Proclamations*, 1:251; War Dept. to Paddock, Aug. 15, 1861, *OR*, ser. 3, vol. 1, p. 414.

30. Lass, *Navigating the Missouri*, 195–96; *Omaha Daily Telegraph*, Aug. 3, 5, 1861; *Omaha Daily Nebraskian*, Aug. 7, 1861.

31. *Nebraska Advertiser*, June 27, July 4, July 25, 1861.

32. Rhoades diary, NSHS; Dudley, *Roster of Nebraska Volunteers*, 116–17; *Nebraska Advertiser*, Aug. 1, 1861.

33. Rhoades diary, NSHS; Henry Koenig to Mother, Dec. 26, 1861, Koenig papers, NSHS; *Nebraska Advertiser*, Aug. 8, 1861; *Nebraska City News*, Aug. 10, 1861. No copy of a Frémont order concerning the First Nebraska is found in the *OR*. The statement that he had issued such an order appeared in the newspapers. At this time the Western Department was authorized to accept as many three-year regiments as might be offered, and Frémont did accept offers of regiments from the governors of Indiana and Illinois on July 29. *OR*, ser. 1, vol. 3, pp. 400, 414.

34. *Nebraska Advertiser*, Mar. 27, 1862, Aug. 17, 1865. The elder Thompson was a Tennessee native, but all his children, including Robert, had been born in Missouri, according to the 1860 census of Brownville, Nebraska Territory, National Archives Microfilm Publication M653, roll 665.

35. Gillespie letters, Aug. 16, 19, 1861, *Nebraska Advertiser*, Aug. 29, 1861; Henry Koenig to Mother, Dec. 26, 1861, Koenig papers, NSHS.

36. *Nebraska Advertiser*, Aug. 15, 1861. Pvt. Thomas Keen, for example, enlisted "with the promise to not be taken outside of the territory." Keen to Sister, Aug. 24, 1861, in Potter, "I Thought It My Duty," 136.

37. Gillespie letter, July 25, 1861, *Nebraska Advertiser*, Aug. 1, 1861.

38. "Incident of the Civil War," *Nebraska State Journal* (Lincoln), Mar. 5, 1905; "General Thayer Tells How the Original First Nebraska Enlisted and Fought," *Omaha Sunday World-Herald*, May 10, 1901.

39. Newby to AAG, Western Dept., Sept. 14, 1861, Fort Kearny letterbook, NSHS.

40. Martin Stowell letters, *Nebraska Advertiser*, Oct. 24, Nov. 7, 1861.

41. Lide Patrick to Joseph Barker Jr., Jan. 20, 1863, in Snoddy, Combs, Marks, and Weber, *Their Man in Omaha*, 1:53.

42. *Falls City Broad Axe*, Aug. 27, Nov. 19, 1861.

43. *Nebraska Advertiser*, Aug. 8, 22, 29, 1861.

44. Filbert, *The Half Not Told*, 36, 48–49; *Nebraska Advertiser*, Sept. 12, 1861; "Romulus" letter, Sept. 11, 1861, *Nebraska City News*, Sept. 14, 1861.

45. "Romulus" letter, Sept. 11, 1861, *Nebraska City News*, Sept. 14, 1861.

46. *Nebraska Advertiser*, Sept. 19, 1861.

47. *Nebraska Advertiser,* Oct. 3, 17, 1861.

48. *Falls City Broad Axe,* Oct. 15, 29, 1861.

49. *Council Bluffs (IA) Nonpareil,* Dec. 21, 1861; *Nebraska Advertiser,* Dec. 19, 1861.

50. *Falls City Broad Axe,* Oct. 29, 1861; *Nebraska Advertiser,* Dec. 19, 26, 1861.

51. *Missouri Democrat* (St. Louis), Aug. 20, 1861, quoted in *Nebraska City News,* Aug. 31, 1861; Thomas E. Keen to Sister, Sept. 9, 1861, in Potter, "I Thought It My Duty," 136.

52. "G" (John Gillespie) letter, July 4, 1861, *Nebraska Advertiser,* July 11, 1861; Rhoades diary, NSHS; Tipton letter, Aug. 29, 1861, *Nebraska Advertiser,* Sept. 5, 1861.

53. Rhoades diary, NSHS; *Nebraska Advertiser,* Oct. 3, 1861, citing *Missouri Democrat* (St. Louis), Sept. 23, 1861.

54. The Rhoades diary, NSHS, provides a journal of the march to Springfield. Frémont's tenure as commander of the Western Department and his dismissal are discussed in Gerteis, *Civil War St. Louis,* 136–61. The soldiers' reaction is noted in Henry Koenig to Mother, Georgetown, Missouri, Dec. 26, 1861, Koenig papers, NSHS.

55. "Nat" letter, Dec. 9, 1861, *Platte Valley Herald* (Plattsmouth), Dec. 19, 1861; "More Again" letter, Jan. 15, 1862, *Nebraska Advertiser,* Jan. 30, 1862.

56. William Polock described the First Nebraska's role in the Milford campaign in a December 22, 1861, letter, extracted in the *Nebraska Advertiser,* Jan. 9, 1862; see also "More Again" letter, Jan. 15, 1862, *Nebraska Advertiser,* Jan. 30, 1862. Correspondence and reports about the skirmish are in *OR,* ser. 1, vol. 8, pp. 37–42, 437–47.

57. "B," letter in *Missouri Democrat,* Jan. 6, 1862, reprinted in *Omaha Tri-Weekly Nebraska Republican,* Jan. 15, 1862.

58. "Army Correspondence" to the *Tri-Weekly Nebraska Republican,* extracted in *Nebraska Advertiser,* Feb. 6, 1862; "Setting a Black Man Free," *Nebraska State Journal,* Mar. 19, 1905.

59. Fulton, "Freighting and Staging," 262.

60. The *Nebraska Republican,* Oct. 24, 1861, reported completion of the telegraph line: "The posts which bear aloft the wires . . . are so many *guide posts* on the grand thoroughfare which is soon to be opened up between the Atlantic and the Pacific Oceans." The same route was certain to be selected for the Pacific Railroad. "Nature has so ordained it and remains only for Associated Enterprize to execute the fiat."

61. Lass, *From the Missouri to the Great Salt Lake,* 114–20, 122–26, 129.

62. Morton-Watkins, *Illustrated History,* 1:462; Lewis, *Messages and Proclamations,* 1:159–66.

2. 1862

1. The January 31, 1862, issue of the *First Nebraska Volunteer* is in the Nebraska State Historical Society collections. The *Nebraska City News*, June 29, 1861, reprints an exchange from the *Omaha Nebraskian* that identifies Provost as "a brother knight of the stick and rule with whom we have worked many a day."

2. Casualty data are compiled from Dudley, *Roster of Nebraska Volunteers*, and Compiled Service Records. McPherson, *Ordeal by Fire*, 233–34, discusses causes and casualties of disease during the Civil War. The comment about the hospitals is in Keen to sister, Jan. 25, 1862, in Potter, "I Thought It My Duty," 137.

3. *Nebraska Advertiser*, Jan. 2, 1862; *Nebraska City News*, Jan. 4, 1862. Cleveland may have been Marshall Cleveland, who operated primarily in Kansas and Missouri. Historian Albert Castel characterized him as "an ex-convict and professional jayhawker," whose band consisted mostly of criminals and ruffians. Castel, *Civil War Kansas*, 58. Cleveland was killed in May 1862. *Nebraska City News*, May 24, 1862.

4. Capt. John A. Thompson to U.S. Dist. Attorney, Omaha, Jan. 15, 1862, and Thompson to AG Lorenzo Thomas, Jan. 28, 1862, Fort Kearny letterbook, NSHS.

5. *Nebraska Advertiser*, Jan. 9, 1862, quoting *Omaha Nebraskian*, n.d.; *Nebraska Advertiser*, Jan. 23, 1862.

6. Lewis, *Messages and Proclamations*, 1:219; *Laws of Nebraska*, Eighth (Ter.) Session, 167–68, 173–75.

7. *Nebraska Advertiser*, Jan. 30, 1862.

8. "Publius" letter and editorial, *Nebraska Advertiser*, Jan. 23, 1862; "Oscar" letter, *Nebraska Advertiser*, Feb. 6, 1862.

9. "X.Y." letter and editorial, *Nebraska Advertiser*, Feb. 6, 1862.

10. Stowell letter, *Nebraska Advertiser*, Jan. 23, 1862.

11. *OR*, ser. 1, vol. 13, pp. 547–48; *Nebraska Advertiser*, Feb. 6, 13, 1862.

12. *Laws of Nebraska*, Eighth (Ter.) Session, 89–92.

13. *Tri-Weekly Nebraska Republican*, Jan. 15, 1862; *Laws of Nebraska*, Eighth (Ter.) Session, 105, 110, 115, 125–26. Some sources say that Greene County had actually been named for a Cass County, Nebraska, politician and not, as the legislature evidently assumed, for U.S. Senator James Green, a Democrat from Missouri. See Morton-Watkins, *Illustrated History*, 1:274n1; *Journal of the Council*, 209 (re: House File 184).

14. Logan, *Roster*, 4:845.

15. The campaign against Forts Henry and Donelson is thoroughly analyzed in Cooling, *Forts Henry and Donelson*.

16. Joseph H. Bronson, Fort Henry TN, Feb. 14, 1862, to Ella Chubbuck, Binghamton NY, Bronson papers, NSHS.

17. For Nebraska soldiers' commentary on their movements to Fort Donelson, see "More Again" letters, *Nebraska Advertiser*, Feb. 20, Mar. 6, 1862; Martin Stowell letters, *Nebraska Advertiser*, Feb. 20, 27, Mar. 6, 1862. Thayer's report is in the *OR*, ser. 1, vol. 7, p. 252.

18. Cooling, *Forts Henry and Donelson*, 162–76.

19. *OR*, ser. 1, vol. 7, pp. 237–38.

20. Francis I. Cramer to Mother, Feb. 19, 1861, *Page County Herald*, Mar. 7, 1862.

21. Thayer report, *OR*, ser. 1, vol. 7, p. 253; Keen to Sister, Mar. 25, 1862, in Potter, "I Thought It My Duty," 141; "X.Y." letter, *Nebraska City News*, Mar. 1, 1862. Dudley, *Roster of Nebraska Volunteers*, gives the men killed in action as John Whitaker, Company D; George Steward, Company G; and John Pangburn, Company I. Interestingly, none had been Nebraskans at the time of their enlistment. Whitaker and Steward enlisted at Syracuse, Missouri, and Pangburn was an Iowan from Page County.

22. Wallace report, *OR*, ser. 1, vol. 7, p. 238.

23. Potter, "I Thought It My Duty," 140.

24. A review of the significance of the Confederate defeats at Forts Henry and Donelson appears in Cooling, *Forts Henry and Donelson*, 276–77.

25. Potter, "Nebraska Cavalryman in Dixie."

26. The best summary of the history of the Fifth Iowa Volunteer Cavalry appears in Logan, *Roster*, 4:845–62.

27. "More Again" letter, Mar. 15, 1862, *Nebraska Advertiser*, Apr. 3, 1862.

28. *OR*, ser. 1, vol. 10, pt. 1, pp. 169–70.

29. Polock recollection, Polock papers, NSHS; *OR*, ser. 1, vol. 10, pt. 1, pp. 169–70. Wallace's performance on this day would become an issue between him and General Grant, with Grant blaming Wallace for being dilatory, and Wallace blaming Grant and his staff for late and contradictory orders. Regardless of who was to blame, Wallace fell out of favor with Grant and was sent to serve elsewhere. Stewart Sifakis, *Who Was Who*, 434–35.

30. Silas Strickland letter, Apr. 12, 1862, *Tri-Weekly Nebraska Republican*, Apr. 30, 1862; "More Again" letter, Apr. 12, 1862, *Nebraska Advertiser*, May 8, 1862.

31. *OR*, ser. 1, vol. 10, pt. 1, pp. 194, 197–98; Compiled Service Records; Polock recollection, Polock papers, NSHS.

32. Strickland letter, Apr. 12, 1862, *Tri-Weekly Nebraska Republican*, Apr. 30, 1862.

33. *OR*, ser. 1, vol. 10, pt. 1, pp. 102, 195; Keen letter, May 11, 1862, in Potter, "I Thought It My Duty," 143.

34. Reports of Wallace, Thayer, and McCord in *OR*, ser. 1, vol. 10, pt. 1,

pp. 169–72, 193–98; *Cincinnati Gazette*, quoted in *Tri-Weekly Nebraska Republican*, Apr. 25, 1862.

35. Compiled Service Records; "Emma Gillespie Born on a Battlefield," *Omaha Sunday World-Herald*, May 16, 1901, 19.

36. John M. Brockman letter, June 19, 1862, *Nebraska Advertiser*, June 26, 1862; *Nebraska City News*, Aug. 30, 1862; W. W. Cox, "My First Trip to Omaha," 75–76; *Nebraska Advertiser*, Aug. 23, 1862.

37. Thomas W. Tipton letter, July 7, 1862, *Nebraska Advertiser*, July 26, 1862.

38. W. A. Polock letter, n.d., *Nebraska Advertiser*, Aug. 9, 1862.

39. GO No. 135, HQ, First Nebraska Regiment, Helena, Aug. 11, 1862, RG18, roll 3, NSHS; Scherneckau, *Marching with the First Nebraska*, 221. A black man named Ben Ellerson had some affiliation with the regiment, according to an affidavit he gave to the provost marshal general's office in St. Louis on April 22, 1863. While walking down the street, Ellerson was asked by a white man what regiment he belonged to, evidently because Ellerson was wearing all or part of a Union uniform. When Ellerson told the man, "I had been with the First Nebraska," the man struck him with a stick, saying "he would hang all Blacks fighting against White men." Miller Boyd III, Missouri State Archives, e-mail to the author, June 16, 2010.

40. "G. H. T" (Thomas H. Griffin) letter, Sept. 27, 1862, and "R. N." (Reynel Noyes) letter, Oct. 1, 1862, *Nebraska Advertiser*, Oct. 18, 1862; "G. H. T" letter, Oct. 20, 1862, *Nebraska Advertiser*, Oct. 25, 1862.

41. Lass, "Nebraska City's Steam Wagon"; Lass, *From the Missouri to the Great Salt Lake*, 116–17, 122–23, 142.

42. *Tri-Weekly Nebraska Republican*, May 21, 1862; Lamb to Hiram Lamb, June 26, 1862, Lamb papers, NSHS.

43. Shannon, *Organization and Administration*, 1:271, 276–79; *Council Bluffs Nonpareil*, Aug. 9, 16, 1862; *Nebraska Advertiser*, Aug. 9, 30, 1862; *People's Semi-Weekly Press* (Nebraska City), Aug. 14, 1862; Lamb to Hiram Lamb, Aug. 28, 1862, Lamb papers, NSHS.

44. Maps outlining the evolution of Nebraska Territory appear in Blaser, "Where Is Nebraska, Anyway?"

45. Craig's tenure as commander of the troops along the central overland routes is reviewed in Robinett and Canan, "Military Career of James Craig." For the Sixth/Eleventh Ohio Volunteer Cavalry, see Robrock, "Eleventh Ohio."

46. Lem Flowers, stage line division agent, and employee Joseph Holloway reported attacks on trains and coaches near Three Crossings, Green River, and Plant's Stations in April. *Tri-Weekly Nebraska Republican*, Apr. 25,

1862. Fort Halleck's establishment is noted in Robrock, "Eleventh Ohio," 26–27.

47. Robinett and Canan, "Military Career of James Craig," 59–60; SO No. 64, Dept. of the Missouri, Nov. 29, 1862, mentioned in *Tri-Weekly Nebraska Republican*, Dec. 13, 1862.

48. At Nebraska City the Union Guards and the Rough and Ready Rangers had organized by the deadline. Lewis, *Messages and Proclamations*, 1:219–20.

49. Lewis, *Messages and Proclamations*, 1:220; Saunders to Stanton, Aug. 25, 1862, and War Dept. to Saunders, Sept. 3, 1862, OR, ser. 3, vol. 2, pp. 457–58, 510.

50. *Council Bluffs Nonpareil*, Apr. 26, 1862; Lamb to Hiram Lamb, June 26, 1862, Lamb papers, NSHS.

51. Saunders to Stanton, Aug. 25, 1862, OR, ser. 3, vol. 2, p. 458; *Council Bluffs Nonpareil*, Sept. 13, 1862. The story of the Minnesota uprising and the resulting military campaigns appears in Jones, *Civil War in the Northwest*; and Carley, *Dakota War of 1862*.

52. Lewis, *Messages and Proclamations*, 1:251–52.

53. Paddock to Stanton, Sept. 6, 1861, OR, ser. 3, vol. 2, p. 521; Stanton to Paddock, Sept. 10, 1862, OR, ser. 1, vol. 13, p. 622.

54. Lewis, *Messages and Proclamations*, 1:253.

55. Pope to Stanton, Sept. 22, 1862, OR, ser. 1, vol. 13, p. 653; SO, Sept. 29, 1862, *Nebraska Advertiser*, Oct. 4, 1862.

56. Editorial, *Nebraska Advertiser*, Aug. 23, 1862.

57. Isaac Coe to Maj. Gen. John S. Bowen, Sept. 10, 1862, RG18, box 1, NSHS.

58. Shannon, *Organization and Administration*, 2:56; Polock letter, Nov. 9, 1862, *Nebraska Advertiser*, Nov. 22, 1862.

59. *Nebraska City News*, Nov. 1, 1862.

60. The origins and muster-in dates of the companies of the Second Nebraska Cavalry are found in Dudley, *Roster of Nebraska Volunteers*. The Paddock Guards of Brownville are mentioned in the *Tri-Weekly Nebraska Republican*, Nov. 20, 1862. A review of enlistment dates from the First Nebraska rosters in Dudley indicates the approximate number of recruits acquired in fall 1862. August Scherneckau, the sole recruit from Hall County, reported that twenty-seven recruits actually reached the First Nebraska to be assigned to companies in early December 1862. Scherneckau, *Marching with the First Nebraska*, 35–36; anonymous soldier's letter, *People's Semi-Weekly Press*, Mar. 5, 1863.

61. *Tri-Weekly Nebraska Republican*, Nov. 25, 1862.

62. Dudley, *Roster of Nebraska Volunteers*, 158–84; *Tri-Weekly Nebraska Republican*, Dec. 13, 1862.

63. Morton-Watkins, *Illustrated History*, 1:472–73. Potts, "Nebraska Territory," 250–55, analyzes Daily's 1862 campaign.

64. Olson, *J. Sterling Morton*, 101–15, provides the best explanation of the complex issue and concludes that Morton was entitled to the seat (109).

65. Morton-Watkins, *Illustrated History*, 1:470.

66. Morton-Watkins, *Illustrated History*, 1:470.

67. While Kinney was the better educated and more polished of the two candidates, Daily was remembered by fellow Nemaha County resident William A. Polock as "a shrewd debater [who] always carried the masses with him." Renner's speech was delivered in Brownville on September 29 and reprinted in the *People's Semi-Weekly Press*, Oct. 6, 1862; see also Potts, "Nebraska Territory," 261. Renner's reference to the homeopathic soup may have referenced Abraham Lincoln's more famous use of the phraseology in his October 13, 1858, debate with Stephen A. Douglas at Quincy, Illinois. Lincoln then characterized Douglas's explanation of popular sovereignty (his Freeport Doctrine) as being as thin as homeopathic soup. See Etulain, *Lincoln Looks West*, 19. The whole idea derives from the practice of homeopathy, an effort to cure disease by administering very minute (i.e., watered-down) doses of a drug that, if given in large doses to a healthy person, would produce symptoms like those of the disease. For a biographical sketch of Kinney, see Morton-Watkins, *Illustrated History*, 2:65–67.

68. *Laws of Nebraska*, Eighth (Ter.) Session, 177. Shorter and Cobb had purchased Mexican War military bounty land warrants and used them to acquire land in Nebraska Territory. Sheldon, *Nebraska: Land and People*, 1:313n.

69. Sheldon, *Nebraska: Land and People*, 1:318; *Nebraska Advertiser*, Dec. 24, 1862, Jan. 17, 1863; *People's Semi-Weekly Press*, Dec. 29, 1862.

70. *Nebraska Advertiser*, Dec. 27, 1862.

71. On August 7, 1862, Omaha merchant William Koenig wrote to his mother in Germany, noting that steamboats on the Missouri River "are often stopped by the enemy and robbed." Koenig papers, NSHS. On March 28, 1863, guerrillas attacked the steamboat *New Sam Gaty* just east of Kansas City, killed two soldiers and several black deckhands, and destroyed government property, including three hundred sacks of flour being shipped to Nebraska Territory for the Second Nebraska Volunteer Cavalry. *OR*, ser. 1, vol. 22, pt. 2, p. 183; *Nebraska Advertiser*, Apr. 2, 1863.

3. 1863

1. For the winter campaign of the Army of Southeastern Missouri, see Bradbury, "This War Is Managed Mighty Strange."

2. Potter, "I Thought It My Duty," 150–51.

3. Scherneckau, *Marching with the First Nebraska*, 50; "Zouave," Twenty-third Iowa Volunteer Infantry, Jan. 26, 1863, *Council Bluffs (IA) Bugle*, Feb. 18, 1863.

4. Scherneckau, *Marching with the First Nebraska*, 85.

5. "Nebraska" letter, Mar. 20, 1863, *Tri-Weekly Nebraska Republican*, Mar. 30, 1863.

6. Fortunately Company H had its chronicler in Pvt. August Scherneckau, the literate German immigrant who enlisted from the Grand Island settlement in fall 1862. His sprightly account of Company H's St. Louis sojourn is in *Marching with the First Nebraska*.

7. Scherneckau, *Marching with the First Nebraska*, chap. 8; Potter, "I Thought It My Duty," 156. At the same time the Nebraska soldiers were performing their escort duty, Grant was winning battles at Raymond, Jackson, Champion's Hill, and Big Black River as prelude to besieging Vicksburg. McPherson, *Ordeal by Fire*, 316–17.

8. The Marmaduke raid is the subject of Bailey, "Texans Invade Missouri."

9. Lt. Col. William Baumer commanded the First Nebraska during the engagement. Colonel Livingston was in St. Louis and was ordered to lead reinforcements to Cape Girardeau, where he arrived just as the battle was over. Baumer's report, as well as that of Chief of Artillery Charles Meisner, is in *OR*, ser. 1, vol. 22, pt. 1, pp. 260–61, 267–69.

10. Report of Col. Oscar H. La Grange, *OR*, ser. 1, vol. 22, pt. 1, p. 265. Baumer's report of the Chalk Bluff pursuit is in *OR*, ser. 1, vol. 22, pt. 1, pp. 269–70.

11. Olson and Naugle, *History of Nebraska*, 161.

12. A. J. Hanscom to J. Sterling Morton, Jan. 31, 1863, Morton papers, NSHS.

13. *Nebraska City News*, Sept. 27, 1862.

14. *People's Semi-Weekly Press*, Sept. 29, 1862.

15. "More Again" letter, Feb. 7, 1862, *Nebraska Advertiser*, Feb. 13, 1862; Reynel Noyes letter, Oct. 1, 1862, *Nebraska Advertiser*, Oct. 18, 1862.

16. *Omaha Nebraskian*, quoted in *Tri-Weekly Nebraska Republican*, Jan. 21, 1863; *Omaha Nebraskian*, Sept. 11, 1863, quoted in Olson, *J. Sterling Morton*, 126; *Council Bluffs Nonpareil*, May 23, 1863.

17. *People's Semi-Weekly Press*, Jan. 5, 8, 1863.

18. Morton-Watkins, *Illustrated History*, 2:377. Olson, *J. Sterling Morton*, chap. 9, provides a summary of the role of northern "Peace" Democrats, such as Clement L. Vallandigham of Ohio, who were labeled Copperheads for their attacks on the administration. Vallandigham was banished to the Confederacy for "seditious activity."

19. *Nebraska City News*, June 21, 1862.

20. *Nebraska City News*, quoted in *People's Semi-Weekly Press*, Feb. 2, 1863; *People's Semi-Weekly Press*, Feb. 5, 1863. Issues of the *Nebraska City News* are not extant for 1863, but that paper's position and commentary can often be gleaned from its rival.

21. *People's Semi-Weekly Press* Feb. 19, Mar. 16, 1863; *Nebraska Advertiser*, Mar. 5, 1863.

22. *People's Semi-Weekly Press*, Feb. 9, Mar. 9, 1863.

23. *People's Semi-Weekly Press*, Apr. 6, 1863.

24. Olson, *J. Sterling Morton*, 119–20. Union Department of Ohio commander Gen. Ambrose Burnside had issued an order proscribing "treason, expressed or implied," under which he had Vallandigham arrested following the latter's May 1 speech denouncing the war. McPherson, *Ordeal by Fire*, 345–46.

25. *Council Bluffs Bugle*, June 3, 1863.

26. *Council Bluffs Bugle*, June 3, 1863. Morton was arguing that administration policies such as emancipation had "aided rebellion" by increasing the South's resolve and reducing any chance of compromise.

27. *Council Bluffs Bugle*, June 3, 1863. Morton's speech also included many of the arguments in the "Democratic Address" issued May 8, 1862, by fourteen members of the House of Representatives. Morton, then in Washington DC awaiting the outcome of his contest against Samuel G. Daily for the Nebraska delegate's seat stemming from the election of 1860, had a hand in drafting the address. Olson, *J. Sterling Morton*, 117–18. The address is published in the May 24, 1862, *Nebraska City News*.

28. George L. Miller to Morton, Feb. 10, 1863, cited in Olson, *J. Sterling Morton*, 122.

29. Minutes of the Brownville Union Club, 1863, RG4524, NSHS; *Nebraska Advertiser*, May 7, 1863.

30. *Nebraska Advertiser*, May 14, 1863; McPherson, *Ordeal by Fire*, 273–74.

31. [Five men] of Hendricks Precinct, Otoe County, Nebraska Territory, to Morton, June 17, 1863, Morton papers, NSHS.

32. The *Nebraska City News* and the *Nebraska Advertiser* also waged verbal warfare. For example, *News* editor Harvey called *Advertiser* editor T. R. Fisher "the fanatical genius who animates the abolition paper at Brownville," while Fisher branded Harvey's *News* as "a sheet that has given un-

mistakable evidences of sympathy with the rebels from the commence-
ment of the war." *Nebraska Advertiser*, July 16, 1863.

33. Fort Kearny letterbook, NSHS; *Nebraska Advertiser*, Mar. 26, 1863;
Tri-Weekly Nebraska Republican, Feb. 13, 1863. Furnas had been instrumental in recruiting for the First Nebraska in 1861, and in April 1862 he had
been commissioned colonel of a regiment of loyal Indians formed to re-
assert federal control in Indian Territory (Oklahoma). After experiencing
many hardships and problems, Furnas resigned his commission as colonel of the First Regiment of Indian Home Guards on September 7, 1862.
See Farb, "Military Career of Robert W. Furnas."

34. D. D. Belden to Joseph Barker Jr., Dec. 2, 1863, in Snoddy, Combs,
Marks, and Weber, *Their Man in Omaha*, 1:56–57; Morton-Watkins, *Illustrated History*, 2:266, 324.

35. Lass, *From the Missouri to the Great Salt Lake*, 124–37, passim; Morton-
Watkins, *Illustrated History*, 2:324–25; Lamb to Hiram Lamb, Nov. 17, 1863,
Lamb papers, NSHS.

36. *Tri-Weekly Nebraska Republican*, Feb. 18, 1863.

37. Pope to HQ, Feb. 18, 1863, OR, ser. 1, vol. 22, pt. 2, p. 117; Halleck to
Curtis, Mar. 2, 1863, OR, ser. 1, vol. 22, pt. 2, p. 137.

38. Paddock to Halleck, Mar. 2, 1863, and Saunders to Halleck, Apr. 11,
1863, OR, ser. 1, vol. 22, pt. 2, pp. 137, 211, 260; Halleck to Saunders, Apr.
18, 1863, OR, ser. 1, vol. 22, pt. 2, p. 224.

39. Robinett and Canan, "Military Career of James Craig," 62; *Tri-
Weekly Nebraska Republican*, June 15, 1863.

40. *Tri-Weekly Nebraska Republican*, Apr. 17, 1863; *Nebraska Advertiser*, Apr.
23, 30, 1863.

41. Pope to Halleck, July 27, 1863, OR, ser. 1, vol. 22, pt. 2, pp. 403–6.

42. Pope to Halleck, May 18, 1863, OR, ser. 1, vol. 22, pt. 2, p. 288. Jones,
Civil War in the Northwest, 57–74, describes the Sibley/Sully 1863 campaign.

43. "From the Neb. 2nd," HQ, Fort Pierre, Aug. 7, 1863, *Nebraska Advertiser*, Sept. 5, 1863; Henry Pierce diary, June 27, 1863, in Rowen, "Second
Nebraska's Campaign," 27.

44. *Council Bluffs Bugle*, Aug. 6, 1863; Pierce diary, Aug. 4, 1863, in
Rowen, "Second Nebraska's Campaign," 38.

45. Jones, *Civil War in the Northwest*, 67–69.

46. Pierce Diary, Sept. 3, 1863, in Rowen, "Second Nebraska's Campaign," 47. Jones, *Civil War in the Northwest*, 70. Military casualty totals are
given variously in the Furnas and Pierce diaries in Rowen, "Second Nebraska's Campaign," and in Dudley, *Roster of Nebraska Volunteers*. The Second Nebraska casualties as noted in Sully's official report are six killed
and fourteen wounded. OR, ser. 1, vol. 22, pt. 1, p. 561. A letter from Lt.

H. M. Atkinson published in the September 28, 1863, *Tri-Weekly Nebraska Republican* lists the casualties by name.

47. The muster-out dates and locations of the companies of the Second Nebraska are found in Dudley, *Roster of Nebraska Volunteers.*

48. "Attack on Pawnee Agency, Nebraska," *OR*, ser. 1, vol. 22, pt. 1, p. 278; R. T. Beall to Robert Knox, adjutant general of Nebraska, Nov. 21, 1865, RG18, box 2, NSHS; S. F. Watts letter, *Council Bluffs Bugle*, July 15, 1863; Wishart, *Unspeakable Sadness*, 180.

49. John Loree to H. B. Branch, superintendent of Indian affairs, Sept. 30, 1863, *ARCIA*, 1863, p. 255; Crawford, *Rekindling Camp Fires*, 36.

50. *OR*, ser. 1, vol. 22, pt. 2, pp. 397, 406; Logan, *Roster*, 4:1253; Ware, *Indian War of 1864*, 45.

51. Mulhair, *Ponca Agency*, 19–21; Wishart, *Unspeakable Sadness*, 151–53; "Affair with Ponca Indians," Maj. Herman H. Heath, Dakota City, Nebraska Territory, to Brig. Gen. Thomas McKean, Omaha, Dec. 20, 1863, *OR*, ser. 1, vol. 22, pt. 1, pp. 768–69.

52. George Armstrong, Feb. 3, 1864, to AAG, Dist. of Nebraska, *OR*, ser. 1, vol. 34, pt. 2, p. 235; Edwin M. Stanton to J. P. Usher, June 14–15, 1864, quoted in Mulhair, *Ponca Agency*, 21; Logan, *Roster*, 4:1280; Wishart, *Unspeakable Sadness*, 152–53. John J. Pattison was a member of Company B and kept a diary, which mentions that some soldiers had been sent from Dakota City to Niobrara on September 5, 1863. There are no entries in Pattison's diary from November 29, 1863, through March 6, 1865, hence no reference to the killing of the Poncas. Pattison, "With the U.S. Army," 82.

53. "Marching On," *Nebraska Advertiser*, June 11, 1863.

54. McPherson, *Ordeal By Fire*, 355–56; Shannon, *Organization and Administration*, 2:104.

55. *Nebraska Advertiser*, July 30, 1863. George Armstrong was provost marshal for the District of Nebraska in early 1863; he was superseded by O. F. Davis in May. *Tri-Weekly Nebraska Republican*, Mar. 4, May 13, 1863. Regulations governing military provost marshals are found in *OR*, ser. 3, vol. 3, pp. 125–46.

56. *Nebraska City Daily Press*, Dec. 14, 16, 1863.

57. *Council Bluffs Nonpareil*, May 9, June 6, 1863; *OR*, ser. 3, vol. 3, p. 494.

58. *Nebraska Advertiser*, May 14, 1863.

59. *Nebraska Advertiser*, June 11, July 30, 1863.

60. *Nebraska Advertiser*, July 25, 1863; *Report of the Adjutant General of Kansas*, 1:173, 175; *Nebraska City Daily Press*, Nov. 2, 4, 1863.

61. SO No. 95, Dist. of Nebraska, Oct. 28, 1863, *Nebraska City Daily Press*, Nov. 10, 23, 1863.

62. Ware, *Indian War of 1864*, 7, 55.

63. Athearn, "Across the Plains in 1863," 237.

64. Scherneckau, *Marching with the First Nebraska*, 160.

65. Scherneckau, *Marching with the First Nebraska*, 195, 195n. Fort Davidson still survives as the focal point of a Missouri State Park, with a visitor center interpreting the 1864 Battle of Pilot Knob.

66. *Nebraska Advertiser*, July 30, 1863; Livingston to Saunders, Aug. 31, 1863, RG18, box 2, NSHS.

67. GO No. 191, *OR*, ser. 3, vol. 3, pp. 414–16.

68. *Nebraska Advertiser*, Aug. 22, 1863; Saunders to Hughes, RG18, box 2, NSHS; *Tri-Weekly Nebraska Republican*, Sept. 28, 1863.

69. *Nebraska Advertiser*, Sept. 5, 1863.

70. Scherneckau, *Marching with the First Nebraska*, 198, 210–12; *OR*, ser. 1, vol. 22, pt. 2, pp. 621, 623; Company I morning report, Oct. 1863, RG18, roll 3, NSHS.

71. Halleck to Schofield, Oct. 10, 1863, *OR*, ser. 1, vol. 22, pt. 2, p. 627; Scherneckau, *Marching with the First Nebraska*, 222–36, passim.

72. Scherneckau, *Marching with the First Nebraska*, 222, 222n; Circular, HQ First Nebraska, Camp Gamble, Nov. 3, 1863, RG18, roll 3, NSHS; Donovan to Livingston, Nov. 11, 1863, Livingston papers, NSHS.

73. SO No. 317, Dept. of the Missouri, Nov. 20, 1863, and SO No. 213, State of Missouri Adjutant General's Office, Nov. 20, 1863, both in Livingston papers, NSHS; John B. Gray to Edwin M. Stanton, Sept. 16, 1864, *OR*, ser. 3, vol. 4, p. 729.

74. Fisk to Schofield, *OR*, ser. 1, vol. 22, pt. 2, p. 707.

75. Schofield to Livingston, Nov. 30, 1863, and SO No. 327, Dept. of the Missouri, Nov. 30, 1863, *OR*, ser. 1, vol. 22, pt. 2, pp. 725–26.

76. Schofield to Livingston, Nov. 30, 1863, and SO No. 327, Dept. of the Missouri, Nov. 30, 1863, *OR*, ser. 1, vol. 22, pt. 2, pp. 725–26.

77. Scherneckau, *Marching with the First Nebraska*, 231–33.

78. Scherneckau, *Marching with the First Nebraska*, 236–38.

79. Scherneckau, *Marching with the First Nebraska*, 240–41; Livingston to Dept. of the Missouri, Dec. 25, 1863, *OR*, ser. 1, vol. 22, pt. 2, p. 750.

80. *Tri-Weekly Nebraska Republican*, Dec. 4, 1863.

81. Daily to Livingston, Dec. 29, 1863, Livingston papers, NSHS; Blaser, "Where Is Nebraska, Anyway?" 8, 9, 11.

4. 1864

1. Lewis, *Messages and Proclamations*, 1:167.

2. Lewis, *Messages and Proclamations*, 1:176. The early Nebraska enabling acts are discussed in Watkins, "How Nebraska Was Brought into the Union," 381–83.

3. Lewis, *Messages and Proclamations*, 1:180.

4. Olson, *J. Sterling Morton*, 129; Morton speech, *Council Bluffs Bugle*, June 3, 1863; Miller to Morton, Feb. 9, 1864, Morton papers, NSHS.

5. *Nebraska Republican*, Jan. 29, 1864.

6. *Nebraska Republican*, Jan. 29, 1864.

7. *Laws of Nebraska*, Ninth (Ter.) Session, 164–69, 281–82.

8. *Nebraska Advertiser*, Jan. 28, Feb. 4, 25, 1864.

9. SO No. 5, HQ, Dist. of Nebraska, RG500, Records of the U.S. War Department, roll 7, NSHS; *Nebraska Advertiser*, Feb. 11, 25, 1864.

10. GO No. 10, Dist. of Nebraska, Mar. 19, 1864, *Nebraska City Daily Press*, Feb. 26, Mar. 23, 1864.

11. *Nebraska City Daily Press*, Feb. 20, 26, Mar. 7, 11, Apr. 29, 1864; *Nebraska Advertiser*, May 5, 1864; OR, ser. 1, vol. 34, pt. 3, pp. 217, 262.

12. OR, ser. 1, vol. 34, pt. 2, pp. 7, 342, 463–64, vol. 41, pt. 3, pp. 981–82.

13. Pope to Curtis, Mar. 14, 1864, and Curtis to Pope, Mar. 18, 1864, OR, ser. 1, vol. 34, pt. 2, pp. 606–7, 652; Curtis to Mitchell, Apr. 18, 1864, OR, ser. 1, vol. 34, pt. 3, p. 217. Jones, *Civil War in the Northwest*, chap. 5, covers the 1864 campaign in Dakota.

14. Lass, *From the Missouri to the Great Salt Lake*, 168–69.

15. Lamb to Hiram Lamb, May 7, June 5, 1864, Lamb papers, NSHS; *Nebraska Republican*, Aug. 19, 1864.

16. *Council Bluffs Nonpareil*, June 18, 1864; Ware, *Indian War of 1864*, 274; *Nebraska Advertiser*, Aug. 4, 1864; Larson, "Across the Plains ," 8.

17. *Nebraska City Daily Press*, Apr. 28, 1864; Col. William O. Collins to Brig. Gen. Robert Mitchell, Apr. 26, 1864, OR, ser. 1, vol. 34, pt. 3, pp. 304–5. A good overview of the situation along the overland routes and the Indian reaction is found in McDermott, *Circle of Fire*, chap. 1. Jonathan Blanchard traveled to the Idaho/Montana goldfields via the Platte Valley and Bozeman routes in the spring of 1864 and described both the immense emigration and its effect on the Indians. Keller, "1864 Overland Trail."

18. John A. Evans, governor of Colorado Territory, to Curtis, Dept. of Kansas, May 28, 1864, OR, ser. 1, vol. 34, pt. 4, pp. 97–99; "Minutes of a Council, June 8, 1864," OR, ser. 1, vol. 34, pt. 4, pp. 459–60.

19. Mitchell to Evans, July 4, 1864, OR, ser. 1, vol. 41, pt. 2, p. 168.

20. The Enabling Act appears in the *Nebraska Republican*, Apr. 29, 1864, and in *Statutes at Large*, 13:47–50.

21. *Omaha Nebraskian*, May 27, 1864, quoted in Morton-Watkins, *Illustrated History*, 1:483.

22. *Nebraska Republican*, June 3, 1864.

23. *Nebraska Republican*, May 20, 1864.

24. Watkins, "How Nebraska Was Brought into the Union," 388–97.

25. *Statutes at Large*, 13:30–35, 47–50; Etulain, "Abraham Lincoln," 15–16.

26. *Nebraska Advertiser*, July 7, 1864.

27. *Nebraska City Daily Press*, July 6, 1864, reprinted in *Nebraska Advertiser*, July 21, 1864; *Nebraska Republican*, July 22, 1864.

28. Scherneckau on February 26 mentioned receiving "the only mail since we left Rolla," including two letters from Nebraska dated November 28 and 30, 1863. He also mentioned the supply problems, as do numerous military reports. See, e.g., Scherneckau, *Marching With the First Nebraska*, 262, 266; Livingston to Colonel Richmond, Feb. 4, 1864, *OR*, ser. 1, vol. 34, pt. 2, pp. 241–42.

29. McPherson, *Ordeal by Fire*, 391.

30. The text of the proclamation appears in the *Batesville Bazoo*, Feb. 6, 1864, a small newspaper published by the men of the First Nebraska. The only known issue is in the Missouri Historical Society, St. Louis.

31. Mobley, *Making Sense*, 143–44; Livingston to AAG, [Dept. of Arkansas], Apr. 16, 1864, *OR*, ser. 1, vol. 34, pt. 3, p. 181.

32. GO No. 323, AG's Office, Sept. 28, 1863, in *Army and Navy Journal* 1 (Oct. 10, 1863): 108; Scherneckau, *Marching with the First Nebraska*, 296n. The Compiled Service Records and Dudley, *Roster of Nebraska Volunteers*, record the black "undercooks." The "remarks" for December 31 on the Company K morning report for December 1865 noted that Smith had deserted while on furlough at Omaha. RG 18, roll 3, NSHS.

33. Livingston to AAG, Feb. 10, 1864, *OR*, ser. 1, vol. 34, pt. 1, p. 131; GO No. 6, Dist. of Northeastern Arkansas, Jan. 11, 1864, *OR*, ser. 1, vol. 34, pt. 2, pp. 65–67.

34. Scherneckau, *Marching with the First Nebraska*, 254–55. He may have meant the first enemy soldier he had seen killed, though perhaps he had not personally witnessed any of the summary executions of "bushwhackers" during the First Nebraska's march to Batesville.

35. *OR*, ser. 1, vol. 34, pts. 1, 2, 3 contain the correspondence and reports of activities in the District of Northeastern Arkansas from January through May 1864. Scherneckau, *Marching with the First Nebraska*, 252–60, provides an eyewitness account of the scout and action at Sylamore Mountain.

36. Livingston to AAG, Apr. 16, 1864, *OR*, ser. 1, vol. 34, pt. 3, p. 181; Scherneckau, *Marching with the First Nebraska*, 266.

37. GO No. 13, Batesville, Jan. 20, 1864, and Tipton to Livingston, May 1, 1864, both in Tipton file, Compiled Service Records.

38. Livingston to AAG, Apr. 16, May 12, 1864, *OR*, ser. 1, vol. 34, pt. 3, pp. 181, 562–63; Scherneckau, *Marching with the First Nebraska*, 277.

39. Mobley, *Making Sense*, 164–68; DeBlack, *With Fire and Sword*, 108–17; Steele to Livingston, May 22, 1864, *OR*, ser. 1, vol. 34, pt. 3, pp. 718–19. While the First Nebraska was at Jacksonport, the men published at least two issues of another camp newspaper, the *Reveille*. The issue of May 3, 1864, is on display in the museum at Jacksonport State Park.

40. Livingston to AAG, Mar. 18, 1864, *OR*, ser. 1, vol. 34, pt. 2, pp. 646–47; "Abraham" letter, Apr. 2, 1864, *Nebraska Advertiser*, May 5, 1864; De-Black, *With Fire and Sword*, 105–6. The figure of 837 Rebels captured or killed by Livingston's troops was reported in the *St. Louis Democrat*, June 17, 1864, reprinted in *Nebraska Republican*, June 24, 1864.

41. Sutherland, "Guerrillas," 140.

42. Circular and GO No. 18, GO No. 20, HQ, First Nebraska, DeVall's Bluff, June 1, 4, 9, 1864, RG18, roll 3 and box 3, NSHS.

43. *Nebraska Republican*, June 24, 1864; Scherneckau, *Marching with the First Nebraska*, 298; Edward Rosewater diary, June 28, 1864, Rosewater papers, American Jewish Archives, Cincinnati OH.

44. Livingston to "Fellow Citizens," July 4, 1864, *Nebraska City Daily Press*, July 20, 1864.

45. Tipton to Livingston, July 8, 1864, Livingston papers, NSHS; Rolfe, "Overland Freighting," 287–88; Maddox, "Freighting Reminiscences."

46. William Polock letter, July 1, 1864, *Nebraska Advertiser*, July 21, 1864; Scherneckau, *Marching with the First Nebraska*, 286; *Nebraska Republican*, July 15, 1864.

47. *OR*, ser. 1, vol. 41, pt. 2, p. 284.

48. Lt. Col. William Baumer to Gov. Alvin Saunders, n.d., excerpt in *Nebraska Republican*, July 15, 1864.

49. *Nebraska Republican*, Aug. 19, 1864; Lt. Lewis Lowry to Col. Robert R. Livingston, Omaha, Nov. 15, 1864, RG18, box 2, NSHS.

50. Circular, Office of the Commissary of Musters, Little Rock AR, Aug. 18, 1864, and George W. Sprague to editor, Aug. 29, 1864, in *Nebraska Advertiser*, Sept. 15, 1864.

51. Lt. Lewis Lowry, Camp near Ashley's Station AR, to Livingston, Aug. 20, 1864, Livingston papers, NSHS; Johnson reminiscence, NSHS.

52. Chaplain Thomas Tipton, writing from Omaha on September 20, 1864, reported the acting governor's intercession; *Nebraska Advertiser*, Sept. 22, 1864. See also SO No. 245, Dept. of Arkansas, Oct. 7, 1864, *OR*, ser. 1, vol. 41, pt. 3, p. 680; Lowry to Livingston, Nov. 15, 1864, RG18, box 2, NSHS.

53. Polock letter, Sept. 18, 1864, *Nebraska Republican*, Sept. 30, 1864; Po-

lock to Lt. F. A. McDonald, adjutant, First Nebraska Cavalry, Oct. 14, 1864, cited in Potter, "First Nebraska's Orphan Detachment." It was common for both sides to release ("parole") prisoners of war soon after their capture to avoid having to guard and feed them or to avoid the risk of encumbering the tactical operations of columns such as Shelby's cavalry. Under the conventions of war, paroled prisoners could not be returned to duty in their own army until they were "exchanged" on paper for an equivalent number of parolees from the other side.

54. Potter, "First Nebraska's Orphan Detachment," 38.

55. Potter, "First Nebraska's Orphan Detachment," 38–39.

56. Mitchell to Lt. J. A. Wilcox and Mitchell to Curtis, July 27, 1864, OR, ser. 1, vol. 41, pt. 2, pp. 428–29. The name of the post at Cottonwood Canyon had been changed to Fort Cottonwood on May 18, 1864.

57. Organization of Troops, Dist. of Nebraska, Aug. 31, 1864, OR, ser. 1, vol. 41, pt. 2, pp. 981–82.

58. Saunders to Curtis, July 28, 1864, and Mitchell to C. S. Charlot, July 29, 1864, OR, ser. 1, vol. 41, pt. 2, pp. 447, 462–63.

59. Halleck to Curtis, July 30, 1864, OR, ser. 1, vol. 41, pt. 2, p. 483.

60. "The Indians," *Army and Navy Journal* 2, no. 50 (Aug. 5, 1865).

61. Halleck to Grant, Aug. 17, 1864, OR, ser. 1, vol. 41, pt. 2, p. 739.

62. George K. Otis and Ben Holladay, "Testimony as to the Claim of Ben Holladay for Loss and Damages Sustained by Him on the Overland Stage Line . . . ," 1861–66, Senate Misc. Document 19, 46th Cong., 2nd sess., Dec. 17, 1879; Etulain, *Lincoln Looks West*, 44–45; Annual Message of the President, Dec. 6, 1864, OR, ser. 3, vol. 4, p. 978. Omaha telegrapher Edward Rosewater helped transmit the 16,500-word Nevada Constitution over the wires on October 21, a process that took about twelve hours. Rosewater diary, Oct. 21, 1864, Rosewater papers, American Jewish Archives, Cincinnati OH.

63. Various sources are available on these raids, including Green, Murphy, and Gilbert, "Incidents of the Indian Outbreak"; Becher, *Massacre along the Medicine Road*; Mitchell to Curtis, Aug. 8, 1864, OR, ser. 1, vol. 41, pt. 2, p. 612; Ware, *Indian War of 1864*; and Hagerty, "Indian Raids."

64. Curtis to Saunders, Aug. 23, 1864, *Nebraska Republican*, Aug. 26, 1864; Stolley, "History of the First Settlement of Hall County," 55–57; Lamb to Hiram Lamb, Sept. 4, 1864, Lamb papers, NSHS. Stolley blamed the thefts on the company commander, "Captain Davis" [Capt. James B. David]. Earlier, men from David's company had stolen items from fellow soldiers of the Eleventh Ohio Cavalry at the Post of Columbus. In March 1865 Colonel Livingston censured David and his men and ordered them to pay for the goods stolen from the Ohio soldiers. The transgressions

of this particular company may explain why they were sent to garrison a temporary post on the South Loup River north of Fort Kearny in May 1865, which the soldiers called "Fort Banishment." See GO No. 7, HQ, East Subdist. of Nebraska, Mar. 13, 1865, RG18, roll 3, NSHS; and Howell, "Post South Loup Fork." For other depredations by volunteer soldiers, see Ludwickson, "A Far Worse Scourge."

65. *Nebraska Republican*, Sept. 9, 1864; *Nebraska Advertiser*, Aug. 18, Sept. 1, 1864. Agent Robert W. Furnas reported that the Santees appeared on the Iowa side of the Missouri River and killed several Winnebagos who had moved onto the Omaha Reservation. After the attack, Furnas ordered the construction of a blockhouse.

66. *Nebraska Advertiser*, Sept. 1, 1864; Report of Col. Robert R. Livingston, East Subdist. of Nebraska, to AG, Nov. 1, 1864, *OR*, ser. 1, vol. 41, pt. 1, p. 832; *Nebraska City Daily Press*, Aug. 10, 1864; Charles F. Porter letter, Aug. 8, 1864, *Nebraska Republican*, Aug. 12, 1864.

67. Lt. John Gilbert of the militia and Capt. Edward Murphy recalled the episode in separate accounts appearing in Green, Murphy, and Gilbert, "Incidents of the Indian Outbreak." Official documents are in *OR*, ser. 1, vol. 41, pt. 2, pp. 672, 691, 693, 721.

68. GO No. 2, Fort Kearny letterbook, NSHS.

69. SO No. 74, Dist. of Nebraska, Aug. 11, 1864, Livingston papers, NSHS; *OR*, ser. 1, vol. 41, pt. 2, p. 765; *Nebraska Republican*, Aug. 26, 1864.

70. Lewis, *Messages and Proclamations*, 1:223; Edward Rosewater diary, Aug. 15, 1864, Rosewater papers, American Jewish Archives, Cincinnati OH; *Nebraska Republican*, Aug. 19, 1864; Dudley, *Roster of Nebraska Volunteers*, 212–21; Fort Kearny letterbook, NSHS.

71. John Pratt, AAG, Omaha, to Mitchell, Aug. 18, 1864, *OR*, ser. 1, vol. 41, pt. 2, p. 765; Curtis to Saunders, telegram, Aug. 23, 1864, *Nebraska Republican*, Aug. 26, 1864; William Stolley to brother, Sept. 10, 1864, published as Stolley, "Defense of Grand Island."

72. RG500, Records of the U.S. War Department, roll 12, NSHS; *OR*, ser. 1, vol. 41, pt. 2, pp. 864, 981; Mattes, *Great Platte River Road*, 474–79.

73. *OR*, ser. 1, vol. 41, pt. 1, pp. 243–44, and vol. 41, pt. 3, p. 36.

74. Ware, *Indian War of 1864*, 325; Report of Lt. Thomas Flanagan, Sixteenth Kansas Cavalry, Nov. 1864, *OR*, ser. 1, vol. 41, pt. 1, p. 246.

75. *OR*, ser. 1, vol. 41, pt. 3, p. 494; Ware, *Indian War of 1864*, 310.

76. Mitchell to Curtis, Oct. 5, 1864, *OR*, ser. 1, vol. 41, pt. 3, p. 652; Lamb to Hiram Lamb, Oct. 9, 1864, Lamb papers, NSHS.

77. Livingston report, Nov. 1, 1864, *OR*, ser. 1, vol. 41, pt. 1, pp. 825–29, describes both the troop disposition and the facilities at these Platte Valley posts.

78. Report of Col. Robert R. Livingston to AAG, Dist. of Nebraska, Dec. 1, 1864, *OR*, ser. 1, vol. 41, pt. 1, p. 836; Livingston to commanders, Nov. 28, 1864, *OR*, ser. 1, vol. 41, pt. 1, p. 838.

79. Livingston report, Nov. 1, 1864, *OR*, ser. 1, vol. 41, pt. 1, p. 830; GO No. 6, HQ, East Subdist. of Nebraska, Oct. 18, 1864, RG18, roll 3, NSHS.

80. The events and casualties are described in Livingston's reports of November 1 and December 1, 1864, and by reports of his subordinates, all found in *OR*, ser. 1, vol. 41, pt. 1, pp. 825–32, 833–37, 838–49.

81. McDermott, *Circle of Fire*, 158; Ware, *Indian War of 1864*, 254.

82. Halleck to Curtis, July 30, 1864, and Curtis to Halleck, Aug. 30, 1864, *OR*, ser. 1, vol. 41, pt. 2, pp. 483, 944.

83. Livingston report, Nov. 1, 1864, and William Ivory report, Oct. 17, 1864, *OR*, ser. 1, vol. 41, pt. 1, p. 842; GO No. 5, East Subdist. of Nebraska, Oct. 17, 1864, RG18, roll 3, NSHS.

84. Lt. Charles Thompson to AAG, Omaha, Dec. 2, 1864, *OR*, ser. 1, vol. 41, pt. 1, pp. 848–49. For a detailed discussion of army horse problems during the 1864–65 plains campaigns, see Potter, "Horses."

85. John Pratt, AAG, to Livingston, Oct. 17, 1864, *OR*, ser. 1, vol. 41, pt. 4, p. 62.

86. Livingston to post commanders, Oct. 17, 1864, *OR*, ser. 1, vol. 41, pt. 4, pp. 62–63; Livingston report, Nov. 1, 1864, *OR*, ser. 1, vol. 41, pt. 1, pp. 830–31.

87. W. M. Albin to W. P. Dole, Oct. 1, 1864, *ARCIA*, 1864, p. 348–49. Wishart, *Unspeakable Sadness*, chap. 6, "Life on the Reservations in the 1860s," provides a good overall summary of the plight of the Nebraska reservation tribes during the war years.

88. *ARCIA*, 1864, pp. 350–56, 377, 382–83; Wishart, *Unspeakable Sadness*, 156, 174.

89. *Nebraska Republican*, June 3, 1864; McPherson, *Ordeal by Fire*, 407.

90. W. H. H. Waters letter, June 4, 1864, *Nebraska City Daily Press*, June 13, 1864.

91. *Nebraska Republican*, July 1, 1864; *Nebraska Advertiser*, June 30, July 7, 1864.

92. McPherson, *Ordeal by Fire*, 441.

93. T. W. Bedford to Morton, Aug. 3, 1864, Morton papers, NSHS.

94. Miller sketch in Morton-Watkins, *Illustrated History*, 2:719; *Omaha Nebraskian*, Sept. 26, 1864, reported in Morton-Watkins, *Illustrated History*, 1:492.

95. *Nebraska Republican*, Aug. 26, 1864.

96. Thomas R. Tipton to Thomas J. Majors, Sept. 20, 1864, Majors papers, NSHS; *Nebraska Republican*, Sept. 9, 1864; *Nebraska City Daily Press*, Oct. 4, 1864.

97. *Nebraska Advertiser,* Sept. 15, 1864.

98. W. H. Lamb to Hiram Lamb, Oct. 9, 1864, Lamb papers, NSHS; Pollock to editor, Sept. 26, 1864, *Nebraska Republican,* Oct. 7, 1864.

99. Morton-Watkins, *Illustrated History,* 2:377–78, 719; *Nebraska City Daily Press,* Oct. 7, 1864.

100. Morton-Watkins, *Illustrated History,* 1:493; report of vote of Nebraska soldiers at Nashville (in Fifth Iowa Cavalry), *Nebraska Republican,* Oct. 28, 1864; J. G. Megeath, Omaha, Oct. 12, 1864, to J. Sterling Morton, Morton papers, NSHS; " R. N." (Reynel Noyes) letter, Oct. 11, 1864, *Nebraska Republican,* Oct. 21, 1864. When the First Nebraska was mustered out in July 1866, the *Nebraska City News* claimed some of the discharged soldiers expressed jubilation that they could "now vote as we like." There seems to be no way to verify whether or not officers may have pressured soldiers to vote a certain way in either the 1864 or 1866 territorial elections. The suggestion of coercion in 1866 may have been another effort by the Democrats to discredit the soldier vote in the June 2 election for a state constitution and state officers, which proved crucial to Republican success. The Democrats' main argument against counting the soldier vote rested on some evidence that Iowa soldiers serving in the First Nebraska had voted illegally.

101. *Nebraska Republican,* Nov. 11, 1864; Ware, *Indian War of 1864,* 268: William A. Polock letter, Sept. 28, 1864, *Daily Missouri Democrat,* Sept. 29, 1864. McPherson, in *Ordeal by Fire,* 457, noted, "No other society had tried the experiment of letting its fighting men vote in an election that might decide whether they were to continue fighting."

102. Miller to Morton, Oct. 15, 30, 1864, Morton papers, NSHS.

103. *Nebraska City Press,* Oct. 20, 1864; *Daily Nebraska City News,* Dec. 3, 1864; Olson, *J. Sterling Morton,* 130–32.

5. 1865

1. Lewis, *Messages and Proclamations,* 1:182. See McDermott, *Circle of Fire,* 15–22, for a detailed summary of the raid. O'Brien and rancheman Jack Morrow reported the raid in letters published in the January 13, 1865, issue of the *Nebraska Republican.* The Indians' side of the story is told by George Bent in *Life of George Bent,* chap. 7, "The Great Raids."

2. Ware provides a detailed account of the expedition in *Indian War of 1864,* 329–55. See also Mitchell to Curtis, Jan. 29, 1865, telegrams received, Dept. of Kansas, RG393, Records of U.S. Army Continental Commands, courtesy of John D. McDermott. For the raids, see McDermott, *Circle of Fire,* 27; Hyde, *Life of George Bent.*

3. McDermott, *Circle of Fire,* 28–34, summarizes the February 2 raid; Ware, *Indian War of 1864,* 352–75, provides an eyewitness account.

4. McDermott, "We Had a Terribly Hard Time"; Bleed and Scott, "Archeological Interpretation."

5. McDermott, "We Had a Terribly Hard Time"; Bleed and Scott, "Archeological Interpretation."

6. Livingston to Dodge, ca. Feb. 9, 1865, enclosed with Dodge to Pope, Feb. 9, 1865, *OR*, ser. 1, vol. 48, pt. 1, pp. 793–94; Livingston report, Fort Kearny, Feb. 18, 1865, *OR*, ser. 1, vol. 48, pt. 1, pp. 88–90.

7. Livingston report, Fort Kearny, Feb. 18, 1865, *OR*, ser. 1, vol. 48, pt. 1, pp. 89–91; GO No. 4, East Subdist. of Nebraska, Feb. 15, 1865, RG18, roll 3, NSHS.

8. B. M. Hughes to Curtis, Oct. 10, 1864, *OR*, ser. 1, vol. 41, pt. 3, p. 768; Livingston report, Nov. 1, 1864, and Livingston report, Dec. 1, 1864, *OR*, ser. 1, vol. 41, pt. 1, pp. 832, 836–37; Mitchell to Curtis, Feb. 3, 1865, *OR*, ser. 1, vol. 48, pt. 1, p. 735; Mitchell to Dodge and Livingston to Dodge, Feb. 9, 1865, *OR*, ser. 1, vol. 48, pt. 1, pp. 793–94.

9. C. F. Porter letter, Fort Rankin, Colorado Territory, Feb. 6, 1865, *Nebraska Republican*, Feb. 17, 1865.

10. "Capitol Correspondence," Feb. 4, 1865, *Nebraska Advertiser*, Feb. 9, 1865.

11. Grant to Halleck, Nov. 30, 1864, *OR*, ser. 1, vol. 41, pt. 4, p. 716; Grant to Lincoln, Dec. 7, 1864, *OR*, ser. 1, vol. 41, pt. 4, pp. 784–85.

12. GO No. 294, *OR*, ser. 1, vol. 41, pt. 4, p. 749; GO No. 11, *OR*, ser. 1, vol. 48, pt. 1, p. 686. See Jones, *Civil War in the Northwest*, for the full story of Pope as commander of that department. His reassignment and the creation of the Department of the Northwest is at 11–12.

13. McDermott, *Circle of Fire*, 49.

14. Saunders to Stanton, with enclosure, Jan. 17, 19, 1865, *OR*, ser. 1, vol. 48, pt. 1, p. 568, 589.

15. Holladay to Stanton, Oct. 15, 1864, *OR*, ser. 1, vol. 41, pt. 3, p. 903; Pope to Halleck, Feb. 6, 8, 1865, *OR*, ser. 1, vol. 48, pt. 1, pp. 760, 778; GO No. 80, Mar. 28, 1865, *OR*, ser. 1, vol. 48, pt. 1, p. 1285; GO No. 4, Dist. of the Plains, Apr. 8, 1865, *OR*, ser. 1, vol. 48, pt. 2, pp. 54–55.

16. Mitchell to Dodge and Dodge to Mitchell, Feb. 28, 1865, *OR*, ser. 1, vol. 48, pt. 1, pp. 1014–15.

17. Pope to Halleck and Halleck to Pope, Feb. 6, 1865, *OR*, ser. 1, vol. 48, pt. 1, pp. 760–61; Mitchell to Dodge, Feb. 9, 1865, *OR*, ser. 1, vol. 48, pt. 1, p. 793. The story of the Confederate prisoners of war who enlisted in Union service is told in D. Brown, *Galvanized Yankees*. For the Pawnee Scouts, see Danker, " North Brothers."

18. SO No. 41, Dept. of the Missouri, Feb. 10, 1865, *OR*, ser. 1, vol. 48, pt. 1, pp. 807–8.

19. GO No. 4, East Subdist. of Nebraska, Feb. 15, 1865, RG18, roll 3, NSHS; Livingston to Col. Thomas Moonlight, Feb. 15, 1865, *OR*, ser. 1, vol. 48, pt. 1, p. 853; Organization of Troops in the Dept. of Missouri, East Subdist. of Nebraska, Feb. 28, 1865, *OR*, ser. 1, vol. 48, pt. 1, p. 1040; *Nebraska Republican*, Feb. 24, 1865; Mitchell to Dodge, Mar. 10, 1865, *OR*, ser. 1, vol. 48, pt. 1, p. 1144.

20. Scherneckau, "Soldiering in the Platte Valley."

21. Hadley, "Plains War," 278; Scherneckau, "Soldiering in the Platte Valley," 42.

22. Ivory to Lt. F. A McDonald, Mar. 25, 1865, Ivory file, Compiled Service Records.

23. Lewis, *Messages and Proclamations*, 1:189.

24. Morton-Watkins, *Illustrated History*, 1:497; Lewis, *Messages and Proclamations*, 1:181; "Capitol Correspondence," *Nebraska Advertiser*, Feb. 9, 1865.

25. *Nebraska Advertiser*, Feb. 16, 23, 1865; *Nebraska Republican*, Feb. 17, 1865; *Laws of Nebraska*, Tenth (Ter.) Session, 161–62.

26. *Tri-Weekly Nebraska Republican*, May 7, 1862, Dec. 4, 1863; *Nebraska City Daily Press*, Aug. 15, 1864; *Nebraska Advertiser*, Feb. 2, 16, 1865.

27. *Nebraska Advertiser*, May 5, 1864; Gerteis, *Civil War St. Louis*, 230–32.

28. *Nebraska Republican*, Mar. 3, Apr. 21, May 26, 1865. The *Nebraska Republican* of May 5, 1865, published an April 27 letter from First Nebraska surgeon William McClelland listing supplies furnished him by the St. Louis Sanitary Committee for distribution to the solders at the Post of Omaha and at Fort Kearny. They included writing supplies, books, games and puzzles, canned goods, crackers, and patent medicines.

29. *Nebraska Republican*, Apr. 14, June 2, 1865; Tipton, "Forty Years in Nebraska," 67. Tipton also said Nebraska women had contributed $10,000 to the 1864 sanitary fair in St. Louis.

30. *Nebraska Republican*, Mar. 3, 10, 1865; *Nebraska Advertiser*, Mar. 16, 1865.

31. *Daily Nebraska City News*, Apr. 11, 1865.

32. *Nebraska Republican*, Apr. 7, 14, 21, 1865.

33. Griffin letter, *Nebraska Republican*, Apr. 28, 1865. He was adapting Aesop's fable about the farmer and the snake to make his point.

34. *Nebraska Advertiser*, Apr. 13, 1865.

35. Scherneckau, "Soldiering in the Platte Valley," 25; "Nemaha" letter, Apr. 18, 1865, *Nebraska Advertiser*, Apr. 27, 1865.

36. Scherneckau, "Soldiering in the Platte Valley," 26; *Nebraska Advertiser*, Apr. 20, 1865.

37. *Nebraska Herald* (Plattsmouth), Apr. 19, 1865; *Nebraska Republican*, Apr. 21, 1865.

38. "M" letter, May 22, 1865, *Nebraska Republican*, June 2, 1865; Scherneckau, "Soldiering in the Platte Valley," 26.

39. Scherneckau, "Soldiering in the Platte Valley," 26; Morton diary, Apr. 15, 1865, quoted in Olson, *J. Sterling Morton*, 133; *Nebraska City News*, Apr. 22, 1865.

40. Saunders to Samuel Maxwell, May 9, 1865, Maxwell papers, NSHS. According to Saunders, the signed commission reappointing him as territorial governor was found on Lincoln's desk when the president's office was opened after the assassination. The commission is in the NSHS museum collections.

41. OR, ser. 1, vol. 48, pt. 2, pp. 60, 101; D. Brown, *Galvanized Yankees*, 22; Scherneckau, "Soldiering in the Platte Valley," 32.

42. Dudley, *Roster of Nebraska Volunteers*, 227–29; *Nebraska Republican*, May 12, 1865; Farb, "Robert W. Furnas as Omaha Indian Agent," 189, 291.

43. Dodge to Vincent, May 22, 1865, OR, ser. 1, vol. 48, pt. 2, p. 545; Grant to Pope, May 24, 1865, OR, ser. 1, vol. 48, pt. 2, p. 582.

44. OR, ser. 3, vol. 4, pp. 1280–81.

45. Olson, *Red Cloud*, 13–14; Edwin Stanton to J. R. Doolittle, June 15, 1865, OR, ser. 1, vol. 48, pt. 2, pp. 895–96; Mardock, "Plains Frontier and the Indian Peace Policy," 188–91.

46. Connor to Dodge, Apr. 14, 1865, Connor to Dodge, Apr. 29, 1865, Dodge to Pope, May 15, 1865, and Dodge to Connor, May 19, 1865, OR, ser. 1, vol. 48, pt. 2, pp. 101, 246, 453, 515.

47. Dodge to Pope, report, July 18, 1865, OR, ser. 1, vol. 48, pt. 1, p. 332; Connor to Dodge, July 21, 1865, OR, ser. 1, vol. 48, pt. 2, p. 1112.

48. Connor to Dodge, June 24, 1865, OR, ser. 1, vol. 48, pt. 2, p. 988; Dodge to Pope, May 26, 1865, OR, ser. 1, vol. 48, pt. 2, p. 612; Dodge report, July 18, 1865, OR, ser. 1, vol. 48, pt. 1, p. 333; Dodge to Connor, July 7, 1865, OR, ser. 1, vol. 48, pt. 2, p. 1064.

49. Dodge to Pope, Aug. 2, 1865, OR, ser. 1, vol. 48, pt. 2, p. 1158; Lass, *From the Missouri to the Great Salt Lake*, 168, 170–71, 175, based on Nebraska City Board of Trade Report for 1865 in *Nebraska City News*, Mar. 31, 1866. Steamboat landing data for 1865 is given in *Nebraska City News*, Mar. 10, 1866. Nebraska City merchant D. P. Rolfe provides statistics on wages and prices related to overland freighting at this time in "Overland Freighting," 287–91.

50. Ware, *Indian War of 1864*, 101–2; Scherneckau, "Soldiering in the Platte Valley," 34.

51. Daniel Goodman, Fort Kearny, to Hannah Hinman, June 17, 1865, Capron papers, NSHS; Pope to AAG, June 3, 1865, OR, ser. 1, vol. 48, pt. 2, p. 751; Edwin Nash, "Foot of Black Hills," to Robert W. Furnas, July 11, 1865, Furnas papers, NSHS.

52. Lamb to Hiram Lamb, Oct. 13, 1865, Lamb papers, NSHS; Ware, *Indian War of 1864*, 273.

53. Lt. W. R. Bowen, "Report of Depredations," Oct. 31, 1865, *OR*, ser. 1, vol. 48, pt. 2, p. 1251; D. Brown, *Galvanized Yankees*, 21; Potter, "Congressional Medal of Honor," 249.

54. D. Brown, *Galvanized Yankees*, 23–28, covers this incident in some detail. Livingston's assessments are found in Edwin Nash to AAG, May 28, 1865, endorsement, and Livingston report, July 5, 1865, HQ, East Subdist. of the Plains, *OR*, ser. 1, vol. 48, pt. 1, pp. 279–80, 316–17.

55. McDermott, *Circle of Fire*, 57–58. Company F of the First Nebraska Veteran Volunteer Cavalry, Company D of the First Battalion, and a detachment of Company A, First Battalion, made up the Nebraska contingent. *OR*, ser. 1, vol. 48, pt. 2, p. 275.

56. Report of Capt. John L. Wilcox, near Julesburg, Colorado Territory, June 21, 1865, in Logan, *Roster*, 4:1254–56; Pattison, "With the U.S. Army," 85; Hyde, *Life of George Bent*, 209–12.

57. These events in the North Subdistrict of the Plains are thoroughly covered in McDermott, *Circle of Fire*, chaps. 5, 6. A briefer summary is found in McChristian, *Fort Laramie*, chap. 12.

58. Edward D. Smith letter, camp near Laramie Station, Dakota Territory, Aug. 4, 1865, *Nebraska Advertiser*, Aug. 24, 1865. Another report of this raid is in *OR*, ser. 1, vol. 48, pt. 1, p. 357.

59. Vital Jarrot to D. N. Cooley, commissioner of Indian affairs, Aug. 8, 1865, ARCIA, 1865, p. 434.

60. GO No. 86, Apr. 2, 1863, and GO No. 182, June 20, 1863, contained the regulations for consolidating regiments. *OR*, ser. 3, vol. 3, pp. 112–13, 389–90.

61. See chap. 4 for Livingston's recruiting efforts in summer 1864. Descriptive Book of Recruits, Dist. of Nebraska, Jan.–Dec. 1864, file 6568, and Wilcox to Lorenzo Thomas, Sept. 6, 1864, Letters Sent, Dist. of Nebraska, Feb. 1863–Aug. 1865, file 6532, both in RG110, Records of the Provost Marshal General's Bureau, Kansas and Nebraska, National Archives and Records Administration, Central Plains Region, Kansas City, Missouri.

62. Livingston to Wilcox, Apr. 3, 1865, with Dodge endorsement, Apr. 14, 1865, in Endorsements Sent and Received, May 1863–Aug. 1865, file 6534, and W. W. Lowe to district provost marshals, Apr. 18, 21, 1865, and Lowe to O. F. Davis, May 3, 1865, Office of the Chief Mustering Officer, Letters sent, 1863–1866, file 6500, all in RG110, Records of the Provost Marshal General's Bureau, Kansas and Nebraska, National Archives and Records Administration, Central Plains Region, Kansas City, Missouri.

63. Documents relating to this incident are found in Miller's file, Compiled Service Records, roll 17.

64. Livingston to Pratt, Mar. 10, 1865, RG18, box 2, NSHS. For the regulations, see GO No. 86, Apr. 2, 1863, and GO No. 182, June 20, 1863, *OR*, ser. 3, vol. 3, pp. 112–13, 389–90.

65. Griffin to AAG McDonald, May 1, 1865, RG18, box 2, NSHS; Seaton to Livingston, Apr. 27, 1865, Livingston papers, NSHS.

66. H. M. Atkinson to Robert W. Furnas, June 30, 1864, Furnas papers, NSHS; *Nebraska Republican*, July 28, 1865.

67. First Nebraska officers to governor, Apr. 26, 1865, RG18, box 2, NSHS; W. McClelland to Livingston, May 4, 1865, Livingston papers, NSHS; GO No. 2, July 18, 1865, in Patrick, *Report*, 18.

68. SO No. 65, War Dept., June 22, 1865, Livingston file, Compiled Service Records; resolution, July 12, 1865, *Nebraska Republican*, July 21, 1865; "Communicated," July 19, 1865, *Nebraska Republican*, July 28, 1865. Brevet rank was an honorary commission used in the days before medals and campaign badges were authorized to recognize meritorious service. Russell, "Some Thoughts on Brevet Commissions." It should be noted, however, that hundreds of volunteer and regular army officers were awarded brevet rank at the end of the Civil War, suggesting that "faithful" service was likely the primary criterion.

69. Weatherwax to Livingston, July 14, 1865, Livingston papers, NSHS; "Communicated," July 19, 1865, *Nebraska Republican*, July 28, 1865.

70. Connor to Dodge, July 21, 25, 1865, *OR*, ser. 1, vol. 48, pt. 2, pp. 1112, 1123; GO No. 20, East Subdist. of the Plains, July 20, 1865, RG18, box 2, NSHS. Heath's military record is found in Heitman, *Historical Register*, 1:519.

71. "R" letter, Fort Kearny, July 30, 1865, *Nebraska Republican*, Aug. 11, 1865.

72. GO No. 4, Mil. Div. of the Mississippi, St. Louis, July 10, 1865, and GO No. 2, Dept. of the Missouri, July 21, 1865, *OR*, ser. 1, vol. 48, pt. 2, pp. 1070, 1112.

73. In his November 1, 1865, report, Dodge catalogued some 4,740 troops representing nine regiments that had been "sent from the East and South [to the Great Plains] and mustered out without any benefit of account having been derived from their service." Some of them had gone as far west as Fort Kearny before returning to Fort Leavenworth for discharge. *OR*, ser. 1, vol. 48, pt. 1, p. 346.

74. Grant to Pope, June 19, July 29, 1865, *OR*, ser. 1, vol. 48, pt. 2, p. 933, and vol. 48, pt. 1, p. 364; McDermott, *Circle of Fire*, 75–76.

75. Cole report to Grant, Feb. 10, 1867, *OR*, ser. 1, vol. 48, pt. 1, pp. 366–67.

76. Palmer, "History of the Powder River Expedition," 203.

77. McDermott, *Circle of Fire*, 77.

78. Connor to Dodge, Aug. 19, 1865, *OR*, ser. 1, vol. 48, pt. 2, p. 1217; Mc-Dermott, *Circle of Fire*, chaps. 7, 9; and McChristian, *Fort Laramie*, 243–47 summarize the campaign. A soldier identified only as "W" provided an eyewitness account dated October 6, 1865, to the *St. Joseph MO Herald*, reprinted in the *Nebraska City News*, Oct. 28, 1865.

79. GO No. 20, Dept. of the Missouri, Aug. 22, 1865, *OR*, ser. 1, vol. 48, pt. 2, p. 1201; Pope to Wheaton, Aug. 23, 1865, *OR*, ser. 1, vol. 48, pt. 2, p. 1207; McDermott, *Circle of Fire*, 140–44.

80. McDermott, *Circle of Fire*, 166–67.

81. Edwin Nash to Robert W. Furnas, Sept. 25, 1865, Feb. 9, 1866, Furnas papers, NSHS; D. Brown, *Galvanized Yankees*, 133–36; Danker, *Man of the Plains*, 37; Dudley, *Roster of Nebraska Volunteers*, 222, 227.

82. *Omaha Weekly Herald*, Oct. 27, 1865; Utley, *Frontiersmen in Blue*, 339–40. In a postwar reminiscence Dodge charged that ignorance of frontier conditions by administration officials and Indian Bureau efforts to undermine the credibility of military commanders in the West led to the "fatal mistake" of stopping the campaigns. Dodge, *Battle of Atlanta*, 105–8.

83. Mardock, "Plains Frontier and the Indian Peace Policy," 189; Dodge report, Nov. 1, 1865, *OR*, ser. 1, vol. 48, pt. 1, p. 344.

84. Ellis, *General Pope and U.S. Indian Policy*, 33, 37, 41–42.

85. Palmer, "History of the Powder River Expedition," 229; William R. Bowen, Fort Kearny, to John Q. Lewis, Fort Laramie, Oct. 31, 1865, *OR*, ser. 1, vol. 48, pt. 2, p. 1251; Pattison, "With the U.S. Army," 87; Dudley, *Roster of Nebraska Volunteers*, 36–37, 40–41.

86. "E" letter, Fort Kearny, Nov. 12, 1865, and Joseph Richey letter, Fort Kearny, Nov. 15, 1865, in *Nebraska Republican*, Dec. 1, 1865.

87. "E" letter, Fort Kearny, Nov. 12, 1865, and Joseph Richey letter, Fort Kearny, Nov. 15, 1865, in *Nebraska Republican*, Dec. 1, 1865; "Manuscript History of Company A," RG18, NSHS; Pattison, "With the U.S. Army," 87.

88. Clarke, "Freighting," 303–5. During negotiations at Fort Laramie the following year, Spotted Tail, Swift Bear, and other Brules admitted to the raid on Clarke's train, although they had likely been more interested in capturing the livestock than in killing white men. Unlike other Plains bands and leaders, these Brules had concluded that it was futile to resist American expansion. For the November 6 skirmish, see "Manuscript History of Company H," RG18, NSHS. Harrison Johnson was mustered out with the regiment in 1866 and settled in Lincoln, where he lived until his death in 1900. His son, John Johnson, took exquisite photographs documenting Lincoln's African American community in the early twentieth century. See Zimmer and Davis, "Recovered Views," 58–114.

89. Pope, HQ, Dept. of the Missouri, to Maj. Gen. W. T. Sherman, Mil. Div. of the Mississippi, Aug. 15, 1865, OR, ser. 1, vol. 48, pt. 2, p. 1183–84; *Army and Navy Journal* 2, no. 41 (June 2, 1866): 663.

90. AAG to Pope, Dec. 18, 1865, RG18, box 2, NSHS; Scherneckau, "Soldiering in the Platte Valley," 44–45; Company H morning report, September 1865, RG18, roll 3, NSHS.

91. Company H morning report, September 1865, and SO No. 153, HQ, Fort Sedgwick, Dec. 10, 1865, both in RG18, roll 3, NSHS; W. W. Ivory, Julesburg, Colorado Territory, to Lt. W. C. Majors, Dec. 10, 1865, RG18, box 2, NSHS. Lohnes's desertion and the tragic story of his postwar years are reviewed in Potter, "Congressional Medal of Honor."

92. Ivory to Majors, Dec. 10, 1865, RG18, box 2, NSHS.

93. Grant to Pope, Oct. 26, 1865, and Pope to Grant, Oct. 26, 1865, OR, ser. 1, vol. 48, pt. 2, p. 1244; Scherneckau, "Soldiering in the Platte Valley," 46; Carrington, *Absaraka*, 33, 65.

94. *Nebraska Republican*, July 28, 1865; *Omaha Daily Herald*, Aug. 29, 1878. The "great idea" quote is from the *Omaha Weekly Herald*, Feb. 2, 1866. Morton-Watkins, *Illustrated History*, 2:107, credits the first rail of the Union Pacific, "and so the first railway track in Nebraska," as being laid on July 10.

95. *Nebraska Republican*, May 5, 26, 1865.

96. *Omaha Weekly Herald*, Oct. 20, 1865; *Nebraska Daily Republican*, Oct. 10, 12, 1865.

97. *Omaha Weekly Herald*, Nov. 17, 1865; Lamb to Hiram Lamb, Nov. 11, 1865, Lamb papers, NSHS.

98. "Valedictory," *Nebraska City News*, Aug. 5, 1865.

99. *Nebraska City News*, May 27, June 10, 1865; "Newspaper Tilt," *Nebraska Republican*, June 16, 1865; *Nebraska City Daily Press*, Sept. 22, 1864.

100. *Nebraska City News*, July 1, 1865. For the Missouri constitution of 1865, see Gerteis, *Civil War St. Louis*, 310–12.

101. *Nebraska Advertiser*, July 6, 1865.

102. McPherson, *Ordeal by Fire*, 498–502, 501–2n. Republicans in the three states voted for the amendments by heavy majorities, but virtually all Democrats voted no. *Nebraska Republican*, Nov. 10, 1865.

103. *Nebraska City News*, July 8, 1865.

104. *Nebraska City Press*, July 5, 1865, quoted in *Nebraska Republican*, July 14, 1865. President Franklin Pierce appointed Estabrook as U.S. attorney for Nebraska Territory in 1854. In 1859 he was elected territorial delegate to Congress on the Democratic ticket, but his election was challenged by the Republican contender, Samuel G. Dailey, and the Republican House of Representatives awarded Daily the seat in May 1860. Estabrook had early favored black suffrage when he was a member of the Wisconsin

Constitutional Convention in 1847–48, a precursor to switching his affiliation to the Republican Party in the 1860s. Morton-Watkins, *Illustrated History*, 1:411–15, 646–48.

105. *Nebraska Republican*, July 7, 1865; *Nebraska Advertiser*, July 13, 1865.

106. *Nebraska City News*, June 7, 1862. Harvey's comments appeared in connection with an 1862 speech by Illinois Democratic congressman William A. Richardson "against the usurpations of the Abolitionists." Richardson had been one of the fathers of the Kansas-Nebraska Act of 1854 and later served briefly as Nebraska territorial governor.

107. *Nebraska City News*, Sept. 16, 1865.

108. *Nebraska City News*, Aug. 5, 1865; Olson, *J. Sterling Morton*, 134–35.

109. A survey of territorial journalism appears in Morton-Watkins, *Illustrated History*, 2:336–78.

110. *Nebraska Republican*, Aug. 25, 1865.

111. W. Brown, "George L. Miller and Nebraska Statehood," 303; Miller to Morton, July 12, 1865, Morton papers, NSHS. U.S. senators were elected by the state legislatures until the Seventeenth Amendment was ratified in 1913.

112. E. B. Chandler to Morton, July 16, 1865, T. M. Bedford to Morton, Sept. 17, 1865, and Miller to Morton, Aug. 29, 1865, Morton papers, NSHS.

113. Miller to Morton, Aug. 15, 1865, Morton papers, NSHS. The *Nebraska Republican*, Jan. 26, 1866, published President Johnson's January 12, 1866, message to Congress summarizing events relating to Colorado statehood.

114. McPherson, *Ordeal by Fire*, 504–5; *Nebraska Republican*, Sept. 22, 1865.

115. *Nebraska City News*, Sept. 30, 1865; Woolworth to Morton, Sept. 16, 19, 1865, Morton papers, NSHS.

116. *Nebraska Advertiser*, Sept. 28, 1865.

117. *Nebraska Advertiser*, Sept. 28, 1865.

118. *Plattsmouth Sentinel*, quoted in *Nebraska Advertiser*, Sept. 21, 1865; *Nebraska Advertiser*, Sept. 28, 1865.

119. Morton-Watkins, *Illustrated History*, 1:504; *Plattsmouth Herald*, Sept. 27, 1865, quoted in *Nebraska Advertiser*, Oct. 5, 1865.

120. *Nebraska Daily Republican*, Dec. 15, 1865.

121. Party affiliation data compiled from council and house votes on the 1866 state constitution as given in *Nebraska City News*, Feb. 10, 1866, and *Omaha Weekly Herald*, Feb. 16, 1866.

122. *Nebraska Daily Republican*, Oct. 11, 1865; *Nebraska Advertiser*, Oct. 19, 1865; Miller to Morton, Oct. 20, 1865, Morton papers, NSHS. A woman identified only as "Stella" visited Nebraska City in October 1865 and re-

ported that "the majority of the people I saw were southerners. . . . Those who would not meet my eye I set down as 'rebs,' 'deserters,' 'bushwhackers,' 'guerrillas,' etc. for there are any amount of them there." [Stella], "Letter from the Interior."

123. *Nebraska Daily Republican*, Nov. 15, 1865. On October 13, Bvt. Brig. Gen. Herman Heath, still in command of the East Subdistrict of Nebraska, became the nominal editor of the *Republican*. Heath was a War Democrat who favored statehood and supported Johnson's reconstruction policy, thus his views were not inconsistent with the *Nebraska Republican*'s previous editorial stance. Given Heath's military responsibilities (e.g., his leadership of the October–November Indian campaign in southwestern Nebraska), it is likely that many of the *Republican*'s editorials were written by Edward B. Taylor, the former editor, or E. A. McClure, who remained partners in the firm. In the summer of 1865 Taylor had been appointed superintendent of Indian affairs for the Northern Superintendency.

124. *Omaha Weekly Herald*, Dec. 15, 1865.

125. *Nebraska Advertiser*, quoted in *Nebraska Daily Republican*, Dec. 30, 1865.

126. Potts, "Nebraska Statehood and Reconstruction," 75. One of the petitions is illustrated on page 77.

127. "Klc" [D. H. Kelsey], Washington DC, Dec. 20, 1865, *Nebraska Herald* (Plattsmouth), Jan. 3, 1866.

6. 1866

1. H. D. Hathaway to Maxwell, Jan. 22, 1866, Maxwell papers, NSHS.

2. Gere, "Admission of Nebraska," 164, notes that the debates over statehood "were ingeniously engineered so as to make it appear that purely economic and financial principles were at stake." The references to capitalists and "penury" are found in a letter by "Taxpayer" in the June 3, 1864, *Nebraska Republican*, demonstrating that the pro-state arguments, like those opposing statehood, had changed little by 1866. A cogent overview of the various points of view is given by Potts, "Nebraska Statehood and Reconstruction," 74. For Nevada statehood see Etulain, "Abraham Lincoln," 16. Nevada population data is from Walker, *Compendium of the Ninth Census*, 8. The ratio of population to representation in the U.S. House of Representatives is found in Stonebraker, *Nebraska Blue Book*, 356.

3. *Nebraska Daily Republican*, Jan. 3, 1866.

4. *Nebraska Daily Republican*, Jan. 3, 1866.

5. Lewis, *Messages and Proclamations*, 1:199.

6. Lewis, *Messages and Proclamations*, 1:199–200; *Nebraska City Press*, quoted in *Nebraska Daily Republican*, Jan. 3, 1866; Potts, "Nebraska Territory," 281. Experience Estabrook was quoted in the *Omaha Herald*, July 9, 1875, saying that the group that drafted the constitution met in his office.

7. *Nebraska Daily Republican*, Jan. 19, 1866.

8. *Omaha Weekly Herald*, Jan. 19, 1866.

9. Bennett to Morton, Jan. 10, 1866, Morton papers, NSHS.

10. *Nebraska Daily Republican*, Feb. 5, 6, 7, 1866, published the legislative proceedings. The council vote with party affiliation appears in the *Nebraska City News*, Feb. 10, 1866, and the house vote with affiliation is found in the *Omaha Weekly Herald*, Feb. 16, 1866. Several sources refer to the "secret committee," none of which provide clear documentation of its membership. See Woolworth, "Address to the Public," 1:529–36, 511; Estabrook, quoted in the *Omaha Herald*, July 9, 1875.

11. Olson and Naugle, *History of Nebraska*, 139–40; *Nebraska City Press*, quoted in *Omaha Weekly Herald*, Feb. 23, 1866. McPherson, *Ordeal by Fire*, 81, notes that before the Civil War only the New England states (except Connecticut) allowed black suffrage.

12. *Omaha Weekly Herald* supplement, Feb. 23, 1866; *Nebraska City News*, quoted in *Omaha Weekly Herald* supplement, Feb. 23, 1866; "Open for Conviction" letter, *Nebraska City News*, Mar. 17, 1866.

13. Johnson, Jan. 12, 1866, message to Congress, *Nebraska Republican*, Jan. 26, 1866.

14. *Nebraska City Press*, quoted in *Omaha Weekly Herald*, Feb. 23, 1866.

15. *Nebraska City News*, Feb. 3, 1866; *Omaha Weekly Herald*, Feb. 9, 1866.

16. *Nebraska Advertiser*, Mar. 1, 1866; *Nebraska Daily Republican*, Feb. 6, 1866.

17. The overview of Johnson versus the congressional Republicans is drawn from McPherson, *Ordeal by Fire*, 508–14; and Potts, "Nebraska Statehood and Reconstruction," 73–74. The quote is from Experience Estabrook to *Nebraska Daily Republican*, Feb. 6, 1866, regarding the "status of states lately in revolt."

18. *Omaha Weekly Herald*, Mar. 9, 1866.

19. Algernon S. Paddock, Omaha, to William H. Seward, Feb. 13, 1866, enclosing resolution, Territorial papers; *Nebraska Daily Republican*, Feb. 22, 1866; *Nebraska Advertiser*, Mar. 1, 1866.

20. *Nebraska Daily Republican*, Mar. 3, 1866; *Nebraska Herald*, Feb. 28, Mar. 21, 1866.

21. This summary is drawn from McPherson, *Ordeal by Fire*, 515–17.

22. Morton-Watkins, *Illustrated History*, 1:519; *Nebraska Advertiser*, May 10, 1866; *Nebraska City News*, Apr. 28, 1866.

23. Miller to Morton, Mar. 12, 1866; J. W. Paddock to Morton, Apr. 10, 1866, Morton papers, NSHS.

24. *Nebraska Statesman*, quoted in *Nebraska Republican*, May 4, 1866.

25. Morton-Watkins, *Illustrated History*, 1:520, draws the convention proceedings from the *Nebraska Advertiser*, Apr. 26, 1866.

26. *Nebraska Advertiser*, Apr. 26, 1866, quoted in Olson, *J. Sterling Morton*, 142; *Omaha Weekly Herald*, Apr. 27, 1866.

27. *Nebraska Advertiser*, May 3, 10, 1866; *Nebraska Republican*, May 18, 1866. Colorado Territory's population in 1870 was 39,864. Walker, *Compendium of the Ninth Census*, 8.

28. See, for example, the Morton-Butler exchanges in *Omaha Daily Republican*, May 24, 1866.

29. *Omaha Weekly Herald*, June 1, 1866.

30. *Omaha Daily Republican*, June 1, 1866.

31. See Morton-Watkins, *Illustrated History*, 1:521–22, for a sketch of Train. The *Nebraska Advertiser*, May 17, 1866, reported Train's appearance in Brownville with Morton and Miller.

32. Lt. Charles Strong, "Journal of Expedition," kept by Lt. Charles Strong, No. 4009, Everett D. Graff Collection of Western Americana, Newberry Library, microfilm copy, MS4093, NSHS.

33. Lt. Charles Strong, "Journal of Expedition," no. 4009, Everett D. Graff Collection of Western Americana, Newberry Library, microfilm copy, MS4093, NSHS. The dead soldier was Pvt. Jesse Rowley; see Logan, *Roster*, 4:1475. A second journal of this expedition is by Pattison, "With the U.S. Army," 88–91. Fort Cottonwood had been renamed Fort McPherson on January 20, 1866, in honor of Union general James B. McPherson, killed at the Battle of Atlanta on July 22, 1864.

34. *Nebraska Daily Republican*, Jan. 27, 1866; *Nebraska Republican*, Mar. 30, 1866.

35. Mattes, *Great Platte River Road*, 234–35, summarizes the Eighteenth Infantry's time at Fort Kearny on the Platte.

36. Olson, *Red Cloud*, 28–34.

37. Olson, *Red Cloud*, 38–39; ARCIA, 1866, pp. 208, 211.

38. *Omaha Herald*, quoted in Olson, *Red Cloud*, 38.

39. "Table of the Vote, June 2, 1866," in Morton-Watkins, *Illustrated History*, 1:534.

40. Morton-Watkins, *Illustrated History*, 1:527–34; *Nebraska Herald*, June 13, 1866. A review of the Rock Bluffs canvassing board's decision and that of County Clerk Spurlock is provided by David Marquette, a prominent minister in Nebraska's Methodist Episcopal Church, who concluded that the decision not to count the Rock Bluffs vote was the proper one.

It should be noted that Marquette was not an entirely disinterested observer, since he was the brother of Republican congressional candidate T. M. Marquett (who did not use the final "e" in his name). Morton-Watkins, *Illustrated History*, 2:549–54n.

41. *Nebraska City News*, June 30, 1866. Adolph Moncray, or Monterey, was allegedly listed on the poll book of Company A, but Dudley, *Roster of Nebraska Volunteers*, 18–19, shows him as being mustered out for disability in 1863. Several of the soldiers listed in Captain Murphy's affidavit enlisted in Page County, Iowa, which likely remained their official residence. During U.S. Senate debate on the Nebraska admission bill in July 1866, Senator James Doolittle of Wisconsin credited Capt. Lewis Lowry of the First Nebraska as confirming that Iowa soldiers voted in the Nebraska election; cited in Watkins, "How Nebraska Was Brought into the Union," 412–13.

42. *Nebraska Republican*, June 8, 1866.

43. Woolworth's address appears in Morton-Watkins, *Illustrated History*, 1:529–36. Olson, *J. Sterling Morton*, 142–44, gives an accessible review of this episode. Woolworth argued that the entire soldier vote should be thrown out, rather than just the votes of the First Nebraska soldiers whose legal residence was elsewhere. Yet he wanted all Rock Bluffs precinct votes counted, even though there was at least circumstantial evidence that some of them were also cast by nonresidents.

44. *Nebraska Republican*, July 6, 13, 1866; Porter to Morton, June 28, 1866, Morton papers, NSHS; *Omaha Weekly Herald*, June 22, 1866.

45. HQ, Dept. of the Missouri, SO No. 3, June 10, 1866, RG18, box 2, NSHS; *Omaha Weekly Herald*, June 29, 1866; Joseph Barker Jr. to "My Dear Folkses," June 19, 1866, in Snoddy, Combs, Marks, and Weber, *Their Man in Omaha*, 1:123. The "stampeeders" Barker mentions were evidently disillusioned miners returning from the Colorado goldfields.

46. *Omaha Weekly Herald*, June 29, July 13, 1866; *Nebraska City News*, July 13, 1866.

47. *Nebraska Republican*, July 6, 1866. The number of original First Nebraska men still serving at the regiment's mustering out on July 1, 1866, was compiled from data in Dudley, *Roster of Nebraska Volunteers*.

48. Pattison, "With the U.S. Army," 91–93; D. Brown, *Galvanized Yankees*, 142; Paul, "Galvanized Yankee"; Jensen, *Voices of the American West*, 2:210, 216. Grenville Dodge recalled that three-quarters of the Galvanized Yankees remained in the West after they were discharged, though he gave no specific evidence. Dodge, *Battle of Atlanta*, 143.

49. Lewis, *Messages and Proclamations*, 1: 261–64. The Fourteenth Amendment did not grant universal male suffrage.

50. Woolworth, "Address to the Public," 1:531; Marquette, quoted in Morton-Watkins, *Illustrated History*, 2:549–54n; Potts, "Nebraska Territory," 294.

51. *Nebraska Republican*, July 13, 1866; Charles H. Gere, Omaha, to Mariel Clapham, July 27, 1866, Gere papers, NSHS.

52. *Nebraska Republican*, July 13, 1866; *Omaha Weekly Herald*, July 13, 1866. Legislator Charles H. Gere went on the excursion and reported that the train passed over a mile of track that had been laid that very day, "while we were running out to the spot." Gere to Mariel Clapham, July 27, 1866, Gere papers, NSHS.

53. Lass, *From the Missouri to the Great Salt Lake*, 179–81; Joseph Barker Jr. to "My dear mother," Nov. 3, 1866, in Snoddy, Combs, Marks, and Weber, *Their Man in Omaha*, 1:218; *Nebraska Republican*, Apr. 20, 1866.

54. Lass, *From the Missouri to the Great Salt Lake*, 183, 186–88. In 1860 Nebraska City was slightly larger than Omaha, the former with 1,922 residents and the latter with 1,883, according to the 1860 census. In the fall of 1866 newspapers estimated Omaha's population at eight thousand to eighty-five hundred, with Nebraska City's at about seven thousand. *Omaha Daily Republican*, Oct. 18, 1866. From that time on the disparity widened dramatically. In 2007 Nebraska City's population was estimated at slightly over seven thousand by the League of Nebraska Municipalities and the Nebraska Department of Economic Development, nearly identical to that of 1866.

55. *Nebraska Advertiser*, July 19, 26, 1866.

56. Bakken, "Chronology of Nebraska Statehood," 87; *Nebraska Advertiser*, Aug. 2, 1866.

57. This summary is drawn from Potts, "Nebraska Statehood and Reconstruction," 77–78; and McPherson, *Ordeal by Fire*, 518. On April 9, 1866, just before the Union Party convention in Plattsmouth, Robert S. Knox of Omaha identified Kellogg, Taylor, and Paddock as "twaddlers" unfaithful to the Republican Party and its principles. Knox to Samuel Maxwell, Apr. 9, 1866, Maxwell papers, NSHS.

58. Ware, *Indian War of 1864*, 11, 96; and Logan, *Roster*, 4:8, 102, 1253, 1261, treat Heath's military career. He was mustered out on May 17, 1866. Ware disliked him intensely and called him "a self-important, dictatorial wind-bag."

59. Heath, Washington DC, to "Col. Cooper, Prv. Secy. to the President," May 12, 1866, Territorial papers; *Nebraska Herald*, Aug. 1, 1866.

60. Potts, "Nebraska Statehood and Reconstruction," 78; *Nebraska City Daily Press*, quoted in *Nebraska Herald*, Aug. 1, 1866; *Nebraska City News*, Oct. 14, 1865.

61. *Nebraska Herald*, Aug. 1, 1866; Olson, *J. Sterling Morton*, 145, quoting Miller in *Omaha Weekly Herald*, Aug. 24, 1866.

62. Sheldon, *Nebraska Constitutions*, 194.

63. Morton-Watkins, *Illustrated History*, 1:539–42.

64. The Philadelphia convention resolutions appear in the *Omaha Weekly Herald*, Aug. 31, 1866; *Omaha Daily Republican*, Oct. 8, 1866; *Nebraska Herald*, Sept. 19, 1866.

65. *Nebraska Republican*, supplement, Sept. 21, 1866.

66. Morton and Miller to Johnson, Nebraska appointments file, Territorial Papers, cited in Potts, "Nebraska Statehood and Reconstruction," 83n40, n42; Richardson to Morton, June 13, 1866, Morton papers, NSHS.

67. McPherson, *Ordeal by Fire*, 518–20, is the basis for this summary of the National Union Party and Johnson's role in molding public opinion before the fall 1866 elections. News of the riots made it into the Nebraska newspapers; see, e.g., *Nebraska Advertiser*, May 10, 1866. The *Nebraska Herald* of September 19, 1865, editorialized on "Our National Disgrace."

68. Joseph Barker Jr. to "My dear mother, father, and all," Oct. 3, 1866, in Snoddy, Combs, Marks, and Weber, *Their Man in Omaha*, 1:201; *Omaha Daily Republican*, Oct. 8, 1866.

69. *Nebraska Advertiser*, Sept. 13, Oct. 4, 1866.

70. *Nebraska City News*, Sept. 22, 1866.

71. Returns appear in the *Nebraska Republican*, Nov. 2, 1866.

72. *Nebraska City News*, Oct. 13, 1866; *Omaha Weekly Herald*, Oct. 19, 1866; Miller to Morton, Oct. 20, 1866, Morton papers, NSHS.

73. A. C. Dodge to O. H. Browning, Sept. 5, 1866, and J. W. Paddock to Andrew Johnson, Sept. 24, 1866, both in Territorial papers. The Nebraska patronage and its relation to the Nebraska political campaigns of 1866 are discussed in Berwanger, *West and Reconstruction*, chap. 3, esp. 93–99.

74. J. W. Paddock to Morton, Nov. 6, 1866, Morton Papers, NSHS; John Taffe, Omaha, to Samuel Maxwell, Nov. 15, 1866, Maxwell papers, NSHS; Potts, "Nebraska Statehood and Reconstruction," 78, 83n44.

75. Seymour, "Western Incidents."

76. Joseph Barker Jr. to "My Dear Good Mother," Oct. 29, 1866, in Snoddy, Combs, Marks, and Weber, *Their Man in Omaha*, 1:211; Olson and Naugle, *History of Nebraska*, 161; *Omaha Daily Republican*, Oct. 25, 1866.

77. Watkins, "How Nebraska Was Brought into the Union," 417. The "too great importance" quote is from the *Chicago Republican*, reprinted in the *Nebraska Republican*, Nov. 16, 1866.

7. 1867

1. Potts, "Nebraska Statehood and Reconstruction," provides much of the basis for this discussion. See also Webster, "Controversy," 370.

2. The debate as recorded in the *Congressional Globe* is discussed in Watkins, "How Nebraska Was Brought into the Union," 417–26; and Potts, "Nebraska Statehood and Reconstruction," 80.

3. Saunders, Washington DC, to Seward, Dec. 10, 1866, Territorial papers.

4. Lewis, *Messages and Proclamations*, 1:243.

5. *Nebraska Republican*, Jan. 18, 1867; *Omaha Weekly Herald*, Jan. 18, 1867. See also the legislative proceedings of January 18 and 22 as printed in the *Omaha Weekly Republican*, Jan. 25, 1867.

6. Morton-Watkins, *Illustrated History*, 2:57–59.

7. Morton-Watkins, *Illustrated History*, 2:58–60.

8. *Laws of Nebraska*, Twelfth (Ter.) Session, 20.

9. The *Omaha Weekly Republican*, Feb. 22, Mar. 1, 1867, and the *Omaha Weekly Herald*, Feb. 22, 1867, contain lengthy columns covering the legislative deadlock. Joseph Barker wrote his family on March 4, 1867, that the South Platte section had tried to gain two-thirds of the seats in the legislature and stalled the Omaha appropriation bill "to carry their point." Snoddy, Combs, Marks, and Weber, *Their Man in Omaha*, 1:254–55.

10. Watkins, "How Nebraska Was Brought into the Union," 426–29.

11. *Omaha Weekly Herald*, Jan. 18, 1867; *Omaha Weekly Republican*, Jan. 25, 1867.

12. *Nebraska Advertiser*, Jan. 31, 1867.

13. Potts, "Nebraska Statehood and Reconstruction," 83n65; *Journal of the House*, Twelfth (Ter.) Session, 96–98; *Nebraska Herald*, Jan. 30, 1867.

14. *Chicago Journal*, n.d., in *Omaha Weekly Republican*, Jan. 25, 1867.

15. Potts, "Nebraska Statehood and Reconstruction," 80–81.

16. *Journal of the House*, Twelfth (Ter.) Session, 198–201.

17. D. M. Kelsey letter, Feb. 9, 1867, *Nebraska Herald*, Mar. 6, 1867. Marquett was elected to Nebraska's seat in the House of Representatives of the Thirty-Ninth Congress at the June 2, 1866, election but could not take office until statehood was achieved. The term for which he had been elected would expire when the Fortieth Congress convened in special session on March 4, 1867. In the October 1866 territorial election Marquett was elected territorial delegate and John Taffe was elected representative for the Fortieth Congress, one or the other to take office depending on the statehood outcome. After Nebraska's admission on March 1, 1867, Marquett was seated in the House of Representatives of the Thirty-Ninth Congress on March 2 and served two days. When the Fortieth Congress opened on March 4, Taffe was sworn in as congressman from Nebraska. Morton-Watkins, *Illustrated History*, 3:3–4.

18. *Nebraska Advertiser*, Feb. 14, 1867; Lewis, *Messages and Proclamations*, 1:226–27.

19. *Omaha Weekly Herald*, Feb. 15, 22, 1867; *Nebraska Advertiser*, Feb. 14, 1867. The question of Congress's authority to impose the "fundamental condition" on Nebraska without a vote of the people came up in 1872, when a defendant in Omaha challenged the right of an African American to sit on a jury. In *Brittle v. the People* (Woolworth, *Reports of Cases*, 2:198–240) the Supreme Court ruled two to one that it was too late to question the validity of the method under which Nebraska had been admitted to statehood. The majority, Judges Lake and Crounse, held that the U.S. Constitution did not prescribe the method by which states were to be admitted and that how and by whom the state constitution had been formed was of no consequence. "When the fact of admission is established, the courts are bound by it and cannot go behind it." Dissenting Judge Mason argued that the "fundamental condition" was without force and effect because the people had not voluntarily entered the Union "with a constitution amended by the erasure of the word 'white.'" Morton-Watkins, *Illustrated History*, 3:122–23.

20. Lewis, *Messages and Proclamations*, 1:203–4.

21. *Omaha Weekly Herald*, Mar. 1, 1867; *Nebraska Herald*, Mar. 6, 1867; *Journal of the House*, Second State Session, 41–54.

22. "Speech of the Hon. I. N. [*sic*] Hascall," *Omaha Weekly Republican*, Mar. 1, 1867.

23. "Speech of the Hon. I. N. [*sic*] Hascall," *Omaha Weekly Republican*, Mar. 1, 1867.

24. "Speech of the Hon. I. N. [*sic*] Hascall," *Omaha Weekly Republican*, Mar. 1, 1867.

25. *Nebraska City News*, Mar. 9, 1867; *Omaha Weekly Herald*, Mar. 1, 1867; *Omaha Weekly Republican*, Mar. 1, 1867.

26. *Omaha Daily Herald*, Mar. 28, 1867.

27. *Omaha Weekly Herald*, Apr. 5, 1867. Saunders would be elected U.S. senator from Nebraska in 1876. Joseph Barker Jr.'s letters from Omaha during the late 1860s and early 1870s in volume 2 of Snoddy, Combs, Marks, and Weber, *Their Man in Omaha*, reflect alliances having much more to do with economic development and speculation than with straight party politics.

28. *Omaha Weekly Republican*, Mar. 8, 1867. The black population of Nebraska at statehood was fewer than a thousand, based on the 789 African Americans enumerated by the 1870 U.S. Census, and only males age twenty-one or older would have been eligible to vote. Table 42, "Nebraska—Race and Hispanic Origin: 1860 to 1900" in Gibson and Jung, "Historical Census Statistics," 60, accessed June 10, 2010, http://www.census.gov/population/www/documentation/twps0075.html.

29. *Omaha Weekly Herald*, Mar. 8, 1867; *Omaha Daily Herald*, Mar. 7, 1867. The *Daily Herald*, Mar. 9, 1867, estimated the number of potential black male voters in the city at fifty.

30. *Omaha Weekly Republican*, Mar. 8, 1867; *Laws of Nebraska*, Twelfth (Ter.) Session, 20. The state constitution provided that territorial laws "now in force shall remain in force until altered, amended, or appealed [*sic*] by the legislature" and wherever the word *territory* appeared in the statutes, it would be construed to mean *state*.

31. *Nebraska Herald*, Apr. 3, 1867.

Epilogue

1. Olson and Naugle, *History of Nebraska*, 143; Sheldon, *Nebraska: Land and People*, 1:368.

2. Sheldon, *Nebraska: Land and People*, 1:368.

3. Potts, "Nebraska Territory," 314–41.

4. Morton-Watkins, *Illustrated History*, 3:25.

5. Sheldon, *Nebraska: Land and People*, 1:579.

6. See Wishart, *Unspeakable Sadness*, for the full story.

7. Following Morton's death in 1902, Furnas prepared a eulogy published by the state historical society. Furnas recalled the two men's first meeting in 1856, when both were editors of newspapers "differing radically in politics." They made a brief reference to their "political altercations," said Furnas, and then "[w]e mutually agreed to never talk politics, nor write, or indulge in them personally," an agreement that "was sacredly observed." Furnas, "J. Sterling Morton," 152.

8. Wax, "Robert Ball Anderson," 163–92; Potter, "Congressional Medal of Honor," 251–53.

9. Zimmer and Davis, "Recovered Views," 63; Andreas, *History of Nebraska*, 1075.

10. *Omaha Daily Republican*, June 29, 1866.

11. U.S. Department of the Interior, Bureau of the Census, *Compendium*. Michael Bon Doll of Beatrice is the last known Union veteran to die in Nebraska. *Beatrice Daily Sun*, Dec. 24, 1948.

BIBLIOGRAPHY

Unpublished Sources

Bronson, Joseph H. Papers. RG3288. Nebraska State Historical Society, Lincoln.

Brownville (Nebr.) Union Club. Records. RG4524. Nebraska State Historical Society, Lincoln.

Capron, Edwin. Papers. RG3521. Nebraska State Historical Society, Lincoln.

Compiled Service Records. First Nebraska Volunteer Infantry/Cavalry. National Archives microfilm publication M1787. RG 94. Records of the Office of the Adjutant General. Copy at Nebraska State Historical Society, Lincoln.

Dale, Raymond E., comp. "Otoe County Pioneers: A Biographical Dictionary." 10 vols. Unpublished typescript, 1961–65. Nebraska State Historical Society, Lincoln.

Descriptive Book of Recruits, District of Nebraska, Jan.–Dec., 1864. RG110. Records of the Office of the Provost Marshal General's Bureau, Nebraska and Kansas. National Archives, Central Plains Region, Kansas City.

Endorsements Sent and Received, Mar. 1863–Aug. 1865. RG110. Records of the Office of the Provost Marshal General's Bureau, Nebraska and Kansas. National Archives, Central Plains Region, Kansas City.

Fort File. RG77. Records of the Office of the Chief of Engineers. National Archives.

Fort Kearny, Nebraska. Letterbook. RG505, roll 6. Nebraska State Historical Society, Lincoln.

Furnas, Robert W. Papers. RG1, SG10. Nebraska State Historical Society, Lincoln.

Gere, Charles Henry. Papers. MS302. Nebraska State Historical Society, Lincoln.

Johnson, Joseph. Reminiscence. RG3436. Nebraska State Historical Society, Lincoln.

Koenig, William. Papers. RG090. Nebraska State Historical Society, Lincoln.

Lamb, Squire. Papers. RG1561. Nebraska State Historical Society, Lincoln.

Latta, W. S. Papers. RG4352. Nebraska State Historical Society, Lincoln.

Letters Sent, District of Nebraska, Feb. 1863–Aug. 1965. RG110. Records of the Office of the Provost Marshal General's Bureau, Nebraska and Kansas. National Archives, Central Plains Region, Kansas City.

Letters Sent, Office of the Chief Mustering Officer, 1863–1866. RG110. Records of the Office of the Provost Marshal General's Bureau, Nebraska and Kansas. National Archives, Central Plains Region, Kansas City.

Livingston, Robert R. Papers. RG129. Nebraska State Historical Society, Lincoln.

Ludwickson, John. "Roster of Nebraska Territorial Militia in the Pawnee War, 1859." Typescript. Copy in author's possession.

Majors, Thomas J. Papers. RG2189. Nebraska State Historical Society, Lincoln.

Manuscript History of Company A and Company H, First Nebraska Volunteer Infantry/Cavalry. RG18. Records of the Nebraska Military Department. Nebraska State Historical Society, Lincoln.

Maxwell, Samuel. Papers. MS428. Nebraska State Historical Society, Lincoln.

Morning reports. First Nebraska Volunteer Infantry/Cavalry. RG18. Records of the Nebraska Military Department. Nebraska State Historical Society, Lincoln.

Morton, J. Sterling. Papers. MS7, roll 3. Nebraska State Historical Society, Lincoln.

Muster rolls, Nebraska militia companies. RG18. Records of the Nebraska Military Department. Nebraska State Historical Society, Lincoln.

Nash, Edwin. Letters. In Robert W. Furnas Papers, RG1, SG10. Nebraska State Historical Society, Lincoln

Order books. First Nebraska Volunteer Infantry/Cavalry. RG18. Records of the Nebraska Military Department. Nebraska State Historical Society, Lincoln.

Polock, William A. Papers. RG1323. Nebraska State Historical Society, Lincoln.

Population Schedules, Eighth Census of the United States: Nebraska Territory, 1860. National Archives microfilm publication M653, roll 665.

Post returns and orders. RG500. Records of the U.S. War Department. Nebraska State Historical Society, Lincoln.

Potts, James B. "Nebraska Territory, 1854–1867: A Study of Frontier Politics." PhD diss., University of Nebraska–Lincoln, 1973.

Rhoades, Albert K. Diary. RG1386. Nebraska State Historical Society,
Lincoln.

Rosewater, Edward. Papers. Manuscript collection no. 503. Jacob Rader
Marcus Center of the American Jewish Archives, Cincinnati, Ohio.

Strong, Charles. "Journal of Expedition." Everett D. Graff Collection, no.
4009. Newberry Library, Chicago. Microfilm copy at Nebraska State
Historical Society, Lincoln.

Territorial papers: Nebraska, 1854–1867. National Archives microfilm
publication M228, roll 1. Records of the U.S. State Department.

Published Articles, Books, and Government Documents

Abbott, O. A. "Recollections of a Pioneer Lawyer." *Nebraska History* 11
(Jan.–Mar. 1928): 3–64; (Apr.–June 1928): 65–113; (July–Sept. 1928):
115–177.

Andreas, A. T., comp. *History of Nebraska*. Chicago: Western Historical Co.,
1882.

Annual Report of the Commissioner of Indian Affairs for the Year 1861. Washington DC: GPO, 1861.

Annual Report of the Commissioner of Indian Affairs for the Year 1862. Washington DC: GPO, 1863.

Annual Report of the Commissioner of Indian Affairs for the Year 1863. Washington DC: GPO, 1863.

Annual Report of the Commissioner of Indian Affairs for the Year 1864. Washington DC: GPO, 1865.

Annual Report of the Commissioner of Indian Affairs for the Year 1866. Washington DC: GPO, 1866.

Athearn, Robert G., ed. "Across the Plains in 1863: The Diary of Peter
Winne." *Iowa Journal of History* 49 (July 1951): 221–40.

Bailey, Anne J. "Texans Invade Missouri: The Cape Girardeau Raid, 1863."
Missouri Historical Review 84 (Jan. 1990): 166–87.

Bakken, Douglas. "Chronology of Nebraska Statehood." *Nebraska History*
48 (Spring 1967): 81–90.

Becher, Ronald. *Massacre along the Medicine Road: A Social History of the Indian War of 1864 in Nebraska Territory*. Caldwell ID: Caxton, 1999.

Berwanger, Eugene H. *The West and Reconstruction*. Urbana: University of
Illinois Press, 1981.

Blaser, Kent. "Where Is Nebraska, Anyway?" *Nebraska History* 80 (Spring
1999): 3–14.

Bleed, Peter, and Douglas D. Scott. "Archeological Interpretation of the
Frontier Battle at Mud Springs, Nebraska." *Great Plains Research* 19
(Spring 2009): 13–25.

Bowles, Samuel. *Across the Continent.* New York: Hurd and Houghton, 1865.

Bradbury, John F., Jr. "'This War Is Managed Mighty Strange': The Army of Southeastern Missouri, 1862–63." *Missouri Historical Review* 87 (Oct. 1994): 28–47.

Bray, Kingsley M. *Crazy Horse: A Lakota Life.* Norman: University of Oklahoma Press, 2006.

Brisbin, Gen. James S., ed. *Belden, the White Chief; or, Twelve Years among the Wild Indians of the Plains.* Cincinnati: C. F. Vest, 1870.

Brown, D. Alexander. *The Galvanized Yankees.* Urbana: University of Illinois Press, 1963.

Brown, Wallace. "George L. Miller and the Struggle over Nebraska Statehood." *Nebraska History* 41 (Dec. 1960): 299–318.

Carley, Kenneth. *The Dakota War of 1862: Minnesota's Other Civil War.* 2nd ed. St. Paul: Minnesota Historical Society Press, 2001.

Carrington, Margaret K. *Absaraka: Home of the Crows.* Edited by Milo M. Quaife. Chicago: R. R. Donnelly and Sons, 1950.

Castel, Albert. *Civil War Kansas: Reaping the Whirlwind.* Lawrence: University Press of Kansas, 1997.

Clarke, Henry T. "Freighting: Denver and Black Hills." *Nebraska State Historical Society Publications* 10 (1902): 299–312.

Colton, Ray C. *The Civil War in the Western Territories: Arizona, Colorado, New Mexico, and Utah.* Norman: University of Oklahoma Press, 1959.

Cooling, Benjamin Franklin. "The First Nebraska Infantry Regiment and the Battle of Fort Donelson." *Nebraska History* 45 (June 1964): 131–46.

——. *Forts Henry and Donelson: The Key to the Confederate Heartland.* Knoxville: University of Tennessee Press, 1987.

Cox. W. W. "The Beginning of Lincoln and Lancaster County." *Nebraska State Historical Society Publications* 3 (1892): 85–100.

——. "My First Trip to Omaha." *Nebraska State Historical Society Publications* 10 (1902): 69–82.

Crawford, Lewis F. *Rekindling Camp Fires: The Exploits of Ben Arnold (Connor).* Bismarck ND: Capital Book Co., 1926.

Curtis, Earl G. "John Milton Thayer." *Nebraska History* 28 (Oct.–Dec. 1947): 255–38; 29 (Mar. 1948): 55–68; (June 1948): 134–50.

Curtis, Ken. "Producing a Gold Rush: National Ambitions and the Northern Rocky Mountains, 1853–1863." *Western Historical Quarterly* 40 (Autumn 2009): 275–97.

Danker, Donald F. "Columbus: A Territorial Town in the Platte Valley." *Nebraska History* 34 (Dec. 1953): 275–88.

——. *Man of the Plains: Recollections of Luther North.* Lincoln: University of Nebraska Press, 1961.

——. *Mollie: The Journal of Mollie Dorsey Sanford in Nebraska and Colorado Territories, 1857–1866*. Lincoln: University of Nebraska Press, 1959.

——."The North Brothers and the Pawnee Scouts." *Nebraska History* 42 (Sept. 1961): 161–80.

Danziger, Edmund J., Jr. "Civil War Problems in the Central and Dakota Superintendencies: A Case Study." *Nebraska History* 51 (Winter 1970): 387–410.

DeBlack, Thomas A. *With Fire and Sword: Arkansas, 1861–1874*. Fayetteville: University of Arkansas Press, 2003.

Dodge, Grenville M. *The Battle of Atlanta and Other Campaigns, Addresses, Etc.* Council Bluffs IA: Monarch, 1911.

Dudley, Edgar S. "Notes on the Early Military History of Nebraska." *Nebraska State Historical Society Publications* 2 (1887): 166–96.

——. *Roster of Nebraska Volunteers from 1861 to 1865*. Hastings NE: Wigton and Evans, 1888.

Dyer, Frederick H. *A Compendium of the War of the Rebellion*. Des Moines IA: Dyer, 1908.

Ellis, Richard N. "Civilians, the Army, and the Indian Problem on the Northern Plains, 1862–1866." *North Dakota History* 37 (Winter 1970): 20–39.

——. *General Pope and U.S. Indian Policy*. Albuquerque: University of New Mexico Press, 1970.

Etcheson, Nicole. "Where Popular Sovereignty Worked: Nebraska Territory and the Kansas-Nebraska Act." In *The Nebraska-Kansas Act of 1854*, edited by John R. Wunder and Joann M. Ross, 159–81. Lincoln: University of Nebraska Press, 2008.

Etulain, Richard W. "Abraham Lincoln: Political Founding Father of the American West." *Montana, the Magazine of Western History* 59 (Summer 2009): 3–22.

——, ed. *Lincoln Looks West: From the Mississippi to the Pacific*. Carbondale: Southern Illinois University Press, 2010.

Farb, Robert C. "The Military Career of Robert W. Furnas." *Nebraska History* 32 (Mar. 1951): 18–41.

——. "Robert W. Furnas as Omaha Indian Agent, 1864–1866," Pt. 1. *Nebraska History* 32 (Sept. 1951): 186–203.

Fellman, Michael. *Inside War: The Guerrilla Conflict in Missouri during the American Civil War*. New York: Oxford University Press, 1989.

Filbert, Preston. *The Half Not Told: The Civil War in a Frontier Town*. Mechanicsburg PA: Stackpole Books, 2001.

Fulton, William. "Freighting and Staging in Early Days." *Nebraska State Historical Society Publications* 10 (1902): 261–64.

Furnas, Robert W. "J. Sterling Morton." *Nebraska State Historical Society Publications* 15 (1907): 147–53.

Gendler, Carol. "Territorial Omaha as a Staging and Freighting Center." *Nebraska History* 49 (Summer 1968): 103–20

Gere, Charles H. "Admission of Nebraska into the Union." *Nebraska State Historical Society Publications* 1 (1885): 162–73.

Gerteis, Louis S. *Civil War St. Louis.* Lawrence: University Press of Kansas, 2001.

Gibson, Campbell, and Kay Jung. "Historical Census Statistics on Population Totals by Race, 1790 to 1990, and by Hispanic Origin, 1970 to 1990, for the United States, Regions, Divisions, and States." Working paper no. 56. Washington DC: U.S. Census Bureau, 2002.

Goodwin, Doris Kearns. *Team of Rivals: The Political Genius of Abraham Lincoln.* New York: Simon and Schuster, 2005.

Green, James, E. B. Murphy, and John Gilbert. "Incidents of the Indian Outbreak of 1864." *Nebraska State Historical Society Publications* 19 (1919): 1–28.

Greene, Jerome A. *Fort Randall on the Missouri, 1856–1892.* Pierre: South Dakota Historical Society Press, 2005.

Gregory, John S. "Early Days at the Salt Basin." *Nebraska State Historical Society Publications* 15 (1907): 102–8.

Hadley, C. B. "The Plains War in 1865." *Nebraska State Historical Society Publications* 10 (1902): 273–78.

Hagerty, Leroy W. "Indian Raids along the Platte and Little Blue River, 1864–1865." *Nebraska History* 28 (Oct.–Dec. 1947): 240–50.

Harmer, Marie U., and James L. Sellers. "Charles H. Van Wyck: Soldier-Statesman of New York and Nebraska." *Nebraska History* 12 (Apr.–June 1929): 83–128; (July–Sept. 1929): 190–246; (Oct.–Dec. 1929): 322–73; 13 (Jan.–Mar. 1932): 3–36.

Heitman, Francis B. *Historical Register and Dictionary of the U.S. Army.* 2 vols. Washington DC: GPO, 1905.

Holmes, Louis A. *Fort McPherson, Nebraska, Fort Cottonwood, N.T.: Guardian of the Tracks and Trails.* Lincoln: Johnsen, 1963.

Howell, Alice Shaneyfelt. "Post South Loup Fork." *Buffalo Tales* 14 (July–Aug. 1991): 1–5.

Hyde, George E. *Life of George Bent, Written from His Letters.* Edited by Savoie Lottinville. Norman: University of Oklahoma Press, 1968.

Jensen, Richard E., ed. *Voices of the American West.* Vol. 2, *The Settler and Soldier Interviews of Eli S. Ricker, 1903–1919.* Lincoln: University of Nebraska Press, 2005.

Jones, Robert Huhn. *The Civil War in the Northwest.* Norman: University of Oklahoma Press, 1960.

Josephy, Alvin M., Jr. *The Civil War in the American West.* New York: Alfred A. Knopf, 1991.

Journal of the Council. Eighth (Ter.) Legislative Session, 1861–62. Omaha: Taylor and McClure, 1862.

Journal of the House of Representatives. Twelfth (Ter.) Legislative Session, 1867. Omaha: Barkalow Bros., 1867.

Journal of the House of Representatives. Second State Legislative Session, 1867. Omaha: St. A. D. Balcombe, 1867.

Keller, Robert H., Jr. "The 1864 Overland Trail: Five Letters from Jonathan Blanchard." *Nebraska History* 63 (Spring 1982): 71–86.

Kennedy, Joseph C. G. *Preliminary Report on the Eighth Census.* Washington DC: GPO, 1862.

Larson, T. A., ed. "Across the Plains in 1864 with George Forman: A Traveler's Account." *Annals of Wyoming* 40 (Apr. 1968): 5–22.

Lass, William E. *From the Missouri to the Great Salt Lake: An Account of Overland Freighting.* Lincoln: Nebraska State Historical Society, 1972.

——. *Navigating the Missouri: Steamboating on Nature's Highway, 1819–1935.* Norman: Arthur H. Clark, 2008.

——. "Nebraska City's Steam Wagon." *Nebraska History* 79 (Spring 1998): 24–33.

Laws of Nebraska. Seventh (Ter.) Legislative Session, Begun at Omaha, Dec. 5, 1860. Nebraska City: Thomas Morton, 1861.

Laws of Nebraska. Eighth (Ter.) Legislative Session, Begun at Omaha, Dec. 7, 1861. Omaha: Taylor and McClure, 1862.

Laws of Nebraska. Ninth (Ter.) Legislative Session, 1864. Omaha: Taylor and McClure, 1864.

Laws of Nebraska. Tenth (Ter.) Legislative Session, 1865. Omaha: Taylor and McClure, 1865.

Laws of Nebraska. Twelfth (Ter.) Legislative Session, 1867. Omaha: Barkalow Bros., 1867.

Laws of Nebraska. First, Second, and Third Legislative Sessions, 1866–67. Omaha: St. A. D. Balcombe, 1867.

Lewis, John G. W., ed. *Messages and Proclamations of the Governors of Nebraska.* Vol. 1. Lincoln: Nebraska State Historical Society, 1941.

Logan, Guy E., comp. *Roster and Record of Iowa Soldiers in the War of the Rebellion.* Vol. 4. Des Moines IA: State Printer, 1910.

Ludwickson, John. "'A Far Worse Scourge than the Indians': Volunteer Cavalry in Northeast Nebraska." In *Papers of the Thirteenth Dakota*

History Conference, edited by H. W. Blakely, 547–58. Madison SD: Dakota State College, 1982.

Luebke, Frederick C. "Time, Place, and Culture in Nebraska History." *Nebraska History* 69 (Winter 1988): 150–68.

Maddox, Porter. "Freighting Reminiscences." *Nebraska State Historical Society Publications* 10 (1901): 296–97.

Mardock, Robert W. "The Plains Frontier and the Indian Peace Policy, 1865–1880." *Nebraska History* 49 (Summer 1968): 187–201.

Mattes, Merrill J. "Fort Mitchell, Scotts Bluff, Nebraska Territory." *Nebraska History* 33 (Mar. 1952): 1–34.

——. *The Great Platte River Road: The Covered Wagon Mainline via Fort Kearny to Fort Laramie*. Lincoln: Nebraska State Historical Society, 1969.

McChristian, Douglas C. *Fort Laramie: Military Bastion of the High Plains*. Norman: Arthur H. Clark, 2008.

McDermott, John D. *Circle of Fire: The Indian War of 1865*. Mechanicsburg PA: Stackpole Books, 2003.

——. "'We Had a Terribly Hard Time Letting Them Go': The Battles of Mud Springs and Rush Creek, February 1865." *Nebraska History* 77 (Summer 1996): 78–88.

McPherson, James M. *Ordeal by Fire: The Civil War and Reconstruction*. New York: McGraw-Hill, 1982.

——. *Tried by War: Abraham Lincoln as Commander in Chief*. New York: Penguin Press, 2008.

Mobley, Freeman K. *Making Sense of the Civil War in Batesville-Jacksonport and Northeast Arkansas, 1861–1874*. Batesville AR: Author, 2005.

Morton, J. Sterling, succeeded by Albert Watkins. *Illustrated History of Nebraska*. 3 vols. Lincoln: Jacob North, 1905–1913.

Mulhair, Charles. *The Ponca Agency*. Niobrara NE: Author, 1992.

Nebraska Blue Book, 2008–09. Lincoln: Clerk of the Legislature, 2009.

Olson, James C. *J. Sterling Morton*. 1942. Reprint, Lincoln: Nebraska State Historical Society Foundation, 1972.

——. *Red Cloud and the Sioux Problem*. Lincoln: University of Nebraska Press, 1965.

Olson, James C., and Ronald C. Naugle. *History of Nebraska*. 3rd ed. Lincoln: University of Nebraska Press, 1997.

Palmer, Henry E. "History of the Powder River Indian Expedition of 1865." *Nebraska State Historical Society Publications* 2 (1887): 197–229.

Patrick, John R. *Report of the Nebraska Adjutant General, January 1871*. Des Moines IA: Mills, 1871.

Pattison, John J. "With the U.S. Army along the Oregon Trail, 1863–66." *Nebraska History* 15 (Apr.–June 1934): 79–93.

Paul, R. Eli. *Blue Water Creek and the First Sioux War, 1854–1856*. Norman: University of Oklahoma Press, 2004.

——, ed. "A Galvanized Yankee along the Niobrara River." *Nebraska History* 70 (Summer 1989): 146–57.

Pedersen, James F., and Kenneth D. Wald. *Shall the People Rule?: A History of the Democratic Party in Nebraska Politics, 1854–1972*. Lincoln NE: Jacob North, 1972.

Potter, James E. "A Congressional Medal of Honor for a Nebraska Soldier: The Case of Private Francis W. Lohnes." *Nebraska History* 65 (Summer 1984): 245–56.

——. "The First Nebraska's Orphan Detachment and the Skirmish at Grand Prairie, 1864." *Nebraska History* 81 (Spring 2000): 35–39.

——. "Horses: The Army's Achilles Heel in the Civil War Plains Campaigns of 1864–65." *Nebraska History* 92 (Winter 2011): 158–69.

——, ed. "'I Thought It My Duty To Go': The Civil War Letters of Thomas Edwin Keen, First Nebraska Volunteer Infantry." *Nebraska History* 81 (Winter 2000): 134–69.

——, ed. "A Nebraska Cavalryman in Dixie: The Letters of Martin Stowell." *Nebraska History* 74 (Spring 1993): 22–31.

Potts, James B. "Nebraska Statehood and Reconstruction." *Nebraska History* 69 (Summer 1988): 73–83.

——. "North of 'Bleeding Kansas': The 1850s Political Crisis in Nebraska Territory." *Nebraska History* 73 (Fall 1992): 110–18.

Report of the Adjutant General of the State of Kansas, 1861–65. Vol. 1. Topeka: J. K. Hudson, 1896.

Robinett, Paul M., and Howard V. Canan. "The Military Career of James Craig." *Missouri Historical Review* 66 (Oct. 1971): 49–60.

Robrock, David P. "The Eleventh Ohio Volunteer Cavalry on the Central Plains, 1862–1866." *Arizona and the West* 25 (Spring 1983): 23–48.

Rolfe, D. P. "Overland Freighting from Nebraska City." *Nebraska State Historical Society Publications* 10 (1902): 279–93.

Rowen, Richard D., ed. "The Second Nebraska's Campaign against the Sioux." *Nebraska History* 44 (Mar. 1963): 3–53.

Russell, Don. "Some Thoughts on Brevet Commissions—and Custer." *The Chicago Westerners Brand Book* 16 (Sept. 1959): 1–2.

Scherneckau, August. *Marching with the First Nebraska: A Civil War Diary*. Translated by Edith Robbins. Edited by Edith Robbins and James E. Potter. Norman: University of Oklahoma Press, 2007.

——. "Soldiering in the Platte Valley, 1865: A Nebraska Cavalryman's Diary." Edited by James E. Potter and Edith Robbins. *Nebraska History* 91 (Spring 2010): 16–51.

Seymour, Silas. "Western Incidents Connected with the Union Pacific Railroad." *Nebraska History* 50 (Spring 1969): 27–54.

Shannon, Fred Albert. *The Organization and Administration of the Union Army, 1861–1865.* 2 vols. Cleveland: Arthur H. Clark, 1928.

Sheldon, Addison E. *Nebraska: The Land and the People.* Vol. 1. Chicago: Lewis, 1931.

——, comp. *Nebraska Constitutions of 1866, 1871, and 1875.* Lincoln: Nebraska Legislative Reference Bureau/Nebraska State Historical Society, Sept. 1920.

Sifakis, Stewart. *Who Was Who in the Union.* New York: Facts on File, 1988.

Smith, Duane A. *The Birth of Colorado: A Civil War Perspective.* Norman: University of Oklahoma Press, 1989.

Snoddy, Donald D., Barry Combs, Bob Marks, and Del Weber, eds. *Their Man in Omaha: The Barker Letters.* Vol. 1, *1860 to 1868.* Omaha: Douglas County Historical Society, 2004.

Statutes at Large of the United States of America. Vol. 13. Boston: Little, Brown, 1866.

[Stella]. "Letter from the Interior of Nebraska." *Nebraska State Historical Society Publications* 6 (1894): 46.

Stolley, William. "Defense of Grand Island." *Nebraska History* 16 (Oct.–Dec. 1935): 221–27.

——. "History of the First Settlement of Hall County, Nebraska." Special issue, *Nebraska History* (Apr. 1946): 1–90.

Stonebraker, Orville M., comp. *Nebraska Blue Book, 1899–1900.* Lincoln: State Journal, 1899.

Sutherland, Daniel E. "Guerrillas: The Real War in Arkansas." In *Civil War Arkansas: Beyond Battles and Leaders,* edited by Anne J. Bailey and Daniel E. Sutherland, 133–53. Fayetteville: University of Arkansas Press, 2000.

Thavenet, Dennis. "The Territorial Governorship: Nebraska Territory as Example." *Nebraska History* 51 (Winter 1970): 411–24.

Thayer, John M. "The Pawnee War of 1859." *Nebraska State Historical Society Publications* 10 (1902): 231–46.

Tipton, Thomas W. "Forty Years in Nebraska: At Home and in Congress." *Nebraska State Historical Society Special Publication* (1902): 1–570.

U.S. Department of the Interior, Bureau of the Census. *Compendium of the Eleventh Census, 1890.* Pt. 3. Washington DC: GPO, 1897.

——. *Manufactures of the United States in 1860.* Washington DC: GPO, 1865.

U.S. Senate. *Testimony as to the Claim of Ben Holladay for Losses and Damages Sustained by Him on the Overland Stage Line during the Years 1862, 1863, 1864, 1865, and 1866.* Misc. doc. 19, 46th Cong., 2nd sess., 1879.

Utley, Robert M. *Frontiersmen in Blue: The United States Army and the Indian, 1848–1865.* New York: Macmillan, 1967.

Wagner, David E. *Patrick Connor's War: The 1865 Powder River Indian Expedition.* Norman: Arthur H. Clark, 2010.

——. *Powder River Odyssey: Nelson Cole's Western Campaign of 1865, The Journals of Lyman G. Bennett and other Eyewitness Accounts.* Norman: Arthur H. Clark, 2009.

Walker, Francis A. *Compendium of the Ninth Census.* Washington DC: GPO, 1872.

Ware, Eugene F. *The Indian War of 1864.* Edited by Clyde C. Walton. Lincoln: University of Nebraska Press, 1960.

The War of the Rebellion: A Compilation of the Official Records of the Union and Confederate Armies. 128 vols. Washington DC: GPO, 1880–1901.

Watkins, Albert. "How Nebraska Was Brought into the Union." *Nebraska State Historical Society Publications* 18 (1917): 375–434.

Wax, Darold D. "Robert Ball Anderson, Ex-slave, a Pioneer in Western Nebraska, 1884–1930." *Nebraska History* 64 (Summer 1983): 163–92.

Webster, John Lee. "Controversy in the United States Senate over the Admission of Nebraska." *Nebraska State Historical Society Publications* 18 (1917): 345–74.

White, John B. "Published Sources on Territorial Nebraska: An Essay and Bibliography." *Nebraska State Historical Society Publications* 23 (1956).

Wishart, David. "Age and Sex Composition on the Nebraska Frontier, 1860–1880." *Nebraska History* 54 (Spring 1973): 106–19.

——. *An Unspeakable Sadness: The Dispossession of the Nebraska Indians.* Lincoln: University of Nebraska Press, 1994.

Woolworth, James M. "Address to the Public [1866]." In Morton, *Illustrated History of Nebraska*, 1:529–36.

——. *Reports of Cases in the Supreme Court of Nebraska.* Vol. 2. Chicago: Callaghan, 1873.

Zimmer, Edward F., and Abigail Davis. "Recovered Views: African American Portraits, 1912–1925." *Nebraska History* 84 (Summer 2003): 58–114.

INDEX

Page numbers in italic refer to illustrations.

Abbott, Othman A. (lt. gov., 1877–79), 287
abolition and abolitionists, 56; Democrats' hatred of, 83–84, 93, 214, 218; Harvey's hatred of, 88, 212, 324n106; J. S. Morton's hatred of, 89–91, 119, 222. *See also* emancipation; slavery
accidents, 45, 247; drownings, 60; falls, 37, 60; shootings, 36, 182
Adamsville (TN), Wallace's division in, 57
"Address to the Public" (Woolworth), 244–45
African Americans, *278*; civil rights for, 234, 279–81; colonization of, 213; expulsion of, from Nebraska City, 88; proposed exclusion of, from Nebraska, 86–88; riots by, 258–59; school segregation of, 267–68. *See also* African American soldiers; contrabands; freedmen's rights; slavery; suffrage: for African Americans
African American soldiers: attitudes toward, 72, 93, 118, 128, 157; pragmatic basis for, 89; service of, in 1st Nebraska, 61, 130, 195, 206, 289, 302n39; service of, in Union army, 84, 85, 195
Ajax. *See* Harvey, Augustus
alcoholic beverages. *See* Union army: alcohol abuse in

Alder Gulch (IDT, later MTT), gold discoveries in, 65
Alkali Station: Indian attacks at, 154, 205; soldiers at, 176
allegiance, oaths of. *See* loyalty oaths
Allen, J. B., disloyal conduct of, 181
Allen, William V. (U.S. senator), 287
American Indians, 11, 77, 289; 1861 threats by, 18–19, 21; 1862 threats by, 64, 65, 66, 67, 74; 1863 Dakota campaign against, 96–101; 1864 Plains war against, 124–26, 138, 140–56, 165; 1865 peace initiative toward, 186–87, 200, 203, 241; 1865 Powder River campaign against, 185–204; 1865 raids by, 167–71, 190–93, 204–6; 1865 Republican Valley campaign against, 168, 169, 172; 1866 campaign against, 239–40; 1870s wars of, 289; perceived Secessionist influence among, 25, 66, 145; Pope's policy toward, 97–98; postwar dispossession of, 285; soldiers' attitudes toward, 193; U.S. policy toward, 204. *See also specific tribes*
Anderson, Robert Ball (African American homesteader, soldier), 289
Antietam, Battle of (1862), emancipation spurred by, 75
Appomattox (VA), Lee's surrender at, 181, 246–47
Arapaho Indians, 11, 125, 140, 193; at Ft. Laramie, 241–42; at Sand Creek, 167; at Tongue River, 202

Arbor Day, origin of, 288

Arcadia (MO), 1st Nebraska in, 108

Arkansas, 108, 194; 1st Nebraska in, 82, 112–14, 128–34; irregular warfare in, 113–14, 129, 131–34, 137; Marmaduke's raid from, 81–82; martial law in, 131; mutiny in, 137–38; Price's raid from, 149; Shelby's raid from, 110–11, 133; Union soldiers from, 130, 133, 139

Armstrong, George (Maj.), Ponca killings investigated by, *94*, 102, 308n55

Army of Northern Virginia (Confed.), 123, 141

Army of Southeastern Missouri, under Davidson, 78, 79

Army of the Potomac, Army of Northern Virginia besieged by, 141

Army of the Southwest, 1st Nebraska attached to, 60–61

Army of Western Missouri, 37

Ash Hollow, 148; Battle of Blue Water Creek near, 170

Astoria (OR), 289

Atchison County (MO): Secessionists in, 26–27, 33; Unionists in, 33, 34, 106

Atkinson, Henry M. (Adj.), *94*; 2nd Nebraska defended by, 196

Atlanta (GA), capture of, 123, 141, 161

Bad Wound (Oglala Sioux), Mitchell's council with, 125

Balcombe, St. A. D. (of *Nebraska Republican*), 261, 262; suffrage views of, 269–70

Baltimore (MD), Union Party convention in, 157

banishment of Confederate sympathizers, 80–81

Bannack City (IDT, later MTT): gold discoveries near, 65, 95, 101, 123

Barker, Joseph, Jr.: description of 1st Nebraska by, 246; description of Omaha by, 262–63; description of politics by, 259

Batesville (AR): Confederates captured at, 79; District of Northeastern Arkansas headquartered at, 112, 113, 128, 129, 130; supply lines to, 132; Union withdrawal from, 133

Battle Creek (NE), 13

Baumer, William (Lt. Col.), 24; in 1st Nebraska, 197, 198–99

Beatrice (NT): Jayhawkers near, 35; militia in, 145–46

Beauvais' Ranche, soldiers at, 176

Beaver Creek, 148

Bedford, Thomas W., 158–59, 217–18

Belden, David D. (legislator, Omaha mayor), 6

Belden, George P. (soldier), biography of, 289

Bellevue (NT), 3, 9

Bellevue *Nebraska Times*, on statehood, 227

Bennett, J. B., statehood supported by, 229

Benton Barracks (St. Louis), 1st Nebraska in, 32, 50

Big Blue River, 287

Bighorn Mountains, 201, 242

Big Sandy Creek, 143

Black, Samuel (terr. gov., 1859–61), 13, 294n5; Daily's election certified by, 71–72; farewell message of, 6; Pawnee War misconduct of, 13; slavery bill vetoed by, 4, 294n5; volunteers organized by, 18

Black Hills, 192, 201

Black Republicans (nickname for anti-slavery Republicans), 73, 86–88, 93, 214

Black River, 133

blacks. *See* African Americans; African American soldiers

black soldiers. *See* African American soldiers

Blackwater Creek. *See* Milford (MO), skirmish at

Blue Water Creek, Battle of (1855), 11, 170

Boettner Park (Brownville), historical plaque in, 290

Booth, John Wilkes, 184

bounties as military recruiting incentive: for reenlisted veterans (1863), 109–11; for three-year recruits (1862), 68

Boutwell, George (U.S. congressman), amendment by, 269, 271, 273

Bowen, A. (surgeon), *94*

Bowen, Leavitt L., militia commanded by, 12

Box Butte County (NE), 289

Boyd County (NE), formation of, 283

Bozeman, John M., Bozeman Trail named for, 125

Bozeman Trail, 125, 202; fortification of, 241–42, 250–51

Breckinridge, John C., as presidential candidate, 4

Bridger, Jim, Indians described by, 153

bridges: over Loup River, 188; over Missouri River, 268, 276–77; over Platte River, 241

Brown, B. Gratz (U.S. senator), suffrage amendment by, 265–66

Brown, Charles H., (Omaha mayoral candidate), 278

Brown, Joseph R. (Gen.), steam wagon of, 62

Brown, R. H. (Lt. Col.), 1866 Indian campaign of, 239–40

Brownville (NT), 85, 193; 7th Iowa in, 121–22; African Americans in, *278*; first homestead claim filed at, 83; freighting from, 9, 26; Handley's murder in, 106; historical plaque in, 290; Jayhawkers and anti-Jayhawkers in, 34, 35–36, 46, 48, 49, 120–21; Knights of the Golden Circle in, 92–93; Lincoln mourned in, 182–83; militia in, 19, *22*, 23, 33–34, 64–65, 69;

Morton-Butler debate in, 238; political conventions in, 255; recruiting in, 136; refugees in, 21, 33; R. Thompson's arrest in, 28; Secessionists in, 26–27, 28, 33, 124; soldier relief in, 179; steamboats in, 17; telegraph reached by, 6; Union clubs in, 92; victory celebrations in, 181–82

Brownville Home Guards, 19. *See also* militia (in Nebraska)

Brownville *Nebraska Advertiser*, *22*, 94, 215–16, 293–94n4; on 1st Nebraska, 30, 110; on 2nd Nebraska, 68, 97; on 7th Iowa, 121–22; on African American suffrage, 223, 232, 270, 273; on call to arms, 15; on contrabands, 104; on Democratic Party platforms, 158, 161, 237; on elections, 5, 157–58, 161, 180, 220, 222, 259; on flag presentation, 23; on Freedmen's Bureau, 251–52; on Handley's murder, 106; on Harvey's disloyal conduct, 128, 212; on Indians, 74, 97, 145, 193; on Jayhawking and anti-Jayhawking, 34, 46, 48; on J. S. Morton, 220; on Knights of the Golden Circle, 92–93; on Lincoln administration, 180; on President Johnson, 233, 251–52, 259; on recruiting, *22*, 68; on Secessionists, 5, 33, 105–6, 121; on statehood, 223, 227; on telegraph, 6; on victory celebrations, 182

Brownville Union Club, 92

Brule (NE), 176

Brulé Sioux Indians, 167; in Battle of Blue Water Creek, 11; at Cottonwood Springs, 125; at Ft. Laramie, 192, 241, 242; in raids on Pawnee, 63; in skirmish at Pawnee Agency, 101, 102

Buchanan, James (U.S. pres.), 1, 3, 4, 220

Buckrau, Henry (Cpl.), wounding of, at Shiloh, 58

Bull Run, First Battle of (1861), 30

Bull Run, Second Battle of (1862), 173–74

burnetizer, logs soaked in, 208–9

bushwhackers. *See* irregular warfare

Butler, David (first state gov., 1867–71), 235, 237–38, 243, 247–48, 274, 276; impeachment of, 284

Byram brothers, freight hauled by, 62

Cairo (IL), Union base at, 31, 51

Calhoun, John C., Calhoun Co. named for, 50

Calhoun County (NT, later Saunders Co.), 49–50

Cameron, Simon (U.S. sec. of war), 18; misleading letter from, 20, 30

Camp Collins, 140

Camp Cook, 2nd Nebraska at, 94, *98*

Camp Rankin. *See* Fort Sedgwick

Camp Saunders, 2nd Nebraska at, 71

Camp Shuman. *See* Fort Mitchell

Camp Wheaton, 240

Cantonment McKean. *See* Fort Cottonwood

Cape Girardeau (MO), 1st Nebraska in, 79–82, 108

Cape Girardeau (MO), Battle of (1863), 81–82, 108, 305n9

Captain Buck's Jayhawkers, near Falls City, 35

Carondelet (MO), gunboats constructed at, 110

Carr, Eugene A. (Maj. Gen., 3rd Brigade, 2nd Corps), 137

Carrington, Henry (Col.), 241; Red Cloud's defeat of, 242

Cass County (NT): 1866 election fraud in, 243–45, 248; legislative speaker from, 268–69; Republicans in, 221, 222

Castor River, bridge on, 82

Celia (escaped slave), 2

cemeteries: Steele Cemetery (Falls City), 290; Wyuka Cemetery (Lincoln), 289–90

Central Overland and Pikes Peak Express, in Platte Valley, 41

Central Superintendency, crop failure in, 156

Chalk Bluff skirmish (1863), 82

Chancellorsville, Battle of (1863), 107

Chandler, E. B., attitude of, toward statehood, 217

Chapman, John, 238

Charleston (SC), Union capture of, 180

Chase, DeWitt (Cpl.), killing of, by Indians, 205

Cheyenne Indians, 11, 18, 19, 125; in 1865 raids, 140, 191, 193; at Ft. Laramie treaty council, 241–42; Moonlight's pursuit of, 191–92; during Powder River Expedition, 202; at Sand Creek, 155, 167

Chicago (IL), 92; Democratic convention in, 158, 161; sanitary fair in, 179, 180

Chicago Journal, 271

Chicago Platform. *See* Democratic Party Platform of 1864

Chivington, John M. (Col.), at Sand Creek, 155, 167, 193

Chivington, Rebecca S., soldier relief by, 179

Clarinda (IA), flag from, 22

Clarke, Henry T., oxen stolen from, 205, 322n88

Cleveland, Grover (U.S. pres.), 288

Cleveland, Marshall (Union Jayhawker), 46, 47, 48, 300n3

clothing and equipment, 27; for 1st Nebraska cavalry, 111, 146; for 1st Nebraska infantry, 36; shoes, 78; uniforms, 25, 131

Cobb, W. R., confiscation of property of, 73, 304n68

Coe, Isaac, in territorial militia, 68

Coffman, Jacob (Pvt.), *70*

Cole, Nelson (Col.), in Powder River Expedition, 201–2

Colhapp, John (of *Nebraska Advertiser*),

182; on African American suffrage, 213, 232, 270; on A. S. Paddock, 259; on Freedmen's Bureau, 251–52; on Missouri refugees, 212; on President Johnson, 233, 234, 251–52; on victory celebrations, 182

Colhoff, George W. (5th U.S. Volunteers), 247

Collins, Caspar (2nd Lt.), killing of, by Indians, 193

Collins, William O. (Lt. Col.), 192, 193; Plains service of, 63–64, 125, 150, 170, 191

Colorado (steamboat), 146, 208

Colorado Territory, 35, 140, 174; constitutional suffrage restriction in, 231, 232, 237; formation of, 8, 63, 115; Indians in, 125, 167, 168; Secessionists in, 105; statehood for, 118, 127–28, 216, 218, 223, 265, 269, 272

Columbus (KY), Confederate stronghold at, 55

Columbus (NT), 7, 19, 283; 2nd Nebraska at, 94; bridge at, 188; railroad junket to, 250

Comanche Indians, Sioux attacked by, 125

Comstock, Francis J. (Lt.), resignation of, 103

Confederate army: desertion from, 107, 139; Nebraskans in, 7, 294n12; surrender of, 181, 246–47. *See also* irregular warfare: in Arkansas; irregular warfare: in Missouri

Confederate War Department, 17

Confiscation Acts for escaped slaves, 61

Congregational Church, 180

Connor, Ben, white depredations described by, 101

Connor, Patrick Edward (Brig. Gen.), 197, 198, 200; 1865 Powder River Expedition of, 174–75, 185–88, 192, 200–202, 204, 241

conscription: avoidance of, by fleeing to Nebraska, 62–63, 64–65, 66, 103–5, 108–10, 121, 124, 145; exemption from, 104–5, 108; provisions for, in Enrollment Act of 1863, 62–63, 104–5, 111–12, 121; resistance to, 118. *See also* recruiting

consolidation, of 1st Nebraska Veteran Volunteer Cavalry with 1st Battalion, Nebraska Veteran Volunteer Cavalry (1865), 194–99, 221

Constitutional Convention of 1864, 126–28, 158, 177, 216–17, 219

contrabands: in 1st Nebraska, 61; at Ft. Davidson, 108; from Missouri, 104. *See also* African Americans; refugees

Copperheads. *See* Peace Democrats

Corinth (MS), Union campaign against, 56, 57, 59

Cottonwood Canyon, 102

Cottonwood Springs: 2nd Nebraska at, 97; 7th Iowa at, 102, 107; Mitchell's council with Sioux at, 125

Council Bluffs (IA), 15, 65, 89–91; as railroad terminus, 114

Council Bluffs Nonpareil: on emigration, 105; on flight to avoid conscription, 124; on Omaha *Daily Nebraskian*, 86

Council File 32 for state constitution, 229

Courthouse Rock, 169

courts-martial: for 7th Iowa soldiers, 103

Cozad (NE), 150

Craig, James (Gen.), Plains service of, 64, 69, 97

Cramer, Francis, at Ft. Donelson, 54

Crawford, George N., frivolous amendment by, 274

Creighton, Edward, telegraph built by, 41, 146

Creighton, Hiram (Sgt.), killing of, by Indians, 191

Crounse, Lorenzo (state gov., 1893–95), postwar career of, 287

Crow Indians, 101

Crump's Landing (TN), 1st Nebraska at, 57, 60

Cumberland River, Ft. Donelson on, 51

Cuming, Thomas B. (terr. gov., 1854–55, 1857–58), militia organized by, 11, 12

Cuming City (NT), soldier relief in, 180

Curran, Sterritt (Capt.), recruiting by, 67, 68, 69

Curtis, Samuel R. (Gen.), 122, 123; commanding Army of the Southwest, 60–61; commanding Dept. of Kansas, 103, 122, 173; commanding Dept. of the Missouri, 69, 78, 96, 97; commanding Dept. of the Northwest, 173; Curtis Horse named for, 50; in Indian wars, 140–50, 153, 154; military ability of, 141–42

Curtis Horse (Fifth Iowa Volunteer Cavalry): Civil War service of, 51, 56; merger of Nebraska cavalry battalion into, 50

Daily, Darah (Mrs. Samuel G.), fundraising by, 23

Daily, Samuel G.: as delegate to Congress, 23, 71–73, 158, 304n67, 323–24n104; as proponent of statehood, 114–15; as speaker in Brownville, 92; as visitor to White House, 157

Dakota City (NT), 140, 156

Dakota Territory, 187, 200; 1862 Indian scare in, 66; 1863 Indian campaign in, 96–101, 108, 124, 174; formation of, 8, 63, 115

Davenport (IA), 7th Iowa in, 102

Davidson, John W. (Brig. Gen.): Ft. Davidson named for, 108; Missouri campaign of (1862–63), 78–79

Davis, Jefferson (Confed. pres.), 17, 105, 181, 184

Davis, Sarah, soldier relief by, 179

Dawes, Henry (U.S. congressman, senator), 269

Dayton (OH), anti-Lincoln newspaper in, 89

Decatur (NT), soldier relief in, 180

Dellone, Andrew, as candidate for treasurer, 256

Democratic Club, J. S. Morton's address to, 89–91

Democratic Party, 50, 16, 118, 160; abolition hated by, 83–84; African American suffrage opposed by, 214–16, 223, 231–32, 269, 270, 273, 277–78; fall campaigns of, 42, 72, 157–65, 216–22, 235–39, 243–45, 248, 255–62; newspapers of, 5, 16, 84, 85–86, 92, 126–27, 181, 210–17, 243, 246, 259–60, 273; perceived disloyalty of, 86, 92–93, 128; platforms of, 158–62, 219, 220, 236–37, 256; postwar eclipse of, 260–61, 285, 287–88; prewar ascendancy of, 1–2; pro-Johnson stance by, 232–34, 246, 252, 254; Radical Republicans hated by, 72, 84, 89–91; Reconstruction views of, 256; soldier relief opposed by, 178; splits of, 3, 4, 83–84, 158, 235–37; statehood views of, 126–28, 216–19, 223, 225–30, 235–37, 273, 274–75. *See also* Peace Democrats; War Democrats

Democratic Party Platform of 1864, 158–59, 161–62

Denver (CT), 125; freighting to, 62; gold mining near, 26; Indian threat to, 125, 140, 168, 169, 171, 176

Department of Arkansas, 133, 134, 199–200; mutiny in, 137–38

Department of Kansas, 64, 103, 122, 138, 141; Indians in, 125; martial law in, 49; merger of, into Dept. of the Missouri, 64, 173; recruiting in, 65

Department of the Missouri, 64, 69, 96, 199–200; under Curtis, 69, 78; desertion from, 206; under G. M. Dodge, 173, 174, 195; headquarters of, in St. Louis, 80, 173; under Pope,

200, 206, 207; under Rosecrans, 173; under Schofield, 110, 111, 112

Department of the Northwest, 67, 69; 2nd Nebraska assigned to, 96–97; under Curtis, 173; under Pope, 67, 69, 123, 174

Department of the Ohio, 199–200

Department of the Plains. *See* District of the Plains

Department of the Platte, headquarters of, in Omaha, 251

Department of the West: under Frémont, 27, 31, 37; under Harney, 21

desertion, 289; from 1st Nebraska, 45, 78, 130, 200, 206–8, 247, 289; from Confederate and Union armies, 104, 107, 122, 124, 139; halting of, by provost marshals, 104–5, 121, 124

DeVall's Bluff (AR), 112, 133, 134, 136, 137, 138; mutineers confined at, 137–39

diaries: of H. Pierce, 99; of J. S. Morton, 184; of Scherneckau, 207; of Winne, 107

Direct War Tax: exemption from, 73–74; levy of, by Congress, 42, 114

disease among soldiers, 247; chills and fevers, 46, 61; diphtheria, 36; measles, 45, 46; mumps, 45–46; scurvy, 149; "typhoid pneumonia," 40

District of Central Missouri under Pope, 40

District of Colorado, 155

District of Nebraska, 102, 174–75, 195; under Craig, 64, 97; East Subdistrict of, 149–50, 153, 175, 205, 253; under McKean, 106, 122; under Mitchell, 122–23, 140, 146, 152, 154, 168; West Subdistrict of, 149–50; under Wheaton, 240

District of Northeastern Arkansas, under Livingston, 112, 130–34

District of Southeastern Missouri, under Fisk, 112

District of the Plains, 174, 185, 187, 200, 202; East Subdistrict of, 190, 198; North Subdistrict of, 191

District of Utah, 174

Dobytown. *See* Kearney City (NT)

Dodge, Augustus C. (U.S. senator), 261

Dodge, Grenville M. (Gen.), 173, 174, 175, 176, 191, 200; Indian policy criticized by, 204; Powder River Expedition of, 185–88, 200; recruiting disallowed by, 195

Donovan, Catherine (Mrs. Edward, hospital matron), 59–60

Donovan, Edward (Lt.), 59; recruiting by, 111, 136

Doolittle, James R. (U.S. senator), Indian peace policy of, 187, 241

Dougherty, William (undercook), 130

Douglas, Stephen A.: as architect of Nebraska Act, 263; as presidential candidate, 4

Douglas County (NT), 235; Democrats in, 221–22; recruiting quota for, 67

Douglass, Frederick, 236

Dover (TN), Ft. Donelson near, 53

Downs, Hiram P., territorial militia commanded by, 12, 17

draft. *See* conscription

Durant, Thomas (Union Pacific vice pres.), 250

Eddyville (IA), Iowa Railroad in, 42

Edmunds, George (U.S. senator), suffrage amendment by, 266, 269, 271

Edmunds, Newton (DT gov.), Indian peace policy of, 187, 241

education: grants of public land for, 226, 228; racial integration of, 267–68; Nebraska Territory's lack of, 10

Eighteenth United States Infantry, 208, 239–41

elections (presidential): of 1860, 4–6; of 1864, 91, 119–20, 134, 142, 156–59, 163, 165, 180, 212

Eleventh Missouri Volunteer Cavalry, in Arkansas, 112, 113, 130

Eleventh Ohio Volunteer Cavalry, Plains service of, 63–64, 101, 125, 140, 147, 148, 150, 170, 192, 193

Eliza (escaped slave), 2

Elkhorn River, 13; railroad built to, 208; white settlement along, 283

Ellis, Richard N. (historian), 204

Elwood, Fred (Sgt.), Indians fought by, 206

emancipation: Antietam as spur to, 75; compensation for, 91; Democratic hostility toward, 72, 89–91, 93, 118; pragmatic basis for, 89; proclamation of, 72, 74–75, 82–91, 157. *See also* abolition and abolitionists; slavery

emigration, 264; gold as cause of, 105, 107, 123, 124–25, 190; increase of, 62, 103–7, 123–24, 190, 217, 223, 284, 285; jumping-off points for, 42; reversal of, 190

Enrollment Acts. *See* conscription

Estabrook, Caroline, soldiers feted by, 25

Estabrook, Experience, 25; defeat of, for delegate to Congress, 71; suffrage views of, 213–14, 231, 323–24n104

Eubanks, Isabelle, capture of, by Indians, 143

Eubanks, Lucinda, capture of, by Indians, 143

Evans, John (CO terr. gov.), 125

Fairbury (NT), 283

Falls City (NT): 2nd Nebraska in, 106–7; 7th Iowa in, 121; Jayhawkers and anti-Jayhawkers in, 35, 121; historical marker in, 290; home guards in, 35; Missouri refugees in, 32

Falls City *Broad Axe*: on Civil War crisis, 6; on Missouri refugees, 32

Falls City *Southern Nebraskian*, on statehood, 227

"Farmer," view of, on Morton-Butler debate, 238

Fetterman Massacre (1866), 242

Fifteenth Amendment (U.S. Constitution), 281

Fifth Iowa Volunteer Cavalry. *See* Curtis Horse (Fifth Iowa Volunteer Cavalry)

Fifth United States Volunteer Infantry, 203, 247

Fifty-eighth Ohio Volunteer Infantry, at Ft. Donelson, 51; at Shiloh, 57

Fifty-sixth Ohio Volunteer Infantry, at Shiloh, 57

fires, prairie, 154–55, 168

First Battalion, Nebraska Veteran Volunteer Cavalry, 50, 103; consolidation of, with 1st Nebraska Veteran Volunteer Cavalry, 194–99; formation of, 109–111; Plains service of, 123, 140, 147, 150, 190, 191; recruiting for, 109–111, 135

First Illinois Light Artillery, at Ft. Donelson, 53

First Nebraska Veteran Volunteer Cavalry: African Americans in, 61, 130; Arkansas campaign of, 112–14, 128–34; consolidation of, with 1st Battalion, Nebraska Cavalry, 194–99; desertion from, 45, 78, 130, 200, 206–8, 247, 289; discharge of, 245–47; flag of, *199*; furlough of, 130, 134–37, 146, 194; historical markers for, 290; Lincoln mourned by, 182–83; mounting of, 110–11; mutiny of, 128–34, 198, 241; orphan detachment of, 138–40; Plains service of, 140–56, 170, 176–93, 204–8, 239–40; postwar careers of, 286, 288–89; recruiting for, 112, 135–36, 194–95; voting by, 163, 242, 243–44

The First Nebraska Volunteer (Georgetown MO), 45

First Nebraska Volunteer Infantry, 179; in Arkansas, 60–62; in Mississippi, 57–59; in Missouri, 37–41, 45–46,

50, 74, 77, 81–82, 108; mounting of, 110–11; operations of (1862–64), *29*; organization of, 21, 23–25, 286, 288–89; provost marshal service of, 80–81, 110; recruiting for, 65–69, 108–11, 303n60; removal of, to Ft. Leavenworth, 27, 28, 30, 64; in Tennessee, 50–56. *See also* First Nebraska Veteran Volunteer Cavalry

First United States Cavalry, at Ft. Kearny, 21

Fisher, T. R. (of *Nebraska Advertiser*), 105–6, 306–7n32

Fisk, Clinton B. (Brig. Gen.), Dist. of Southeastern Missouri under, 112

flags, 82, 183; of 1st Nebraska, 88, *199*; destruction of, in St. Joseph, 21; above Gray's store, 16; Harvey's abuse of, 128; presentation of, to soldiers, 22–23, 198–99, 297n21; at Union Pacific ceremonies, 114, 209

Florence (NT): militia in, 19; outfitting in, 9; soldier relief in, 179

Fontanelle (NT), Sioux attack near, 12

foraging. *See* supplies and supply lines

Ford's Theater, 182

Forman, George, Secessionists noted by, 124

Fort Blakely, battle at (1865), 287

Fort Connor, construction of, 201–2, 203

Fort Cottonwood (later Fort McPherson), in Plains Indian wars, 140, 147, 148, 149, 150, 152, 168, 170–71, 176, 182, 189, 239–40

Fort Davidson, construction of, 108, 309n65

Fort Donelson: 1st Nebraska in battle for, 50–55, *55*, 58, 59, 60; Union victory at, 55–56

Fort Halleck, 95; establishment of, 64; Indian raids near, 193

Fort Henry, Union capture of, 50, 51, 53, 56

Fort Kearny (on the Platte), 7, 8, 18, 21, 63, 102, 103, 107, 140, 159, 247, 251; 2nd Nebraska at, 69–71, 94–95, 98; 18th U.S. Infantry at, 208, 240–41; artillery accident at, 182; bridge at, 188, 241; emigration and travel through, 62, 149, 190; freighting through, 62, 188; Jayhawking at, 46; "Laramie Loafers" at, 192; Lincoln mourned at, 182–83; militia ordered to, 147; mutiny at, 198; perceived Secessionist threat to, 18, 20, 21, 31; in Plains Indian wars, 143, 145, 146, 147, 148, 150, 152, 153, 154, 170, 175, 176, 185, 191, 197; prairie fire near, 155; slavery at, 2; telegraph reached by, 6; troops withdrawn from, 16–17, 20; voting at, 162, 163, 242, 243–44

Fort Laramie, 7, 63, 64, 95; emigration through, 124, 125; Grattan Massacre near, 10–11; "Laramie Loafers" at, 192; mutiny at, 201; in Plains Indian wars, 147, 150, 169, 170, 171, 175, 185, 187, 188, 190, 191–92, 193, 200–204; treaty negotiations at, 241–42; troops withdrawn from, 16; Upper Platte Agency near, 11, 101, 193

Fort Leavenworth, 16, 64, 146, 149, 240, 247; 1st Nebraska at, 27, 28, 30; 3rd U.S. Infantry at, 191; in Powder River Expedition, 188; Secessionist threat to, 17, 21; Union depot at, 17, 27

Fort Lyon, 21, 208

Fort McPherson. *See* Fort Cottonwood

Fort Mitchell, *148*, 171; establishment of, 122–23, 147; troops from, at Mud Springs, 170

Fort Phil Kearny (DT), Fetterman Massacre at, 242

Fort Pierre (DT), 99

Fort Randall, 7, 18; 2nd Nebraska at, 98–99; troops withdrawn from, 16–17, 19, 20

Fort Riley, 148, 175

Fort Sedgwick, in Plains Indian wars, 167–69, 176, 185

Fort Sumter, bombardment of, 6, 15

Fort Wise. *See* Fort Lyon

Fourteenth Amendment (U.S. Constitution), 255, 281; criticism of, 266; pending ratification of, 234, 247–48, 270

Fourth Arkansas (Union) Mounted Infantry, 130, 133

Fourth Missouri Volunteer Cavalry, at Cape Girardeau, 80

Fourth United States Artillery, withdrawal of, from Ft. Randall, 20

Fouts, William (Capt.), killing of, by Indians, 192

Fowler, J. S. (U.S. senator), suffrage views of, 270

Freedmen's Bureau, veto of bill for, 232, 251

freedmen's rights, 213–16, 232

Freeman, Daniel, first homestead claim filed by, 83

Freeman, Thomas R. (Col.), Confederate forces of, 131

Free Soil, in Kansas Territory, 3

freighting, 26, 63, 104, 136; from Brownville, 9, 26; from Nebraska City, 62, 95, 123, 188, *189*; from Omaha, 9, 26, 41, 42, 95, 123, 188; through Platte Valley, 41–42, 188; from Plattsmouth, 188; after rail competition, 250–51

Fremont (NT), 7

Frémont, John C. (Gen.): 1st Nebraska ordered to St. Louis by, 27, 30, 298n33; campaign of, for president, 3; ineptitude of, at Lexington, 37; removal of, by Lincoln, 37; Western Dept. commanded by, 31

Fremont County (IA), 106

Frenchman Creek, Indians along, 205

fundamental condition. *See* Nebraska Constitution: suffrage requirements of

furloughs, as military recruiting incentives, 109, 111, 130, 134–37, 146

Furnas, Robert W. (Col.), 16, 23, 30, *94*, 307n33; Arbor Day proclamation by, 288; call to arms by, 15; as Indian agent, 156, 262, 286; military service of, 34, 94–95, 98, 196, 307n33; Missouri Secessionists denounced by, 26–27; *Nebraska Advertiser* edited by, 5, 15; postwar career of, 286, 288; rivalry of, with J. S. Morton, 288, 333n7

Galvanized Yankees. *See* United States Volunteers (Confederate prisoners of war)

Gantt, Daniel (terr. dist. atty.), 243

GAR. *See* Grand Army of the Republic

Garber, Silas (state gov., 1875–79), 287

Garton, Elijah, killing of, by Indians, 205

Garton, H. B., killing of, by Indians, 205

Gaskill, Albert, killing of, by Indians, 205

General Order No. 1, for volunteers, 18

General Order No. 3, for recruiting quotas, 67

General Order No. 77, for reducing armed forces, 186

Genoa (NT), Pawnee Agency near, 98, 101, 203

Georgetown (MO), 1st Nebraska in, 37–41, 45–46, 50

Georgia, 3rd Nebraska in, 287; Sherman's march through, 123, 134, 141, 200

Gere, Charles H. (legislator), 248, 250

Germans: in Grand Island, 7–8, 143, 147, 289; in Nebraska City, 73, 88–89; in St. Louis, 80; in Union Rifle Co., 19, 23–24

Gettysburg, Battle of (1863), as turning point, 117

Gibson, Robert, accidental death of, 36

Gillespie, Emma, "daughter of the regiment," 60

Gillespie, John (Pvt.): as auditor, 220, 221, 235, 255, 286; at Crump's Landing, 60

Gillespie, Sarah (Mrs. John), 60

Gillette, Lee (Capt.), as 1st Nebraska's recruiter, 67, 68, 69

Gilman's Ranche, soldiers at, 176

gold rush, 74, 104, 105, 107, 124–25, 136, 237, 285; to Alder Gulch, 65; to Bannack City, 65, 95, 123; to Denver, 26; to Montana, 65, 124, 202; to Pike's Peak, 8; to Salmon River, 65, 66, 95

Goodman, Daniel (Pvt.), emigrants described by, 190

Goodrich, St. John, as candidate for treasurer, 220

Grand Army of the Republic (GAR), 290, 291

Grand Island (NT), 283; 7th Iowa at, 143; Germans at, 7–8, 143, 147, 289; militia at, 19

Grand Prairie (AR) skirmish (1864), 138, 286

Grant, Ulysses S. (Gen.), 36, 60, 149, 286; Indian wars policy of, 142, 186; in Mississippi, 57–59, 78, 108; in Tennessee, 50–56; troop reduction by, 200, 207–8; in Virginia, 123, 134, 180–81

Grattan, John (Lt.), 10–11. *See also* Grattan Massacre

Grattan Massacre (near Ft. Laramie, 1854), 10–11

Gray, [?], Secessionist flag above store of, 16

Greene County (NT, later Seward Co.), 49, 300n13

Green River, Indian raids near, 64

Griffin, Thomas (Lt.): letter from, 181; troop consolidation condemned by, 196

Griggs, John Colby (5th U.S. Volunteers), 247

Grigsby, Washington (undercook), 130

Gruwell, James (Cpl.), killing of, by Indians, 205

guerrillas. *See* irregular warfare

gunboats: at Ft. Donelson, 51, 53; at Ft. Henry, 51, 53; at Shiloh, 51; at St. Louis, 80, 110

Hadley, D. B., alcohol abuse described by, 186–87

Hale, [?] (Col., Jayhawker), 34

Hall County (NT), recruiting quota for, 69

Halleck, Henry W. (Gen. in Chief), in Plains Indian wars, 96, 141–42

Handley, Nathan, killing of, 106

Hannibal (MO), 1st Nebraska in, 28

Hannibal and St. Joseph Packet Line, 26, 28, 188

Hannibal and St. Joseph Railroad, 9, 26, 28, 123; Secessionist threats to, 17

Hanscom, Andrew J., abolitionists hated by, 83

Harney, William S. (Gen.), 21; at Battle of Blue Water Creek, 11

Harvey, Augustus, *87,* 306–7n32; African American suffrage opposed by, 210–14, 324n106; disloyal conduct of, 128; Lincoln mourned by, 184; Missouri residents invited to Nebraska by, 212, 222; *Nebraska City News* edited by, 86, 87, 184, 210; racist language of, 86–89, 215; rivalry of, with Waters, 210; school bill sponsored by, 267–68; statehood views of, 235–36, 272

Hascall, Isaac, statehood supported by, 274–75

Hathaway, H. D., G. L. Miller satirized by, 243

Heath, Herman (Bvt. Brig. Gen.): condemnation of (1866), 261, 329n58; East Subdistrict of Nebraska commanded by, 198, 205, 253; Indians pursued by, 205; mutiny suppressed by, 198; *Nebraska Republican* edited by, 323, 253, 325n123; President Johnson

Heath, Herman (*continued*)
  supported by, 233–34, 253–54, 258;
  Sumner amendment opposed by, 232
Hedrick, [?], execution of, 139
Helena (AR), 78; 1st Nebraska in, 60–62
Henderson, Anderson (undercook), 130
Herndon House Hotel, 23; concerts at,
  for soldier relief, 179; Sherman at,
  209; soldiers at, 24
Hitchcock, Phineas W. (U.S. senator),
  272; election of, as delegate to
  Congress, 159, 162–63; postwar
  career of, 287
Hoffman, John B. (Indian agent), 103
holidays and anniversaries, as
  experienced by soldiers: Christmas,
  113, 128; Decoration Day, 291;
  Inauguration Day, 180; Independence
  Day, 13, 25, 60, 213, 231; New Year's,
  77–78; Washington's Birthday, 13
Holladay, A. S. (Republican legislator), 178
Holladay, Ben, Central Overland and
  Pikes Peak Express owned by, 41, 142,
  174
Holliday, Peter (undercook), 130
Holly, Charles F., slaves owned by, 2
Holt County (MO), Secessionists in,
  26–27, 33, 34
home guards. *See* militia (in Missouri);
  militia (in Nebraska)
Homestead Act, 74, 82–83, 117;
  Buchanan's opposition to, 3;
  emigration affected by, 104, 223,
  284, 285; first claim filed under, 83;
  Republican support for, 3–4, 72
Hood, John Bell (Gen.), Tennessee
  invaded by, 172
Horse Creek, battle at (1865), 192
horses: comparison of, with Indian
  horses, 147, 152–54; lack of food for,
  132; lack of, for Plains commands
  (1864–65), 177, 187, 202; poor
  quality of, 111, 154, 177, 190, 205;
  procurement of, 153; theft of, 206–7

hospitals, 58, 59–60, 289–90; poor
  quality of, 46
Hughes, B. M., of Overland Stage Line,
  171
Hughes, W. W. (terr. adj. gen.), 146
Hunter, David (Gen.), Dept. of Kansas
  under, 49
Huntsman's Echo (Wood River Center),
  16, 18
Hutton, James (Pvt.), *39*
Hutton, John (Pvt.), *38*

Idaho Territory, 140; formation of, 95,
  115, 283; gold discoveries in, 65, 125.
  See also Bannack City; Salmon River
Independence (MO), Secessionists in, 27
Independence County (AR), 1st
  Nebraska in, 113
Indian Territory, 200; loyal Indian
  regiment in, 94–95, 307n33
Internal Revenue Act of 1862, 74
Iowa: provost marshal of, 63; residents
  of, in Nebraska Territory, 3;
  Secessionists in, 97; soldiers of, in
  1st Nebraska, 24–25; soldiers of, in
  Nebraska, 163, 244; Unionists from, 34
Iowa Railroad, 42
Irish, O. H., 236
Ironton (MO), 1st Nebraska in, 108
irregular warfare, 59, 110; in
  Arkansas, 113–14, 129, 131–34, 137;
  in Missouri, 26, 31, 40, 77–79; in Otoe
  Co., 106
Ivory, William H. (Capt.): favoritism
  protested by, 207; horses described
  by, 177
Izard, Mark W. (terr. gov., 1855–57), 12
Izard County (NT, later Stanton Co.), 49

Jackson, [?] (Pvt.), killing of, by Indians,
  152
Jackson, William Henry, painting by,
  148
Jacksonport (AR): 1st Nebraska in, 133;
  skirmish at (1864), 131

James River, 99

Jamestown (ND), 100

Jarrot, Vital (Indian agent), 193

Jayhawking, 103, 107; A. Saunders's
proclamation against, 47, 49; at Ft.
Kearny, 46; in Johnson Co., 47; justice
for, 47–48; in Kansas, 35, 49; in
Missouri, 34, 35; in Nemaha Co., 35–
36, 46, 120–21; in Otoe Co., 46, 47–48,
120–22; in Richardson Co., 35, 121

Jefferson, Thomas, language of, in
party platform, 236

Jefferson City (MO), 1st Nebraska in, 37,
51, 110

Johnson, Andrew (U.S. pres.), 159, 184,
210, 213; civil rights act vetoed by,
234; Colorado admission bill vetoed
by, 237, 265; Democratic attitudes
toward, 232–34, 236, 246, 248;
Freedmen's Bureau bill vetoed by,
232, 233, 251; Miller-Morton visit
to, 254–55; Nebraska admission bill
signed by, 273, 275, 276; Nebraska
admission bills vetoed by, 252, 254–
55, 265, 271–72, 274–75; Nebraska
supporters of (1866), 252–62, 266;
Reconstruction views of, 212–13,
218–20, 225, 231, 232–33, 252, 256,
258, 266, 275; Republican attitudes
toward, 233–34, 235, 252–53

Johnson, Harrison (undercook), 130,
206, 289, 322n88

Johnson, Joseph E. (of *Huntman's Echo*),
16; Indian threat discounted by, 18–19

Johnson, O. F. (Mrs.), flag sewed by, 22

Johnson Clubs, formation of (1866), 252

Johnson County (NT), Jayhawking in, 47

Jordan, Robert C., as candidate for
territorial librarian, 256

Julesburg (CT), 149, 150, 154, 170, 185,
205; 1st Nebraska at, 207; 7th Iowa
at, 163; Indian raids on, 143, 167–69,
170; prairie fire near, 155; telegraph
constructed to, 41; voting at, 163

Kansas, 222–23; freighting from, 251;
hostile Indians in, 125, 140–49, 154,
168, 205, 239–40; Jayhawkers in, 34,
35; loyal Indian regiment in, 94–95;
martial law in, 49; mutineers from,
201; recruiters from, 109

Kansas City (MO), 149

Kansas-Nebraska Act, 263, 279;
comparison of, with 1867 admission
bill, 271; Missouri Compromise
repealed by, 2

Kansas Territory: civil strife in, 2–3;
proposed annexation to, of South
Platte region, 3

Kearney City (NT): Jayhawkers in, 46;
Secessionists in, 31

Keen, Thomas (Pvt.), descriptions by: of
Davidson, 78–79; of Ft. Donelson, 54;
of Shiloh, 58; of uniforms, 36

Kellogg, William (terr. chief justice),
227, 230, 236, 243, 252

Kelly, [?] (Pvt.), killing of, by Indians, 152

Kelsey, D. M., passage of Nebraska
admission bill described by, 272

Kennard, Thomas P. (sec. of state,
1867–71), 235

Kentucky: settlers from, 8; Union
campaigns in, 63

Keokuk (IA), Nebraska cavalry battalion
in, 32

Kinney, John F., as candidate for
delegate to Congress, 72–73, 304n67

Kiowa Indians, Sioux attacked by, 125

Kirkham, Robert M., slaves owned by, 2

Knights of the Golden Circle: in
Nemaha Co., 92–93; in Otoe Co., 93

Kountze, Augustus (terr. treas., 1861–
67; state treas., 1867–69), 220–21,
235, 255

Krumme, Henry (Capt.), Indians
trailed by, 205

Ladies' Soldiers' Aid Society (Omaha),
179

Lakota Indians. *See* Sioux Indians

Lamb, Caroline (Mrs. Squire), 143
Lamb, Squire, 6, 95, 143, 161, 294n11;
comments of: on emigration, 66,
123–24, 190; on railroads, 209; on
refugees, 63; on stagecoaches, 150;
on wartime conditions, 143–45,
313–14n64
Lamb, William, 190, 209; Democratic
Party platform described by, 161–62
Land-Grant College Act, 74
Lane, James H. (Gen.), recruiting by, 65
"Laramie Abortion," treaty negotiation
of, at Ft. Laramie, 241–42
"Laramie Loafers," Sioux at Ft.
Laramie, 192, 241
Laws, Gilbert L. (U.S. congressman), 287
Lee, Fitzhugh (Gen.), celebration of
surrender of, 182
Lee, Robert E. (Gen.), 117, 123, 134, 141;
celebration of surrender of, 181–82
Lewellen (NE), 11
Lexington (MO), 40; capture of, 33, 37.
See also Lexington (MO), Battle of
Lexington (MO), Battle of (1861), 33, 37
Lexington (NE), 151
Lincoln (NE): state capital at, 284, 286;
Wyuka Cemetery in, 289, 290
Lincoln, Abraham (U.S. pres.), 18, 41, 72,
128, 178; assassination of, 182–84; call
for volunteers by, 15, 19; Daily-Waters
visit to, 157; Democratic attitudes
toward, 18–19, 83–84, 89–93, 126,
128, 214; demotion of Frémont by, 37;
elections of, to presidency, 4, 91, 119–
20, 134, 142, 156–59, 163, 165, 180,
212, 279; Emancipation Proclamation
by, 74, 82–86, 118; J. S. Morton's
criticism of, 89–91; last official act of,
185, 319n40; Nebraska capital named
for, 289; overland communications
stressed by, 142; Proclamation of
Amnesty and Reconstruction by, 129,
134; railroad terminus selected by,
114

Little Blue River, 124, 155; Indian
attacks along, 143, 145, 146, 152, 191
Little Blue Station, 154
Little Missouri River, 201
Little Priest (Winnebago), in Powder
River Expedition, 203
Little Rock (AR), 133, 137, 138; capture
of, 129; Union campaign against, 78,
108
Livermore, Mary (Mrs.), and
Northwestern Sanitary Commission,
180
Livingston, Robert R. (Maj./Col./Bvt.
Brig. Gen.), 60, 114, 196, 290; in
Arkansas, 61, 112–14, 129–34, 137–
38; discharge of, from 1st Nebraska,
197–98, 253, 321n68; in militia,
17; in Missouri, 80, 110–12, 111; in
Plains Indian wars, 141, 145, 146,
148, 149, 150, 152, 154, 155, 170–76,
191; postwar career of, 286, 288;
recruiting by, 109–12, 135, 194–95
Lodge Pole Creek, 169, 207
Lohnes, Francis (Pvt.): desertion of,
207; Medal of Honor awarded to, 191;
postwar career of, 289
Long, Samuel, shooting of, 35
Loree, John (Indian agent), 101
Louisiana Territory, slavery banned in, 2
Loup River, 19; bridge across, 188; ferry
across, 7
Lowry, [?] (Jayhawker), 47
Loyal National League, in Brownville, 92
loyalty oaths, 28; in Arkansas, 129–30,
134; in Brownville, 92, 106; in
Nebraska City, 105; in Omaha, 128,
181
Lutheran Church, 221

Major General Sherman (locomotive),
208, 209
Majors, Alexander, slaves owned by, 2
Majors, Thomas J. (Maj.), postwar
career of, 286
Manderson, Charles (U.S. senator), 287

maps: 1st Nebraska's theater of operations (1861–64), *29*; Central and Northern Plains (1865), *169*; Post of Plum Creek, *151*

Marengo (IA), Iowa Railroad at, 42

Marmaduke, John S. (Gen.), raid into Missouri by, 81–82

Marmaduke's Raid. *See* Cape Girardeau (MO), Battle of

Marquett, Turner M., 255, 272, 331n17

martial law: in Arkansas, under 1st Nebraska, 131; in Kansas, 49

Marysville (KS), Jayhawkers near, 35

McClellan, George B. (Gen.), as candidate for president, 138, 158–59, 161, 163

McClelland, William (1st Nebraska's surgeon), 58, 318n28

McCord, William D. (Lt. Col.): death of, 60; at Shiloh, 57, 59

McDermott, John D., horses in Plains Indian wars described by, 153

McFadden, Joseph, Pawnee Scouts under, 147, 148

McKean, Thomas J. (Brig. Gen.), Plains service of, 97, 106, 122

McNally, Christopher (Col., 3rd U.S. Volunteer Inf.), 185

McPherson, Elizabeth (Mrs. John), fundraising by, 23

McPherson, John (Dr.), 23; Secessionist harbored by, 120–21

McRae, Dandridge (Gen.), Confederate forces of, 131

Medal of Honor: to Lohnes, 191, 207, 289; to Vifquain, 287

Medicine Bow Mountains, mail routes near, 64

Medicine Creek, R. H. Brown's 1866 campaign near, 240

Memphis (TN), 1st Nebraska in, 60; riots in, 258

Merchants Line of steamboats, 123

Methodist Church, 10

Michigan, volunteer cavalry from, in Indian wars, 186

Mickey, John (state gov., 1903–7), 287

Midway Station, 1st Nebraska at, 176, 177, 182, 183, 189, 207

Miles, D. S. (Col.), at Ft. Leavenworth, 21, 296n7

Milford (MO) skirmish (1861), 40

Military Division of the Mississippi, 209; formation of (1865), 199–200

Military Division of the Missouri, formation of (1865), 173

military leadership assessments, 24; of Curtis, 141–42, 173; of Davidson, 78–79; of Livingston, 61; of Rosecrans, 173

militia (in Missouri), 17, 21, 31, 33. *See also* Missouri State Guard

militia (in Nebraska), 17, 31, 68; compensation for (1865), 178; conscription for (1862), 49, 64–65; organization of, 11–12, 17–18, 33–34; Pawnee War service of, 13; Plains service of, 145–46, 148, 150, 168; quality of (1857), 12–13; recruiting for, 17–26, 105, 146–47

Miller, [?] (ranche owner), 176, 177

Miller, George L., 119, *160*, 222, 238, 262, 267; African American suffrage opposed by, 231, 273, 275; A. Saunders praised by, 276; defeat of, for delegate to Congress, 159, 161–65, 215, 260–61; Northwest secession opposed by, 92; *Omaha Herald* edited by, 160, 215; postwar career of, 288; President Johnson supported by, 233, 254, 258; railroad praised by, 209; Rock Bluffs election fraud condemned by, 243; statehood views of, 217, 218, 222–23, 229, 235, 237, 275–76

Miller, John (Pvt.), death of, 36

Miller, John, racial attitudes toward, 195

Miller, William H.: African American suffrage supported by, 213–14, 231; newspapers edited by, 161, 213

Minnesota, 99; 1862 Indian conflict in, 64, 65, 66, 96, 102; suffrage restriction in, 213

Mississippi, Union campaign in, 57–59

Mississippi River, 51, 55; 1st Nebraska's scouts along (1862), 61; fall of Vicksburg along, 108, 117; Secessionist threats to traffic on, 44, 112; supplies transported on, 133; troops transported on, 51, 79–80

Missouri, 3, 8; 1st Nebraska in, 37–40, 45–46, 50, 74, 77–82; 1st Nebraska recruits from, 111–12; contrabands from, 104; irregular warfare in, 31, 74, 304n71; Jayhawking in, 34, 35; Marmaduke's raid into, 81–82; Price's raid into, 149, 172; refugees from, 21, 32, 34, 63, 103, 106, 107, 122, 124, 190; residents of, invited to Nebraska Territory, 212, 222; Secessionist threats from, 18, 21, 26–27, 33, 80, 97, 110–11, 133; slavery in, 40–41

Missouri Compromise, repeal of, 2

Missouri River, 7, 8, 135, 208; bridging of, 268, 276–77; drownings in, 47–48, 60; freighting from, 188–89; Nebraska Territory bounded by, 1; Secessionist threats to traffic on, 17, 41; steamboats on, 9, 26, 27; Sully's 1863 campaign along, 96–101, 108; white settlement along, 283

Missouri State Guard: battle at Wilson's Creek won by, 37; Springfield threatened by, 31. *See also* militia (in Missouri)

Mitchell, Robert B. (Gen.), 122, 123, 171, 176; 1864 Plains service of, 140–50; 1865 Republican Valley expedition of, 168, 169, 172, 239; Indian threat described by, 125–26; reassignment of, 174–75

Mobile Bay, Union victory at, 161

Montana Territory, 174; gold discoveries in, 65, 124, 202

monuments and memorials, to Civil War events and people, 290

Moonlight, Thomas (Col.), Plains service of, 191–93

"More Again" (newspaper corresp.), 85

Morgan's Mill (AR) skirmish (1864), 131

Mormons, 9, 26, 42, 174; emigration to Utah by, 62, 123, 124; perceived Secessionist influence among, 25

Morton, J. Sterling (terr. gov., 1858–59, 1861; terr. sec., 1858–61), 13, 23, *90*, 262, 293n3; in 1864 election, 157–65; in 1865 election, 220, 222; as Arbor Day founder, 288; as candidate for delegate to Congress, 71–72, 89, 256, 258, 259, 260; as candidate for governor, 236, 237–39, 243, 244, 260, 288; as candidate for U.S. Senate, 250, 260; in Cleveland administration, 288; as foe of abolition, 83; as mourner for Lincoln, 183–84; as *Nebraska City News* editor, 215; as NSHS leader, 288; as opponent of African American suffrage, 215, 231–32, 259–60; as opponent of statehood, 157–58, 217, 219, 229, 230, 235, 254–55, 275; as Peace Democrat, 89–93, 119, 157–59, 164, 254; as rival of Furnas, 288, 333n7; as supporter of Northwest secession, 92; as supporter of President Johnson, 254, 258

Morton, Nancy (Mrs. Thomas), capture of, by Indians, 143, *144*

Morton, Thomas (emigrant), killing of, by Indians, 143, 144

Morton, Thomas (publisher), 88, 210

Mount Olive (AR), 1st Nebraska in, 131–32

Mount Vernon Academy (later Peru State College), 286

Mt. Pleasant (IA), 19

Mud Springs, 207; skirmish at (1865), 169–71, 193

Mullally's Ranche, 150; Indian attack near, 152, 190; prairie fire near, 155

Murphy, Edward B. (Capt., 7th Iowa), 145–46

Murphy, Frank, as candidate for auditor, 256

Murphy, John P. (Capt.), and votes cast by Iowa soldiers, 244

mutiny: by 1st Nebraska, 77–78, 137–38, 198; by Kansas troops, 201

Nance, Albinus, (state gov., 1879–83), 287

Nash, Edwin (Capt.), Omaha Scouts under, 185–86, 190, 203

Nashville (TN), evacuation of, 55–56, 165

National Union Convention, 252–53, 254, 256

Nebraska Act. *See* Kansas-Nebraska Act

Nebraska cavalry battalion (1860–61): formation of, 25–26; merger of, into Curtis Horse, 50; removal of, to St. Louis, 31–32. *See also* Curtis Horse (Fifth Iowa Volunteer Cavalry)

Nebraska City (NT), 7, 9, 13, 165; 2nd Nebraska in, 106–7; 7th Iowa in, 121–22; African Americans driven from, 88; Estabrook's speech in, 213, 231; flags in, 22, 128; freighting and travel from, 9, 26, 41, 62, 95, 123, 149, 188–89, *189*, 151; Germans in, 88; Jayhawkers and anti-Jayhawkers in, 47–48; Lincoln condemned in, 86; militia in, 19, 23, 64–65; murder in, 106; newspapers in, 86–89; outfitting in, 123; political conventions in, 159, 236; population of, 251, 329n54; Secessionists in, 105, 222, 324–25n122; slavery in, 2; soldier relief in, 180; steamboats in, 9, 17, 123; steam wagon in, 62; territorial capital proposed for, 3; victory celebration in, 181

Nebraska City Guards, 19, 23, 297n21. *See also* militia (in Nebraska)

Nebraska City *Nebraska Statesman*, on statehood, 236

Nebraska City News, 210, 267; on 1st Nebraska's discharge, 246; on African Americans, 86–88, 210–12, 215; on elections, 5, 244; on emancipation, 84; on Kountze's candidacy for treasurer, 220–21; on Lincoln administration, 86–88, 128, 184; on recruiting, 68–69; on state constitution, 230, 235; on statehood, 227, 275; on victory celebration, 181

Nebraska City *Press*, 157, 210, 211; on emancipation, 85, 86; on G. L. Miller, 161; on horse thieves, 107; on Jayhawkers and anti-Jayhawkers, 122; on *Nebraska City News*, 88–89; on salaries of state officials, 230; on statehood, 227, 228; on suffrage, 213–14; on "whites only" voting clause of state constitution, 231

Nebraska City Rangers, 19. *See also* militia (in Nebraska)

Nebraska Constitution, 285; adoption of (1866), 227–30, 234, 235, 237, 243–45, 273–75, 284; suffrage requirements of, 230, 235, 252, 265–66, 269, 271–72, 273, 274–75, 332n19

Nebraska Enabling Act of 1864, 118, 120, 126, 127, 245, 272

Nebraska Hall of Fame, 288

Nebraska Legislature (state): First sess. (1866), 237, 240, 245, 247–51, 255; Second sess. (special, 1867), 273–75

Nebraska Legislature (terr.), 1, 2, 3, 73–74; First sess. (1855), 11–12; Second sess. (1855–56), 10; Eighth sess. (1861–62), 4, 36, 42, 47, 49–50; Ninth sess. (1864), 114, 117–20; Tenth sess. (1865), 167, 171, 177–78; Eleventh sess. (1866), 216, 221, 222, 226, 227–28; Twelfth sess. (1867), 255, 266–69, 272

Nebraska State Historical Society founders, 288

Nebraska statehood, 185, 218; arguments against, 118, 126–27, 216–17, 222, 226, 325n2; arguments for, 118, 126–27, 177, 225–26, 227–28, 236, 274–75, 325n2; Democratic attitudes toward, 126–28, 216–19, 222, 225–30, 235–37, 269; elections for, 4, 227–30, 234, 235, 237, 242–45, 258; enabling act for (1864), 115, 120, 126, 231, 272; Harvey's opposition to, 210–12; newspaper coverage of (1866), 226–27; passage of congressional bill for, 269–70; petitions to legislature for, 223, 228; President Johnson's veto of, 252, 254–55; proclamation of, 273, 275, 276; rejection of (1864), 126, 127–28, 158, 177, 216–17, 219, 228; Republican attitudes toward, 126–28, 216–19, 222–23, 225–27, 269–70; Wade's sponsorship of, 252, 264, 265

Nebraska State Seal, *280*, 281

Nebraska Supreme Court (terr.), 1, 287

Nebraska Territory, 1, 200; African American suffrage in, 210–15, 218, 270, 271, 273, 277–81; attitudes of, carried over to statehood, 284; attitudes of, toward emancipation, 84–91; dividing of, 8, 63, 115; military history of (1854–59), 10–13, 294–95n13; Missourians invited to, 212; prewar conditions in, 1–13, 295n19; postwar conditions in, 223–24; Secessionist threat to, 17, 18; wartime conditions in, 41–44, 197, 223–24, 226

Negroes. *See* African Americans; emancipation; slavery

Nemaha City Home Guards, 34. *See also* militia (in Nebraska)

Nemaha County (NT), 23; Jayhawkers and anti-Jayhawkers in, 35–36, 46, 48; militia in, 33–34; purported treason in, 92–93; refugees in, 21; Republicans in, 221, 222; soldier relief in, 179

Nemaha County Cavalry, 34. *See also* militia (in Nebraska)

Nevada Territory, statehood for, 118, 127–28, 142, 217, 226

New Madrid (MO), Confederates in, 31

New Mexico, Indians from, at White House, 157

New Orleans (LA): riots in, 258–59; steamboats from, 188–89

New York Tribune, 60

Niobrara (NT): Indian scare in, 66; Poncas killed near, 102–3, 193

Niobrara River, 283; killings near, 103

Norfolk (NE), 283

North, Frank (Capt.), Pawnee Scouts under, 175, 202, 239, 289

North, Luther, postwar career of, 289

Northern Superintendency, under Taylor, 241

North Platte (NT), Union Pacific built to, 251

Northwest Confederacy, proposal of, by Peace Democrats, 92–93

Northwestern Sanitary Commission, 180

Northwestern Sanitary Fair (Chicago), 180

Noyes, Reynel (Sgt.), Emancipation Proclamation praised by, 85

Nuckolls, Stephen F., slaves owned by, 2

Oak Grove (NT), 143

O'Brien, Nicholas (Capt.), Camp Rankin defended by, 168

O'Fallon's Station, 176; Indian attack near, 204–5

Ogallala (NE), 205

Oglala Sioux Indians, 167; at Cottonwood Springs, 125; at Ft. Laramie treaty council, 192, 241–42

Ohio River, gunboats on, 51

Omaha (locomotive), 250

Omaha (NT), 6, 7, 17, 19, 154, 201; 1st
Nebraska in, 21, 22–25, 27, 30, 32, 65,
97, 135, 137, 138, 140, 146, 153, 196,
245–47, 290; 2nd Nebraska in, 97,
101; African Americans in, 277–79,
281; description of (1866), 262–63;
deserters in, 107; feting of soldiers
in, 22–23, 25, 196, 246; freighting
and travel from, 9, 26, 41, 42, 62, 95,
123–24, 149, 188; levy bill for, 268–
69, 331n9; Lincoln mourned in, 183;
mail service to and from, 26, 176;
military headquarters in, 64, 71, 150,
151; outfitting in, 95, 123; political
meetings in, 60, 233, 238; railroads
in, 71, 114, 150–51, 185, 208–9, 217,
223–24, 227, 262–64; Secessionist
flag in, 16; soldier relief in, 179–89;
territorial capital at, 3, 8, 15, 47,
74, 127, 177, *184*, 226, 284; victory
celebrations in, 180, 181. *See also* Post
of Omaha
Omaha (steamboat), 19, 60
Omaha *Daily Nebraskian*, 45, 215,
293–94n4; on 1860 election, 5; on
anti-Jayhawker bill, 47; on disloyal
conduct, 181; on emancipation,
85–86; on statehood, 126
Omaha *Daily Telegraph*, on Ft. Sumter
bombardment, 15
Omaha Herald, 160, 215, *216*, 262, 275,
276; on 1st Nebraska's discharge,
246; on African American suffrage,
273, 277–78; on A. S. Paddock, 267;
on election of 1866, 260–61; on
Ft. Laramie Treaty (1866), 242; on
Indians, 203; on Morton-Butler
debate, 238; on President Johnson,
233, 253–54; on proposed state
constitution, 230; on railroads, 209;
on Rock Bluffs election fraud, 243;
on statehood, 222, 227, 229, 230, 269,
273, 275–76
Omaha Indians, 11, 19, 102, 103, 186,
262, 285, 286; food scarcity among,
155–56; killing of, by soldiers, 156;
raids on, by Sioux, 145; soldier relief
by, 180
Omaha *Nebraska Republican*, 216,
241, 253, 258, 261, 262, 272; on 2nd
Nebraska, 95, 97, 196; on African
American suffrage, 213, 232, 269–70,
277; on A. S. Paddock, 256, 267;
on county name changes, 50; on
disloyal conduct, 181; on elections,
161, 163, 221–22, 238, 244, 259,
262; on Lincoln's assassination,
183; on McClellan's nomination for
president, 161; on military rivalries,
196; on Omaha Scouts, 186; on
overland mail service, 176; on Peace
Democrats, 119–20; on President
Johnson, 233–34; on soldier suffrage,
129; on statehood, 127, 217, 222,
226–27, 228–29, 242–43, 263, 271, 276;
on war's beginning, 16
Omaha Scouts, Plains service of, 185–
86, 190, 201, 203
One Hundred and Twenty-fifth U.S.
Colored Infantry, 289
Order No. 77, 186
Otoe County (NT): Democrats in, 221,
222; fraudulent voting in, 245;
Jayhawking and anti-Jayhawking
in, 47–48; militia in, 68; purported
treason in, 93; recruiting quota for, 67
Oto-Missouria Indians, 11, 19, 102;
food scarcity among, 155–56
Overland Stage Line, 171
Ozarks, 1st Nebraska in (1862–63), 78–80

Pacific Railroad, 37, 71, 165, 299n60
Pacific Railroad Act, 72, 74, 114, 117
Pacific Telegraph Company, 146
Paddock, Algernon S. (terr. sec.,
1861–67), 138, 178, 236, 240, *257*, 262;
condemnation of (1866), 256–58, 259;
Indians and Secessionists feared by,
25, 66, 96; Lincoln mourned by, 183;

Paddock, Algernon S. (*continued*)
nomination of, for Congress, 256;
postwar career of, 287, 288; President
Johnson supported by, 252, 354;
recruiting by, 66–67; school bill
vetoed by, 268; state constitution
drafted by, 230; twelfth legislature
addressed by, 266–67

Paddock, Emma (Mrs. Algernon S.),
soldier relief by, 179

Paddock, J. W., 261

Paddock Guards, 34, 69. *See also* militia
(in Nebraska)

Paddock Riflemen, 19. *See also* militia
(in Nebraska)

Page County (IA), 1st Nebraska soldiers
from, 24, 244

Painter, Hettie K. (Dr.), 289–90

Panic of 1857, 9

Papillion Creek, 209

Paris (TN) skirmish (1862), 56

paroles and exchanges. *See* prisoners
of war

partisans. *See* irregular warfare

Patrick, Eliza "Lide," fears of, for
soldier brother, 32

Patterson (MO), 1st Nebraska in, 69

Pawnee Agency: 2nd Nebraska at, 98,
101; 7th Iowa at, 147; Pawnee Scouts
at, 203

Pawnee City (NT), G. L. Miller at, 162

Pawnee Indians, 11, 102, 192; food
scarcity among, 155–56; purported
attacks by, along Little Blue, 91;
Sioux raids on, 19, 63, 101, 155. *See
also* Pawnee War of 1859

Pawnee Ranche, 155

Pawnee Reservation, 191

Pawnee Scouts: under McFadden, 147;
under North brothers, 175, 239, 240,
289; in Powder River Expedition, 201,
202, 203

Pawnee War of 1859, 13

Paxton (NE), 205

pay: of Pawnee Scouts, 147; of soldiers,
32, 68, 135; of state officials, 229, 230

Peace Democrats, 120, 190, 212,
221–22, 233, 254, 256, 267; election
of 1864 influenced by, 158–65;
Lincoln opposed by, 83–84, 88–91;
Northwest Confederacy proposed
by, 92–93; Taylor's criticism of, 119.
See also Morton, J. Sterling: as Peace
Democrat; Vallandigham, Clement L.

Pearman, John W. (Maj.), *94*;
Secessionists arrested by, 105

Penniston, [?] (ranche owner), 176, 177

Penniston and Miller's Ranche, 1st
Nebraska at, 176, 177

Penn Medical College, 289

Peru (NT): fundraising in, 23; militia
in, 34; Mt. Vernon Academy in, 286;
shooting in, 35; Stowell in, 56

Peru Home Guards. *See also* militia (in
Nebraska)

Petersburg (VA), siege of (1864–65), 141,
180

Philadelphia (PA), National Union
Convention in, 252, 254, 256

Phillips, Wendell (abolitionist), 91

Pierce, Franklin (U.S. pres.), political
patronage of, 1

Pierce, Henry (Cpl.), 1863 Dakota
campaign described by, 99

Pike's Peak, gold discoveries at, 8

Pilot Knob (MO), 78, 112; 1st Nebraska
in, 28, 36, 37, 79, 108, 110, 139

Pilot Knob Mountain, 1st Nebraska at,
108

Pittsburg Landing, Battle of. *See* Shiloh,
Battle of

Platte Bridge Station, Indian attack
at, 193

Platte River, 151, 176; bridging of,
188, 241; Indians near, 101, 125, 167,
170, 190, 192; mail routes along, 64;
political division by, 3, 71, 227, 248,
268, 284

Platte Valley: Confederates in, 107, 242; emigration and freighting through, 41, 62, 123–24, 149, 188–89, 202; Indians in, 18–19, 102, 124–26, 140–56, 168, 190, 204, 206; prairie fires in, 154–55; railroad relocation from, 222–23; road ranches in, 16; white settlement in, 8, 283

Plattsmouth (NT), 9, 60, 224, 272, 286; African American suffrage in, 279; freighting and travel from, 188, 251; historical marker in, 290; militia in, 18, 22, 24; political conventions in, 156–58, 219–20, 235, 256, 261; soldier relief in, 180

Plattsmouth *Nebraska Herald*, 216, 221; on Edmunds-Boutwell amendment, 171; on G. L. Miller, 243; on office seekers, 253–54; on President Johnson, 234; on statehood, 227

Plattsmouth Sanitary Committee, 180

Plattsmouth Sentinel, on Union convention, 220

Plum Creek, 150, 152; Indian attack near, 143. *See also* Post of Plum Creek

Pole Creek Station, Indian attack near, 205–6

Polock, William A. (Sgt./Lt.): 1st Nebraska extolled by, 68; capture and imprisonment of, 138–40, 163; Livingston described by, 61; Peace Democrats criticized by, 162; postwar career of, 286; recruiting by, 136; Shiloh described by, 57

Ponca Indians, 11, 19; food scarcity among, 156; killing of, near Niobrara, 102–3, 193

Pony Express, eclipse of, by telegraph, 42

Pope, John (Gen.), 40, 69, 123, 206, 207–8; and 2nd Nebraska, 67, 96–97; attitude of, toward disloyal emigrants, 190; attitude of, toward Indians, 97–98, 204; campaign of, in Dakota Territory (1863), 96–101, 124; campaign of, near Powder River (1865), 185–86, 200–202; campaign of, in Upper Missouri region (1864), 123

Poppleton, Andrew J.: as candidate for U.S. Senate, 250; as prospective candidate for delegate to Congress, 72

Poppleton, Caroline (Mrs. Andrew J.), soldier relief by, 179

popular sovereignty, 4, 280; establishment of, by Kansas-Nebraska Act, 2, 271

Porter, Charles F. (Capt.), Indians described by, 172

Porter, James R., fraudulent voting described by, 245

Porter, John R., Council File No. 32 introduced by, 229

Post of Omaha, 181, 318n28

Post of Plum Creek, in Plains Indian wars, *151*, 176

Poteet, [?], assault and robbery of, 121

Potomac River, 44

Potts, James B. (historian), 284

Potts, John (Capt.), Confederates routed by, 137

Powder River: Indians near, 167, 169, 175, 185, 190, 192, 200, 201, 202; military posts along, 241, 242

Powder River Expedition (1865), 185–204, 239, 241

Prairie Dog Creek, 148

Presbyterian Church, 9, 182–83

Price, Sterling (Gen.), 28, 33, 40, 41, 97, 222; Missouri State Guard commanded by, 31; raids by, 149

prisoners of war: Confederate soldiers as, 40, 80, 175; execution of, by 1st Nebraska, 113, 131, 132, 134; Nebraska soldiers as, 136, 138–40, 163, 312–13n53. *See also* United States Volunteers (Confederate prisoners of war)

prisons, military, in St. Louis, 80, 110

Proclamation of Amnesty and
Reconstruction (Lincoln), 129, 134
Promontory Summit (UT), 209
Provost, Charles E. "Provy" (Lt.), 45,
300n1
provost duty, 1st Nebraska assigned to,
80–81, 110
Provost Marshal General, recruiting
controlled by, 104–5, 195
provost marshals: of Iowa, 63; of
Nebraska Territory, 104–6, 121, 181,
195

Quinn, John H. (Cpl.), accidental death
of, 37

Radical Republicans, 256; Democrats'
hostility toward, 72, 260; J. S.
Morton's hostility toward, 89–91,
260; President Johnson's hostility
toward, 225, 233–34, 252, 258–59,
261; Reconstruction plans of, 232,
265
Rangers. *See* militia (in Missouri);
militia (in Nebraska)
Reconstruction, 225, 232; Democratic
views of, 219, 256; President
Johnson's views of, 212–13, 218–20,
256, 258, 275; Republican views of,
213, 219–20, 256
recruiting, 65, 81, 118; for 1st
Battalion, Nebraska Cavalry, 109–11,
135; for 1st Nebraska, 61–62, 64–69,
108–11, 135–38, 194–95, 303n60;
for 2nd Nebraska, 61–62, 67–69;
for militia, 17–26, 146–47. *See also*
conscription
Red Buttes, Indian attack at, 193
Red Cloud (Oglala Sioux): at Fetterman
Massacre, 242; at Ft. Laramie treaty
council, 241–42
Red Cloud Agency, 247
Redick, John I., 238
Red River Expedition, failure of, 123,
133

refugees, 77, 124; from Arkansas, 133;
from Missouri, 21, 32, 33, 62–63, 104,
106, 190. *See also* African Americans;
contrabands
relief, for soldiers and their families:
misdirection of, for 1st Nebraska
parolees, 139–40; no appropriations
for, 50, 178. *See also* United States
Sanitary Commission; women: relief
efforts for soldiers by
Renner, Frederick (Dr.), Kinney
demonized by, 73, 304n67
Republican Party, 5, 83, 84, 88, 178;
1861 campaign of, 42; 1862 campaign
of, 71–73, 74; 1864 campaign of, 119,
156–65; 1865 campaign of, 216–22;
1866 campaign of, 235, 243–45, 248,
255–62; accusations of disloyalty by,
93, 128; African American soldiers
supported by, 89, 120; African
American suffrage supported
by, 212–15, 232, 269–71, 274–75,
277–79; attitude of, toward President
Johnson, 233–34, 251, 252–62, 266;
formation of, 3, 4; J. S. Morton's
criticism of, 89–91; newspapers of,
5, 16, 84, 85, 119, 126–28, 210–17,
243, 256–58; platforms of, 157,
159–61, 219–20, 235, 255, 256;
postwar dominance of, 267, 285–86;
Reconstruction views of, 232, 252,
256, 265; slavery opposed by, 4, 120;
statehood views of, 126–28, 216–20,
225–27, 235, 274–75. *See also* Black
Republicans; Radical Republicans
Republican River: Indians near,
101, 125, 146, 154, 205; Mitchell's
campaigns near, 148–49, 167, 168,
172; prairie fires near, 155; R. H.
Brown's campaign near, 240
Reynolds, Milton W. (of *Nebraska City
News*), 5
Richardson, Albert D. (newspaper
corresp.), 60

Richardson, William A. (terr. gov., 1858), 254, 258, 324n106

Richardson County (NT), 289; Jayhawkers and anti-Jayhawkers in, 35; murder in, 106

Richmond (VA), capture of, 63, 181, 182

Ritchie, Alexander, disloyal conduct of, 181

road ranches, 8, 62; alcohol at, 176–77; attacks on, by Indians, 143, 168, 170; fortification of, by soldiers, 150; supplies for, 95, 123, 188. *See also specific ranches*

Rock Bluffs (NT), 1866 election fraud at, 243–45, 248, 327–28n40

Rock Island (IL), arsenal at, 175

Rockport (MO), 33

Rocky Mountains, 1; gold rush to, 7, 8, 9, 65–66, 74, 95

Roggensack, John (Pvt.), wounding of, at Shiloh, 58

Rolla (MO): 1st Nebraska in, 112, 113; Union base in, 78

"Romulus" (newspaper corresp.), 33, 34

Roper, Laura, capture of, by Indians, 143

Rosecrans, William S. (Gen.), leadership ability of, 173

Rosewater, Edward, recruiting described by, 146

Rowley, [?], killing of, by Indians, 240

Rulo (NT), robbery at, 121

Rush Creek, skirmish near (1865), 170–71, 193

Russell, Majors, and Waddell, U.S. Army contract with, 9

Rutherford, George (Capt.), Confederate forces of, 131

sabotage of telegraph, 26

Salem (NT), murder in, 106

Salmon River, gold discoveries along, 65, 66, 95

Salt Lake City (UT), 66, 202; mail service to, 8; Mormons in, 62, 123; stagecoaches to, 62; telegraph built to, 41

Sand Creek Massacre (1864), 155, 167, 203; investigation of, 187, 193

Sand Hill Station, Indian attack near, 205

Santa Fe Trail, Indian depredations along, 125

Santee Sioux Indians, 99; 1862 uprising of, in Minnesota, 64, 65, 66, 96, 102; Omahas raided by, 145, 314n65

Sapp, W. F. (Lt. Col.), *94*

Saunders, Alvin (terr. gov., 1861–67), 24, 25, *43*, 69, 74, 95, 96, 114, 191, 197, 243, 246, 262, 267; 1st Nebraska's discharge sought by, 240; anti-Jayhawking efforts by, 36, 47, 49; change in election law approved by, 268; Indians feared by, 25, 96, 141, 147, 174, 178; legislature addressed by, 42, 117–19, 168, 171, 177–78, 227–28, 273; militia organized by, 19–20; Omaha boosted by, 276–77; possible removal of, as governor, 253, 258, 261; postwar career of, 276–77, 288; reappointment of, as governor, 185, 319n40; recruiting by, 19–20, 25–26, 65, 109, 146–47; Saunders Co. named for, 49; state constitution drafted by, 228, 230; statehood supported by, 177, 227, 266

Saunders, Marathena (Mrs. Alvin), soldier relief by, 179

Saunders Flying Artillery, 19, 23. *See also* militia (in Nebraska)

Savannah (GA), 165

Scherneckau, August (Pvt.), 242; in Arkansas, 113, 131, 132; in Missouri, 79, 80, 110, 111, 305n6; in Oregon, 289; in Plains Indian wars, 176, 177, 182–83, 185, 189, 207, 208

Schofield, John M. (Gen.), Dept. of the Missouri under, 110, 112

Scott, Winfield (Gen.), 18

Scott's Bluff, Camp Shuman near, 147, 148

Seaton, John S. (Lt.): as candidate for auditor, 220, 221; as soldier, 196, 221

Secession, 5, 6, 15, 119; effect of, on Democrats, 83–84; proposal of, for Old Northwest, 92–93; nullification of, 212; threats of, 5

Second Corps, Third Brigade of, 1st Nebraska soldiers in, 137

Second Missouri Light Artillery: in Arkansas, 112, 113; at Cape Girardeau, 80, 81; on the Plains, 186, 201

Second Nebraska Volunteer Cavalry, 70, 94, 98, 105, 111, 135; Dakota campaign of (1863), 96–101, 108; formation of (1862), 67–69, 74, 77, 93–96; historical marker for, 290; pejorative attitudes toward, 109, 196; postwar careers of, 286, 289; provost duty of, 106-7

Second United States Cavalry, Plains service of, 239–40

Second United States Dragoons: at Ft. Kearny, 20; in Pawnee War, 13

Second United States Infantry, at Ft. Kearny, 16

Sedalia (MO), 37

Selby, George W., killing of, by Indians, 205

Senate Bill 456 for statehood, 264

Seventh Iowa Volunteer Cavalry, 253; depredations by, 143, 313–14n64; discharge of, 247; "Laramie Loafers" attacked by, 192; Mud Springs defended by, 170; Plains service of, 102, 107, 123, 124, 140, 143, 145–47, 148, 149, 150, 168, 190, 198, 205, 239–40; Poncas killed by, 102–3; provost duty by, 121–22; voting by, 163

Seventy-sixth Ohio Volunteer Infantry, at Ft. Donelson, 51, 54

Seward, William H. (U.S. sec. of state), 114; Seward Co. named for, 49

Shamblin, Lafayette, murder of, 106

Shelby, Joseph O. (Gen.), 137; 1st Nebraska soldiers captured by, 138–39; Missouri raid by, 110–11, 133

Sheldon, Addison E., Nebraskans described by, 285

Shenandoah River Valley, Confederate offensive in, 158, 161

Sherman, William Tecumseh (Gen.), 200; Georgia campaign of, 123, 134, 149, 161, 165; railroad promoted by, 209

Shiloh, Battle of (1862), 1st Nebraska in, 57–59, 60

Shorter, Eli, proposed confiscation of property of, 73, 304n68

Shorter County (NT), later Lincoln Co., 49

Shreveport (LA), Red River campaign against, 123

Sibley, Henry (Gen.), 1863 campaign of, against Sioux, 98, 99

Sioux City (IA), 283; 2nd Nebraska in, 94, 96, 98

Sioux Indians, 11, 18, 19, 101, 102, 140, 155, 193, 283; in Dakota Territory, 96–101; in Fontanelle, 12; at Ft. Laramie treaty council, 241–42; in Grattan Massacre, 10–11; in Powder River country, 202, 203. See also Brulé Sioux Indians; Oglala Sioux Indians; Santee Sioux Indians; Yankton Sioux Indians

Sioux Lookout, 189

Sixteenth Kansas Volunteer Cavalry, Plains service of, 148, 185

Sixth Iowa Volunteer Cavalry, at White Stone Hill, 100

Sixth Kansas Volunteer Cavalry, deserter from, 106

Sixth Ohio Volunteer Cavalry. See Eleventh Ohio Volunteer Cavalry

Sixty-eighth Ohio Volunteer Infantry, at Ft. Donelson, 51

slavery, 16, 183; Democratic attitude toward, 4, 127; destruction of, after Emancipation Proclamation, 72, 74, 82–91; effect of Kansas-Nebraska Act on, 263, 279; in Kansas Territory, 2–3; in Missouri, 40–41, 212; in Nebraska Territory, 2, 4, 280, 294n5; Republican attitude toward, 4, 120; war's effect on, 61. *See also* abolition and abolitionists; contrabands; emancipation; Thirteenth Amendment

Slocum, Merritt (Cpl.), shooting of, 139

Smith, Alfred (undercook), 130

Smith, Ed (Sgt.), Indian raids described by, 193

Smith's Ranche (NT), 190; Medal of Honor awarded for service at, 191

Smoky Hill River, 223; Indians near, 125

Solomon River, 148, 240

South Carolina, 86; secession of, 5, 6, 15

South Pass, 150

Spanish American War, 287

Spotted Tail (Brulé Sioux): at Cottonwood Springs, 125; at Ft. Laramie treaty council, 241

Springfield (MO), 31, 37, 40. *See also* Wilson's Creek, Battle of

Spurlock, Burwell, in Rock Bluffs election fraud, 243

Spurlock, Isabella, soldier relief by, 180

stagecoaches: escort of, by soldiers, 150, 171, 175–76, 185, 206, 207; gold shipped by, 95; Indian threats to, 18, 64, 141, 142, 150, 152, 155, 168, 170–71, 193, 206, 302n46; mail service by, 8, 26, 41, 64, 97; stations of, 8, 62, 95, 143, 147, 168

Stanley, Frances (Cpl.), killing of, by Indians, 205

Stanton, Edwin (U.S. sec. of war), 65, 66–67, 174, 182; Stanton Co. named for, 49

steamboats, 74, 304n71; transporting emigrants to jumping-off points, 42; transporting freight and passengers, 17, 26, 41, 123, 188–89; transporting gold, 95; transporting military supplies, 98–99, 129, 131, 132, 133, 201; transporting soldiers, 17, 19, 23, 27, 28, 32, 51, 56–57, 79. See also *Colorado*; *Omaha*; *Westmoreland*; *West Wind*

steam wagon, in Nebraska City, 62

Steele, Frederick (Gen.), 40, 61, 138; failure of Red River campaign of, 133

St. Francis River, skirmish near, 82

Stinking Water Creek, Indian attack near, 205

St. James (NT), Wiseman killing near, 99, 102

St. Joseph (MO), 23, 156; 1st Nebraska in, 23–24, 27, 28; railroads in, 17, 26; refugees from, 33; Secessionist militia in, 17, 21, 33; stagecoaches from, 26; steamboats from, 188; U.S. flag destroyed in, 21

St. Louis (MO): 1st Nebraska in, 28, 30, 32, 36, 37, 51, 61, 130, 135; banishment from, 80–81; Confederate threat to, 81; Curtis Horse in, 50; military headquarters in, 21, 69, 80, 173; parolees in, 139–40, 163; provost duty in, 80–81, 110–11; sanitary fair in, 179, 318n28; steamboats from, 9, 26, 123, 188–89

St. Louis and Iron Mountain Railroad, 28, 36

St. Louis District, under Curtis, 50

Stolley, William, soldiers' thievery described by, 143, 313–14n64

Stowell, Martin (Sgt. Maj.), 48–49; death of, 56

Strickland, Silas (reg. adj.), Shiloh described by, 58

suffrage, 256; for African Americans, 210–15, 218–19, 223, 230–32, 235, 237, 252, 260, 265–66, 268–75, 277–81, 332n28; for Nebraska soldiers, 117, 120, 162–63, 221, 243–44, 316n100. *See also* Fourteenth Amendment; Nebraska Constitution: suffrage requirements of; Territorial Suffrage Act
Sully, Alfred (Gen.), 1863 campaign of, against Sioux, 98–100, 102
Summers, Samuel (Col.), stockade constructed by, 146
Sumner, Charles (U.S. senator), 91; suffrage amendment by, 231, 232, 236, 252, 265
supplies and supply lines, 40, 95; disruption of, for Powder River Expedition, 187–88, 200, 201, 203; lack of, for Davidson's Missouri campaign, 78–79; lack of, for Livingston's Arkansas campaign, 113, 129, 131, 132; lack of, for Pope's Dakota Territory campaign, 99
Sweet, James, 236
Sweetwater River, 140; mail routes along, 64
Sylamore Mountain (AR) skirmish (1864), 131, 132
Syracuse (MO), 1st Nebraska in, 37

Taffe, John (Maj.), 255, 262, 272, 331n17; in 2nd Nebraska, 4, 94, 286
Taylor, Edward B., 183, 272; discharge of, as Indian agent, 261–62; Ft. Laramie treaty negotiated by, 241–42; *Nebraska Republican* edited by, 119–20, 258, 261, 262, 325n123; President Johnson supported by, 252, 253, 261–62
telegraph, 6, 180; construction of, 41–42, 299n60; Indian threat to, 141, 142, 168, 169; repair of, by soldiers, 171; sabotage of, in Missouri, 26
Temple, J. H., killing of, by Indians, 204–5

Tennessee, 117, 188; Grant's 1862 campaigns in, 50–56; Hood's 1864 invasion of, 172; readmission to Union of, 270; settlers from, 8
Tennessee River, Grant's army along (1862), 51, 56, 57
Territorial Suffrage Act, 270, 271, 273, 278–79
Texas, invasion of, 123
Thayer, John M. (Col./Brig. Gen.), 52, 56, 71, 238, 272; 1st Nebraska commanded by, 25, 27; election of, as U.S. senator, 248–50, 251, 262, 274; escaped slave rescued by, 40–41; at Ft. Donelson, 51–56; Indians pursued by, 12, 13; militia commanded by, 12–13, 17, 18; postwar career of, 286; promotion of, after Shiloh, 60, 71; reminiscence by, of 1st Nebraska's removal to Ft. Leavenworth, 30; at Shiloh, 57–59
Third Missouri Volunteer Cavalry, at Cape Girardeau, 80
Third Nebraska Volunteer Infantry, in Spanish American War, 287
Third United States Volunteer Infantry, Plains service of, 185, 190, 191
Thirteenth Amendment (U.S. Constitution), 126, 142, 178, 213, 244
Thirty-Ninth Congress: First sess., 252; Second sess., 255, 264
Thompson, Charles (Lt.), Army horses described by, 154
Thompson, J. D. N. (Capt.), in Brownville militia, 23, 28, 298n34
Thompson, John A. (Capt.), at Ft. Kearny, 46
Thompson, M. Jeff: Missouri militia organized by, 17; U.S. flag destroyed by, 21
Thompson, Robert, arrest of, 28, 298n34
Thurston, John M. (U.S. senator), 287

Tipton, Rachael (Mrs. Thomas),
fundraising by, 23
Tipton, Thomas, 23, *249*, 270;
discharge of, 197; election of, as U.S.
senator, 248–50, 251, 262; Lincoln
eulogized by, 183; postwar career of,
286, 288; recruiting by, 136; service
of, with 1st Nebraska, 36, 132–33, 249
Tongue River, Arapaho killed near, 202
Train, George Francis: equal suffrage
opposed by, 239; soldier relief by, 179;
statehood supported by, 238–39
transcontinental railroad: Republican
support for, 3, 165; terminus selected
for, 114. *See also* Union Pacific Railroad
treaties at Ft. Laramie (1866), 241–42
Twelfth Missouri Volunteer Cavalry:
in 1866 Indian campaign, 239–40; in
Powder River Expedition, 201
Twenty-third Indiana Volunteer
Infantry, at Shiloh, 57
Two Strike (Brulé Sioux), Mitchell's
council with, 125
Tyler, [?] (Lt.), in Nemaha Co., 34
Tyler, Charles (Capt.), at Ft. Kearny,
20–21

undercooks. *See* African American
soldiers: service of, in 1st Nebraska
Underground Railroad, 2
uniforms. *See* clothing and equipment
Union army, 141; alcohol abuse in, 31,
79, 176–77; attitude of, toward trans-
Missouri, 141–42; demobilization
of, 186, 194; Nebraskans in, 7,
294–95n13; organization of, 15–26;
postwar desertion from, 206–8;
recruiting for, with bounties and
furloughs, 68, 109–111, 134; veterans
of, in Nebraska, 286–87, 291, 333n11.
See also conscription
Union Home Guards, 35. *See also*
militia (in Nebraska)
Union Jayhawkers, 46. *See also*
Jayhawking: in Nemaha Co.

Union League, Secessionist attacked
by, 120
Union League against Jayhawking, 46.
See also Jayhawking: in Otoe Co.
Union Pacific Railroad, 114, 185,
208–9, 215, 217, 222–23, 239, 251, 267;
junkets on, for dignitaries, 250, 262,
263, 264
Union Party. *See* Republican Party
Union Rifle Company, of Germans, 19,
23–24. *See also* militia (in Nebraska)
United States Bureau of Indian Affairs:
peace policy of, 200; restitution
approved by, 156
United States Census: of 1860, 2, 8,
9–10, 67, 295n17; of 1890, 291
United States Department of the
Interior, Indian policy of, 186–87, 204
United States Department of War, 96,
102; 1st Nebraska discharged by,
240; conscription and recruiting
by, 19–20, 25–26, 62–63, 65, 66, 109;
during Plains Indian wars, 141, 146,
153, 175, 204; troop consolidation
and reduction by, 186, 187, 194–95,
200, 203
United States forces in Kansas and the
territories, under G. M. Dodge, 200
United States Land Office at
Brownville, 83
United States Navy gunboats, 51, 80, 110
United States Sanitary Commission,
179
United States Volunteers (Confederate
prisoners of war), 175, 239, 247; 3rd
U.S. Volunteer Infantry, 185, 190, 191;
5th U.S. Volunteer Infantry, 203, 247
Upper California Crossing, alcohol
abuse at, 176–77
Upper Platte Agency, 11, 101, 193
Utah Territory: District of Utah
headquartered in, 174; Kinney in,
72–73; Mormons in, 9; railroad built
to, 209

Vallandigham, Clement L., as Peace Democrat, 84, 89, 91, 92, 93, 119, 158, 163, *164*, 165, 258, 306n18, 306n24

Van Buren (MO), 1st Nebraska in, 78

Vanderwater, William, disloyal conduct of, 181

Van Wyck, Charles (U.S. senator), 287

Vicksburg (MS), Union campaign against, 78, 81, 108, 117

Vifquain, Victor, Medal of Honor awarded to, 287

Virginia, 107, 134, 158, 161; campaign in, to capture Richmond, 63, 181, 182; settlers from, 8

Von Eaton, Felix, Jr., killing of, 106

Wade, Benjamin (U.S. senator), 263; Nebraska admission bill sponsored by, 252, 264, 265, 272

Walker, James, as first African American to vote in Nebraska, 278

Walker, Samuel (Col.), in Powder River Expedition, 201–2

Wallace, Lew (Gen.): at Ft. Donelson, 51–55; at Shiloh, 57–59, 301n29

War Democrats: G. L. Miller as, 92; Heath as, 253; Lincoln supported by, 83–84, 88; McClellan as, 158; President Johnson as, 212; Republican wooing of, 157

Ware, Eugene F. (Lt.), 153, 163; description of deserters by, 107, 124; description of reverse emigration by, 190; description of trail dust by, 189

Washington (DC), 219, 224; A. Saunders in, 25, 266; B. Holladay in, 142; Heath in, 253; Lincoln's funeral in, 183; Miller-Morton visit to, 254–55; S. G. Daily in, 71, 157; Secessionist threats to, 44; Thayer in, with statehood document, 274

Washington County (NT), sawmill in, 208–9

Waters, William H. H., 157; of *People's Press*, 85, 107, 210, 211; rivalry of, with Harvey, 88–89, 210, *211*

Watson, [?] (Jayhawker), 47

Waugh's Farm (AR) skirmish (1864), 131

Weatherwax, Thomas (Capt.), discharge desired by, 198

Western Department. *See* Department of the West

Western Sanitary Commission, 179

Western Stage Company, 26, 42

Westmoreland (steamboat), 135

Westport, Battle of (1864), Confederate defeat at, 149

West Wind (steamboat), 1st Nebraska on, 27, 28

Wheaton, Frank (Gen.), 202; Camp Wheaton named for, 240

Whig Party, former members of, as Republicans, 3

Whistler (Oglala Sioux), Mitchell's council with, 125

The White Chief (Belden), 289

Whiteman's Fork. *See* Frenchman Creek

White River, 113; as supply route, 129, 132, 133

"whites only" voting clause: in Colorado constitution, 231, 237; in Nebraska constitution, 230, 235, 252, 274–75

White Stone Hill, Battle of, 1863, 99, *100*, 101, 286, 290

Whitewater River bridge, 82

Wilcox, John (Lt.), troop consolidation recommended by, 194

Williamsburg, Battle of (1862), 287

Wilson's Creek, Battle of (1861), 37

Wind River Mountains, 192

Winne, Peter, emigrants described by, 107

Winnebago Indians, 185–86; at Omaha reservation, 156, 185–86, 190. *See also* Omaha Scouts

Winnebago Indian Scouts. *See* Omaha Scouts

Wiseman, Henson (Pvt.), killing of family of, 99, 102

Wiseman, Phoebe Ann (Mrs. Henson), killing of family of, 99

women, 135; fears of, for loved ones, 32; feting of soldiers by, 22–23, 25; flags presented to soldiers by, 22, 198–99; husbands accompanied to battlefronts by, 59–60; killing or capture of, by Indians, 99, 143; relief efforts for soldiers by, 178–80

Women's Relief Corps, GAR women's auxiliary, 290

Wood River, Squire Lamb's road ranche along, 6, 66, 95, 143, 161, 190, 209

Wood River Center (NT), 18, 123, 296n4

Woolworth, James M., on state constitution, 244–45; on statehood, 118–19

Wynn's Ferry Road, Confederate escape along, 53, 54

Wyoming Territory, 286

Yankton (DT), 99

Yankton Sioux Indians, 99

Yates, Frank, at Red Cloud Agency, 247